NGUGI WA THIONG'O

Kenyan dramatist and novelist Ngugi wa Thiong'o is regarded as one of the most influential African writers today, not only for his creative work but also for his criticism of wider cultural issues – isues such as nation and narration, power and performance, language and identity, empire and postcoloniality. Simon Gikandi's study offers a comprehensive analysis of all Ngugi's published work and explores the development of the major novels and plays against a background of colonialism and decolonization in Kenya. Gikandi places the works in a context that examines the way they engage with the changing history of Africa. Tracing Ngugi's career from the 1960s through to his role in shaping a radical culture in East Africa in the 1970s and his imprisonment and exile in the 1980s, this book provides fresh insight into the author's life and the historic events that produced his work.

Simon Gikandi is Professor of English Language and Literature at the University of Michigan. He was born in Kenya and educated there, the United Kingdom and the United States. His previous books include *Reading Chinua Achebe: Language and Ideology in Fiction* (1991), *Writing in Limbo: Modernism and Caribbean Literature* (1992), and *Maps of Englishness: Writing Identity in the Culture of Colonialism* (1996). He is editor (with Abiola Irele) of the forthcoming *Cambridge History of African and Caribbean Literature*.

CAMBRIDGE STUDIES IN AFRICAN AND CARIBBEAN
LITERATURE

Series editor: Professor Abiola Irele, Ohio State University

Each volume in this unique series of critical studies will offer a comprehensive and in-depth account of the whole *œuvre* of one individiaul writer from Africa or the Caribbean, in such a way that the book may be considered a complete coverage of the writer's expression up to the time the study is undertaken. Attention will be devoted primarily to the works themselves – their significant themes, governing ideas and formal procedures, biographical and other background information will thus be employed secondarily, to illuminate these aspects of the writer's work where necessary.

The emergence in the twentieth century of black literature in the United States, the Caribbean, and Africa as a distinct corpus of imaginative work represents one of the most notable developments in world literature in modern times. This series has been established to meet the needs of this growing area of study. It is hoped that it will not only contribute to a wider understanding of the humanistic significance of modern literature from Africa and the Caribbean through the scholarly presentation of the work of the major writers, but also offer a wider framework for the ongoing debates about the problems of interpretation within the disciplines concerned.

Already published

NGUGI WA THIONG'O

SIMON GIKANDI

CAMBRIDGE
UNIVERSITY PRESS

PUBLISHED BY THE PRESS SYNDICATE OF THE UNIVERSITY OF CAMBRIDGE
The Pitt Building, Trumpington Street, Cambridge, United Kingdom

CAMBRIDGE UNIVERSITY PRESS
The Edinburgh Building, Cambridge CB2 2RU, UK
40 West 20th Street, New York, NY 10011-4211, USA
477 Williamstown Road, Port Melbourne, VIC 3207, Australia
Ruiz de Alarcón 13, 28014 Madrid, Spain
Dock House, The Waterfront, Cape Town 8001, South Africa

http://www.cambridge.org

First published 2000
Reprinted 2002

Printed in the United Kingdom at the University Press, Cambridge

Typeset in Baskerville 11/12.5 pt [VN]

A catalogue record for this book is available from the British Library

Library of Congress Cataloguing in Publication data
Gikandi, Simon
Ngugi wa Thiongi'o / Simon Gikandi.
p. cm. – (Cambridge studies in African and Caribbean literature)
Includes bibliographical references and index.
ISBN 0 521 48006 X
1. Ngãgã wa Thiong'o, 1938–Criticism and interpretation. 2. Kenya–In literature.
I. Title. II. Series.
PR9381.9.N45 Z67 2000
823 21–dc21
99–043662

ISBN 0 521 48006 X hardback

To my teachers, Okot p'Bitek
and Henry Owour Anyumba, in memoriam

Contents

Preface

This was a book that I resisted writing for both personal and intellectual reasons. Although separated by a generation, Ngugi and I share a common colonial and postcolonial background, one whose most defining characteristics are the "state of emergency" declared by the British government in Kenya in 1952, the euphoria of independence in the 1960s, the emergence of the student democratic movement at the University of Nairobi in the 1970s, and the consolidation of the undemocratic postcolonial state in the 1980s. Given this background, I felt, for a long time, that I did not have enough distance from Ngugi's works to be able to develop the kind of systematic critique of his works that I wanted. At the same time, however, I felt that more than any other African writer Ngugi needed the kind of sustained critique that would take his readers beyond the simple politics of identity that have come to dominate so much postcolonial theory and criticism.

At a time when postcolonial theory seems to have lost interest in local knowledge, history, and context, I thought a critique of Ngugi's works was an ideal way of bringing the referent back into literary studies. But once I had decided to write a book that would foreground how a specifically African context weaves its way into Ngugi's texts, I was confronted with a serious theoretical problem: does an insider's knowledge of the conditions in which works are produced help or deter critique? In writing this book I have tried as much as possible to eschew the role of the native informant. At the same time, however, I have found it difficult to repress or transcend the insider's knowledge that is the logical product of the common referent Ngugi and I share. I have sometimes used this "insider information" to reject some dominant interpretations of

Ngugi's works; but I hope I have not used it to foreclose other possible interpretations of his extensive and diverse *œuvre*.

On a more personal level, Ngugi's works have been more important to my intellectual development than those of any other African writer. It was through reading his novels that I effectively learnt the significance of textual knowledge in the making and unmaking of colonial culture. The Church of Scotland Mission at Tumutumu where I was born and spent my childhood and youth had been the epicenter for two events that frame the politics of culture in Ngugi's early novels – the "female circumcision" controversy of the 1920s and the "Mau Mau" insurgency of the 1950s. And yet, in the culture of my colonial childhood and postcolonial youth, these events were effectively muzzled by both the departing colonizers and their postcolonial successors. For many postcolonial readers of my generation, it was through a reading of Ngugi's novels that "unspeakable" colonial events entered postcolonial discourse. Later, in the 1970s, Ngugi's novels and essays would provide my generation with a framework for understanding the politics and poetics of underdevelopment. These works articulated and dramatized the crisis of independence in uncompromising ways. They also provided their readers with a grammar for articulating the need for social and civil rights in a postcolonial situation often defined and driven by ephemeral material concerns and power politics.

I would like to thank Abiola Irele for recognizing Ngugi's significance in the world of African and postcolonial letters and for his insistence that this was a book I had to write. I am grateful to Ngugi and Gitahi Gititi for providing me with the Gikuyu edition of *Matigari* at a time when this text was in danger of disappearing from the literary scene. My comprehension of the history of colonialism and nationalism in East Africa – the key to understanding Ngugi's works – has been enhanced by conversations with David William Cohen and Luise White and from reading the works of Charles Ambler, John Lonsdale, and Atieno Odhiambo. For biographic and bibliographic information on Ngugi and his works I have relied heavily on the work of Carol Sicherman, especially *Ngugi wa Thiong'o: The Making of a Rebel*. I would like to thank Mako Yoshikawa for her help and support. As usual I am grateful to my wife and children for providing relief and disruption from the rigors of intellectual work.

Chronology

1938   Ngugi born 5 January in Limuru, Kenya.

1947–48   Attends Church of Scotland Mission (CSM) at Kamaandura, Limuru.

1948–55   Attended Manguu Gikuyu Independent (Karing'a) School.

1955–59   Student at Alliance High School, Kikuyu.

1959–64   Student at Makerere University College, Uganda.

1960   Publication of "The Fig Tree" in *Penpoint*, the literary magazine of the English Department at Makerere.

1961–64   Columnist for *Daily Nation* and *Sunday Nation*.

1962   Production of *The Black Hermit* at the Ugandan National Theatre, Kampala. Attends the Makerere Conference of African Writers of English Expression.

1964   Enters Leeds University. Publication of *Weep Not, Child*.

1965   Publication of *The River Between*.

1966   Attends International Pen conference in the United States.

1967   Attends conference of Afro-Asian Writers in Beirut, Lebanon. "This Time Tomorrow" is broadcast on the BBC African Service. Publication of *A Grain of Wheat*. Becomes Special Lecturer in English at University College, Nairobi.

1968   Visiting Lecturer, University College, Dar es Salaam.

1969   Resigns from University College, Nairobi.

1970–71   Visiting Associate Professor at Northwestern University.

1971   Returns to University College, Nairobi.

1972   Publication of *Homecoming*.

1973   Promoted to Senior Lecturer and Head of the Department of Literature at the University of Nairobi. Awarded the Lotus Prize at the Afro-Asian Writers Conference at Alma Ata, Khazakhstan.

1975   Publication of *Secret Lives*.

1976   Attends International Emergency Conference on Korea in Tokyo. *The Trial of Dedan Kimathi* performed at the Kenya National Theatre in Nairobi. Promoted to Associate Professor. Publication of *Petals of Blood*.

1977   *The Trial of Dedan Kimathi* performed at FESTAC '77 in Lagos, Nigeria. *Ngaahika Ndeenda (I Will Marry When I Want)* performed at Kamĩrĩĩthũ. Detained at Kamiti Maximum Prison.

1978   Adopted by Amnesty International as a prisoner of conscience. Released from detention.

1980   Publication of Gikuyu editions of *Ngaahika Ndeenda* and *Caitaani Mutharabaini (Devil on the Cross)*.

1981   Publication of *Detained* and *Writers in Politics*.

1982   Denied permission to produce *Maitu Njugira* at the Kenyan National Theatre. Publication of English editions of *I Will Marry When I Want* and *Devil on the Cross*. Ngugi is forced into exile in Britain.

1983   Publication of *Barrel of a Pen*.

1984   Delivers Robb Lectures at the University of Auckland, New Zealand. Visits Zimbabwe.

1985   Keynote Address at the African Literature Association, Northwestern University.

1985–86 Studies film-making in Sweden. Publication of the Gikuyu edition of *Matigari ma Njiruungi*. Government confiscates all available copies from the publisher. Publication of *Decolonising the Mind*.

1987   Chairman of Umoja, umbrella organization of Kenyan dissident groups in exile.

1990–92 Visiting Professor at Yale University.

1993   Appointed Professor of Comparative Literature and Performance Studies at New York University. Publication of *Moving the Centre: The Struggle for Cultural Freedom*.

1994   Edits and publishes *Mũtiiri*, a Gikuyu journal of culture.

1997   Publication of revised edition of *Writers in Politics*.

Introduction: reading texts and contexts

Several paths are open to the reader who wants to examine Ngugi's literary and critical works in their historical and cultural context: one can choose, for example, to read them as specific commentaries on the African experience as it emerges from colonial domination and moves into the theatre of independence and postcoloniality. One could read these works from the ideological perspective provided by the author himself through his essays and social commentaries. Or one could choose to analyze Ngugi's major novels as a series of experiments in narrative form, experiments driven by the author's search for an appropriate style for representing an increasingly complex social formation. Whatever approach the reader prefers, however, several questions and problems immediately come to mind: what is the relationship between Ngugi's texts and their contexts? Indeed, what is Ngugi's immediate context? Are his novels and plays to be read as attempts to come to terms with a Gikuyu culture trying to reinvent itself in face of the problems and opportunities provided by British colonialism as it establishes its hegemony over the peoples of Central Kenya? Or are these narratives to be read as part of a larger project trying to will an independent Kenyan nation into being?

Reading Ngugi's works through his ideological pronouncements may be convenient to some readers and critics, but it is a process that presents its own theoretical problems: how do we respect his strong views on the nature of literary production, the function of culture, and the relation between art and politics without repressing the significant contradictions that are equally important to the shape and function of his novels and plays?[1] This critical problem is ultimately compounded by the fact that, while it

seems easy to differentiate the early Ngugi (the student of English
literature, the admirer of D. H. Lawrence and the "great tradition") from the later Ngugi (the disciple of Marx and Fanon and
the advocate of socialist realism), this difference is not as simple as
it appears to be, or as numerous critics make it out to be. There is
no simple chronological framework for explaining Ngugi's literary
career.[2] On the contrary, his literary works are best read as a
continuous – and often agonized – search for the narrative forms
that might best represent the complex culture of postcolonial
Africa and as a reflection of the contradictions inherent in any
attempt to synthesize aesthetic forms and cultural formations in a
continuous state of flux. Ngugi's mature works suggest a confident
break with his literary past, but this past continues to haunt his
ideological pronouncements and narrative practices.[3] In this
chapter, I will examine the social and cultural forces that characterize Ngugi's own attempt to come to terms with his colonial
background and his postcolonial present.

To understand the relation between Ngugi's texts and their
context, we need, among other things, to have a clear sense of the
ways in which his life is wrapped up with the cultural history of
Kenya since the 1920s, and how this history is, in turn, woven into
his novels and plays. For as I will argue later in this chapter, if
Ngugi's ambition is to produce narratives that bear witness to the
historical experience – he defines the author as "a kind of sensitive
needle" which registers "with varying degrees of accuracy and
success, the conflicts and tensions in his changing society" – the
reader's challenge is to understand how the author's idea of the
historical has shaped his own identity as an African writer and how
his narratives have shaped the way two generations of postcolonial
readers have come to understand their history.[4] While some of the
best critical works on Ngugi's novels and plays have given us a
profound sense of the context in which they were produced, very
little attention has been paid either to how this context has shaped
the form of his works or how our notion of this context – cultural
nationalism, "Mau Mau," or neo-colonialism in Kenya – has been
overdetermined by Ngugi's discourse. Another purpose of this
chapter, then, is to displace our notion of context as what Michael
Taussig has called "a secure epistemic nest in which our knowl-

edge eggs are to be safely hatched."[5] Instead of reading the historical context as the key to understanding Ngugi's texts, or as an objective source of knowledge, I want to provide a different kind of contextualization, one that establishes "our enormously confused understanding of history and what is meant by history?"[6] I want to explore how Ngugi's texts represent or mediate the reader's understanding of Kenya's contested history.

NGUGI AND THE DRAMA OF (POST)COLONIALISM

An obvious place to start is one of Ngugi's earliest comments on the tenuous relation between African writers and their history: "The novelist is haunted by a sense of the past. His work is often an attempt to come to terms with 'the thing that has been,' a struggle, as it were, to sensitively register his encounter with history, his people's history."[7] According to Ngugi, African writers are haunted by their past simply because the historical narratives that they thought would make their experiences more intelligible have instead confronted them with the opacity of the past. The turn to fiction, then, is one important way of clarifying the confusions created by historical events: "A writer responds with his total personality to a social environment that changes all the time."[8] And yet the idea that fiction can be a conduit of understanding and a means of confronting the past calls into question the veracity and objectivity of the history which fiction is charged with representing. But as numerous advocates of the "new historicism" have argued, the distinction between history and fiction is itself paradoxical: the narrativization of history is, after all, engendered by the author's desire to go beyond simple historicism. How does the novelist represent history without compromising it or becoming imprisoned in the past?[9]

Ngugi's first attempt to deal with this problem is to place himself at the junction where history (the context) and his writings (the text) meet. We can explore this juncture more clearly by examining three autobiographical moments in which Ngugi presents the writing self as the mediator of contexts and texts. The first instance can be found in one of Ngugi's earliest attempts to connect his autobiography to history and the paradoxical claims it makes on the writing self. Here, Ngugi begins by positing the condition of the possibility of his identity as a writer at the point when he confronts the material condition of his family, namely its state of marginality in relation to a colonial plantation: "I grew up in a small village. My father and his four wives had no land. They lived as tenants-at-will on somebody else's land... Just opposite the ridge on which our village was scattered were the sprawling green fields owned by the white settlers."[10] The opposition between the peasant and the settler appeals to Ngugi's imagination because it provides powerful metaphors for the historical struggle between the colonizer and the colonized. This struggle becomes, in effect, the key to understanding the history of colonial and postcolonial Kenya.

Beyond this opposition, however, there is a more subtle reflection on the nature of the colonial relationship, a melancholic moment that connects the author to his colonial childhood through memory and the emotion it conveys:

One day I heard a song. I remember the scene so vividly: the women who sang are now before me – their sad faces and their plaintive melody. I was then ten or eleven. They were being forcibly ejected from the land they occupied and sent to another part of the country so barren that people called it the land of black rocks. This was the gist of their song:
    And there will be great great joy
    When our land comes back to us
    For Kenya is the country of black people
    And you our children
    Tighten your belts around your waist
    So you will one day drive away from this land
    The race of white people
    For truly, Kenya is a black man's country.
They were in a convoy of lorries, caged, but they had one voice. They sang of a common loss and hope and I felt their voice rock the earth where I stood literally unable to move.[11]

What may appear to be a self-indulgent autobiographical account can be seen, on closer examination, to be an important technique for connecting the reader to some of the central tropes in Ngugi's early works – exile and displacement, the emotive language of nationalism in Kenya, and the politics of decolonization.

How do texts and contexts interplay in this instance? For one, Ngugi identifies with the dispossessed on their way to exile precisely because their state of displacement mirrors that of his own family; indeed, the scene of deprivation is vividly recalled almost twenty years later because of its powerful emotion of loss, an emotion that readers will recognize as indispensable to the form and meaning of Ngugi's early novels. Secondly, as I have argued elsewhere, the discourse of emotions is central to Ngugi's narrative practice because of its deep roots in Gikuyu nationalist songs and Christian hymns (*nyimbo*), songs whose plaintive melodies simultaneously recall the losses of the native land and the prophetic moment of return and restoration.[12] Finally, the occasion which Ngugi witnessed at the age of ten or eleven was itself a major historical event, one of the defining moments of nationalism in Central Kenya: the peasants he had seen in a convoy of lorries were Gikuyu squatters evicted from the Olenguruone settlement on their way to forced exile in the semi-desert landscape of Yatta in Eastern Kenya.

As historians of nationalism in Central Kenya have noted, Olenguruone, itself the site of a major confrontation between the colonial state and Gikuyu squatters over land rights and representation, inaugurated the phase of armed resistance to colonialism, leading, shortly after, to the declaration of the state of emergency in Kenya. The significance of the squatters' defiance against colonial authority, notes Tabitha Kanogo, "lay mainly in its pivotal role as a rallying point for Kikuyu unity against the colonial government and the Olenguruone crisis was largely important in strengthening the people's commitment to the single goal of dislodging the colonial government."[13] But if Olenguruone was to become "a symbol of Kenyan anti-colonial resistance," it was because of the melancholic discourse it generated and the influence this had in stirring nationalist emotions; as a discursive event Olenguruone was propelled by twin themes – loss and prophetic expectations – which were to become the defining sentiments of the cultural grammar of nationalism in Central Kenya when Ngugi was coming of age.[14] These themes dominate his early works, most notably *The River Between* and *Weep Not, Child*.

But if Ngugi is writing about a defining moment of his political culture – and a key integer of his relationship to this culture – why does he not provide his readers with a fuller historical account for these events? Why does he not introduce the heroic struggle at Olenguruone in more concrete terms? Why is the historical context taken for granted? The most obvious explanation is that Ngugi's main interest is in the images generated by history rather than the historical event itself. This answer, however, does not explain Ngugi's omission of the concrete historical event, for as the rest of the essay indicates, Ngugi's search is for precisely the kinds of histories repressed by the colonial library: "The song I heard as a child then spoke of things past and things to come. I was living in a colonial situation but I did not know it."[15] Here, as is often the case in his early works, Ngugi is caught between two contending texts, the Gikuyu song promoting themes of national restoration and a colonial historiography which seeks to repress such themes. While Ngugi's sympathies were perhaps always with the nationalist cause, he had to struggle for many years to figure out the appropriate style for representing the history of colonialism from the perspective of its victims.

This problem can be clarified by referring to a second autobiographical moment. This one comes from Ngugi's seminal introduction to *Secret Lives*, his collection of short stories, a collection which, because it spans most of his writing career, is defined as "my creative autobiography":

My writing is really an attempt to understand myself and my situation in society and history. As I write I remember the nights of fighting in my father's house; my mother's struggle with the soil so that we might eat, have decent clothes and get some schooling; my elder brother, Wallace Mwangi, running to the cover and security of the forest under a hail of bullets from colonial policemen; his messages from the forest urging me to continue with education at any cost; my cousin, Gichini wa Ngugi, just escaping the hangman's rope because he had been caught with live bullets; uncles and other villagers murdered because they had taken the oath; the beautiful courage of ordinary men and women in Kenya who stood up to the might of British imperialism and indiscriminate terrorism. I remember too some relatives and fellow villagers who carried the gun for the whiteman and often became his messengers of blood. I remember the fears, the betrayals, Rachael's tears, the moments of despair and love and kinship in struggle and I try to find the meaning of it all through my pen.[16]

What we have here is a catalogue of the conflicting events and emotions that have gone into the making of the writer: the troubled and impoverished household and a mother's struggle to educate her children, the bitter struggle between nationalists and loyalists, and the mixed feelings of fear and betrayal created by the state of emergency. And while Ngugi has clear ideas about the historical origins and implications of these events, he sees himself caught in the middle of an interpretative dilemma: how does one make sense of a past that still haunts the writer in the postcolonial present? It is in this context that the act of writing is posited as an instrument of finding the meaning "of it all."

One might, of course, ask why Ngugi struggles to give meaning to events that would appear to be self-evident, especially in 1975 when he wrote the preface to *Secret Lives*. Had not his discovery of Marxism and its language of class consciousness and ideological struggle provided him with the appropriate language for understanding the Kenyan past? Had not the decade of decolonization in Kenya clarified the terms of independence and thus the meaning of the nationalist struggle against colonial domination? The truth is, while Marxism provided Ngugi with an instrument for understanding postcolonial culture, it could not account for, or indeed give meaning to, historical events which the author himself had witnessed, experiences which, as he noted in the passage cited above, came back to his mind every time he tried to write about the past. Indeed, decolonization in Kenya had made the writer's relationship with the past more complicated for an unexpected reason: the ruling elite was so afraid of its immediate past that it was busy reinventing an alternative version of "Mau Mau" and the state of emergency in order to legitimize its position.[17]

But there is an even more important reason why Ngugi posits his writing career as a continuous struggle to understand himself in a colonial and postcolonial situation defined by compromised histories: even as the novelist draws on his own subjective experiences to invest his version of the past with moral authority, the astute reader cannot fail to notice the gap that separates him from this past. Ngugi writes from the position of one who remembers the recent African past vividly, but he does not seem to be connected to this past except through its remembrance and – ultimately – its representation in narrative. If Ngugi's works seem to be driven by an ardent desire for the historical, it is because history, even the history of events experienced first-hand, seems to be blocked by the narratives designed to represent it. This blockage comes from two sources: first, the events which Ngugi considers to be central to his own understanding of Kenyan history – land alienation, colonial terror, and nationalist resistance (or "Mau Mau") – were, until the publication of his works, considered to be absences, voids, or silences.[18] Secondly, because Ngugi was a student in a privileged colonial school and university college when the events he remembers took place, he was never part of their immediate context. He was connected to the drama of history through his family and class, but separated from them through his colonial education.

This separation is succinctly captured in a third autobiographical moment, this time an essay on the Biggles series of adventure stories popular in British colonial culture. Ngugi cannot help recalling his initial encounter with the Biggles stories at Alliance High School, at the height of the "Mau Mau" war in Kenya, as a strange case of imperial irony:

I met Squadron-Leader James Bigglesworth, DSO DFC MC, at one time of the Royal Flying Corps, Later the Royal Air Force, and known to his readers as simply Biggles, at Alliance High School, in Kenya, back in 1956. It was a colonial school in a colonial world. The school, founded by an Alliance of Protestant Missions way back in the thirties, was the leading elitist school for African children. Its motto, "Strong to Serve," expressed the ideals of the school: to produce leaders who, of course, had the necessary character and knowledge to faithfully serve King and Empire... It was a school where Kipling's poem "If" was so very important. And of course Shakespeare...[19]

The central irony here relates to Ngugi's anxieties about his own relationship to the Englishness represented by Bigglesworth and colonial culture: had he, in the security of the colonial school, come to identify with the forces of civilization against the barbarism of nationalism that lay just outside the gates of Alliance High School?[20] Did he turn to writing fiction as a way of reconciling the world represented by his parents and brothers, struggling against British colonialism, to the imagined ideals of Biggles's Englishness? In reading Bigglesworth's pro-imperialist books in 1955 and 1956,

Ngugi was caught in what he aptly describes as "a drama of contradictions":

> Biggles, the flying ace and squadron leader of the Royal Air Force, could have been dropping bombs on my own brother in the forests of Mount Kenya. Or he could have been sent by Raymond of Scotland Yard to ferret out those who were plotting against the British Empire in Kenya. Either way he would have been pitted against my own brother who, amidst all the fighting in the forest, still found time to send messages to me to cling to education no matter what happened to him. In the forests they, who were so imbued with a sense of Kenya nationalist patriotism, had celebrated my being accepted into the same Alliance High School where I was to meet Biggles, an imaginary character so imbued with a sense of British patriotism.[21]

Here, as in the other autobiographical moments considered above, the drama of colonial contradictions cuts several ways: the colonial text (the adventures of Biggles) seeks to promote an unquestioning identification with Englishness in the African student's mind; but this identification can only be achieved by negating one's specific social and historical context, and even betraying kin at war with British colonialism. The nationalists have taken up arms against colonial governance and rule – and by extension the culture of Englishness – but they still take time off to celebrate the author's admission into the citadel of colonial culture in Kenya. What, then, is the connection between "nationalist patriotism" and "British patriotism"? Ngugi has to create imaginary narratives to make sense of it all.

In calling attention to Ngugi's personal investment in his texts and contexts, my goal here is not to posit his writing as purely subjective or continuously self-reflective; on the contrary, my intention is to show how he sees his own relationship to the defining moments of colonialism and postcolonialism in Kenya as connected to larger ideological questions. In trying to understand himself (in colonial culture), Ngugi produces narratives in which individual experiences become collectivized, as it were. Indeed, the most radical distinction between Ngugi's earlier works and his mature novels, as we shall see in subsequent chapters, is his shift from the bourgeois notion of the subject of the novel as an individual struggling in a world that has – in Georg Lukács's

famous term – been "abandoned by God" to the Marxist notion of
novelistic characters as embodiments of historical forces which
they must understand and control to retain their identity.[22]

In these circumstances, the later Ngugi would seem to fit
Frederic Jameson's controversial notion of the Third World artist
in the era of multinational capitalism. Jameson's argument – or
"sweeping hypothesis," as he calls it – is that what Third World
cultural productions "seem to have in common and what distinguishes them radically from analogous cultural forms in the first
world," is their allegorical function: these productions are to be
read as *"national allegories"* because they reject the radical split,
common in Western realist and modernist novels, "between the
private and the public, between the poetic and the political,
between what we have come to think of as the domain of sexuality
and the unconscious and that of the public world of classes, of the
economic, and of secular political power."[23] While most of the
criticism directed at Jameson's postulation is well founded, there is
no doubt that for writers like Ngugi, the ideal mode of cultural
production is one which overcomes the split between the private
and public realms.[24] His emphatic claim is that the best kind of
writing is done in the name of the nation and the social collective:
"A nation's literature which is a sum total of the products of many
individuals in that society is then not only a reflection of that
people's collective reality, collective experience, but also embodies
that community's way of looking at the world and its place in the
making of that world."[25]

Because Ngugi has so clearly located his later works in what
Jameson calls the "life-and-death struggle with first-world cultural
imperialism,"[26] his novels and plays can be seen as an attempt to
establish the forms in which the story of the struggle between the
global narrative of capital and local stories of resistance can be
told. For this reason, the problems that haunt Ngugi's works –
questions of language, power, and knowledge – are as much about
literary form as they are about ideological preferences. Jameson
identifies this problem succinctly when he notes that if the dilemma of radical writers like Ngugi, especially after the "poisoned
gift of independence," is how their ideological "passion for change
and social regeneration" can find appropriate narrative agents,

then what we are dealing with here is "also very much an aesthetic dilemma, a crisis of representation."[27] Indeed, given Ngugi's struggle with the crisis of representation in his non-fictional writings, it is surprising that so many critics have written on his ideological dilemma as if it were independent of aesthetic problems.[28]

Ngugi's most agonizing reflections on the ideology of literature inevitably seek resolution in the aesthetic: for example, in talking about the effect of the land in an early interview with Dennis Duerden (January 1964), Ngugi notes that the centrality of the land to people in Kenya derives not so much from its materiality, or even economic possibilities, but from "something almost akin to spiritual" effects.[29] Several years later, in his Marxist phase, when political economy had become central to his conception of literary culture, Ngugi could still claim that literature "is of course primarily concerned with what any political and economical arrangement does to the spirit and the values governing human relationships."[30] Even when he conceived literature as a primarily collective enterprise in what may be considered his orthodox Marxist phase in the 1970s and 1980s, Ngugi could not negate his belief in the close relationship between collective identity and aesthetic forms: literature is "a reflection on the aesthetic and imaginative planes, of a community's wrestling with its total environment to produce the basic means of life, food, clothing, shelter, and in the process creating and recreating itself in history."[31]

In this concern with the land and the values that it supports, we can detect another crucial drama of contradictions in Ngugi's conception of literary production: on the one hand, he defines literature as a collective enterprise that is affected by a community's wrestling with its environment, and he conceives the writer as a person defined by his or her engagement with the interests of this community; on the other hand, however, he wants art to maintain a certain autonomy and the artist to sustain a certain imaginative subjectivity. Ngugi's dilemma here is simply this: how can the category of the aesthetic (or what he constantly refers to as the imagination) provide access to the political and social questions that have preoccupied him since he started writing in the early 1960s?

While a lot has been written on these political and social
problems – and how they enter Ngugi's fiction – very little consideration has been given to the aesthetic dimension of these
questions.[32] The reason for this dissociation of the aesthetic from
political forms arises, as Terry Eagleton has argued in a different
context, from the indeterminate nature of aesthetic forms and
their traditional association with ahistorical categories such as
universality and autonomy.[33] And yet, the aesthetic provides one
of the most important points of entry into the questions which, in
Eagleton's words, "are at the heart of the middle classes' struggle
for political hegemony" and are inseparable "from the construction of the dominant ideological forms of modern class-society,
and indeed from a whole new form of human subjectivity appropriate to that social order."[34] One of Ngugi's major achievements
as a writer arises from his sensitive understanding of the complex
relation between aesthetics and politics in modern society.

But if the aesthetic is central to the construction of the kind of
bourgeois hegemony Ngugi writes against, then it has to be incorporated as an agent of the oppositional. To quote Eagleton again,
the aesthetic "provides an unusually powerful challenge and alternative to these dominant ideological forms, and is in this sense an
eminently contradictory phenomenon."[35] In the very contradic-
toriness of the aesthetic – or the imagination – is to be found
Ngugi's continuous search for forms that might bridge three sets of
gaps which emerge every time he tries to use his novels or plays to
make sense of the recent history of colonial and postcolonial
Kenya: the gap between the everyday experience of rural peasants
and urban workers and the art forms of the middle class (the novel
or drama); the chasm between the experience of reification in class
society and the writer's utopian desire for a "non-alienated mode
of cognition"; and the break between the functional authority of
art (its need to serve an ideological interest) and its inherent
autonomy (the fact that art derives its identity from its ability to
transcend its conditions of possibility).[36]

CULTURE AND THE CRISIS OF REPRESENTATION

My central argument up to this point is that the relationship
between Ngugi's life, his works, and context is not as simple as he

himself makes it out to be; on the contrary, this relationship is defined by a series of contradictions and a complex aesthetic ideology. These contradictions are, of course, not unique to Ngugi; on the contrary, they reflect the social and cultural forces that were responsible for the creation of the modern colonial subject. Ngugi may prefer to represent himself as the son of peasants, but his core identity has been constructed by his colonial education and (post)colonial class position. The writer is, in fact, placed in a situation where he has to negotiate three social positions in order to establish his authority: the split between his subjective experience and his public commitments, the inscrutability and dissonance of the history that generates his work, and the tension between the bourgeois aesthetic and the realities of class society. While Ngugi's writing career has undergone some radical transformations, most evident in his rejection of Christianity and his adoption of Marxism, the splits noted above persist and are important in explaining many of the choices he has made as a writer in regard to such contentious issues as art and ideology, language and culture. Instead of trying to explain these problems away, or seek resolutions to them in the powerful ideological statements the author has given us, I have chosen to foreground them as the conditions that enable Ngugi's works.

Sustaining the contradictory moments that make Ngugi's narratives possible is important for another reason: the changing form of his fiction – from the romanticism of his early works to the socialist realism of his later novels, for example – can be explained by his own sense of the crisis of representation he encounters every time he tries to account for the African condition during and after colonialism. But since this alone does not explain the changes in Ngugi's fiction, our more immediate problem is how to read the crisis of colonial history and subjectivity as it is presented in the form of his works. While previous studies of Ngugi's works have read his development as a writer either in terms of his changing ideologies (from English liberalism to Marxism), or his switch of narrative forms (from romantic poetics to realism), I have adopted an approach that seeks to acknowledge the explicit changes in Ngugi's aesthetic ideology while tracing the implicit continuities in his novels and plays.[37] I have hence adopted a theoretical framework that brings Ngugi's historicism into what I hope is a productive encounter with his residual formalism.

Two assumptions lie behind my reading of what might be characterized as Ngugi's aesthetic ideology: first, since the novelist's primary topic is history, we need, as John Frow has urged us to do, to build a fuller conception of "the historicity of the text, accounting not merely for its pastness but also for its productive interaction with historically distinct systems."[38] While Frow's concern here is primarily with the function of literary texts in relation to other texts, my focus is more on the relation between works of art and their historical context: how do Ngugi's works enter into a creative interaction with the history they seek to represent? In order to address this problem, I make a second assumption: because the interaction between Ngugi's texts and the historical narrative changes as his career develops, it is important to sketch out an internal (intertextual) relation between his works. Let me elaborate on these assumptions.

We can begin to consider the historicity of Ngugi's texts by making a simple observation: that in spite of the predominance of Gikuyu mores and norms in his works, Ngugi rarely invokes a precolonial Gikuyu world to counterbalance the devastating effects of colonial modernity. True, the Gikuyu people constitute a major referent in Ngugi's works: they are his primary cultural field and experience; their institutions provide the stage in which the central political and cultural conflicts in the author's work and thought are fought out. But Ngugi is unique among African writers of his generation in his refusal to invoke a precolonial world as the site of a stable culture and identity. The reason for this refusal arises, perhaps, from Ngugi's recognition of how difficult it is to discuss a Gikuyu culture outside the colonial relationship. For this reason, any attempt to read Ngugi's works in relation to a Gikuyu ontology or aesthetic (the way we read Soyinka in relation to a Yoruba normativity, for example) is bound to fail. And this is not because Ngugi has no interest in this kind of normativity; indeed his works in Gikuyu are marked by a desire to find aesthetic forms that exist outside the bourgeois ideologies inherited from the colonial school.

The situation Ngugi finds himself as an African writer using the

English language, or a member of the postcolonial elite writing in
an African language, is far more complex than the above opposition between Gikuyu and bourgeois worlds might suggest. Now, it
has become convenient in some political circles to label Ngugi a
Gikuyu nationalist; but whatever the merits or demerits of such a
claim, it must begin by confronting the ambiguous character of its
frame of reference.[39] For in spite of attempts by Gikuyu nationalists since the 1920s to construct and sustain the myth of a Gikuyu
Volksgeist (nyumba ya Mumbi) it is impossible to talk of a Gikuyu
culture outside the discourse of colonialism. Although Gikuyu
temporality inscribes itself by invoking an ancient history – *hingo ya
ndemi na mathathi* – the people who have come to be known under
this corporate identity invented themselves to meet the challenges
of colonial rule and domination.

This does not mean that there were no Gikuyu people before
colonialism. The Gikuyu were joined by a common language,
common kinship descent, and shared belief systems; but this identity was not corporate or centralized; there was no need for social
organization around overarching social, cultural, or government
organizations. Indeed, at the end of the nineteenth century when
the Gikuyu first came into contact with the Europeans, they were
essentially a fluid, acephalous, culture, organized around sub-clans
(mbari) and distant memories of a common descent. As Godfrey
Muriuki notes in *A History of the Kikuyu*, the heads of *mbari*, often
powerful individuals and agrarian pioneers *(athamaki)*, were often
the centers of economic and moral authority.[40] And if Gikuyu
identity would appear to have been "parochial," as John Lonsdale
has argued, it was not in the sense of being narrow-minded, but
simply diocesan.[41] It was in the crucible of colonialism – both in
resistance and collaboration – that a Gikuyu group consciousness
emerged in the early decades of the twentieth century. Gikuyu
identity thus came to be formed in – and shaped by – what
Georges Balandier has aptly called the dialectic of the colonial
situation rather than in a Manichean opposition to colonial rule
and governance.[42] With the establishment of colonial rule in 1895,
notes Muriuki, the way was open "for all the new forces that were
to influence the development of the Kikuyu this century":

Administrators, settlers, traders and missionaries poured into the Kikuyu country bringing with them what was, in the Kikuyus' eyes, a new and strange way of life with its sometimes incomprehensible demands and ideas. Gradually the Kikuyu realized that they had to come to terms with the new order and the period between the last decade of the nineteenth century and the end of the First World War witnesses the attempt, on their part, to adjust themselves to rapidly changing circumstances and environment.[43]

While Gikuyu cultural nationalism in works such as *The River Between* might express its strongest sentiments in the form of a desire for something before colonialism, the lives of the colonized subjects in this novel, as in other fictional works from Central Kenya, are dominated by the reality of colonial rule. Indeed, what appears in novels such as *The River Between* to be a precolonial history, is only history (in the modern sense of the word) to the extent that it is appropriated to counter the culture of colonialism and its historiography. Within this context, the past is not spoken about in any concrete terms until it begins to be invoked to resist colonialism; the authority of a precolonial history is derived not from its ability to illuminate the past, but for its prophetic potential. Constructed around a figure such as Mugo wa Kibiro, as is the case in *The River Between*, history is driven by what is aptly referred to as "visions of the future."[44] The foundational histories of the Gikuyu – including the histories invoked in Ngugi's novels – arise from a concerted attempt, started by cultural nationalists in the 1920s, to interpret and reinterpret specific instances of colonial rule and governance.

This does not mean that we have to read these events purely as discourses; on the contrary, to the extent that colonialism was a palpable political, social, and cultural project, it created certain realities and events that were to transform Gikuyu culture in tangible ways. At the top of these realities and events was the power and authority of the colonial state: colonial rule was rationalized by the imposition of a new and powerful bureaucratic state; as the arbiter of race, class, and clan conflict "the colonial state occupied centre stage in Kenya, symbolically and materially standing over colonial society."[45] For a decentralized *polis* like that of the Gikuyu, the function of the state as the primary instrument of social transformation was seen as a radical sign of rupture. From the moment colonial rule was established, as a witness to the coming of colonial power was to recall in old age,

the state of things began to change more and more rapidly, and ceased to be at all like it was in the olden days. The country became like a new country that was unknown to us, and one of the things that caused the most serious trouble was the way in which we began to have our lands taken away from us by the White Government, and that started to happen after my people began to seek education.[46]

What we see in this elder's lament is the same kind of dual response to colonialism we read in *The River Between* when Chege urges his son to go to the mission school and "Learn all the wisdom and all the secrets of the white man. But do not follow his vices. Be true to your people and the ancient rites."[47] The colonial government and the white men are posited simultaneously as a threat to Gikuyu interests (especially in relation to land tenure) and as indispensable agents of change and salvation. Indeed, while nationalist histories were later to rewrite the moment of colonial conquest as one of radical loss and alienation, it is important to bear in mind that colonialism offered the Gikuyu innumerable opportunities, not only redefining their power within the new colonial space by giving them access to increasingly internationalized networks of trade, but also abetting their frontier expansionism, opening up lands, especially in the Rift Valley, which could not have been accessible to them without the agency of colonial settlement.

While Ngugi's later novels cast the relation between the Gikuyu and the British in familiar Manichean terms – the colonized and the colonizer separated by opposed identities and interests – the more ambivalent portrait in the early works, especially *The River Between*, seems to be closer to the historical record. Both colonizer and colonized were engaged in acts of cultural translation, trying to invent their traditions and selves in relation to the realities of the other. The British colonial authority – with the help of Christian missionaries – sought to reorganize the Gikuyu according to the central doctrines of colonial modernity, positioning them in a cultural grid which emphasized white supremacy and the benign authority of colonization. The Gikuyu, in turn, carefully remade and rewrote their cultural narratives and moral economy to fit into the structures privileged by colonialism, creating an identity for themselves as a "tribe," valorizing centralizing narratives of common descent, calling attention to a common mythological pantheon, and privileging histories and temporalities that would put them, morally and conceptually, on equal terms with their colonizers.

But if colonialism offered the Gikuyu unprecedented privileges – largely because they were so quickly colonized – why did they so easily elaborate mechanisms and discourses of resistance against colonialism?[48] Or to put the question another way, why did the young men who flocked to the colonial school at the beginning of *The River Between* become transformed into formidable foes of colonial domination at the end of the novel? The answer is to be found in two closely related issues that dominate Ngugi's novel – land and the notion of cultural integrity. Because the land is posited as the defining symbol of Gikuyu culture and identity, its loss under colonialism triggers at least three forms of cultural discourses: a melancholic discourse that derives its moral authority from the loss of ancestral lands; an eschatological discourse that posits the recovery of these lands as the precondition for the restoration of Gikuyu selfhood; and a nationalist discourse that uses the loss of land as the impetus for political struggle.

No matter how powerful the discourse of land might be in Ngugi's novels, however, it needs to be put in its proper context: how did the Gikuyu transform the figure of the lost lands into the key for understanding their moral system and sense of selfhood? How did they come to represent themselves as the custodians of other people's lost lands and colonized landscapes? And given the fact that the Gikuyu lost less land to colonial settlement than their Maasai neighbors, why did they invest so much sentiment in this loss? The rational answer to these questions – that the Gikuyu sense of land loss was deep and abiding because they lost control over lands they continued to occupy as squatters – does not explain the emotive nature of the issue.[49] If land was the "spiritual principle" of Gikuyu culture, as Jomo Kenyatta was to argue in *Facing Mount Kenya* (1938), it was because it had become the conduit

through which the Gikuyu negotiated their relationship with the new colonial order – and even among themselves – over important issues of moral authority, temporality, and emplacement.[50]
When colonialism challenged the Gikuyu demand for tenure rights in the 1920s, it was not simply questioning their narratives of ownership and possession, but their notions of the past and the future; it was a threat to their emergent sense of self and a violation of the integrity of their social body. While the testimonies and representations which Gikuyu families presented to the Kenya Land Commission of 1932 were ostensibly about property rights and land tenure, they were ultimately about questions of historicity and identity.

Nothing illustrates better the centrality of historicity and identity in Gikuyu consciousness than the now famous confrontation between Chief Koinange wa Mbiyu's (up to this time one of the staunchest Gikuyu supporters of colonial rule) and A. L. Block, a prominent white settler. When Block denied the chief's ancestral claim to some of the land which he had appropriated, "Koinange was so angered by Block's testimony that he exhumed the body of his grandfather, which was buried on the alienated land, in order to provide the justification of his mbari's claims."[51] Can there be a more dramatic illustration of one's claim to a social and moral space than the exhumation of an ancestor's body? If the burial of the dead body is a mark of a family's claim to the land – and thus a somber assertion of their identity – it made perfect sense for Koinange to exhume his grandfather's body as an expression of his temporal relationship to the land and his genuine rage at his family's dispossession.

In the end, the Land Commission ruled in favor of colonial rights of settlement, but this ruling was to provide Gikuyu nationalists with their most visible sign of British betrayal and a justification of their rage against colonialism. Indeed, Koinange's transformation from a colonial loyalist to the patron saint of radical nationalism among the Gikuyu is often explained in terms of his disenchantment with the colonial contract on weighty issues such as ancestral claims to land ownership. As he was to note with bitterness, "When someone steals your ox, it is killed and roasted and eaten. When someone steals your land, especially nearby, one can never forget. It is always there, its trees which were dear friends, its little streams. It is a bitter presence."[52] Similar sentiments are to be found in Ngugi's novels.

But this scene of disenchantment with colonialism was more complicated than Koinange and others conceived or represented it. The Gikuyu sense of disillusionment with colonialism was genuine and its consequences lasting, but it was a disenchantment that was performed in the theatre of colonialism in a grammar and context that colonial rule had created. In short, in spite of Koinange's invocation of Gikuyu bodies and mores to press his case, what he wanted, above everything else, were the values that colonialism had introduced among the Gikuyu and privileged as the mark of civilization – individual rights to land and property (Koinange was, after all, a product of colonial missions).

Disenchantment was, nevertheless, to become a trope of cultural expression and a major theme in narratives and songs. And while the trope of the lost lands is repeated over and over in Ngugi's novels, it finds its most dramatic expressions in Chege's "sermon" to Waiyaki in *The River Between*: here, through one of the most powerful narratives of dispossession the "hidden things of the hills" are revealed and the prophecy of revelation and restitution is foregrounded.[53] In this novel, as elsewhere in Ngugi's works, a sense of loss leads to radical disenchantment which is, in turn, posited as the precondition for an eschatological narrative. When he is first exposed to the beauty of the land, Waiyaki is overcome with powerful sentiments of patriotic love; but as he is instructed in the recent history of colonial conquest, this love gives way to an acute sense of loss; finally, he is consoled by the retelling of the ancient prophecy forecasting the emergence of a savior among the people of the hills, a savior who, it is implied, will be a product of the Christian mission at Siriana.

The mixed emotions that the landscape triggers in Waiyaki exemplify how Ngugi's texts are connected to larger cultural narratives. For soon after the Land Commission ruled against Gikuyu families in the 1930s, Koinange, too, had observed, without possibly realizing the ironic nature of his assertion, that Gikuyu sons educated in colonial schools would one day come to a prophetic awakening – "these sons will consider what deceits and cheating their fathers have suffered from the whites and this will lead to mistrust."[54] If we recall that *The River Between* is set in the period in which history and culture had become contentious issues in the colonial encounter in Kenya, then we can understand the kind of relation between texts and contexts that a comprehensive reading of Ngugi's works demands. For what we have in the example above is a situation in which historical events (the Land Commission report) enters Gikuyu legend (the song of Koinange), which ultimately enters Ngugi's works as culture.

And thus to return to the question I raised earlier, Ngugi does not write about precolonial Gikuyu traditions because the issues he is interested in – dispossession and domination – became significant cultural texts at the moment of colonial encounter. Indeed, like the Gikuyu cultural nationalism that was to influence him in his childhood and youth, the idea of culture that dominates Ngugi's early works was created as part of the colonial project, in affiliation or resistance to imperial rule.[55] As Nicholas Dirks has observed, what we recognize as culture in postcolonial literature was not merely produced by the colonial encounter; the concept itself was invented in the context of colonial conquest and rule: "Claims about nationality necessitated notions of culture that marked groups off from one another in essential ways, uniting language, race, geography, and history in a single concept. Colonialism encouraged and facilitated new claims of this kind, re-creating Europe and its others through its histories of conquest and rule."[56]

It is thus important to remember that the claims that were to drive Gikuyu nationalism from the 1920s onwards – claims about nationness, land, and identity – had become important because colonialism made them the litmus test of a modern polity. The main dilemma for Gikuyu nationalists, however, was that the staunchest advocates of culture as an instrument of resistance against colonialism were also the most colonized both because they identified with central facets of colonial modernity and because they derived their primary identity from their conversion to Christianity: "Converts to Christianity were called *athomi*, i.e. literates, the rest were called *Agikuyu*, i.e. the people who remained in the Kikuyu culture."[57] The *athomi*'s dilemma was that while conversion demanded that they give up their Gikuyu identity, it did not offer complete entry into European culture – they were modern subjects who remained marginal to the institutions of political and economic power. What came to be known as cultural nationalism, one of the most important themes in Ngugi's early works, was an attempt by the *athomi* to hollow out a new space of identity between colonial Christianity and Gikuyu tradition, to differentiate culture from colonialism and Christianity from Eurocentricism.

This project reached its apotheosis in the so-called "female circumcision" controversy of 1929, once again, the subject of *The River Between*. While the moral and gender questions surrounding the issue of clitoridectomy are now bound to haunt any discussion of this problem in Ngugi's novel, it is important to contextualize it by noting that if one ritual practice was considered as universal and central to Gikuyu identity, it was that of circumcision and clidectomy. As an earlier European observer of the Gikuyu was to observe,

The festivals and rites associated with both marriage and death hold but a small place in Kikuyu imagination compared to that greatest of all ceremonies whereby the boy becomes a man and the girl a woman. By the rite of circumcision, with its complicated ritual, each individual passes from the condition of simply being the property of Kikuyu parents to that of a member of the Kikuyu nation, with its accompanying rights, privileges, and obligations.[58]

In 1928, when the Church of Scotland Mission demanded that its members renounce clidectomy as a condition of their continued membership in the Church, a large number of *athomi* balked, breaking away to form their own independent churches. The Christian community in Central Kenya thus came to be divided between those who had agreed to sign a pledge renouncing clidectomy (this group came to be known as *kirore*, the signatories) and the breakaway group which labeled itself Gikuyu *karing'a* (pure Gikuyu). The objective of the latter group was, in the words of its manifesto, "to further the interests of the Kikuyu and its members and to safeguard the homogeneity of such interests relating to their spiritual, economic, social, and educational upliftment."[59] Once again, we can see how the main desire of cultural nationalism (a pure Gikuyu identity) was defined by a clear desire for a modern (colonial) identity.

The outstanding questions which these nationalists had to deal with – up until Kenya became independent in 1963 – constitute an important background to Ngugi's novels: how could one simultaneously maintain cultural autonomy while advocating social and economic upliftment as it had been defined by colonial modernity? Indeed, if autonomy was the primary goal of cultural nationalism – and the nationalists' self-description as *Karinga* seemed to suggest so – why did they not just renounce Christianity and colonial modernity altogether instead of trying to construct parallel Gikuyu institutions?[60] The most obvious response to this question – and readers of *The River Between* will recall this vividly – was that cultural autonomy did not imply a return to a precolonial tradition; rather, cultural nationalism was the desire and demand that an autonomous Gikuyu identity be sustained *within* the colonial project; it was the quest for a political license that would allow the "new" Gikuyu subject to be more selective about those aspects of colonial culture to be incorporated into the modern identity. This is the point made vividly by Jomo Kenyatta in his conclusion to *Facing Mount Kenya*, the manifesto of Gikuyu cultural nationalism in the 1930s:

> If Africans were left in peace on their own lands, Europeans would have to offer them the benefits of white civilisation in real earnest before they could obtain the African labour which they want so much. They would have to offer the African a way of life which was really superior to the one his fathers lived before him, and share the prosperity given to them by their command of science. They would have to let the African choose what parts of European culture could be beneficially transplanted, and how they could be adapted.[61]

Cultural nationalism was ultimately an attempt to see how the idea of culture itself could be liberated from colonialism. In this sense, Ngugi's early novels must be seen as part of a project in which culture was being translated and transformed from being an instrument of colonialism to an agency of national liberation. In fact, for the period covered by *The River Between*, culture – or rather its contested meaning and effect – constituted the battleground between the colonizer and the colonized and among the colonial subjects themselves. More significantly, this period saw a concerted attempt by both sides on the colonial cultural divide to redefine the idea of culture itself. Thus, while the first generation of Gikuyu Christians had been eager to identify with colonial culture as a European-derived phenomenon, by the 1930s, new forms of culture were being constituted to challenge the colonial.[62] Colonial subjects had quickly come to realize the extent to which culture constituted the terrain on which questions of identity, self-determination, and agency were fought. The forms of expressiveness that were to emerge during moments of cultural crisis well into the period of independence in the early 1960s were ones in which the claims of colonial rule and its political economy were subverted in dramatic ways.

Consider, for example, the form of the *muthirigu* dance that emerged among the educated classes in the midst of the crisis between missionaries and nationalists over clidectomy. The dance was a spectacular performance in which about 2,000 dancers would move in a circle, singing, often in rousing voices, obscene songs challenging missionary morality and colonial hypocrisy. It was precisely because of this challenge to the new moral order and the state that enforced it, that the dance was banned by the colonial government in January 1930. Another notable cultural phenomenon was the re-emergence of the institution of prophets *(arathi)* who, during the clidectomy crisis, went around the Gikuyu countryside, preaching "the wrath of God on the European and the duplicity of the missions in professing to champion native interests while in league with Europeans generally in scheming to injure those interests."[63] It is significant to note that the inventors of these two traditions – the dance and the narrative of prophecy – were often products of the mission schools and continued to define themselves as Christians even as they defied the missionary establishment.

Two conclusions can be drawn from these events: first, the idea of culture among the educated classes in Central Kenya did not entail any practical return to the past; on the contrary, culture was being reinvented as a project in which Gikuyu beliefs and European systems were brought into a syncretic relationship.

Secondly, the idea of culture in Gikuyu colonial society could not be conceived outside a persistent sense of crisis and grievance: colonialism was both the social formation that had created the literate classes and the agent of their alienation and dispossession. And because Ngugi was born in the midst of this crisis, writing was one way in which he could come to terms with it; in doing so, he could also try and understand the colonial government and the postcolonial state that had often created and proctored this crisis.

CULTURE, WRITING, AND THE STATE

If Ngugi's childhood memories are dominated by images of colonial rule in crisis, it is because he came of age during the state of emergency (1952–61) declared by the British colonial administration in an attempt to control a Gikuyu peasant uprising which came to be referred to as "Mau Mau." Although the political and economical reasons behind the uprising and its consequences on African families and institutions have been discussed thoroughly in numerous books, the meaning of "Mau Mau" in the politics of decolonization in Kenya has become more contested and controversial as its memories have faded into the past.[64] For this reason, understanding the central role "Mau Mau" has come to occupy in Ngugi's works demands a careful separation of the event from the discourse it generated. The events are, after all, not in dispute: the movement started among the displaced squatters of Orenguruone in the Rift Valley around 1948 and spread to the Gikuyu heartland soon after, propelled by massive oathing ceremonies and other clandestine activities. The movement was banned in 1950, forcing its adherents to go underground and to take up arms. In response, the colonial government declared a state of emergency in Kenya on October 20, 1952. Thousands of British troops were brought into the country to control the uprising, which was to continue well into the late 1950s.

The effect of the state of emergency on many Gikuyu families is also not in dispute. Not only was this a period of violence and tribulation *(hingo ya thiina)*, but most of the actual fighting was between kinsmen and women divided between those who fought to maintain the colonial order (the loyalists) and those who opposed it (the rebels). Families were displaced from their ancestral lands and forced to live in massive villages, complete with garrisons, under a state of curfew and strict control of movements from one area to another. Thousands of men and women were also arrested without trial and sent to detention camps in remote parts of Kenya. These detainees would return toward the end of the 1950s and the beginning of the 1960s to find that their families had been broken up, their children expelled from colonial schools, and their land confiscated.

Because Ngugi's family was directly involved in these events, it is only natural that they were to become central themes in his novels. Indeed, his "Mau Mau" novels, most notably *Weep Not, Child* and *A Grain of Wheat* are attempts to come to terms with a traumatic past, sort out its conflicting meanings and emotions, and give voice to a hitherto repressed discourse. And it is precisely as discourse that "Mau Mau" has come to occupy a central place in Ngugi's thoughts, for beyond the historical evidence summarized above, the movement was associated with a certain kind of intellectual terror; it functioned as a "nervous system," a system of fear ruling not only those who were ruled but the rulers too.[65] There is no better illustration of this terror than that scene in *Weep Not, Child* when Ngugi's young protagonist is tortured by a white settler:

> "Have you taken Oath?"
> "I-am-a-school-boy-affendi," he said, automatically lifting his hands to his face.
> "How many Oaths have you taken?"
> "None, sir."
> Another blow. Tears rolled down his cheeks in spite of himself. He remembered the serenity of his school. It was a lost paradise.
> "Do you know Boro?"
> "He's my – brother."
> "Where is he?"
> "I – don't – know."
> Njoroge lay on the dusty floor. The face of the grey eyes had turned red. He never once spoke except to call him Bloody Mau Mau. A few seconds later Njoroge was taken out by the two homeguards at the door. He was senseless. He was covered with blood where the hob-nailed shoes of the grey eyes had done their work.[66]

Until this point in the novel, Njoroge had hoped that he could maintain his "vision of boyhood" and beat back "the chaos that had come over the land" (p. 84); through education and his belief in "the righteousness of God" (p. 94), he could survive the chaos around him and become a properly civil subject. But once colonial terror has engulfed his family, neither his education nor his beliefs can save him; to live in a state of emergency is to be dominated by forces beyond one's control and understanding.

Indeed, what made "Mau Mau" such a difficult phenomenon to represent was that, more than the event itself, the terror surrounding it (and "Mau Mau" was, for both its proponents and opponents, signified by terror) was the way it refused to be contained by the discursive mechanisms of colonial rule. Unable to comprehend it – that is, to establish a causal relationship between the grievances that had dominated the political debate in the Kenya colony since the 1920s and the uprising – the colonial government and its intellectuals were quick to characterize the insurgency as atavistic. In its atavism, "Mau Mau" posed a challenge to both the "imaginative structures" of white supremacy and the moral conduct of the Gikuyu *athomi*.[67] And because "Mau Mau" was the unnamed and unnamable event (even to this day no one knows what the name meant or represented), it signified a certain gap in both European and Gikuyu consciousness. Stories about "Mau Mau" were "passed from mouth to mouth across a nation, from page to page, from image to body," but no one had a real sense of what it meant or represented; not even those who had suffered from it or for it.[68] Unspoken in its own time, "Mau Mau" was to acquire cultural value after decolonization when it became the subject of contention not only among Kenyan intellectuals but also between the state and its subalterns.

Because of Ngugi's later unequivocal claim that "Mau Mau" constitutes the highest point of Kenyan nationalism, it is easy to forget that his own relation to the movement has evolved considerably during his writing career, or that his later works are deliberate attempts to create an intellectual history for the movement as a way of accounting for his prior ambivalence toward it. In Ngugi's earliest works, including *Weep Not, Child* and some of the early stories collected in *Secret Lives*, "Mau Mau" is not defined in terms of heroism or patriotism, but by fear and doubt. The dominant images in these works are of shadows, darkness, and death. As we have already seen, "Mau Mau" is associated with the darkness that falls in the second part of *Weep Not, Child*, destroying Njoroge's dreams and expectations; it is also the source of the "shocks" and "troubles" that "seemed to have no end, to have no cure."[69] In one of Ngugi's early short stories appropriately called "The Martyr," another Njoroge has deep emotional reasons to help "Mau Mau" fighters destroy the white family that expropriated his family's land, but he struggles with his doubts and divisions, unsure whether to kill or save his white employer.[70] In these early works, "Mau Mau" is not an unequivocal figure of insurgency, but a source of an intense moral dilemma.

This moral dilemma can be traced to the implicit tension between Ngugi's own experience as the son of dispossessed peasants sympathetic to the goals of the movement and his commitment to the liberal ideals of colonial culture, including education and Christianity. Ngugi's family was involved with "Mau Mau" in one way or another, but his own position at the time was more ambivalent than his retrospective account might suggest. Clearly, like most educated Gikuyu in the 1950s, he reacted to the outbreak of violence and the consequences of the uprising with a mixture of fear and uncertainty. He might have identified with the goals of "Mau Mau" because, as the child of a *muhoi* (tenant at will), the sentiment of land and freedom struck a strong chord in him; on the other hand, however, he most likely abhorred the movement's practices because, as a devout Christian and a student at the country's leading colonial school, such practices seemed to threaten the order and authority represented by church and school. Like Njoroge in "The Martyr," Ngugi must have been "a divided man and perhaps would ever remain so."[71]

A second phase in Ngugi's relation to the "Mau Mau" movement was evident on the eve of decolonization and in the first two years of Kenya's independence in the early 1960s. While decolonization seemed to function as the eschatological moment of revelation foretold by the cultural nationalists in the 1920s, it was to bring with it renewed doubts about the exact nature and meaning of this revelation and thus the possibility of its betrayal. The central motif in the narratives Ngugi produced between 1963 and

1968 was that of the "homeward journey" made by ex-detainees who returned to their villages with longing and expectation only to discover that home was no longer the hearth they had dreamt it would be, but a site of radical displacement. Instead of seeing independence as a privileged moment of closure in which the past could be commemorated as heroic and justifiable, characters such as Kamau in "The Return" are driven by a sense of bitterness and desolation.[72] The interplay of the motif of return and betrayal structures *A Grain of Wheat*, Ngugi's great novel of postcolonial disenchantment.

It was in his Marxist phase, however, that Ngugi began to deploy " Mau Mau" as the defining moment in Kenya's recent history – the "highest peak" of a "heroic tradition of resistance."[73] In fact, the redefinition of "Mau Mau" that is evident in Ngugi's later works, most notably *Petals of Blood*, cannot be understood outside his adoption of a materialist ideology and aesthetic. Apart from the intellectual need to reconstruct "Mau Mau" to support a Marxist historiography, Ngugi was involved in an ongoing debate among Kenyan intellectuals on the utility of usable pasts and the nature and function of culture in a period of "arrested decoloniz-ation."[74] While Ngugi was to narrativize this struggle in his later works, most notably *Petals of Blood*, as essentially one between radical and conservative historians, it is more meaningful to see it as a struggle between intellectual workers and the postcolonial Kenyan state over the nature of the past they had inherited from colonialism. For what the Kenyan state had managed to do, especially under the leadership of Jomo Kenyatta, who had emerged from colonial detention in the early 1960s to become president, was to neutralize "Mau Mau" by universalizing its claims and desires.

Thus, while Kenyan society in general and Gikuyu society in particular had been bitterly divided between loyalists and rebels, Kenyatta closed this gap by claiming that all sides had fought for independence. While culture had been the most obvious source of the division between rebels and loyalists with the former "return-ing" to the old ways in their search for alternatives to the colonial order and the latter living in horror of this return as an example of the atavism they had been fighting against for generations,

Kenyatta assured both sides that colonial culture and Gikuyu ways were desirable because of their complementality. Colonial culture was indispensable to the new nation because it sustained the ideals of modernity, individualism, and prosperity; African traditions were important because they secured the moral integrity of the new national community.

In short, African culture, especially one patronized by the state, was no longer to be seen as a threat to modern life. When Kenyatta and Malcolm MacDonald, the last British governor of Kenya, joined a group of Gikuyu peasants to sing the *muthirigu* dance (which had been banned since 1930) in a state ceremony in 1964, the loyalists who now ran the Kenyan state could vividly see that Gikuyu culture could no longer be considered a source of terror.[75] But because Ngugi's radical politics posed a direct challenge to the loyalists' amnesia – they were to detain him without trial in 1977 for trying to commemorate what they considered to be a divisive history – it was inevitable that his reading of the past was going to be different from that of the institutions of the state. In 1963, Ngugi could describe Kenyatta as the embodiment of the spirit of revolt and resistance: "He got support from the peasant masses and urban workers because he was a symbol of their deepest aspirations. To have imprisoned him was futile, because he was himself only a symbol of social forces which could never be finally put down by a gun."[76]

But twenty years later, banished into exile by the postcolonial regime, Ngugi could not reflect on the events that had led to Kenyatta's arrest and imprisonment without a tone of bitterness and regret. He now saw the former president as the embodiment of the betrayal of national consciousness: "Kenyan reactionary scholarship was about to give the final *coup de grâce* to what Kenyatta started when in 1954 at his trial in Kapenguria; he described Mau Mau as an 'evil thing' which 'I have done my best to denounce ... and if all other people had done as I have done Mau Mau would not be as it is now'."[77] How can we explain Ngugi's estrangement from the Kenyatta whom he had idolized in his early works as "the burning spear"? The answer to this question will go a long way to explaining the formal and ideological differences between the novelist's earlier and later works.

Sometime in 1967, as a student at Leeds University, working on *A Grain of Wheat*, his third novel, Ngugi came to the realization that the narrative of independence, which had provided the most obvious structure for his works and thought, was proving to be more vexed than he had anticipated. He awoke to the realization that the promises of nationalism were already being betrayed by the very nationalists who had fought against colonial rule and culture. This realization was brought about by two factors that were to change his notion of culture and his understanding of the function of art as a mediator of social practices – the works of Frantz Fanon and the politics of neo-colonialism in Kenya. More specifically, in reading Fanon's *The Wretched of the Earth*, especially the chapter on the "Pitfalls of National Consciousness," Ngugi came to realize that some of his own fears about the possibility of betrayal were actually being played out in many African states.[78] Fanon's diagnosis of national betrayal provided Ngugi with a critical grammar for explaining the phenomenon of arrested de-colonization. If in the early 1960s Ngugi would leap to the defense of the nationalist movement against its colonial detractors, in the late 1960s he would berate the black bourgeoisie which, on coming to power through negotiated decolonization, "never tried to bring about those policies which would be in harmony with the needs of the 80% of the people ... living below the bread-line standard."[79]

But even before reading Fanon, Ngugi had a good sense of the crisis of independence in Africa (there is enough evidence of this in his first play, *The Black Hermit*): he knew that the euphoria of decolonization was clearly in danger of being misinterpreted and its desires misplaced. But his critique of decolonization remained vague. What Fanon gave Ngugi, among other things, was a sys-tematic explanation of the causes of the failure of decolonization. In reading *The Wretched of the Earth*, he came to realize that in spite of its numerous cultural spectacles, independence, previously posited as "the all-embracing crystallization of the innermost hopes of the whole people," was nothing but an "empty shell, a crude and fragile travesty of what it might have been"; he could comprehend the coming to power of an "underdeveloped middle class" with no economic power and in "no way commensurate with the bourgeoisie of the mother country which it hopes to replace."[80] In Fanon's work, Ngugi could find lucid explanations for the sense of betrayal and disillusionment he was sensing around him. He could understand how the new postcolonial government was seeking to legitimize authoritarianism and ethnic chauvinism instead of instituting democracy and equality; he could see how dreams of Pan-African unity were disappearing quickly into "the mists of oblivion, and a heartbreaking return to chauvinism in its most bitter and detestable form"; he could witness how the party that had mobilized the populace against colonial rule had established itself as "the modern form of the dictatorship of the bourgeoisie, unmasked, unpainted, unscrupulous, and cynical."[81] Fanon's text testified to how easily a leader who had symbolized resistance against colonialism could become transformed into "the general president of the company of profiteers impatient for their returns which constitutes the national bourgeoisie."[82] What one was witnessing as the spectacle of independence unfolded was not the birth of a new African identity, but a radical reversal of the most elementary forms of political and cultural formation. Ngugi's middle works, especially *Petals of Blood* and *The Trial of Dedan Kimathi*, can be read as attempts to find a narrative form for these transformations and reversals.

Clearly, one can begin to understand the changes taking place in Ngugi's notion of the relation between aesthetics and ideology by comparing the treatment of the theme of disillusionment in *A Grain of Wheat* and *Petals of Blood*. For while the two novels were written under the Fanonist ideology discussed above, their discernible differences, especially in techniques of representation, tell us a lot about the changes Ngugi was undergoing as the decade of independence and its euphoria were eclipsed by radical disenchantment. Techniques of representation need to be underscored for two reasons: first, Ngugi's political views, especially after reading Fanon, remained consistent in his later works; discernible shifts and differences were to be found in his rejection of the aesthetic inherited from the liberal Englishness of the Makerere school.[83] After all, if *A Grain of Wheat* was the embodiment of the novel in the "great tradition" – a novel that had successfully subsumed its political concerns beneath literary experimentation – *Petals of Blood* belonged to a tradition that used literary techniques to call attention to its ideological intentions. In addition, if Ngugi's earlier novels had sought to capture the sentiments and feelings of the people and the landscape, as he had told his interlocutors in 1964, by the 1970s he was thinking about how art could be used as an instrument of knowledge and social change.

In *A Grain of Wheat*, as the following passage illustrates, the collective entity – history, the landscape, culture – is important only to the extent that it foregrounds the crisis of the lonely individual:

> They were abandoned in a desert where not even straying mice from the world of men could reach them. This frightened Gikonyo, for who, then, would come to rescue them? The sun would scorch them dead and they would be buried in the hot sand where the traces of their graves would be lost forever. This thought brought more despair to Gikonyo, remembering Mumbi and Wangari: that his identity even in death would be wiped from the surface of the earth was a recurring thought that often brought him into a cold sweat on cold nights. At such times, words formed in prayers would not leave his throat.[84]

Here, as elsewhere in the novel, history (imprisonment), nature (the desert), and culture (the family) are designed to call attention to the subject's search for mooring in a world abandoned by God, or rather the old certainties of colonial culture. In *Petals of Blood*, in contrast, the ethic driving the bourgeois novel is reversed: the deepest crisis of the individual subject – the death of a mother, for example – acquires greater value when it illuminates the crisis of the whole society:

> Karega received the news and his face did not move. But despite attempts to control and contain himself, a teardrop flowed down his left cheek. He watched the drop fall to the cement floor. He was weak in body because of the early beatings, the electric shocks and the mental harassment. These, he could bear. But to hear that his mother was dead – dead! That he would never see her . . . that he had never really done anything for her . . . that she had remained a landless squatter all her life: on European farms, on Munira's father's fields, and latterly a landless rural worker for anybody who would give her something with which to hold the skin together! "Why? Why?" he moaned inside. "I have failed," and he felt another teardrop fall to the cement floor. Then suddenly he hit the cell wall in a futile gesture of protest. What of all the Mariamus of Kenya, of neocolonial Africa? What of all the women and men and children still

weighed down by imperialism? And for two days he would not eat anything.[85]

In looking back at his transition as a novelist in one of the essays collected in *Moving the Center* (1993), Ngugi would explain his movement away from the novel of disillusionment to a more committed and activist tradition by evoking what one may call the crisis of African temporality: what took place in African post-colonial states in the 1970s – political repression, economic crisis, and the emergence of a culture of fear and silence – was, he claimed, "to reveal what really had been happening in the sixties: the transition of imperialism from the colonial to the neo-colonial stage."[86] In the field of literature, the most obvious manifestation of neo-colonialism was the radical split between the African writer and the postcolonial state:

The Kenya that emerged from the seventies is a good illustration of the workings of a neo-colonial state. At the beginning of the decade Kenya was a fairly "open society" in the sense Kenyans could still debate issues without fear of prison. But as the ruling party under Kenyatta, and later under Moi, continued cementing the neo-colonial links to the West, the Kenyan regime became more and more intolerant of any views that questioned neo-colonialism.[87]

The key word here is "neo-colonial" for it suggested, to Ngugi and other radical intellectuals in Africa, that a primary cause of the split between the writer and the state was the latter's rejection of a program of radical transformation and its investment in programs which had been instituted by colonialism. As Colin Leys was to show in *Underdevelopment in Kenya*, an economic and social study that closely parallels *Petals of Blood*, Kenya was the archetypal neo-colonial state: it exemplified the ways in which colonial institutions could survive under the guise of independence; here the political culture of neo-colonialism was not accidental, but was driven by official government policies.[88] Indeed, while Ngugi and his con-temporaries on the political left assumed that neo-colonialism was the betrayal of the dream of independence, the Kenyan state – and the elite that supported it – saw the political economy of the neo-colony, to the extent that it represented a commitment to modernity and modernization, as the *raison d'être* of national liberation. Thus, the very political culture Ngugi was to attack as regressive in both *Petals of Blood* and *The Trial of Dedan Kimathi* was being celebrated by the Kenyan bourgeoisie as the ultimate fulfillment of the state of independence.

The opposition between the writer and the state is a crucial paradigm for understanding Ngugi's later works: while the novelist lamented the emergence of a deracinated African middle class, the Kenyan state saw the "development" programs that it had initiated as essential to the consolidation of the power and authority of the African middle class. While the novelist questioned the efficacy of an African capitalist class dependent on the goodwill of international capital, the state displayed this class as a symbol of Africanization in the key sectors of the economy. While Ngugi advocated and agitated for socialism, the state invoked a rhetoric of socialism to camouflage its unrequited desire for capitalism. And while the author wrote to critique neo-colonial politics as corrupt and corrupting, the colonial state presented the spectacle of power as its most important claim to legitimacy.

Colin Leys has provided us with an accurate description of the spectacle of neo-colonial politics in Kenya in the period covered by *Petals of Blood*:

To [Kenyatta's] court came delegations of all kinds; district, regional, tribal, and also functional. Most of them came from particular districts, often in huge numbers, accompanied by teams of traditional dancers and choirs of schoolchildren, organized and led by MPs and local councillors, and provincial and district officers from the area. They gave displays of dancing and singing; the leaders presented cheques for various causes sponsored by the President and expressed their sentiments of loyalty and respect.[89]

Ngugi would mimic such rituals of power in a memorable passage in *Petals of Blood* where the peasants of Ilmorog "perform" politics with their elected representative:

They trooped to the Jeevanjee Gardens and, as they approached the others, the women ululated the Five Ngemi usually sung for a male child and a returning victorious hero. Within seconds this had attracted a crowd of hangers-on, the hordes of the jobless who normally slept off their hunger at the Gardens and were grateful for any distracting drama, religious, political or criminal. The reception pleased Nderi but did not quite allay his fears. Njuguna introduced him to the crowd as "our prodigal son we sent to bring us back our share from the city," and repeated their call for help in face of the drought. Karega could not quite analyse his attitude to the MP but he, like the others, was hopeful and hung on the MP's lips, closely followed his movements and gestures and eagerly waited for a dramatic solution to their problems.[90]

Beneath Ngugi's determination to capture the realism of neo-colonialism in Kenya, however, were his own nagging doubts about the efficacy of the novelistic project. Educated in the great tradition associated with F. R. Leavis, a tradition in which the efficacy and power of the novel depended on its moral authority, the early Ngugi had not been concerned too much about the political function of his art or its effect on its intended audience. But with his conversion to Marxism sometime in the late 1960s, questions of ideology and audience became paramount. Such questions were also the source of numerous anxieties. By the 1970s, for example, Ngugi was not merely content with representing the narrative of colonialism and decolonization; on the contrary, he wanted to produce narratives that would intervene in the cultural sphere, agitating for – and promoting – change, effectively using literature to rectify what he saw as the failure of national consciousness. As a Marxist, Ngugi identified the working class and the peasantry as the agency of the kinds of changes he envisaged. But textual knowledge was essential in the promotion of change.

Herein lay Ngugi's intellectual dilemma: the novels and plays he was producing in the 1970s, works intended to enhance the agency of workers and peasants, were written in English, a language which many of them could neither read nor understand. As he was to succinctly observe in "Return to the Roots," an essay collected in *Writers in Politics*, the question of language had become central to his intellectual and cultural project as he began to question his previous investment in the institution of literature in English:

To choose a language is to choose a world, once said a West Indian thinker, and although I do not share the assumed primacy of language over the world, the choice of a language already pre-determines the answer to the most important question for producers of imaginative literature: For whom do I write? Who is my audience? . . . The question of audience has a bearing on the next few problems for a writer: What is the subject and content of my works? From whose stand do I look at that content or not?[91]

Ngugi's decision to write in Gikuyu, beginning with his play *Ngaahika Ndeenda* (*I Will Marry When I Want*) and his novel *Caitaani Mūtharabainī* (*Devil on the Cross*), was a clear sign that he had embarked on a project whose goal was not simply to make the working class and peasantry the central subjects of his works, but also the primary readers of his texts.

On the surface, then, the decision to write in Gikuyu was one way of reconnecting with readers and subjects whom Ngugi had valorized in the novels written during his Marxist phase. On another level, however, it is possible to argue that this linguistic conversion was an attempt to reopen the whole debate about national culture in the postcolony and to contest the fetishization of national culture by the Kenyan state. For one of the interesting characteristics of cultural production in Kenya in the 1970s was the ways in which, as Ngugi was to show in *Petals of Blood*, the idea of national culture was being vulgarized by the governing elite which was increasingly turning traditional cultural practices into rituals of power. And if Ngugi's works in English – especially *Petals of Blood* – were written primary for a middle-class readership, it was because he still had faith in the capacity and willingness of the middle class to initiate the kinds of changes he was advocating. Writing in Gikuyu was a threat to this class not so much because it evoked new literary subjects or advocated new radical commitments (the subject and ideology of *Petals of Blood* is the same as that of *I Will Marry When I Want*), but because a discourse across class lines would call into question the political arrangements that secured the political authority of the postcolonial state.

Since Ngugi did not pose any real threat to the established political order in Kenya, one of the questions that readers of his works have to constantly ask is why the state went out of its way to imprison him without trial in 1977 and to eventually force him into exile in 1982. There are several plausible answers to this question: one could argue that, as a Marxist, Ngugi presented the only coherent ideological critique of the politics of neo-colonialism (to be a Marxist in Kenya was to be a heretic); or that his writing in

Gikuyu undermined the covenant between the ruling class and its subalterns by suggesting that there was an alternative to the state, the party, and the president as sources of meaning and authority; or even that his writings, by turning the state itself into a subject of ridicule, were undermining the representational authority of the postcolony.[92] One way of bringing all these issues together, as I hope to do in the last three chapters of this study, is to examine the centrality of the state in Ngugi's aesthetic and ideological practices since the 1980s. What I am proposing, then, is a chronological reading of his works that takes us from the liberal Englishness of his early fiction to the Marxist – and perhaps post-Marxist – engagement with questions of power and society in the theatre of decolonization.

CHAPTER 2

Narrative and nationalist desire: early short stories and The River Between

Ngugi began his writing career under the pressures of three power-ful cultural institutions in colonial Kenya: the Protestant church, which was the major conduit for modern identities in the colonial sphere; the mission school, which, through its valorization of literacy as the point of entry into the culture of colonialism, promoted new narratives of temporality and identity; and Gikuyu cultural nationalism, which manifested itself in the tradition of independent schools that the novelist attended in his youth.[1] For the young Ngugi, each of these institutions held promises of emancipation from the bonds of class and ethnicity, but also presented unexpected dilemmas. One of the major appeals of Protestantism in Central Kenya, for example, was its equation of morality with bourgeois civility: one was not merely a Christian because one believed in a certain doctrine; rather, conversion was apparent in one's ability to live a modern life, a life manifested in a new monetary economy, mode of dress, set of cultural values, and even architecture.

But if Christian conversion was the colonial subject's point of contact with modernity, it also implied a self-willed *dédoublement* from a set of cultural values that had been at the foundation of one's communal identity. Conversion implied the negation of a traditional identity in preference for a modern, quasi-European one, and this was not particularly easy for the Gikuyu who, as we saw in the last chapter, were beginning to consolidate their identity in the wake of colonial rule.[2] Ngugi was thus born into a culture that was eager to embrace colonial modernity, but one that had serious doubts about the wisdom of a radical negation of its newly invented collective identity. Indeed, one of the central themes in

Ngugi's early works is the tension between this desire for modernity and the pull of what appears to be an intractable past.   The hunger for education constitutes a second major theme in Ngugi's works. The predominance of the trope of education and self-making in Ngugi's early works has roots in his biography as much as the culture of colonialism: the Gikuyu who had left their homesteads behind to join Christian-based educational institutions did so in the belief that it was it was only through a mission education that conversion could be rationalized and effected. The relationship between colonial education and Christian conversion – which was also conceived as the entry into modernity – was so close that Gikuyu Christians were defined as *athomi*, the people of the book.[3] But underneath the promise held by the culture of the book, as many of the protagonists in Ngugi's early works come to realize sooner or later, was the fear that education marked an irreversible move away from the existing foundation of identity and community or what came to be known as tradition.[4] As we saw in the last chapter, this anxiety had been responsible for the founding of Gikuyu independent schools in the 1930s. These schools were, however, built on a very problematic philosophical foundation: the belief that one could be educated in the colonial sense and still maintain a certain measure of affiliation with Gikuyu (traditional) culture.

When Ngugi's parents sent him to an independent school for his elementary or primary education, they might have done so in the common belief that such a school could provide their son with a modern education while ensuring his continuous affiliation with his immediate community and culture. But as Ngugi was to show so powerfully in *The River Between*, the idea of community was itself at odds with the individualism on which a modern identity was predicated.[5] Ngugi's early writings – most notably the early stories in *Secret Lives*, *The River Between*, and *Weep Not, Child* – must thus be located in what Raymond Williams has aptly called the border country "between custom and education, between work and ideas, between love of place and an experience of change."[6] The novelist's ideological notions about categories such as custom, work, and time would certainly be transformed in the course of his career, but one constant thread in all his writings would continue be the conflict between his love of place – one identity formed around notions of land, household, and the community (the *mbari*) – and the overwhelming sense of change that defined the moment in which these works were set (the high nationalist period) and the time in which they were written (the advent of decolonization).

BECOMING A WRITER

If a writer's early works are symptomatic of the anxieties that generate a literary career, then it is appropriate to see Ngugi's juvenilia as containing the germs of the questions of displacement and the desire for radical social transformation which mark his more mature works such as *Petals of Blood*.[7] And so it is to his earliest stories that readers are asked to turn in order to understand how the context discussed in the previous chapter finds its way into the very language of Ngugi's fiction. This task must begin with the simple observation that Ngugi's love of place, and his experience of change, generates a certain aesthetic form: it is the love of place that makes his Gikuyu physical and cultural landscape – and its multiple conflicts and identities – the raw materials for the early fiction. But the author's desire to capture this disappearing landscape in writing is often in conflict with his inherited notion about what makes good writing.[8]

This is especially the case in relation to subjectivity. For to capture the essence of a Gikuyu identity as it had been defined by cultural nationalism since the 1920s, the writer needed to conceive his subjects as corporate and affiliative entities, defined by their investment in certain communal values and rites, such as circumcision, and elements of colonial modernity such as education and the cash economy. The desire for a subjectivity defined by communal affiliations, was, however, at odds with the production of the modern novel whose condition of possibility was the existence of a unique individual defined by his or her rejection of communality. Ngugi thus began his career facing a typical novelistic dilemma: how could the modern novelist claim affiliation with a disappearing communal culture and still display his mastery of the language of alienation which, he had been taught at Makerere University College, was the essence of good writing?[9]

Ngugi's earliest fiction is an attempt to resolve this conflict. These stories are defined by the tension between his sense of landscape and inherited forms of fiction. They are, indeed, stories about the gap that separates the author's desire for affiliation with the Gikuyu landscape and the impossibility of representing this desire in modernist form. These stories are about the search for identity and belonging, but they are also dominated by images of darkness, drought, and barrenness. In Ngugi's earliest story, "Mugumo" (originally published as "The Fig Tree"), for example, Mukami's tragedy is foreshadowed and framed by "the lone and savage darkness" that meets her when she decides to leave her husband; in "And the Rain Came Down!," Nyokabi's childlessness functions as a metaphor of emotional barrenness; and in "Gone with the Drought," a landscape scorched by the sun, appears to the narrator to be gripped by "the whiteness of death."[10] As the following example shows, the power of these early stories lies in the opposition between the image of the landscape as simultaneously the source of life and the place of death:

> From ridge up to ridge the neat little shambas stood bare. The once short and beautiful hedges – the product of land consolidation and the pride of farmers in our district, were dry and powdered with dust. Even the old mugumo tree that stood just below our village, and which was never dry, lost its leaves and its greenness – the living greenness that had always scorned short-lived droughts. Many people had forecast doom. Weather-prophets and medicine men – for some still remain in our village though with diminished power – were consulted by a few people and all forecast doom. (*Secret Lifes*, pp. 15–16).

It would be tempting to read these persistent images of darkness, decay, and failure as symbols of the land under colonial domination. But this kind of reading is complicated by the fact that images of darkness, drought, and barrenness in these stories are also marks of the gap that separates the individual from the collective. As a budding writer at Makerere University, Ngugi had been taught that the best kind of writing emerged from a writer's sense of the troubled relation between subjects and their landscape. But in trying to represent the Gikuyu landscape in the same way the writers F. R. Leavis had privileged in *The Great Tradition* were supposed to have done for England, what the novelist seemed to confront was his own separation from the people whose psychology he was trying to represent.[11] While the sense of displacement readers encounter in these early stories can be interpreted as symptomatic of identity under colonial rule, as Ngugi was to argue in his later works, it was also a reflection of another central tenet in the great tradition – the belief that a modern identity was predicated on alienation.

Consider, then, how often in these early stories individual identity – and even heroism – emerges only when solitary subjects confront the terror of the collective will or the dictates of tradition. In "Mugumo," to cite just one example, what makes Mukami the focus of pathos is her lone defiance of the values of the "tribal" hearth. Rather than being defined by her presence in the "courtyard," as Gikuyu tradition would demand, Mukami acquires her distinctive identity when she moves away from the "eternal chorus of mute condemnation" represented by the institution of marriage and the family: "She stood a moment, and in that second Mukami realized that with the shutting of the gate, she had shut off a part of her existence. Tears were imminent as with a heavy heart she turned her back on her rightful place and began to move" (*Secret Lives*, p. 2).

There is no doubt that Mukami's rejection of the traditional configuration of identity is represented as both necessary and dangerous: it is necessary because it is by initiating her own estrangement from the *socius* that she can finally find her true self; it is dangerous because what appears to be self-willed alienation is already a tragic response to collective or institutional demands. Although Mukami seeks to discover herself by rejecting the values of the hearth ("She only wanted a chance to start life anew – a life of giving and not only receiving" [p. 6]), her rebellion is shadowed by a communal "spell" which insists that she has no identity without a husband and a child.

Indeed, one could argue that Mukami escapes from one tradition (that of domesticity) to seek refugee in another (religion). At the end of the story, she has found sanctuary under the scared Mugumo tree, the most obvious symbol of Gikuyu collective interests and desires, where she dreams of lying "asleep under the protecting arms of God's tree" and imagines herself to have been touched by the hand of Mumbi, the legendary mother of the Gikuyu (p. 7). Touched by the hand of divinity, as it were, Mukami decides to sacrifice her individual desires and go back to "my husband and my people" (p. 7). This choice is endorsed by the narrator who had earlier seemed to condone Mukami's estrangement: "It was a new Mukami, humble yet full of hope who said this" (p. 7). Coming to the knowledge that "she was pregnant, had been pregnant for some time," Mukami is now ready to come to terms with herself; but she can only do so through the figures of tradition she had rejected at the beginning of the story:

As Mukami stood up ready to go, she stared with unseeing eyes into space, while tears of deep gratitude and humility trickled down her face. Her eyes looked beyond the forest, beyond the stream, as if they were seeing something, something hidden in the distant future. And she saw the people of Muhoroini, her *aiiru* and her man, strong, unageing, standing amongst them. That was her rightful place, there beside her husband amongst the other wives. They must unite and support *ruriri*, giving it new life. Was Mumbi watching? (p. 8)

This story would appear, then, to be driven by divided intentions. On the one hand, it belongs to a modernist tradition in which subjects are defined by their estrangement from the community. The original version of the story has an important epigraph from D. H. Lawrence, the English master of the theme of identity through alienation; and the story begins by positing subjects whose integrity is threatened by the tyranny of tradition. On the other hand, the story's resolution is an assent to the sentiments of cultural nationalism in which individual desires are subjected to communal interests. In the original version of the story published in the Makerere University journal, *Penpoint*, Mukami decides to go back "to my husband and my tribe."[12] Even in the revised version quoted above, Mukami's return home to her husband and co-wives is explained, not by an appeal to individual desire, but through the language of high nationalism: "They must unite and support *ruriri* [the nation or the race], giving it new life" (p. 8). Reproduction is justified by its capacity to give life to the new nation.[13]

If the moment of closure in a story or a novel is always privileged and contains the code that explains the meaning of the whole narrative, there is more in the above opposition between the assertion of individuality and the pull of collective desires and interests than meets the eye. This opposition is symptomatic of Ngugi's paradoxical location, in his early works, between nationalist sentiment and modern alterity. We can read the last sentence of the passage above as Ngugi's romantic identification with the desires of the *Karing'a* (Gikuyu cultural nationalism) against the authority of the *kirore* (the proponents of colonial modernity). But what does it mean to valorize the call for national unity in narrative techniques borrowed from the modern masters of English literature?

Ngugi's narrative language in the early stories is structured by a simple trajectory: rejected by their families and communities because they cannot – or are unable – to fulfill their assigned cultural functions, the main characters decide to embrace their loss and displacement as the enabling condition for a new identity; but at the end of the story these subjects come to realize that there is no identity outside the locus of community. In "And the Rain Came Down!" the main character, Nyokabi, is, like Mukami, *thata* (barren). And as in the previous story, readers are invited to perceive her childlessness as both the cause and consequence of her displacement. In short, because of her childlessness, Nyokabi is represented simultaneously as a subject who has failed to live up to certain communal expectations about women and as the victim of metaphysical notions about life and reproduction: "Murungu [God] had not answered her cry, her desire, her hope. Her great expectations had come to nought" (*Secret Lives*, p. 10).

Communal demands and individual desires coalesce in unnamable objects usually referred to as spells or curses in the story; when such unnamable things become "too much," characters such as Nyokabi seek sanctuary in the bush, a heterotopic space where "the wildness of the place, and the whole desolate atmosphere seemed to have strangely harmonized with her state of madness" (p. 11).[14] But as in "Mugumo," the moment of self-discovery, of ironic distance from the community, also sets the stage for the subject's realization that there is no selfhood outside the parameters set by the collective culture, that the alternative to home, family, and nation, is social death – the "haunted death of a lonely woman" (p. 11). The story then leads to an expected fantasy or utopian resolution: Nyokabi finds a lost child in the bush; in a state of delirium she takes the child home believing it is her own; but as it turns out, the lost child is that of her husband's younger wife. In rescuing the lost child, however, Nyokabi makes her husband proud, fulfills a maternal function, and finds satisfaction in honor rather than death.

So the story moves from a moment of crisis, through a space of self-reflection, to one of romantic resolution. And in this trajectory, we can see what I consider to be young Ngugi's unfulfilled aesthetic ambition. For what we have in both "Mugumo" and "And the Rain Came Down!" are stories in which local subjects, themes, and landscapes are represented in the language of the modernist novel. These stories are modern in the sense that the act of narration depends on the existence of individuals who have made self-willed attempts to break from tradition. In addition, the narration of this modernizing gesture is predicated on the representation of Gikuyu landscape and cultures as both a source of terror and a threat to enlightenment.

But because Ngugi is not entirely comfortable with the modernist narrative of emancipation through alienation sketched in his early stories, what I have characterized as his romantic resolution to the cultural crisis in these narratives is his way of gesturing to the power of tradition. In order to acquire an identity, his characters must give up their revolt and seek comfort in communal narratives and norms. This is how these early stories come to be structured by recursive and apostrophic moments: the characters always run back to the institutions from which they sought to escape (hence their recursiveness); in doing so they are turned away from their original quest (hence the apostrophic nature of their return).

While it might be convenient to read the romantic resolutions as fabricated attempts to conclude narratives that should ideally be left open-ended, I think they point to Ngugi's first attempt to transcend the great tradition and his ultimate imprisonment in it. Instead of presenting us with stories in which individuals effect a radical break with tradition and start their lives anew, Ngugi returns them to the hearth; in the process he rejects the modernist notion of a privileged and unique identity. At the same time, however, the focalization of these stories remains very ambivalent.

This ambivalence is especially apparent when one turns attention to the question of gender in these stories: for if women such as Mukami and Nyokabi are deprived of their unique identity because they cannot perform the reproductive functions assigned to them by the families and communities, why are they unable to seek the fulfillment of their desires elsewhere, through other means? Writing under the pressures of nationalism, Ngugi seems to share the common creed that individual desires must be sacrificed for the common good.

But this explanation still leaves the cultural politics of these stories unaddressed: where does Ngugi stand on the troublesome questions that were all around him as he wrote these stories at the dawn of independence – questions about nation, culture, and gender? The divided intentions I mentioned earlier seem to leave his position quite ambivalent. Was he living in a colonial situation that he knew nothing about? Or had he turned to imaginative writing as a way of escaping from the violent politics of late colonialism? If the two stories discussed above are considered representative, Ngugi became a writer to escape the harsh politics that had dominated his childhood and youth. While colonialism is very much alive in even the stories that seem to eschew politics, what is notable about colonial culture in these works is its ambivalent terms of reference. This ambivalence raises a simple question: is Ngugi writing against colonialism or Gikuyu traditionalism?

One can address this question from both an ideological and an aesthetic perspective. From an ideological perspective, the early Ngugi was a strong believer in Christian conversion and enlightenment. From an aesthetic perspective, he became a writer at Makerere College, under the tutelage of the latter-day disciples of Matthew Arnold and F. R. Leavis, teachers who believed that literature was above all an instrument of moral change and individual assertion.[15] Ngugi had, however, come of age under the influence of traditional Gikuyu culture and the mandate of cultural nationalism, and the task he had set himself early in his career was simply how to reconcile these ostensibly opposed functions. Becoming a writer was one way of negotiating the ideological and aesthetic demands reflected in the great divide between colonial culture and cultural nationalism.

"The Village Priest" (an early version of *The River Between*) is exemplary in this regard. The story begins by presenting the cartography of the colonial landscape in binary oppositions. Joshua, the village priest, is a representative of colonial culture; his character and deportment symbolize the civility demanded by the discourse of conversion; his evangelical zeal denotes his absolute rejection of Gikuyu traditions; his family is a model of the modern life promoted by colonialism. His house, we are told, was "the only one of its kind along the ridge"; it was "a tin-roofed rectangular building" that stood in stark contrast to the "mud-walled, grass-thatched round huts that were scattered all over the place" (*Secret Lives*, p. 22). Joshua's house symbolizes bourgeois civility and modern architecture in the colonial landscape; there are, in turn, signs of a new epistemology: his unquestioning belief in the power of Christian prayer stands in opposition to the rituals of the rain-maker, which he holds in contempt.

But the drought they seek to alleviate, and the crisis of knowledge and meaning they have to confront, conjoin both priests in a way that redefines their functions in the colonized landscape. The rainmaker's sacrifices seem to have brought about the rain, but his virtual absence from the story indicates his marginality in the colonial economy of representation; Joshua's apparent failure to bring about the end of the drought through prayer seems to call attention to the alienation of his new system of knowledge and belief – and thus the "hollowness and hopelessness" (p. 25) within him. At the end of the story, however, there is no doubt that real power and authority reside in the world represented by the white priest, Livingstone, and that for those who have converted to Christianity, reversion to old rituals is impossible. In this situation of radical division, the narrative voice seems to hover in an empty space between conversion and prophecy, perhaps eager to endorse the rainmaker but aware of the power of the new Christian order (p. 27).

CONVERSION AND PROPHECY: *THE RIVER BETWEEN*

It is impossible to understand the relation between language, narrative, and the politics of colonialism in Ngugi's early work without considering the trope of prophecy and conversion in *The River Between*, his first completed novel. Indeed, whereas the imposition of colonial rule in Central Kenya depended on the conversion of the Gikuyu from the traditions and narratives of their ancestors to the stories of colonial modernity, it was through the discourse of prophecy that nationalists in Central Kenya would seek to reconcile themselves to colonial rule and to create a cultural space in which a future beyond colonialism could be fashioned. It is thus surprising that so many critics of *The River Between* have missed the close relation between the language of the novel and the trope of conversion and prophecy – strange because the novel opens by establishing this relationship quite explicitly:[16]

The two ridges lay side by side. One was Kameno, the other was Makuyu. Between them was a valley. It was called the valley of life. Behind Kameno and Makuyu were many more valleys and ridges, lying without any discernible plan. They were like many sleeping lions which never woke. They just slept, the big deep sleep of their Creator.

A river flowed through the valley of life. If there had been no bush and no forest trees covering the slopes, you could have seen the river when you stood on top of either Kameno or Makuyu. Now you had to come down. Even then you could not see the whole extent of the river as it gracefully, and without any apparent haste, wound its way down the valley, like a snake. The river was called Honia, which meant cure, or bring-back-to-life. Honia river never dried: it seemed to have a strong will to live, scorning droughts and weather changes. And it went on in the same way, never hurrying, never hesitating. People saw this and were happy.

Honia was the soul of Kameno and Makuyu. It joined them. And men, cattle, wild beasts and trees, were all united by this life-stream.[17]

The novel opens by calling attention to the Manichean geography of the colonial situation, but its language also establishes that, beneath the radical separation of Kameno and Makuyu, lie some important connections.[18] The simple sentences of the first paragraph foreground the diachronic relationship between the two communities; the second and third paragraphs conjoin them in a relation of identity and difference.

Several narrative strategies are deployed in the establishment of these connections and disconnections: first, the novel valorizes the position of the addressee – the "you" – who is promised a unified

view of the landscape, but is warned that a descent into the valley
will only expose him or her to the antagonisms that define the two
communities. Secondly, the narrative calls attention to the symbolic nature of Honia, the river of healing, which serves as the
signifier of mutual identity and a mark of radical separation.
Thirdly, while each of the ridges acquires its personality from the
position its leaders take in relation to contested meanings about
traditional pasts and colonial presents, they both articulate their
needs in the language of Christian conversion.

This relationship of identity and difference needs to be under-
lined because it sets up the puzzle that the rest of the novel seeks to
answer: how did two communities with a common past and
culture come to be defined by so much antagonism and such bitter
rivalry? *The River Between* addresses this problem by establishing a
certain fiction or mythology of time, a temporality defined by –
and represented in – the idiom of prophecy, the language of usable
pasts, contested presents, and unknown futures. This is the fiction
we read in Kameno's self-representation as the "chosen place,"
the site of Gikuyu origins and ultimate restoration:

Kameno had a good record to bear out this story. A sacred grove had
sprung out of the place where Gikuyu and Mumbi stood; people still paid
homage to it. It could also be seen, by any who cared to count, that
Kameno threw up more heroes and leaders than any other ridge. Mugo
wa Kibiro, that great Gikuyu seer of old, had been born there. And he
had grown up, seeing visions of the future and speaking them to the many
people who came to see and hear him. (*The River Between*, p. 2)

As John Lonsdale has argued in another context, it is through
an appeal to the prophetic narrative associated with Mugo wa
Kibiro that a Gikuyu historiography is invented and instituted.[19]
What should not be forgotten, however, is that the prophetic trope
– and the narrative of history associated with it – is retrospective
and thus has cogency only to the extent that it is a specific cultural
response to colonialism in general and Christian conversion in
particular.[20]

Significantly, though, Ngugi's novel opens with a now familiar
situation in which myths of origins are haunted by the language of
the Bible and the colonial event. Chege derives his spiritual auth-

ority from his genealogical association with Mugo wa Kibiro, but to the extent that his most important prophecy – the one foretelling the establishment of the Christian mission at Siriana – had been doubted by his community, he is seen as a belated prophet and the guardian of "flickering" or tenuous knowledge (pp. 7–8). In addition, Chege's prophetic account – and Waiyaki's cultural function within it – is overshadowed by Christian conversion in two significant ways: first, the community begins to take the prophecy seriously only when it needs a narrative to help them deal with the crisis Christianity triggers in Gikuyu culture. Secondly, what makes the prophetic moment so crucial to cultural nationalism as it is represented in Ngugi's novel, is its capacity to sustain the utopian longing that defines cultural nationalism, the belief that a moment of restoration exists after colonialism.

In this context, the trope of prophecy in *The River Between* has both a historical and imaginative function: it serves as a symptom of the discontent generated by colonization and as the narrative mode in which a future beyond European conquest can be imagined or be revealed. In Ngugi's novel, the colonized subjects' acute awareness of their temporal dislocation in the new order of things goes hand in hand with the certainty that this situation can be mastered because it has been foreseen and foretold. More importantly, the cultural crisis that is narrated in *The River Between* is triggered by a certain confusion or misunderstanding about the meaning of the ancient prophecy and its efficacy. Very early in the novel, for example, we are told that Chege's despair arose from his realization that the tangible evidence of colonial encroachment was not enough to convince people that the old prophecy has already come to pass: "the white man had come to Siriana, and Joshua and Kabonyi had been converted. They had abandoned the ridges and followed the new faith. Still people shrugged their shoulders and went on with their work..." (p. 8). A prophecy has no authority unless it can be believed; and Chege dies without convincing anyone that the things foreseen in the ancient prophecy had come to pass.

It is hence left to Chege's son, Waiyaki, to try and connect the old world, the one that produced the prophecy, with the symbolic economy of colonialism. Waiyaki's dilemma, however, is caught up in the archetypal problem of the colonized African: he finds himself tenuously connected to his traditional past while holding on to the dream of an autonomous future which cannot be guaranteed. From an early age, he is forced to simultaneously envision and wrestle with pasts and futures in which the realities of colonial rule are intermixed with the sweet dreams of national liberation . Thus, if Waiyaki seems to prefer the image of stable origins – what he calls "the beginning of time" (p. 10) – to the chaos and doubts that are visible in his colonial childhood, it is also because he is aware of the distance between him and the time associated with national heroes such as Demi and Mathathi, whom he seeks to emulate:

Demi na Mathathi were giants of the tribe. They had lived a long way back, at the beginning of time. They cut down trees and cleared the dense forests for cultivation. They owned many cattle, sheep and goats and they often sacrificed to Murungu and held communion with the ancestral spirits. Waiyaki had heard about these two generations of the tribe and he was proud of them. Only he wished he knew what they had looked like. They must have been great and strong to have braved the hazards of the forest. (p. 10)

In the above passage, as in Ngugi's early works as a whole, melancholy and loss structure the subject's reflection on the past. This melancholy is also evident in the numerous instances in the novel when Waiyaki considers his own sense of alienation which, when compared to the cosmic unity of his ancestors, forces him to question his own function within the prophetic tradition he is supposed to embody. Melancholy is, however, also represented as a sign of the tension between the dream of prophetic restoration and the uncompromising power of Christian conversion. For while Waiyaki lives in doubt about the efficacy of the ancient prophecy – can Gikuyu culture ever overcome the contamination ostensibly brought about by Christian conversion? – evangelical Christians such as Joshua are driven by a faith which, because of its reinforcement by the white man's power and "magic," cannot countenance doubt or the possibility of failure. Indeed, *The River Between* is structured not simply by the traditional rivalry between Makuyu and Kameno, but also the subtle contrasts the narrator makes between, on the one hand, Joshua's faith and certainty and, on the other hand, Waiyaki's sense of doubt and crisis.

In spite of the challenges presented by a resurgent traditionalism, Joshua's faith is described as a kind of "possession" built on the authority of radical renunciation. Unlike Waiyaki, who lives in uncertainty, Joshua cannot doubt his new faith or the authority of colonial culture precisely because his new identity is built on his total rejection of Gikuyu culture. Joshua's sense of self – and indeed his location within his new Christian community – is predicated not so much on the promises of colonial culture (his decaying house seems to put this into question), but his innate belief that the "tribe's magic, power and ritual" were signs of darkness and that their cultural narratives were inherently flawed:

His people worshipped Murungu, Mwenenyaga, Ngai. The unerring white man had called the Gikuyu god the prince of darkness . . . Isaiah, the white man's seer, had prophesied of Jesus. He had told of the coming of a messiah. Had Mugo wa Kibiro, the Gikuyu seer, ever foretold of such a saviour? No. Isaiah was great. He had told of Jesus, the saviour of the world. (p. 29)

At the end of the novel, however, Joshua's blind belief represents an important moment of irony in *The River Between*: his authority is challenged by Waiyaki's school, the counter-discourse he constructs around the figure of Mugo, and the resurgence of an emotive narrative of Gikuyu restoration. In addition, while Joshua's message of salvation appears original at first, it is shown, on closer examination, to be a compilation of Christian clichés which, because of their vehemence and uncompromising nature, end up alienating potential converts and readers.

Clearly, Ngugi is more sympathetic to the ideals of Gikuyu restoration embodied by Waiyaki and more skeptical of Joshua's narrative of Christian conversion. This is in marked contrast to the ambivalent stance we detected in "The Village Priest," an earlier version of Joshua's story. But as we have already seen, the discourse of colonial power in *The River Between* is the tangible reality against which all Gikuyu narratives, including the prophetic narrative and the desire for "tribal" restoration, must be measured; all such stories of origin and autonomy are subordinated to the grand narrative of empire. Its own uncertain relation to its cultural landscape and history, to cite one obvious example, defines the narrative of tradition in *The River Between*. Indeed, while the traditional community performs its primary rites of identity such as circumcision in the belief that these constitute historical continuity, the novel calls attention to the tenuous nature of such rites.

Beneath the excitement generated by "tribal" rituals, traditional culture is shown to be nothing more than a series of signs that have become disjointed from their signifiers:

Harvests came and went. They had been good; people rejoiced. Such rich harvests had not been seen for years. Old men sighed with inner fear as they witnessed the hubbub of excitement, throbbing through the ridges, making things tremble. Had they not seen such happenings before in their days of youth?

The elders, then, offered many burnt sacrifices to Murungu. Who did not know what such unusual harvests portended? Who could not remember the great famine that had swept through the hills, spreading its fingers of smoke to all the land of the Gikuyu? That was before the real advent of the white men. Most of the old men had then been young. But they had never forgotten the great wealth and harvests that preceded the famine. (p. 37)

By the end of *The River Between*, when Waiyaki is confronted by stark choices, it becomes apparent to him, as it does to the reader, that the constant clamor for a return to the old ways that dominates the second half of the novel arises from an awareness of loss and displacement. Even what would appear to be the traditionalists' triumph over the Christians – Muthoni's defection to the *Karing'a*, for example – is also the moment when the tenuous authority of the "tribal" narrative is exposed.

A reading of *The River Between* as a nationalist novel must hence begin by acknowledging how the desire for an autonomous national culture is overshadowed by the very economy of colonial rule that it seeks to transcend. Among Ngugi's early works, *The River Between* provides readers of African literature with one of the best illustrations of the compromised context in which nationalist narratives were produced in the era of decolonization. If the reader were to begin with the second chapter of *The River Between*, he or she would encounter one of the most powerful evocations of the dreams and desires of Gikuyu nationalists in the period in which the novel is set (the 1920s) – the desire for cultural purity under-written by a deep emotional investment in the unity of the "tribe."

As we saw in the previous chapter, the rite of circumcision is considered to be the essence of a Gikuyu community; it is the process by which one enters into an associative relationship with the governing *polis*; it is also the occasion when the expression of the individual subject's deep patriotic sentiments and erotic desires is fused with those of a collective entity variously called *aandu* (the people) or *ruriri* (the race or nation). The fusion of individual and communal desires is symbolized by the great dance (*Mambura*) that precedes initiation. The significance of this dance in rites of passage, the process through which identity in performed in precolonial society, has been noted by almost every observer of Gikuyu life.[21] All these commentators have been keen to underscore how the initiates' dance provides a cultural occasion for self-representation in a communal process in which individual and social drives are merged. In Ngugi's representation of the neophytes' dance, there is a crucial foregrounding of the erotic and associative nature of the occasion, of the interplay between *polis* and eros:[22]

The dance was being held at an open-air place in Kameno. Whistles, horns, broken tins and anything else that was handy were taken and beaten to the rhythm of the song and dance. Everybody went into a frenzy of excitement. Old and young, women and children, all were there losing themselves in the magic motion of the dance. Men shrieked and shouted and jumped into the air as they went round in a circle. For them, this was the moment. This was the time. Women, stripped to the waist, with their thin breasts flapping on their chests, went round and round the big fire, swinging their hips and contorting their bodies in all sorts of provocative ways, but always keeping the rhythm. (p. 41)

The significance of the dance, then, is to be found in the license it gives people to express their individual selves in the deepest way possible, but, at the same time, to remind them that this self can only be expressed within the parameters set by the community. The dance is carnivalesque in obvious ways: it offers a forum for individual subjects to forget themselves and the differences – of rank, class, and religion – that have become a marked feature of their society under colonialism. In the course of the neophytes' dance, time is suspended in the eroticism of the moment, and the participants are impelled to exist in what Benedict Anderson, writing on nationalism and culture, has memorably called "empty homogeneous time."[23] Even when the spell is broken with Muthoni's appearance and her attempt to justify her participation in rituals her father has renounced as barbaric, the associative nature of the dance – and hence of circumcision – is accentuated. Muthoni is keen to underscore the fact that her reversion to "tribal" rituals does not imply her rejection of Christianity; her goal, she insists, is to synthesize the two cultures and belief systems.

But if the neophytes' dance represents the last attempt by Gikuyu culture to resist its reorganization under colonial norms, the narrator reminds us that this project is threatened from the start. Indeed, the scenes of erotic associativeness discussed above are preceded – and often punctuated – by a subtext that exposes them as romantic dreams, instances of cultural amnesia, or even dangerous musings. It is important that Chapter Nine opens by again calling the trope of prophecy – the foundation of nationalism in Central Kenya – into question. Nationalism in *The River Between* relies on a prophetic discourse because, as I have already suggested, it is driven by the belief that a new millennium, one in which colonialism will be transplanted by the restoration of national desires and interests, is at hand; but the future which Gikuyu nationalists await is constructed around an idealized past before colonial rule and conquest.

And yet, Chapter Nine of the novel opens with a kind of eschatological fear of both the past and the future. All signs point to a rich harvest, a sign of rebirth which spreads joy through the ridges; but the old men who are supposed to be custodians of national memory "sighed with inner fear as they witnessed the hubbub of excitement, throbbing through the ridges, making things tremble" (p. 37). And just as the expectations of national renewal are rationalized by an idealized past – that of Ndemi and Mathathi which Waiyaki invokes as he prepares to carry out his prophetic role – the elders also base their fears on their reading and (mis)understanding of the past: "Had they not seen such happenings before in their days of youth?" (p. 37). Compared to the legends of Ndemi, which the young neophytes invoke on the eve of their circumcision, the elders' recollections point toward a history witnessed and thus feared. If the prophecy of national restoration in *The River Between* seems to be undermined even as it seems to be celebrated, or if, as Abdul JanMohammed has argued, the major problem of the novel is its inability to represent Waiyaki "unreservedly as a real messiah or whether to portray him as a character whose prophetic calling is a self-delusion," it is because the narrative of history is itself caught between the promise of the messianic and its impossibility.[24]

The narrative Waiyaki has inherited from his father and ancestors is, on one level, quite simple: A "black messiah" will emerge from the hills to restore Gikuyu lands and secure their cultural integrity. By all indications, Waiyaki is this messiah. On another level, however, this narrative is complicated by the conditions in which it is developed and elaborated, a colonial condition in which the ends and means of the messianic project are called into question by forces extraneous to the foundational narratives of the Gikuyu. In order for communal restoration to be effective in the new order, both the means and ends of the prophetic narrative must be inscribed as alienated: the "black messiah" will have to be trained in a "white" school and he must function as an agent of modernity and modernization not of tradition. Thus, Chege, the guardian of the prophecy of restoration, is forced to send his only son, Waiyaki, to the colonial school at Siriana as an acknowledgment that the prophecy itself can only be played out according to the rules established by colonialism. The important lesson here is that the fulfillment of the prophecy demands that the colonized "be wise in the affairs of the white man" (p. 38).

The implication of this dependence on colonial authority is not lost upon Waiyaki or his father. Indeed, Waiyaki's doubts during the circumcision rituals, and his self-censorship in the face of the blatant sexuality of the neophytes' dance, is the most obvious sign of how his education in the colonial schools has alienated him from the central rites of his people. Waiyaki may pretend to lose himself in the frenzy of the neophytes' dance, but we cannot fail to recognize that his language and standards of judgment come out of the missionaries' epistemology, their puritanism and moral censure. Waiyaki feels uneasy and out of place in the dance and something "inside" prevents him from "losing himself in this frenzy"; what others see as an uninhibited expression of self, he sees as evidence of "the chaos created by locked emotions let loose" (p. 42). Although his culture allows him to talk freely about sex and sexuality on this occasion, Waiyaki "was slightly embarrassed by this talk of forbidden things" (p. 42). Waiyaki's alienation in the rituals of circumcision raises two questions that are at the very heart of Ngugi's novel: given his education and conversion, why does he speak the language of cultural restoration? And if his desire is for the return to a precolonial culture, why is his yearning for Gikuyu eroticism censored by the mechanisms of a colonial education?

We can address these questions – perhaps indirectly – by observing a central paradox in Ngugi's early works: on the one hand, Ngugi sees his primary role as a writer on the eve of decolonization as that of representing, in the imagination, an autochthonous African culture that might function as the foundation of the new nation; on the other hand, however, he is aware of the degree to which his Christian beliefs and missionary education continuously block his desire for the idealized cultural body. This paradox accounts for the linguistic stammer we notice every time Ngugi tries to describe seminal Gikuyu rituals such as the rite of being born again (p.12) or circumcision (p. 42). But the novelist's anxieties toward the "tribal" past his works try to recuperate are also apparent in the problematic status of Gikuyu culture itself, located, as it is, at the cusp between colonialism and decolonization. The truth is, while Ngugi privileges culture in the politics of African nationalism because he shares the common belief, expounded by Kenyatta in *Facing Mount Kenya*, that the essence of a postcolonial identity would be sought in the cultural formation that colonialism had interrupted, the idea of culture itself is a very colonial construct.[25]

Indeed, the history of culture in Central Kenya since the 1920s is one long attempt by both European and Gikuyu anthropologists to codify *miikarire* (customs or everyday practices) as cultural constructs.[26] This codification was particularly important for Gikuyu nationalists, because in the absence of a precolonial state, culture was the basis of social organization and identity. But the precolonial Gikuyu did not, of course, understand or represent culture in its modern anthropological sense and it was left up to writers such as Kenyatta and Ngugi to imagine what Gikuyu culture might have been before colonialism, before its representation in European texts. What Kenyatta considered to be culture emerged as much from his recollection of folk beliefs passed on by elders in his family and community as it did from Malinowski's seminar on cultural change at the University of London.

As a student of Kenyatta, as it were, Ngugi's dilemma was how to represent culture as something more than an eclectic collection of folk beliefs and as something distinct from its anthropological definition. In fiction, the novelist had the license to imagine culture as an admixture of both folk beliefs and anthropological practices and to locate it somewhere between a certain mythology of the precolonial past and the colonial present. The notion of prophecy discussed above is part of this attempt to construct culture in the site of "occult instability" between an African culture and its colonial counterpart.[27] For this reason, the prophetic narrative recreates or imagines a scene of cultural restoration that exists both in an idealized past and an imagined future. Furthermore, if Ngugi's first novel seems eager to account for the past and the future, it was because *The River Between* is a work generated by deep anxieties about the "time of its production."[28]

The three temporal periods of the novel – an ideal or idealized Gikuyu past, the colonized present, and the utopian future – are masterfully brought together in the person of Waiyaki, especially in his dual identity as a Gikuyu hero and a messianic, Christian, figure. Named after a legendary Gikuyu leader who had died in the hands of the British imperialists in the 1890s, Waiyaki embodies three strands of cultural nationalism in Central Kenya: the narrative of resistance to colonial rule, Gikuyu moral ideals centered on questions of sacrifice and martyrdom, and the nationalist myth of cultural restoration. But Waiyaki's life is also fashioned after that of Christ: he is the only son of an old man, the subject of an eschatological history, and, as it turns out, the subject who must be sacrificed in order for the "tribe" to be cleansed. In narrative terms, Waiyaki is a character from African oral traditions, represented in allegorical terms and revealed to us as he undergoes rites

of passage. But he is also the unique – and alienated – individual of
the bourgeois novel, often defined by his opposition to the collective desires and discourses of his people. It can be said that the
power of *The River Between* is to be found in Waiyaki's tortured
attempt to perform all these roles and identities at the same time.

Waiyaki's life story is determined by his location at the point
when these roles make conflicting demands on him. From the very
beginning of the novel when we meet him in the fields playing with
other boys, we are asked to consider him both as the new subject of
colonial modernity, a subject who has been liberated from the
demands of traditional authority, and as the charismatic representative of that authority. We are invited to interpret his legendary
gaze – "Not a man knew what language the eyes spoke. Only, if
the boy gazed at you, you had to obey" (p. 10) – as the sign of his
unique individuality and of his supernaturalism. Similarly, the
narrative compels us to read his cultural crisis in the doubleness of
its representation: we can read this crisis as evidence of Waiyaki's
alienation from the rituals of his people, or his investment in them;
we can interpret his relation to the past as vital and continuous, or
as a symptom of temporal discontinuity and cultural atrophy. As a
boy, Waiyaki sees himself as the heir to the heroes of his culture,
heroes such as Ndemi and Mathathi, who came to be considered
"giants of the tribe" for their role in Gikuyu expansionism (p. 10);
but no sooner does he try to assume the role of such legendary
figures than he is confronted by his own sense of inadequacy –
"Something he could not define seemed to gnaw at his soul,
having first crept through the flesh" (p. 11).

Waiyaki's function in the central drama of Gikuyu culture
under colonialism is defined by the gap between his need to
become a full-fledged member of Gikuyu culture in its historical
connectivity and collectivity and the demand placed on him by the
historical reality of colonial rule and conquest, the demand that
nullifies the narratives and rituals that might secure his traditional
identity. During the ceremony of "being born again," for
example, the women hail the boy as the reincarnation of an old
legend: "Old Waiyaki is born / Born again to carry on the ancient
fire" (p. 12). But the discerning reader cannot forget that this
dream of historical continuity is achieved only through a self-

willed act of forgetfulness: "For a time, Waiyaki forgot himself and thought he was Demi, bravely clearing the forest, a whole tribe behind him" (p. 12). When he wakes up in the morning, however, Waiyaki confronts a "strange hollowness in his stomach" (p. 12) as the illusion of historical continuity confronts the reality of colonial alienation. A similar thing happens when Waiyaki undergoes the rituals of circumcision: he momentarily imagines himself as an agent of historical continuity only to wake up to confront the "feeling that he lacked something, that he yearned for something beyond him" (p. 44).

But what exactly does Waiyaki lack? What represents the thing beyond him? If neither the subject nor the narrative respond adequately to these questions, it is because of their aphoristic nature. In other words, what Waiyaki lacks and what he desires cannot be provided by an idealized precolonial past (his emptiness represents his awareness of both his historical belatedness and the ineffectualness of nostalgia), nor by the brave new world promised by colonialism. Waiyaki's task in the novel is actually to negotiate the gap that separates the precolonial world from the colonial one, to imagine a national space between a dying "tribal" culture and an alienating colonialism. As an adult, his quest is for a narrative in which the ancient prophecy can be translated into modernity and the culture of colonialism can be harnessed to the service of tradition.[29] Waiyaki's crisis of identity is generated by his location at the intersection of Gikuyu traditions and colonial culture. In this sense he is a victim of cultural hybridity and crisis.

Waiyaki's journey into the thicket of cultural crisis is, of course, foreshadowed by Muthoni's narrative, a story that is often read as a commentary on the tragedy of biculturalism in a colonial situation, but which I would like to read as an expression of Ngugi's own doubts about the nationalist belief that culture could create a space in which tradition and colonialism can be reconciled. Muthoni occupies an important place in *The River Between* for several reasons: first, she provokes serious doubts about Waiyaki's dream of cultural regeneration and even forces him to question the depth of his commitment to the prophecy he is supposed to embody. Secondly, Muthoni articulates the dilemma of cultural or religious hybridity in a language that greatly contrasts with

Waiyaki's stutters: "I am a Christian and my father and mother have followed the new faith. I have not run away from that. But I also want to be initiated into the ways of the tribe" (p. 43.) In her eloquent defense of cultural hybridity, however – and this is the second point – Muthoni is more aware of the personal risks involved in cultural syncretism and is therefore able to prefigure Waiyaki's dilemma: how can one desire the "tribe" as a source of cultural purity when the very language of identity comes from the culture of colonialism? Muthoni's repetition of her desire – "I want to be a woman made beautiful in the manner of the tribe" (p. 44) – is a symptom of her own deep anxieties about the idea of purity in a culture of contamination. As Mary Douglas would say, the idea of purity is underwritten by a politics of danger.[30]

The third reason why Muthoni is so important in the novel is that in the process of putting her beliefs of cultural hybridity into practice, she illustrates the impossibility of this project. For while she lives and dies as a consequence of her acts and thus comes to exhibit what Ngugi would consider, after Conrad, to be the morality of action, Muthoni cannot translate her desires to others – she is represented, not as a model to be emulated, but as a lonely individual unable to effect change either in the traditional or Christian community. It is precisely because Muthoni cannot transfer her vision, her words, or actions to others – and thus be able to initiate change – that her death becomes such a contentious issue in the culture as different factions try to interpret this death as a prefiguration of their own hermeneutical positions. For Waiyaki's father, for example, Muthoni's death reinforces his own prophetic authority: "Had he not foreseen this drama? Had he not seen the estrangement between father and daughter, son and father, because of the new faith? This was a punishment to Joshua" (p. 54). For the white missionary, on the other hand, this death "forever confirmed the barbarity of Gikuyu customs" (p. 55).

In all cases, however, Muthoni's fate confirms the radical split between the cultures she had tried to reconcile. And if we are to read her death as a commentary on the impossibility of building cultural bridges in the Manichean culture of colonialism, the narrative seems to use her tragedy to prefigure the tragic status of Waiyaki's mission. Indeed, from the death of Muthoni onwards, Ngugi's novel – and Waiyaki's story – become self-consciously split narratives: they are split between the autonomous nation they imagine and the realities they must encounter along the way; and between their subjects' desire to assert the rights of the colonized to secure their own cultural identities and their acute sense of the irreversible changes brought about by colonialism. During Waiyaki's circumcision, for example, people are surprised that he had not been softened by "the white man's education," that he could stand "the traditional ordeal without flinching" (p. 47). These observers are reassured when Waiyaki goes through the ritual without flinching. What they fail to realize, however, is that while education has not softened Waiyaki, it has changed him, that his relation with "tribal" rituals and secrets is marked by distance, even alienation, that the reason why Muthoni's death haunts him and blocks his quest for understanding – "Wherever Waiyaki went, the silent face of Muthoni would come and bar the way" (p. 52) – is because he is cognizant of the impossibility of reconciling the demands of the ancestral prophecy with the needs of the times. Waiyaki's relationship with his past thus comes to be marked by risk rather than satisfaction.

In spite of these dangers, however, Waiyaki follows Muthoni's example and works hard to try and overcome the radical divisions between Makuyu and Kameno. He breaks with the Christian mission at Siriana and sets up an independent school in the belief that a middle path can be found between the ideality of a colonial education and the traditions of the Gikuyu. But here, as he tries to sort out the contradictions of his new life as a man born again into his culture and yet educated at Siriana, Waiyaki is plagued by doubts about the efficacy of hybridity: "why should they who had been educated at Siriana, be so vehement against it? It was just like his father, who had sent him to the Mission to which he had all his life objected" (p. 64). Doubts and anxieties shadow Waiyaki's cultural project precisely because of its implicit contradictions: while the young man sees his new (independent) school as a continuation of the ancient prophecy – "He saw it as something beyond himself, something ordained by fate" (p. 67) – he also realizes that the idea of the school emerges out of his own individual attempt to figure out a modern identity between the competing views and visions of Christianity and Gikuyu culture.

Waiyaki's story – and the idea of an independent school – calls

attention to the inherent tension between the idea of culture as a
collective project and as a manifestation of individual will. While
Waiyaki rationalizes the need for a school in terms of his desire to
serve his community, the school is also his most obvious attempt to
acquire a unique (modern) consciousness against the demands of
traditional authority. The idea of the school is thus inseparable
from his sudden eruption into adulthood: "His father's death had
almost numbed him... He had all of a sudden become a grown
man. He was now on his own. It was in this mood that the idea of
schools had come to him" (p. 67). In the second half of the novel,
then, Ngugi's task is to try and mediate Waiyaki's role as a "savior"
of his community and his distinctly bourgeois identity, his definition as a subject who is defined by radical alienation. The reader,
then, has to shuttle between the hero's conflicting role as the
reconciler of competing factions and as the agent of forms of social
change that engender cultural divisions.

But what are the narrative and ideological implications of
Waiyaki's split personality? From a narrative perspective, Waiyaki
stands as the earliest sign of Ngugi's mastery of the form of the
bourgeois novel. His story, as I noted earlier, is that of a colonial
subject remaking himself both inside and outside the norms defined by his community. In this respect, he is very much like the
heroes of the modernist novels by Lawrence and Conrad that
Ngugi was reading at Makerere University when he wrote his early
works. Like Paul Morel in *Sons and Lovers*, Waiyaki is defined both
by his attempt to merge with his cultural landscape and his desire
to transcend it. Waiyaki sees his mission as essentially one of
service to his community: he represents himself as the embodiment
of the new spirit sweeping the land – the spirit of cultural nationalism. This spirit is in turn embodied by the independent school
which Waiyaki builds, a school which comes to be seen as the
vehicle of cultural autonomy and resurgence: the school is the
"magic" that brings people together; it is the physical manifestation of their "determination to have something of their own
making, fired by their own imagination"; it is the space in which
their souls can find expression outside the prisonhouse of colonialism (p. 68).

And yet the rhetoric celebrating this new spirit can barely

conceal the fact that, as an institution, the school is a vehicle of colonial rule and conquest. More significantly, if the new spirit engendered by the school was intended to overcome the social and cultural gap that was evident at the beginning of the novel, it has not succeeded at all; on the contrary, all attempts to overcome such gaps only lead to greater cultural and religious divisions. Waiyaki founds his school to overcome social division, but ends up being a divisive subject; alienated from both Kameno and Makuyu, he is also divided within himself; unable to fulfill his messianic role, he is represented in terms of an oppressive desire – "the desire to share his hopes, his yearnings and longings with someone" (p. 71) – that is impossible in a situation defined by radical differences.

The challenge he faces here has, of course, already been prefigured by Muthoni's death: how can the associative desires which nationalism demands be fulfilled if the individual subject, the agent of such desires, is not affiliated totally with one community or another? Some of the most powerful moments in the novel emerge when the reader becomes a witness to Waiyaki's inner struggle with this problem: "Waiyaki wondered if he himself fitted anywhere. Did Kabonyi? Which of the two was the messiah, the man who was to bring hope in salvation to a troubled people? . . . He did not quite know where he was going or what he really wanted to tell his people" (pp. 141–42). This "inward turn" as it were, is the very mark of the good novel as defined by the great tradition via Makerere University College. Psychological introspection and a sense of moral crisis that would have satisfied Leavis and his disciples mark Ngugi's novel.

But Ngugi did not invent Waiyaki to fulfill the demands of the Makerere School of English. Beneath the image of a would-be bourgeois hero struggling with his desires as they come into conflict with the moral claims of his culture, is the portrait of the kind of men who championed Gikuyu nationalism in the 1920s and 1930s. These men, the most notable being Jomo Kenyatta, advocated the restoration of old traditions while insisting on the freedom to assert their individual identity and their role as agents of cultural transgression in the name of modernity. These men's attitude toward the notion of tradition was hence ambivalent: they

invoked tradition in their ethnographic work because they saw it as
the counterpoint to colonial modernity; but in their own lives and
experiences, they sought to master modernity as a prerequisite to
communal regeneration. The Gikuyu *polis* could not have an
autonomous identity without a recuperation of precolonial traditions; but autonomy only made sense in its modern rationality.[31]

This ambivalence toward tradition is apparent in Waiyaki's
romance with Nyambura. This romance is important because, as
we have already noted, romantic love is an imaginative mechan-
ism for overcoming the divisions embedded in the *polis*. In an ideal
situation, Waiyaki's marriage to Joshua's daughter would overcome the divisions between Kameno and Makuyu. For this reason, Nyambura occupies an important place in the novel and in
Waiyaki's mind: she is seen as "the shape in his mind that had
refused to melt into nothingness" (p. 74). If Waiyaki were to marry
an "uncircumcised woman," this would represent a radical transgression – and also remaking – of what constitutes a real Gikuyu
person: "Nyambura was not circumcised. But this was not a crime.
Something passed between them as two human beings, untainted
with religion, social conventions or any tradition" (p. 76).

But why would Waiyaki, the champion of tradition, desire a
universal identity – one beyond local beliefs and cultural practices?
The answer to this question is simpler than it first appears:
Waiyaki defines his mission in terms of his traditional duties and
obligation, but it is apparent that he has also become a prisoner of
the very institutions he set out to defend: "His activities were being
watched by everyone. His freedom was being curbed" (p. 81).
When he says that he is driven by fate "to the helm of things,"
Waiyaki seems to acknowledge that his traditionalism is compelled
by the need to carry out an ancestral mission rather than free will.
In many respects Waiyaki's words and actions, and his deepest
desires, are closer to the culture of colonialism and the discourse of
Christian conversion than the traditionalism represented by his
father. He may, for example, have serious doubts about Joshua's
rigid doctrine, but as a teacher he speaks a similar language, the
language of "conversion: new man, new creature, new life" (p. 86);
he may have entered the church in the hope of seeing Nyambura,

but on a deeper level, he defines his work in missionary terms, sees his mission as that of uplifting his people.

So while Waiyaki often speaks the language of patriotism and cultural purity, the novel calls attention to his alienation in the language "of the tribe." It does this by, first, collapsing the ostensible difference between the language of cultural purity, the one that seeks to restore "the purity of the tribe and the ridges" (p. 87), and the language of radical evangelicalism as it is represented in Joshua's church. Both modes of language have become separated from their mission. There is, in addition, a way in which the language of patriotism is undermined at its foundation when the originality of Waiyaki's cultural mission is exposed as a form of repetition and hence a mode of alienation. In one significant scene in the novel, a multitude of people come to listen to Waiyaki: they adore him as "the reincarnation" of their "former dignity and purity" and celebrate his new school as "the symbol of their defiance of foreign ways" (p. 92). This scene of adulation could be read as the representation of a deep desire by the people of the hills to recuperate a precolonial metaphysics, or at least a return to what has been lost through colonialism. But if the sight of a "whole grass compound full of women and men from every corner of the country" sounds familiar, it is clearly because it echoes the scene of "Beatitudes and Woes" in the New Testament. A powerful moment of Gikuyu cultural discourse, a discourse of origins and restoration, is hence exposed as a site of repetition.[32]

My main point here is that part of the power of *The River Between* lies in Ngugi's awareness of how the narrative of communal regeneration is haunted by its borrowed grammar and its indebtedness to the colonial library. I consider this alienation important in the overall scheme of the novel for the simple reason that it is through their displacement from traditional and colonial narratives that people like Waiyaki – and perhaps the author himself – can hollow out a space in which the future nation can be imagined as "something utterly new."[33] Identity is thus sought through alienation and a failed romance.

We can understand the significance of this mode of self-alienation by recalling the argument made by Doris Sommer in *Founda-*

tional Fictions. Sommer's argument is that nationalist novels deploy
an "erotics of politics" in which they project national ideals
grounded in heterosexual love and "in the marriages that provided a figure for apparently nonviolent consolidation during
internecine conflicts"; as a result, romantic passion becomes one of
the ways in which antagonistic nationalist factions sought to merge
and sustain their mutual "national" interest.[34] In nationalist narratives, argues Sommer, romance has gone "hand in hand with
patriotic history" for it is through the figure of eros that such
narratives have fueled "a desire for domestic happiness that runs
over into dreams of national prosperity; and nation-building projects invested private passions with public purpose."[35]

In the case of *The River Between*, it is in the name of patriotism (his
public function) that Waiyaki tries to overcome "personal frustra-
tions and hardships" (his inability to marry Nyambura in the face
of the opposition of his political allies). But it is also in the name of
romance (love as a non-violent merging of interests) that he undertakes the dangerous task of reconciliation: "Waiyaki did not like to
be identified with either side; he was now committed to reconciliation" (p. 110). Reconciliation can now be represented in a language of romance that appears to be above partisan politics. It is
not unusual, in these circumstances, that Waiyaki presents himself
– or is perceived by his followers – as the object of a sublime kind of
love, one above simple interests. He is adored as much for his ideas
as for his erotic voice and seductive eyes (p. 117). Conceived in the
language of love – attraction and seduction – colonial modernity is
made palatable to the colonized. In the end, however, Waiyaki's
attempt to turn his desire for Nyambura into a public instrument
of reconciliation flounders in the face of the multiple contradictions it faces.

I want to suggest that although this failure has often been read
as tragic, it is actually inevitable and central to the overall meaning
and design of *The River Between*. Although Waiyaki bemoans the
fact that his attempts to reconcile Makuyu and Kameno have
degenerated into a vision of darkness and terror (p. 121), and that
he has become the *pharmakon* whom both sides blame for their
woes, there is a sense in which he has brought the two sides to
confront the fact that they are not two distinct cultural entities, but

are actually conjoined by similar spatial and temporal interests. Visualized by Nyambura as the "black messiah" (p. 134), Waiyaki comes to function as the figure of enlightenment and revelation – "It was as if Waiyaki was a revelation, a thing not of this earth" (p. 138).

What exactly does Waiyaki reveal? He reveals two things: he shows that private passion (eros) is not always reconcilable with public duty as Nyambura had hoped (p. 136); and he exposes the terror of cultural puritanism and ancient prophecies and genealogies within the symbolic economy of colonialism ("Your name will be your ruin," one of his friends tells him [p. 140]). Waiyaki may not appear to have revealed anything to himself – "He did not quite know where he was going or what he really wanted to tell his people. He was still in the dark" (p. 142) – but one important role he performs even as he moves toward his apparent crucifixion is to expose the false ideological positions taken by both sides in this dispute: while the traditionalists assume their identity in the name of cultural purity, Ngugi's novel uses a language that already represents them as contaminated by the culture of colonialism. While the Christians claim to have broken away from the "tribal" past, the novel shows how old traditions and customs shadow their beliefs and practices.

Here is Waiyaki at his Gethsemane:

Even Waiyaki was affected by that great hush that fell over the land. He could hear his heart beat and he told himself: I must not fear. And he stood at a raised piece of ground and looked at the people; at their expectant faces and eyes. *Salvation shall come from the hills.* And he saw that many people had come and had filled up the initiation ground and the slopes of the hills. Some had climbed up trees. *A man shall rise and save the people in their hour of need.* And he remembered his father, and Mugo wa Kibiro, Wachiori, Kamiri, Gikuyu and Mumbi. And he remembered Kerinyaga as he had seen it that great day with his father. *l will look up into the hills from whence cometh my help.* Waiyaki prayed that the cold fear that settled in his stomach be removed. Kameno and Makuyu seemed to be staring at him ready to pounce on him. *He shall show them the way; he shall lead them.* (p. 146)

This is one of the most memorable passages in the novel. Its uniqueness, however, is not to be found in the expected quarter –

the depth of Waiyaki's faith in his people and his sense of impeding doom. This passage is unique because of the way it blurs the distinction between the ancient Gikuyu prophecy and the narrative of Christian salvation. After a lifetime trying to negotiate the split between the Christian and Gikuyu versions of salvation, Waiyaki speaks in a language that interposes both so that neither of the two narratives is privileged in his, or the reader's, mind. And thus Waiyaki's uniqueness lies in his unconscious ability to speak eloquently about Gikuyu traditions and histories in the figural language of the King James version of the Christian Bible.[36]

CHAPTER 3

Educating colonial subjects: the "emergency stories" and Weep Not, Child

Ngugi's early stories and novels were written in the shadow of colonial rule in its most violent form – the state of emergency declared in Kenya by the British government on October 20, 1952. The years in which Ngugi was educated and came of age (1952–62) were some of the most difficult and traumatic in his country's history. Apart from the state of emergency that had been imposed by the government in an attempt to repress a nationalist movement that had taken up arms to press its political demands, relationships between the colonizer and the colonized, social classes, families, and institutions, were conducted through modes of unprecedented violence. Kenya thus became a classical example of a political situation in which, to use Fanon's memorable term, violence comes to rule "over the ordering of the colonial world."[1] This is how the theme of violence came to enter Ngugi's early works. This violence can, indeed, be read as the primary mediator of Ngugi's relationship with his colonial situation, the dominant theme in his early works, and the central trope in his tortured struggle to come to terms with his past.

Later in his writing career, after reading Fanon's treatise on violence as a weapon of decolonization, Ngugi would come to interpret the state of emergency in Kenya as the highest point of African resistance against British imperialism. His main argument was that since colonialism had instituted violence as an instrument of conquest and rule, the colonized had no option but to adopt it as the first step in "deciding to embody history" and thus to break down the system of European rule.[2] But when he began to write in the early 1960s, Ngugi's views on the role of violence in a colonial situation were more immediate and personal. In reflecting on the way in which the state of emergency in Kenya had affected him, his family, and community, the novelist was struck mostly by how the colonial regime used violence to create divisions and conflicts in institutions – such as the family and clan – that were supposed to have maintained their integrity through the process of European domination. In this sense, Ngugi was well attuned to the fact that one of the reasons why the Gikuyu people had come to conceive the state of emergency as an apocalyptic event (*hiingo ya thiina*) was not simply because it had introduced chaos into their ordered worlds (colonialism had accomplished this by the 1920s), but because the unprecedented violence of the 1950s called into question the nationalist romance of restoration.

Simply put, what the emergency seemed to do fast and efficiently was debunk the teleology of Gikuyu nationalism, which, as we saw in the previous chapter, had been constructed around the belief that colonialism would one day end and the lost lands and denigrated traditions would be restored. In trying to understand and narrate the troubled 1950s, Ngugi could not help but contrast the havoc the emergency had wreaked on his natal landscape with the vision of a harmonious time and place which was part of the collective imagination before 1952: "I was born and grew up in Kenya. It is a land of hills and valleys; suns and rain; dry sand in the north and snow on the mountains; black and white races and a multiplicity of tribes ... But the contrasts that make the worth and beauty of the land are at the same time the basis of conflicts. Contrasts and conflicts; that fairly summarizes the Kenyan situation."[3] Clearly, at the beginning of his career, Ngugi had become convinced that colonialism in Kenya could only be effectively represented in terms of the rifts and conflicts it engendered and through the dramatization of the radical contrast between the beauty of the landscape and what seemed to be its ill-fated history.

But it is important to note that Ngugi's views on how conflict had come to define colonialism in Kenya were being expressed in 1962, the year of self-government. Indeed, by the time Ngugi came to produce his fictional works, the emergency had been over for almost two years, Kenyatta was prime minister, and decolonization was at hand. Why, then, do Ngugi's emergency stories and his first published novel, *Weep Not, Child*, seem so pessimistic? Why do they read like stories of what Biodun Jeyifo calls, in a different context, "arrested decolonization"?[4] Why was Ngugi's engagement with history at the beginning of his career so tentative, so uncertain? Why did not the coming of independence, the time of production of his novel, generate a celebratory narrative?

WRITING IN A STATE OF EMERGENCY

We can begin to address these questions by looking at some of the "emergency stories" collected in *Secret Lives*. In "Gone with the Drought," which can be read as an allegory of "arrested decolonization," the central image is that of drought, which appears to the narrator as a representation of the "whiteness of death."[5] But while it is clear that this story is meant to be a commentary on violence as the organizing paradigm of the colonial world, the mode of narration adopted here is intended to call attention to the doubts that mark the interregnum between a long history of colonial rule and the moment of decolonization. First of all, the story is built around an opposition that it also sets out to undermine: as a symbol of "white death," the drought stands in contrast to the legendary fertility of the landscape; at the same time, however, the reader is reminded that the very existence of the drought is due to the failure of the rains – clearly a symbol of decolonization – to fall. And in a situation in which the central image of the story could be either a reference to the past or the future, the reader's problems are compounded by the absence of an authorial stance that might help sort out this ambivalent economy of representation.

Secondly, while the story is told in the first person, the narrator is heterodiegetic; he is not part of the situation and events he narrates and does not seem to have any emotional or ideological commitment to the events he narrates. Indeed, while the first-person narrative is traditionally intended to establish close contact between the reader and the story teller, what we have here is a narrator who seeks to disengage us from the sentiments surrounding the events of the story. If the narrator is marginal to the story he tells, so is the central object of his narration, a woman who, because of her presumed madness, has been relegated to the

margins of her community. Since the narrator's attitude toward
the drought at the beginning of the story is as detached as his
representation of the torrential rain that falls at the end of the
story, we can deduce that he is not seeking to affiliate with the
hopes and expectations of his community. On the contrary, his
identification with the mad woman is seen as an act of detachment
from the events surrounding this community, events that are
explicitly situated in 1961, a year which is considered in Kenya's
political history to be the cusp between colonialism and decolonization.

We encounter the same narrative detachment and indeterminacy in "Black Bird." Here, too, the story is told in the first person,
and again the narrator has adopted a heterodiegetic stance. As in
"Gone with the Drought," the narrator tells the story of another
person on the margins of his community as a means of detaching
himself from the normativity of his culture. But there is something
more in this story: its language does not seek to represent or
translate the idiom of cultural nationalism (as is the case in *The
River Between*), or to capture the rhythms of the landscape. The
narrator sets out to display his mastery of Englishness, or more
specifically, the idiom of the public school; it is through this idiom
that the narrator establishes a relationship with the subject of his
story:

At first I was not much attracted to him. Perhaps it was envy on my part.
You see, I was not good at games and I could not shine in any field, not
even in class. A chap who was popular, a favourite with girls and
teachers, was bound to excite the envy of the less fortunate ones. I hated
him. I hated his aloofness and what I thought was proud disdain of all
favours or approaches for friendship.
And then I discovered his isolation. (p. 29)

The narrator and narratee establish a common identity through
their isolation and alienation. The cultural grammar here – of
school ties, mock civility, and friendship – is as removed from the
language of romance in *The River Between* as it is from the local
setting of the story. Indeed, while this story is concerned with
"local color," its narrator speaks a language that, in reminding us
of his acculturation (represented in the best Oxbridge tones) also

calls attention to his alienation from his culture and background. But beneath the language of Englishness that dominates the surface of this story, the narrator's imagination of bourgeois civility and alienation is haunted by the discourse of tradition, or rather, superstition. Another way of presenting this problem is to note that while the narrator of "Gone with the Drought" does not talk about himself explicitly, he tells the story of a person (the medical student) who is so much like him – in education and temperament – that we are inclined to read this character as a surrogate for the narrator. What the two have in common is their modern (colonial) identity represented by science and Christian enlightenment. But this modernity is haunted by its opposite – "tribal superstition" – represented here by the black bird which is, at the same time, the sign of repressed histories and cultures. In their striving for a modern and rational culture, the narrator and the medical student have deliberately detached themselves from their "backward" communities to escape the specter of the past and the deeds of their forefathers, but the story that comes to dominate their lives is that of an albatross, one whose origins coincide with the first decade of colonial rule in Central Kenya (p. 36). At the end of the story, both the narrator and his subject discover that no amount of acculturation can liberate them from the psychological violence engendered by "ceremonies of conquest."[6]

We can now perhaps answer one of the questions raised at the beginning of this section: one of the reasons Ngugi's emergency stories seem so pessimistic is because while the long-awaited moment of decolonization has arrived, promising a radical rupture with the past, the new imagined community of the nation is caught between the threat of repressed traditions and the truncated identities created by colonial modernity. The narrators of the two stories discussed above are symptoms of this problem: educated in the best colonial traditions, they are not English; uprooted from their ancestral traditions, they are not entirely Gikuyu either. They are caught between the *kirore* and *karing'a* identities discussed in the last chapter: they exist both inside and outside the values espoused by modernity and tradition.

This point is reinforced in "A Meeting in the Dark," a tragic

story in which a young educated African shuttles between colonial
and traditional culture, imprisoned by one and alienated from the
other. It is important to note that one of the issues in this story is
the status of narrative itself: what stories or histories will the
decolonized tell of themselves now that colonial rule is almost
over? Will they recover the stories of repressed precolonial pasts or
will they continue to exist on the margins of the grand narrative of
European domination? At the beginning of the story, there is a
clear opposition between the narrative of colonialism, represented
by the Bible, and the stories of the precolonial past. What makes
colonial culture so painful for the main character of this story is the
fact that it is associated with the figure of the father, represented
here as the source of terror and cultural rupture:

He stood at the door of the hut and saw his old, frail but energetic father
coming along the village street, with a rather dirty bag made out of a
strong calico swinging by his side. His father always carried this bag. John
knew what it contained: a Bible, a hymn-book and probably a notebook
and a pen. His father was a preacher. He knew it was he who had stopped
his mother from telling him stories when be became a man of God. His
mother had stopped telling him stories long ago. She would say to him,
"Now, don't ask for any more stories. Your father may come." So he
feared his father. John went in and warned his mother of his father's
coming. Then his father entered. John stood aside, then walked towards
the door. He lingered there doubtfully, then he went out. (*Secret Lives*,
p. 55).

In a pattern that is noticeable in many of Ngugi's texts from this
period, John's tragedy in this story arises from his dislocation from
his father's biblical world (which he associates with "moral torture" [p. 59]) and his inherent alienation – as a Christian – from
the story of "the tribe and its ways" (p. 59), a story he desires but
cannot master because it is forbidden to him. Like many other
nascent nationalists in Ngugi's early works, John seeks to enter the
narrative of "the tribe" by identifying with peasant women who
appear, in his imagination, to be symbols of the "tribal" values he
lost when his father became a convert to Christianity (p. 59). It is
through his romantic relationship with such a woman that John
hopes to overcome his separation from his "tribe" and to restore
the continuity of the narrative interrupted by colonialism (p. 62).

But no sooner has John turned to such associative relationships than his desires are blocked by the Calvinism of both his father and teacher, who remind him that he occupies cultural spaces defined by a different set of codes and standards than the woman he loves, and that he can only transgress these spaces at the expense of what are considered to be the moral and social codes of modernity. He would like to do the right thing and marry Wamuhu, but "She was circumcised and he knew that his father and the church would never consent to such a marriage . . . Marrying her would probably ruin his chances of ever going to university" (p. 65).

What is even more important in this story is the fact that John cannot break away from the moral codes represented by his father – and thus, by extension, the culture of colonialism – because he cannot conceive of an alternative value system or way of recoding the world. True, John dreams of being initiated "in the tribal manner," but such dreams, instead of giving him the courage to break with his father and join the "tribe," only accentuate his sense of being unhomely, and remind him of the ghostliness of his identity in the space he would like to occupy:[7]

John woke up early. He was frightened. He was normally not superstitious, but still he did not like the dreams of the night. He dreamt of circumcision; he had just been initiated in the tribal manner. Somebody – he could not tell his face, came and led him because he took pity on him. They went, went into a strange land. Somehow, he found himself alone. The somebody had vanished. A ghost came. He recognized it as the ghost of the home he had left. It pulled him back; then another ghost came. It was the ghost of the land he had come to. It pulled him forward. The two contested. Then came other ghosts from all sides and pulled him from all sides so that his body began to fall into pieces. And the ghosts were insubstantial. He could not cling to any. Only they were pulling him and he was becoming nothing, nothing . . . (p. 66)

This situation of radical alienation is complicated by the fact that John cannot represent his world except in the terms he has inherited from Calvinism: he cannot, for example, conceive of a relationship with Wamuhu except in an impossible Christian marriage, nor can he contemplate her pregnancy except in terms of guilt and his fall from what the narrator sardonically calls "the heights of 'goodness'"(p. 69). How does this colonial subject resolve his alienation in two worlds? He kills his forbidden love and her unborn child. But in killing Wamuhu and her unborn child, John ends up destroying himself, for it means that he can no longer be considered to be a member of either the Christian or "tribal" community. To the extent that this killing calls attention to John's total loss of identity and selfhood in the space between competing cultures, we can read it as a "suicide tactic," a gesture of self-destruction that foregrounds the stillborn discourse of decolonization; thus, the narrator's death inscribes the impossibility of reconciling Christianity and Gikuyu traditions and beliefs.[8]

This discussion of "A Meeting in the Dark" creates a context for responding to the second and third questions raised above; it enables us to see how Ngugi uses his early novels to draw a close parallel between the narrative of arrested decolonization and the new nation's failure to discover and valorize a usable past. The fate of the main character in this story serves as a reminder of how neither the desire for a precolonial nor a decolonized future can detour the mechanisms of power and social organization instituted by colonialism. If martyrdom and suicide seem to become important leitmotifs in these stories – as in Ngugi's early works as a whole – it is because the second generation of colonized Africans are as marginalized in their ancestral traditions are they are in the world created by colonialism. For subjects such as John, even the simple act of cognition is split between the nostalgia for an impalpable past and the incompleteness of their modern identity. Alternatively, these subjects are destroyed because they assume that their identity and cultural agency depend on their ability to mediate and moderate the violence that characterizes the relationship between the colonizer and the colonized.

Take the case of Njoroge in "The Martyr," a story that can be read as a prototype for *Weep Not, Child*. He finds himself caught in "the wave of violence that had spread all over the country" and the "variety of accounts and interpretations" about the causes of this violence (p. 39); but he has no tools for explicating this violence or defining himself in relation to its historical causes. Initially, this violence seems to signal the collapse of Christian ideologies of conversion and to indicate Njoroge's awakening to something new; ultimately, however, his tragedy arises from his simultaneous emplacement in a dying colonialism and a yet-to-be-born nation-alism. Simply put, Njoroge cannot choose which side to align himself with: on the one hand, Njoroge sympathizes with national-ist sentiments expressed through stories about the loss of the land and the desire for its recovery; pained by these stories of loss – but inspired by the prophecy of restitution – he has no problem understanding the violence directed at white settlers. In addition, as readers of this story will recall, Njoroge has another, equally important motivation for adopting violence: he has a difficult relationship with his employer, Mrs. Hill, whom he detests be-cause she now occupies his family's land and is indirectly respon-sible for his father's death. Njoroge has good reason to see Mrs. Hill dead.

On the other hand, however, Njoroge finds it difficult to carry out the violent acts demanded of him by the nationalists precisely because of his Christian faith. Indeed, the gist of "The Martyr" is Njoroge's inability to kill Mrs. Hill and thus liberate his family's land from the hands of the colonizer. Why does Njoroge find it so difficult to carry out his overwhelming desire to kill Mrs. Hill? His reflection on the dilemma he confronts in this regard contains useful lessons about the moral economy of colonialism from the point of view of its victims. For as Njoroge prepares to kill Mrs. Hill, she is suddenly transformed, in his imagination, from the symbol of colonial oppression "into a woman, a wife . . . and above all, a mother" (*Secret Lives*, p. 44). This shift in the terms of represen-tation presents Njoroge with a complex dilemma:

He could not kill a woman. He could not kill a mother. He hated himself for this change. He felt agitated. He tried hard to put himself in the other condition, his former self and see her as just a settler. As a settler, it was easy. For Njoroge hated settlers and all Europeans. If only he could see her like this (as one among many white men or settlers) then he could do it. Without scruples. But he could not bring back the other self. Not now, anyway. He had never thought of her in these terms. Until today. And yet he knew she was the same, and would be the same tomorrow – a patronizing, complacent woman. It was then he knew that he was a divided man and perhaps would ever remain like that. For now it even seemed an impossible thing to snap just like that ten years of relationship, though to him they had been years of pain and shame. He prayed and wished there had never been injustices. Then there would never have been this rift – the rift between white and black. Then he would never have been put in this painful situation. (p. 45)

The irony of Njoroge's position may not be obvious, but it needs to be underscored. It is precisely because of his belief in categorical imperatives such as woman, wife, and person, that he is unable to liberate himself from political categories such as "settlers and all Europeans." This dilemma is important to understanding Ngugi's early works for both biographical and narrative reasons: from a biographical perspective, Njoroge's struggle to reconcile the Christian imperative with the nationalist demand for vengeance reflects the author's own moral dilemma at the beginning of his career. What we have here is an example of Ngugi, the liberal humanist and devout Christian produced by Alliance High School and Makerere University College, struggling with his other self – the son of a landless Gikuyu boy growing up in the shadow of colonialism. In narrative terms, what we see in "The Martyr," as in the other stories discussed in this section, is the emergence of a narrative method trapped in the author's desire to represent colonial "terror" in the "civil" language of English fiction. The moral dilemma created by colonial violence – and the split narratives it generates – are the key to understanding *Weep Not, Child*.

COLONIAL SCHIZOPHRENIA: *WEEP NOT, CHILD*

Numerous critics of Ngugi's first published novel have commented on how its melancholic probe into the history of the violence that accompanies decolonization is also the author's attempt to understand the "moral arena" in which political debates are carried out in a colonial situation. But before we try to establish the larger moral economy in which Ngugi was forced to confront colonial violence, it is perhaps useful to read the novel on a more basic level – as a very subjective response to the enigma of "Mau Mau" and its contested histories and ambiguous legacies. This kind of reading is important for a simple reason: the publication of Ngugi's novel in 1964 had a tremendous impact on the culture of letters in East Africa and this impact depended, first and foremost, on the autobiographical character of the novel.

Njoroge's life and education so closely paralleled that of the author and his local readers, many of whom had grown up under the state of emergency, that it was sometimes difficult to tell where to draw the line between fact and fiction. But by calling attention to the autobiographical dimension of this novel, it is not my intention to suggest that Njoroge's life is exactly like Ngugi's. Rather, I want to suggest that the early affective power of *Weep Not, Child* depended on many readers' ability to establish this kind of autobiographical contract and to assume that what they were reading about in the novel could very well have been a record of the author's own life. In retrospect, this assumption had been sanctioned by the snippets of autobiography that Ngugi had presented to his readers early in his career. Ngugi's structuring of the novel as a *Bildungsroman* also valorized novelistic conventions intended to invite readers to identify with the protagonist's struggle to establish his identity and to understand a hostile world.[9] Let us explore these two dimensions of the autobiographical contract more closely.

We might begin by recalling that the central aspects of Ngugi's biography revolve around the love and devotion of the mother, the tenuous authority of the father, the hopes and expectations represented by the colonial school, and the concurrent terror and romance of "Mau Mau." As we saw in the introduction, Ngugi's parents were *ahoi*, landless tenants at will; and in a patriarchal culture in which authority was vested in male heads of households and notions of wealth and virtue were derived from the ownership of land, the state of radical displacement engendered by being a tenant was particularly hard on the father. Without the authority represented by ownership of land – which Kenyatta had already defined as the key to understanding the most important elements of Gikuyu identity, including notions of space, time, and self – heads of such households were condemned to states of doubt, recrimination, and guilt.[10]

But more importantly, in the political economy of colonialism, in which fathers were reduced to servitude in the service of white settlers and the new African *kulak* class, it was not unusual for mothers to become the centers around which the marginalized tried to reorganize their cultural institutions. As Ngugi was to note in an important interview with Katebaliwe Amoti wa Irumba, when his father and mother separated in 1946 or 1947, it was the latter who took full responsibility for raising the children:

My parents lived partly on land, cultivating little stretches of land here and there, eking a living, and also working on other people's land for wages. My father and mother separated in 1946 or 1947, and thereafter my mother was the one who took care of us; that is, we three brothers and three sisters. She virtually shouldered *every* responsibility of our struggle for food, shelter, clothing, and education. It was my mother who initially suggested that I go to school. I remember those nights when I would come back home from school, and not knowing that she could not read or write, I would tell her everything that I had learnt in school or read to her something, and she would listen very keenly and give me a word of advice here and there.[11]

The above image of the mother as both the victim of the disruption brought about by colonial alienation and as the agent of a new (class) identity based on Western education is central to the representation of Njoroge as a colonial subject in *Weep Not, Child*. Indeed, maternity and education are intimately connected in the novel. For if Njoroge's tenuous relationship with his family and his community arises from the simple fact that he cannot understand how his father became a *muhoi* (tenant at will) – "Njoroge had never come to understand how his father had become a *muhoi*. Maybe a child did not know such matters"[12] – his story is premised on the belief that it is through the process of growing up and becoming educated that he can understand such complex things. And the process of growing up and becoming educated – the key to self-understanding in the novel – is shown to be only possible through the figure of the mother. It is the mother who weaves simple social processes – being educated and growing up – into a complex knot in which the history of colonialism and African resistance to it is enmeshed with private loss, failure, and mourning.

We can understand the importance of education in the novel if we recall that it is by sending Njoroge to the colonial school that Nyokabi hopes to compensate for her older son who died fighting for the British in World War II. It is through this most colonial instrument that she hopes to overcome the constrictors of colonialism itself and thus encompass "something broader than that which could be had from her social circumstances and conditions" (*Weep Not, Child*, p. 16). So, unlike the father who lives a life of nostalgia, the figure of the mother becomes what one scholar of the *Bildungsroman* has called "the coefficient of optimism."[13] This is, of course, the point made vividly at the end of the novel when, faced by the tattered dreams of his colonial education, Njoroge tries to kill himself only to be called back from the brink of death by his mother's voice: "His mother was looking for him. For a time he stood irresolute. Then courage failed him" (p. 135).

Njoroge had wanted to commit suicide because, having been expelled from school because of his family's involvement with "Mau Mau", he felt he had failed his parents. But his notion of failure is ironic since, as the novel itself clearly shows, Njoroge is a victim of circumstances, of historical forces beyond his control. But Njoroge's sense of failure is meant to be read as tragic precisely because it calls into question his mother's optimistic belief, expressed powerfully at the beginning of the novel, that education would redeem the family. And yet, what appears to be the collapse of the mother's vision of enlightenment through Western education pales in comparison to the father's passiveness and his silence in the face of the multiple challenges the family confronts.

Ngugi's homage to the figure of the mother in *Weep Not, Child* is equally important for the way it helps him undermine, in a systematic and blunt manner, the paradigm of prophetic restoration associated with paternal figures such as Ngotho who patiently continue to work for white settlers while waiting "for the prophecy to be fulfilled" (p. 26). Ngotho has waited so long for the prophecy to be fulfilled that time has cut into his desires and blunted the force of his nostalgia; he has even begun to have second doubts about the ancient prophecy: "Perhaps he and others had waited for too long and now he feared that this was being taken as an excuse for inactivity, or, worse, a betrayal" (p. 28). Against the mother's pragmatic attempt to turn the narrative of colonialism into something new and liberating, the father's stories are driven by a rhetoric of failure that conceals their estrangement from the world they are supposed to mediate. Detached from the history whose authority they were supposed to secure, these stories have become meaningless.

The question of failure is foregrounded in a memorable scene in which Ngotho and Howlands, the European settler who now occupies his ancestral lands, walk from place to place, connected not only by the spaces each lays claim to, but also by common subliminal desires and thoughts:

> They went from place to place, a white man and a black man. Now and then they would stop here and there, examine a luxuriant green tea plant, or pull out a weed. Both men admired this *shamba*. For Ngotho felt responsible for whatever happened to this land. He owed it to the dead, the living and the unborn of his line, to keep guard over this *shamba*. Mr. Howlands always felt a certain amount of victory whenever he walked through it all. He alone was responsible for taming this unoccupied wildness. (p. 31)

The colonizer and colonized walk hand in hand, as it were, separated by a conflicting set of interests, but connected by a common identity: they are both fathers who have failed in their attempts to turn the tragedy of colonization into their personal utopia. Having invested heavily in an allegory of conquest and resistance that has lost its bearings, the two fathers live in the fear that their unspoken desire (that the contested land will be inherited by their respective children) is a kind of wish-fulfillment.

Is Ngotho, then, to be read as the symbol of a colonized and compromised paternity? This is a difficult question to answer partly because, throughout the novel, Ngotho is treated with the measure of respect that a head of household deserves. And yet it is not hard to see that even in the first part of the novel, when he is clearly represented as the center of the family, the very notion of paternal authority is undermined not only by his rebellious sons but also by his wives. While Gikuyu households were traditionally defined by, and identified through, the figure of the father, the crisis point of colonialism, as it is represented in Ngugi's novel, casts fathers such as Ngotho in the role of worthless symbols, subjects who have lost the capacity to hold their houses together and to ensure the success of their progenies.

Indeed, Njoroge does not see his father as either a source of authority or security; this role is assigned to Kamau, his older brother. Njoroge's fear in the novel is not that his father might one day die and leave him an orphan, but that Kamau might be "drawn into the city"; if this were to happen, he reckons, it "would lead to a final break-up and ruin the cosy security which one felt in thinking of home. Kamau was the man of the home" (p. 48). This is an incredible statement to make because, as I have already argued, the Gikuyu traditionally assumed that so long as the father was alive, he was the head of his household. Indeed, a few pages later, we are told that ever since he was a child, Njoroge had seen his father as "the centre of everything" and as the symbol of continuity in a rapidly changing world – "As long as he lived, nothing could go wrong" (p. 50).

How can we explain this apparent contradiction in the novel? Perhaps by making a distinction between Ngotho's purely symbolic function as the head of the household and comparing it to Kamau's role as the person who "seemed to carry the family dumbly on his shoulders" (p. 48). Ngotho remains the titular head of household, but Kamau is charged with the task of maintaining the dream of material progress and psychological liberation that colonialism has disrupted. Kamau's role as the surrogate father – and Nyokabi's significance as a center of optimism – can be better appreciated if we recall that the novel begins by calling attention to Ngotho's inability to assert his authority and affirm his identity both in relation to his older sons and the colonial apparatus of power. The culture holds that land is the key to everything, yet Ngotho seems to have come to terms with his dispossession, much to the chagrin of his radical son, Boro (pp. 26–27). We are told that, for the new generation, education "held the key to the future," but it is left to the mother to fight for this future against the father's indifference (p. 48). The second part of the novel confirms what was already obvious to the reader: that colonialism has diminished the role of the father in the culture as a whole and in his own household; reduced in "stature," Ngotho has been forced into what the narrator calls "a defensive secondary place" (p. 71). In these circumstances, readers are forced to sit and wait for the failed paternal figure (Ngotho) to come to terms with his diminished role in the household: "Even before this calamity befell him," Ngotho reflects on his death bed, "life for him had become meaningless, divorced as he had been from what he valued" (p. 119).

But if colonialism has emasculated the father (this is the way Ngugi and many other African writers of his generation have presented the situation), the resulting narrative is one in which the categories colonial culture seeks to promote – enlightenment, modernity, and rationality – become even more tenuous than they might have been in patriarchal societies.[14] One might assume that because colonial culture is inherently patriarchal, it might seek to secure African masculinity instead of undermining it; but the patrimony colonialism desires is white and for this reason, African fathers, like Ngotho, have to be pacified or be transplanted by white men. As a result, African sons find themselves with fathers whose power and authority have been usurped by white men who, nevertheless, cannot be the source of the "cosy security" one associates with home.

Against this background, Njoroge, like many Africans of Ngugi's generation, is asked to carry out an almost impossible cultural mission: to perpetuate what has become a meaningless historical narrative (one associated with paternity, genealogy, and prophecy) and to construct a new vision of the future, the vision presented by the mother who sends him to school at the beginning of the novel. In both cases, of course, colonialism comes to play a decisive role: it is the imposition of colonial rule that renders the older narratives irrelevant; it is the unquestioned belief that the vision of the future can only be realized through colonial institutions that makes the process of education perilous and suicidal. And it is in reflecting on Njoroge's attempts to fashion a narrative to explain – and perhaps reconcile – what Fanon would call the "reciprocal exclusivity" of the antagonistic colonial sectors that Ngugi tries to transform his own autobiography into an allegory of colonial times.[15]

And yet in spite of this autobiographical dimension, what makes this novel important in Ngugi's development as a writer is the ironic distance he is able to maintain, in the process of narrating the dilemmas presented by a colonial education, between his own subjective experiences and their representation in the novel as someone else's story. Indeed, while he seems to have started writing the novel sharing Njoroge's belief in the efficacy of education, Ngugi quickly turns his attention to the ironic gap between such beliefs and the realities that frustrate them. Ironic discourse enables Ngugi to assert the authenticity of Njoroge's faith in colonial culture and to tentatively establish his distance from that faith, which he once shared. It is significant to note that Ngugi begins his novel with an explicit endorsement of his hero's faith in Christianity and education: "Njoroge came to place faith in the Bible and with his vision of an educated life in the future was blended a belief in the righteousness of God. Equity and justice were there in the world. If you did well and remained faithful to your God, the Kingdom of Heaven would be yours" (p. 49). But almost immediately, the narrator undermines Njoroge's faith in the power of education and the efficacy of cultural translation:

His belief in a future for his family and the village rested then not only on a hope for sound education but also on a belief in a God of love and mercy who long ago walked on this earth with Gikuyu and Mumbi, or Adam and Eve. It did not make much difference that he had come to identify Gikuyu with Adam and Mumbi with Eve. To this God, all men and women were united by one strong bond of brotherhood. (p. 49)

In a passage like this one, the reader can begin to sense how Njoroge's education, intended originally to lead to a "better vision of the future," has instead locked him neatly in the prisonhouse of colonialism. And as we shall later see in this chapter, it is when he is ultimately ejected from the colonial school that Njoroge makes his first step into that harsh, violent, world of colonialism in which, as Fanon aptly put it, the learning of the future emerges.[16]

THE COLONIAL *BILDUNGSROMAN*

But even if there was no close relationship between the central events, characters, and experiences in *Weep Not, Child* and Ngugi's autobiography, we would still have to read the novel from the authority established by a subjective experience, namely Njoroge's troubled relationship with the culture of colonialism. In this regard, it is important to pose a simple question: what does it mean to read Ngugi's novel as a *Bildungsroman*, "a story of the youthful hero's contact with the world and education in life and love"? What kind of narrative contract does a *Bildungsroman* establish between heroes and readers? Jonathan Culler's observations on the function of the *Bildungsroman* in Flaubert's *Sentimental Education* provide us with some useful insights:

The conventions of the genre lead us to expect an opposition between hero and world which will make the plot an intelligible history of resistance and accommodation. Illusions will be destroyed; the world will teach him something, whether he choose to accept its lessons; and the conclusion, as the climax of an encounter with the world, will structure that encounter in ways that give it meaning. What happens to the hero will make clear what was learned or not learned, what price must be paid for social integration and whether it is too high.[17]

Ngugi's novel follows these conventions but resists them, too. It presents us with a hero who is clearly in opposition to a situation that demands both resistance and accommodation. Indeed, the novel opens by presenting Njoroge as a subject caught between the desire to resist the colonial situation and to accommodate himself within its moral economy. The overt theme of the novel is Njoroge's desire for education in the European sense; education is the key to a bourgeois identity and civility, what is referred to as "learning." What Njoroge wants above everything else, we are told at the beginning of the book, is to acquire as much learning as Jacobo's son, John, who is going to England (p. 4). But no sooner has education been associated with a European identity, than we are cautioned about the difference between education and understanding: "You cannot understand a white man," Njoroge is warned (p. 5).

As the rest of the novel goes on to confirm, Njoroge goes to school to learn the limits of both a colonial identity and understanding in a colonial situation. In other words, what will make the plot of this story – and thus the history of colonialism in Central Kenya – intelligible, is Njoroge's ultimate ability to create a space of identity beyond the prisonhouse of imperial domination. But he cannot create this space until his illusions are destroyed. In this sense, the novel follows the conventions of the archetypal European narrative of education by suggesting that the most useful and lasting form of education is negative – the destruction of the hero's illusions about his own sense of integrity and the possibilities of his integration into the world. Where Ngugi's novel departs from the European model is in its recasting of this negative education – and the melancholy it generates – as a departure from the desired site of engenderment rather than the condition that enables a new and autonomous identity. For while the plot of the novel is conventional in many ways – most notably in its movement from the illusion of an education to the melancholy of its impossibility – its trajectory is complicated by what we have already called nationalist desire. *Weep Not, Child* is a text structured by a conflict between the conventions of the *Bildungsroman* – especially a plot that seeks to positivize disenchantment and turn melancholy into a source of individual identity – and the nationalists' belief that even the wayward products of a colonial education can be integrated into a decolonized collective whole. It is worth exploring this conflict in some detail.

A useful place to start is to examine the set of expectations raised by the novel's plot: for Njoroge, school is posited as the instrument of understanding, of social upliftment, and of overcoming the social divisions engendered by colonialism. It is significant that on his first day at school he is defined as *njuka*, a word that literally means a new arrival, but has the connotations of a novice in initiation rites. The association between school and Gikuyu rites of initiation cannot be missed; in fact, when the narrator reminds us that the school has become the most important form of social institution, we cannot but read it as a supplement for traditional rites of passage such as circumcision. For the novice, the school is an object of reverence and worship (p. 14).

More significantly, education is represented as a form of social contract, a set of cultural promises centering on the idea of modernity and the desire for emancipation. For a dispossessed colonial subject such as Njoroge, the school is the agency of reterritorialization: it leads to a new language (p. 16), new mode of dress (p. 17), even a house built in the European style (p. 18). Thus the relationship between education and the promise of modernity comes to be linked very early in the novel: Jacobo may be despised as a colonial stooge, but his household is admired for *Ustaarabu*, a Swahili word that means both proper conduct and civilized behavior (pp. 18–19). The plot of the novel sets out to clarify this African desire for the values of colonial culture, the culture that was responsible for Njoroge's family's displacement in the first place. Njoroge's narrative is plotted by his desire to understand why and how his family lost its land, but he can only reach this understanding by mastering colonial culture. Thus, the more his situation in the violent world of colonial politics becomes tenuous, the more he seeks to be educated: "As he could not find companionship with Jacobo's children (except Mwihaki), for these belonged to the middle class that was rising and beginning to be conscious of itself as such, he turned to reading" (pp. 48–49). Reading is both an attempt to find solace in religion and to imagine a future beyond colonialism: "Njoroge came to place faith in the Bible and with his vision of an educated future was blended a belief in the righteousness of God" (p. 49).

Even when the chaos of the emergency disrupts his family and communal life, Njoroge sees his education as the source of a stable identity and the instrument of achieving what remains of his boyhood vision: "With only a year to go before his examination for entrance to a secondary school, he worked hard at his books and his lessons" (p. 84). When the emergency forces the long rift between Jacob and Ngotho to widen beyond reconciliation, the school brings their children together: "And these two, a boy and a girl went forward each lost in their own world, for a time oblivious of the bigger darkness over the whole land" (p. 96). Even when it has become apparent to the reader that Njoroge's dreams – including the dream of a learned future – are falling apart, he still seeks consolation in the idea of education: "He would always be grateful to his mother, who had first sent him to school, and to Mwihaki" (p. 100).

Toward the end of the novel, however, this implicit faith in the value of education has become complicated as Njoroge's self-emplotment via the colonial school runs into political difficulties that he had not anticipated. As Njoroge's education begins to flounder, the narrative forces us to ask ourselves simple questions: is Njoroge's *Bildungsroman* determined by a series of impossible actions and desires? Is there a sense in which his traumatic experiences – his expulsion from school and his arrest, for example – just prove the fact that there cannot be emancipation within the doctrines of colonial modernity?

These questions are germane to the development of the story both because Njoroge poses them, albeit indirectly, as he tries to account for his own life, but also because they call attention to the impossibility of an autonomous African identity within colonial culture. One needs to be educated in order to be an autonomous bourgeois subject; but education only leads to disillusionment and the breakdown of identity. Thus, Njoroge is grateful for his education, but he also has doubts: "Yet what if he failed? That would be the end of all. What was a future without education?" (p. 100).

The last question forces the reader, if not Njoroge himself, to ask what kind of education he has acquired so far in the book. Njoroge has acquired the magic of literacy and he has come to understand that education is the only way he can become socially mobile given the alienation of his family's lands (pp. 35–39); but in the process of becoming educated, he has also become cognizant of "the indefinable demand" his family and community are making on him (p. 39). What makes his task complicated is that the people who insist on the value of education as an instrument of liberation are also the first to doubt its efficacy: "Education is everything," Ngotho tells his son in a poignant moment in the novel. "Yet he doubted this because he knew deep inside his heart that land was everything. Education was good only because it would lead to the recovery of the lost lands" (p. 39).

The explicit association between education and collective obligations is ironic for another reason: even as Njoroge is sent to school so that he can help the cause of communal restitution, he is already being separated from such obligations. Unlike his father who sees education as meaningless unless it can lead to the recovery of the lost lands, Njoroge cannot conceive his progress in the colonial school as inextricable from his dream of England and the mastery of Englishness – "A knowledge of English was the criterion of a man's learning" (p. 44). But because England and Englishness prove elusive to colonial subjects like Njoroge, the education that was supposed to secure alienated land rights comes to function as a source of disenchantment and further alienation. Thus, *Weep Not, Child* ends up being a novel about disenchantment rather than the consolation promised by its title.

Disenchantment in the novel takes two forms: first, it emerges in

Njoroge's realization that the more educated he becomes, the more alienated he is from the life and love around him; he discovers that the social contract promised by modernity is itself the origin of deterritorialization and nomadism.[18] Secondly, in the process of their education, Njoroge and his cohorts come to the realization that the communal burden they have to bear – the search and institution of an African past and future before and beyond colonialism – is itself an illusion. We can amplify the second form of disenchantment by noting that one of the reasons Njoroge loves reading the Bible more than any other text is because the Old Testament helps him imagine scenes of beginnings and territorialization that colonialism has denied his generation. The Gikuyu story of creation parallels – and is authorized by – the book of Genesis (pp. 22–25). It is through the latter that young Africans can realize the histories that colonialism has repressed. Indeed, by endorsing cultural translation – that is, by allowing the educated person to believe that Gikuyu and Mumbi can be translated into Adam and Eve – colonialism has authorized more palatable stories in place of the older Gikuyu mythologies, stories that have the potential for disrupting the synchronic narrative of colonial rule. For people who live under the spell of such old mythologies are bound to discover, as Ngotho discovers very early in life, that they no longer have any authority because without the land, the basis of Gikuyu metaphysics, the old stories do not make sense any more (p. 39). In the Bible, then, Njoroge finds new narratives that make more sense than his father's old mythologies (p. 49). Njoroge comes to embrace the Christian story of revelation and salvation as an appropriate replacement for the dying prophetic narrative: "there was growing up in his heart a feeling that the Gikuyu people, whose land had been taken by white men, were no other than the children of Israel about whom he read in the Bible" (p. 49).

But what exactly is the status and authority of a discourse that is secondary to the dominant narrative of colonialism? In order to emphasize Njoroge's displacement in both his father's house and the culture of colonialism, Ngugi provides the reader with a lyrical scene of Gikuyu beginnings. As we noted in the first chapter, the story of Gikuyu and Mumbi, the mythological founders of the

Gikuyu, was one of the few integrating factors of this culture before colonization. When Ngotho tells the story of Gikuyu beginnings to his sons, he is trying to commemorate, as it were, a foundational narrative that no longer has authority because it has been driven underground: "It was as if he was telling a secret for the first time, but to himself" (p. 24).

In listening to the story as it is told by his father, Njoroge is both searching for a way to give meaning to his complicated life and to integrate himself with his community at a time of cataclysmic social change; but because this is a de-authorized cultural narrative, he can only imagine it in wistful utopian terms:

Njoroge too could imagine the scene. He saw the sun rise and shine on a dark night. He saw fear, gloom and terror of the living things of the creator, melting away, touched by the warmth of the holy tree. It must have been a new world. The man and woman must have been blessed to walk in the new Kingdom with Murungu. He wished he had been there to stand near Him in His holy place and survey all the land. Njoroge could not help exclaiming,
"Where did the land go?"
Everyone looked at him. (pp. 24–25)

This passage is a good example of the ways in which Njoroge's education is both reconstructive of his culture and deconstructive of it: the overt rhetoric promises the unification of the subject and his hitherto foreclosed history. But beneath such metaphorical gestures of presence and participation is a subtext that underlines the hero's loss and displacement ("he wished he had been there"), and calls attention to his ignorance of the foundational histories of his family ("Where did the land go?"). But if such stories are intended to make Njoroge's family history intelligible, as the conventions of the *Bildungsroman* demand, this intelligibility is achieved at the expense of veracity and originality. As we have already noted, this narrative fashions itself after familiar biblical stories and thus exists as a mode of repetition.

But repetition constitutes an important form of education in the novel, for once he recognizes the historical belatedness of the foundational stories related by his father and his own displacement from such stories, Njoroge can structure his relation with the world in utopian terms, terms that seem closer to his own desires. Indeed, given the realities of colonial and anticolonial violence, he can only justify his faith in education in terms of its compensation. He has to believe that something good will come out of his negative experiences. As the colonial forces set about destroying his father's house, which is now turned into an empty ruin, "a place where stories were no longer told" (p. 81), Njoroge holds on to the illusion of education as compensation for the reification engendered by colonialism.[19] The romance associated with education is momentarily seen as a vehicle of overcoming the reality of colonial terror. Indeed, for a brief instant in the novel, Njoroge imagines education, or rather the colonial school, as the only means of overcoming class and racial divisions: it is at school that Njoroge falls in love with Mwihaki, the daughter of his father's enemy ; it is at school that he discovers the boyhood identity he shares with Stephen, the son of the white settler who will later destroy his father. At one point in the novel it appears as though education can actually lead to the reconciliation of the alienated colonial subject and his equally alienated family and community: when Njoroge passes his elementary school examination, his father feels as if the ancient prophecy might not be dead after all: "For the first time for many years something like a glimmer of light shone in Ngotho's eyes. Here at last was a son who might be a credit to the family ... Njoroge might do something for the family" (p. 104). The community expresses similar sentiments and longings: "The news of his success passed from hill to hill. In spite of the troubled time, people still retained a genuine interest in education ... Somehow the Gikuyu people saw their deliverance as embodied in education" (p. 104). There is even the hope that because education represents such a powerful desire, its value transcends class and racial animus; by his success in the colonial school system, it is believed, Njoroge can be ensconced in the communal fold: "He was no longer the son of Ngotho but the son of the land" (p. 105).

Such utopian aspirations are, however, contained within a narrative mode – and a political reality – that negates both subjective and collective desires. Njoroge's triumph in school takes place against the background of one of the most disheartening events in the history of nationalism in Central Kenya – the arrest and conviction of Jomo Kenyatta. Because believers in the ancient prophecy and even some Christians have turned Jomo into the sign of a postcolonial restoration and future, his trial for sedition is conceivable as a test of these people's will and faith: "Everyone knew that Jomo would win. God would not let His people alone. The children of Israel must win. Many people put all their hopes on this eventual victory" (p. 72). Not unexpectedly, Jomo's conviction for anticolonial activities deflates Njoroge's hopes of a utopian future: "That night Njoroge learnt that Jomo lost. His spirit fell and he felt something queer in his stomach. He did not know what to think" (p. 73).

It is important, then, that from this moment onwards the prophetic paradigm that structured the opening of the novel (as it did in *The River Between*) becomes transformed into a discourse of melancholy, or what the narrator calls lamentation. And thus, a novel that opened with high expectations about the future now comes to be dominated by a sense of irreversible loss and of apocalypse: "The fulfillment of the prophecy seemed to be impossible" (p. 73); "Conditions went from bad to worse"; and the only narratives which now seem to make sense are those which seemed to confirm "the destruction of all life in the world" (p. 91). In the circumstances, in a world in which the only authorized discourse is that of lamentations and apocalypse, Njoroge would be foolish to believe that education can have any redemptive value. But there is a fundamental relation between the melancholy that characterizes the second part of the novel and Njoroge's status and identity as a colonial subject: the language of melancholy marks the process by which the colonial subject comes to accept his nomadism or dispossession in the world; but it is by coming to terms with this nomadism that he begins to initiate an autonomous identity against both his family and colonial culture.

But what are we to make of the ending of the novel – especially Njoroge's aborted suicide? Does this gesture represent his total disillusionment with life under colonialism or his hope that somewhere in the future he can use his education to oppose colonial culture? What does the future portend for this colonial nomad? In his influential discussion of melancholy and oppositionality, Ross Chambers makes three important theoretical points that can help us understand the ending of *Weep Not, Child*: first, he argues that deterritorialization and nomadism, the sense of dispossession from one's space and the awareness "of an unending drifting self," are symptoms of melancholia which, nevertheless, serve an important oppositional function; the nomadic subject moves across "a landscape of identity that has no center," but his or her melancholia is an accusation against the dominant system.[20] Secondly, argues Chambers, melancholy needs to be read "not as the site of a personal unconscious, harboring individual 'anger,' but as the 'place' . . . where a political unconscious becomes readable, in and as the tension of the self and the self-constituting other(s)."[21] Thirdly, although the suicidal desires that melancholy often generates appear to be the subject's radical separation from the world, they are in fact the self's way of getting back at the world.[22] Can there be a more satisfactory revenge on a world that has failed one than its total abandonment?

Clearly, the most important aspect of Njoroge's education is his discovery that what he thought were the centers of his identity – the father, the family, and the school – are empty and deformed modes of desire. Indeed, the sight of the father's broken body is the son's best education in the ways of colonial violence: "His face had been deformed by small wounds and scars. His nose was cleft into two and his legs could only be dragged" (p. 122). Observing his dying father, or rather his tortured body, Njoroge is forced to confront colonial terror and the melancholy it generates:

Ngotho's laughter was cold. It left something tight and tense in the air. By now darkness had crept into the hut. Nyokabi lit the lantern as if to fight it away. Grotesque shadows mocked her as they flitted on the walls. What was a man's life if he could be reduced to this? And Njoroge thought: Could this be the father he had secretly adored and feared? Njoroge's mind reeled. The world had turned upside down. (p. 123)

Once he is arrested and tortured, Njoroge comes to realize that his accomplishments in school offer no protection against the brutality of power. He wakes up from his dream and discovers that what appeared to be "the difficulties of the world" (p. 120) mark the true state of the African subject under colonial terror.

The allegory of a world turned upside down is an appropriate setting for the melancholy that arises when Njoroge discovers that his dream or vision was nothing but a mirage, something that disappears as one comes closer to it. But his melancholy also arises from his cognizance of the gap between his previous notion of self capable of being educated in the colonial way and his "otherness" in a world determined by the colonizer. In other words, Njoroge's final education takes place when he gives up the vision of an unproblematic, educated, and thus colonial identity, and comes to terms with his alterity. In this context, it is interesting to note that his negative experiences – expulsion from school, imprisonment, and torture – are described as the "shocks" that "showed him a different world from that he had believed himself living in" (p. 120). As he holds the rope with which he plans to hang himself, we are told, Njoroge "felt a certain pleasure in holding it. For the first time he laughed alone. And he sat waiting for darkness to come and cover him" (p. 135). He derives pleasure from the cord because, as we saw above, suicide is his ultimate revenge on the world.

Njoroge does not, of course, go through with his suicide. He is pulled back by the call and passion of the mother who still believes in him, the mother who sent him to school at the beginning of the book hoping to bring honor and restitution to her family. And if we remember that education, which was posited at the beginning of the novel as the way out of the prisonhouse of colonialism, has now been discredited as a false illusion because it does not protect one from colonial violence, then the question that is left hanging at the end of the novel is simple but intriguing: what does it mean to be a colonial subject, to organize one's life and desire according to a set of values that are ultimately going to be frustrated? What does it mean to be educated in the ways of colonialism when this kind of educaton only leads to an awareness of one's nomadism, the lack of a stable place of identity in the world? At the beginning of his career, Ngugi had not yet found ideological resolutions to such questions.

CHAPTER 4

Representing decolonization: A Grain of Wheat

It is tempting to read *A Grain of Wheat,* the novel that cemented Ngugi's reputation as a major writer, through the prism established by Frantz Fanon in his critique of colonialism and the perils of decolonization. Indeed, it has often been claimed that Ngugi was in the process of writing this novel when he came across Fanon's *The Wretched of the Earth,* and that it was in this book that he simultaneously discovered the politics of socialism and a grammar for representing colonialism and what has now come to be known as arrested decolonization.[1] It has even been said that Fanon's famous critique of decolonization as an arrested moment – one in which national consciousness has failed to be "the all-embracing crystallization of the inner hopes of the whole people" and has instead become "an empty shell, a crude and fragile travesty of what it might have been" – provided Ngugi with an important epigraphic text for his third novel.[2] And if epigraphs are important because they determine or shape readers' expectations as they enter the text, our entry into Ngugi's novel is guided by a powerful image of a grain that wilts and dies instead of growing into "that body that shall be," and by an authorial note drawing attention to the reality of the situation represented in the novel, a situation in which the peasants who fought against British colonial rule in Kenya "now see all that they fought for being put on one side."[3] Both epigraphs are powerful echoes of Fanon's critique of decolonization.

As numerous commentators have noted, *A Grain of Wheat* dramatizes the many salient and ironic moments when decolonization is revealed as an "empty shell," and the novel is structured by an acute opposition between the expectations raised by nationalism and the realities of compromised decolonization.[4] The novel sets out to tell the story of the struggle against colonialism in Kenya, but this story is told from the vantage point of subjects and narrators troubled by the prospects of arrested decolonization and haunted by the ghosts of colonialism past. The novel strives to will a new postcolonial future into being, but the occasional gestures it makes towards hope and renewal are beset by individual and collective fears and anxieties both about the history that is being left behind and the one that beckons. The most memorable political passages in the novel echo Fanon's image of the new postcolonial state as an edifice collapsing from its faults and cracks in "the process of regression."[5] One such passage, which comes toward the end of the novel, is worth quoting in detail:

Kenya regained her Uhuru from the British on 12 December 1963. A minute before midnight, lights were put out at the Nairobi stadium so that people from all over the country and the world who had gathered there for the midnight ceremony were swallowed by the darkness. In the dark, the Union Jack was quickly lowered. When next the lights came on the new Kenya flag was flying and fluttering, and waving, in the air. The Police band played the new National Anthem and the crowd cheered continuously when they saw the flag was black, and red and green. The cheering sounded like one intense cracking of many trees, falling on the thick mud in the stadium.

In our village and despite the drizzling rain, men and women and children, it seemed, had emptied themselves into the streets where they sang and danced in the mud. Because it was dark, they put oil-lamps at the doorsteps to light the streets. As usual, on such occasions, some young men walked in gangs, carrying torches, lurked and whispered in dark corners and the fringes, really looking for love-mates among the crowd. Mothers warned their daughters to take care not to be raped in the dark. The girls danced in the middle, thrusting out their buttocks provokingly, knowing that the men in corners watched them. Everybody waited for something to happen. This "waiting" and the uncertainty that went with it – like a woman torn between fear and joy during birth-motions – was a taut cord beneath the screams and the shouts and the laughter. (*A Grain of Wheat*, p. 203)

This passage is important for two reasons: first, it is an example of the radical transformation Ngugi had undergone since the publication of his first two novels discussed in the previous chapters: the romance of the land and the prophetic narrative have now given in to a self-conscious ironic discourse; the lyricism of the early works has been transplanted by the prose of uncertainty and disconnection; metaphor has given way to metonym. Secondly, while Ngugi's earlier novels were obsessed with genealogies and beginnings, the focus in *A Grain of Wheat* is on narrative and historical closures and the problems they present to those engaged in the politics of nationalism. In this retrospective narrative, everything is told from the muddled point of view proffered by the end of colonialism; the teleological narrative of nationalism does not begin to make sense until it is subjected to the unexpected turns and twists of decolonization. This privileging of endings in the novel raises intriguing questions about the politics of time in Ngugi's *œuvre*, both the time in which the novel is set and the one in which it is produced.[6]

THE NARRATION OF CRISIS

It is hard to say whether Ngugi started writing *A Grain of Wheat* after encountering Fanon's book, or whether he had already started working on it when he read *The Wretched of the Earth*. Nevertheless, the genealogy of the novel raises questions that are germane to its interpretation: does the (Marxist) aesthetic ideology of the novel mark a radical break with Ngugi's previous narrative and cultural practices? Does this novel initiate the socialist ideology and aesthetic that culminated in later works such as *Petals of Blood* and *Devil on the Cross*? Or is it a continuation of the cultural nationalist project discussed in the previous two chapters, a project that reaches its apotheosis in the troubled temporality of decolonization? There are no categorical answers to these questions. The novel itself is caught between its author's desire to trace the history and consequences of cultural nationalism – and thus provide a paradigm for representing decolonization – and the imperative to proffer a cultural grammar for understanding the new postcolonial state. These ostensibly conflicting intentions are best represented in the novel's split temporality: it seeks to capture the "now time" of decolonization and, at the same time, to recover the high moments of cultural nationalism.

What needs to be emphasized at the outset is that while the epigraphs to the novel and its general tone seem to privilege the trope of arrested decolonization (we are constantly forced to read cultural nationalism from the vantage point of its failure), such Fanonist moves should not conceal the celebratory narrative of decolonization, a powerful story of national *retour* and restoration that lies hidden under the rhetoric of failure that dominates the novel. Passages that capture the uncertainty and doubts triggered by decolonization, such as the one quoted above, need to be read against other equally powerful passages that valorize the authority of cultural nationalism. Such passages are often associated with Kihika, who as a prophetic and visionary figure, continues the project began by Waiyaki in *The River Between*:

Kihika's interest in politics began when he was a small boy and sat under the feet of Warui listening to stories of how the land was taken from black people. That was before the Second World War, that is, before Africans were conscripted to fight with Britain against Hitler in a war that was never their own. Warui needed only a listener: he recounted the deeds of Waiyaki and other warriors, who, by 1900 had been killed in the struggle to drive out the whiteman from the land; of Young Harry and the fate that befell the 1923 Procession; of Muthirigu and the mission schools that forbade circumcision in order to eat, like insects, both the roots and the stem of the Gikuyu society. Unknown to those around him, Kihika's heart hardened towards "these people," long before he had even encountered a white face. Soldiers came back from the war and told stories of what they had seen in Burma, Egypt, Palestine and India; wasn't Mahatma Gandhi, the saint, leading the Indian people against British rule? Kihika fed on these stories: his imagination and daily observation told him the rest; from early on, he had visions of himself, a saint, leading Kenyan people to freedom and power. (*A Grain of Wheat*, p. 83)

The novel raises many doubts about the politics of decolonization, but these need to be read against the great historic promise of nationalism.

Now, the central movement of the novel concerns the nationalists' slow discovery that Mugo, the ostensible hero of independence, was a traitor. But Mugo's exposure as a false prophet takes place – indeed becomes possible – only because independence has initiated a radical reversal of the colonial relationship. The changes brought about by decolonization can be noted through a simple contrast in Ngugi's "poetic" deployment of the prophetic figure of Jomo Kenyatta in this and earlier novels. The gloom that overwhelms the prophetic discourse in *Weep Not, Child* when Jomo Kenyatta loses his case at Kapenguria is repeated in the middle of *A Grain of Wheat*: "Jomo had lost the case at Kapenguria. The whiteman would silence the father and the orphans would be left without a helper" (p. 105). The sense of loss here is deep and the resulting despair and disenchantment among nationalists, such as Gikonyo, are perhaps more profound than that felt by the Ngotho family in *Weep Not, Child*.

There is, however, an important difference in the depiction of this historical moment, a distinction in tone that can be explained by the simple fact that in the time frame represented by *A Grain of Wheat*, this loss is recalled from the vantage point of one of the most poignant moments of nationalist success in colonial Kenya – Kenyatta's triumphant return to Gatundu, his ancestral home, back from colonial jails from where, it had been said by some colonial agents, he would never return. True, Kenyatta's trial and imprisonment are represented in *A Grain of Wheat* as the low point in the nationalist narrative; but on the dawn of independence, this moment is recalled so that it can be supplanted by a triumphant narrative of return: "It had rained the day Kenyatta returned home from England: it had also rained the day Kenyatta returned to Gatundu from Maralal" (p. 178). The narrative mentions the loss of the father in order to mock the dystopic colonial narrative with his triumphant return home from his exile in the desert, a return marked by rain, the symbol of new life.

Now, by calling attention to these scenes of restitution and nationalist apotheosis, it is not my intention to discredit the Fanonist idiom that has come to overdetermine the reading of this novel. The language of disenchantment and betrayal cannot be entirely dismissed as a critical imposition; it has, after all, produced some powerful readings of *A Grain of Wheat* by Peter Nazareth and Grant Kamenju, Ngugi's colleagues from Makerere and Leeds University.[7] But Fanon alone cannot account for the novel's contradictory intentions, especially the split between the romance of cultural nationalism and the disenchantment generated by a failed decolonization. Fanon is important to the later Ngugi, but he is just one of the many contexts which readers of this novel need to keep in mind in order to fully understand its language and politics. Two of these contexts need to be examined more closely.

The first context emerges out of Ngugi's identity as a modern writer: his representation of disenchantment and the rhetoric of failure in *A Grain of Wheat* is not simply an ideological response to the failure of decolonization; rather, it also a key part of his desire to situate himself within the tradition of the modern novel. In this respect, readers should not forgot that the question of disenchantment had already entered Ngugi's narrative practice a few years before he discovered Fanon at Leeds in 1964. It is the major theme in two earlier stories, "The Return" (1962) and "Goodbye Africa" (1964), which should be considered as working prototypes for *A Grain of Wheat*.

In "The Return," for example, a political detainee named Kamau returns to his village upon his release, eager to continue the life that was disrupted by the state of emergency; but instead of finding the new beginnings he had expected, he quickly discovers that the world has moved on without him. The motif of return – its promise and reversal – is important in the story, as in Ngugi's later works, for two closely related reasons: first, the author uses the irony of return (the gap between the romance of *retour* and its overwhelming realities) to call into question one of the most cherished notions in anticolonial discourse – the belief that with the collapse of colonialism, cultures and communities could return to their origins and traditions.

In this story, the romance of return, as it were, has been quickly superseded and undermined by images of a hostile nature and landscape. The detainee's journey back home is serenaded by dust; the way back home is not on the red carpet of welcome but on a road notable for its "hardness" and "apparent animosity."[8] The motif of return thus structures disenchantment by contrasting the ex-detainee's dream of a time before alienation – days of childhood and youth – with his radical alienation from the land and people he left behind. As he approaches his village, the ex-detainee wonders whether the villagers will give him a hero's welcome; after all, he has all the credentials needed of a hero of decolonization (*Secret Lives*, p. 50). What he sees in the faces of the villagers, however, is his own alienation and betrayal: "He left them, feeling embittered and cheated. The old village had not even waited for him. And suddenly he felt a strong nostalgia for his old home, friends and surroundings" (p. 51).

The second way in which the motif of return works in the story is to valorize nostalgia as a way of dealing with radical dislocation: on the eve of decolonization, colonial subjects return home to find out that the world that secured their old identities has collapsed; they hence assume that somehow the world of childhood and youth, the world before the state of emergency, was preferable to the new state of uncertainty engendered by the collapse of colonial rule. Such an assumption is, however, based on a misunderstanding because, as we have already seen in our reading of Ngugi's earlier works, childhood and youth are themselves determined and constrained by colonial culture. Nostalgia is constructed out of illusions; it is, indeed, a symptom of the subjects' coming to an awareness of the final collapse of familiar, though compromised, sites of identity – the old village, the lover left behind, the hearth. In prison, ex-detainees like Kamau had borne the pain of imprisonment well, fortified by the hope that on their return home, "life would begin anew" (p. 52). The reality that greets Kamau once he is back home is a familiar one in Ngugi's narratives of this period: his wife has run away with his best friend and with her have gone "the little things that had reminded him of her and that he had guarded all those years" (p. 54).

Similar themes are played out in "Goodbye Africa," where a white settler, forced to leave the country on the eve of decolonization, tries to exorcise the ghost of colonialism past, including the ghost of one man that he had tortured in prison. What is notable about this story, however, is not the way it struggles to represent colonial *angst*, but Ngugi's systematic attempt to turn disenchantment into cultural or literary value. In other words, at this stage in his career, Ngugi was not interested in arrested decolonization for its political value – as a general critique of the failure of independence – but in the ways in which the themes of failure, disenchantment, and betrayal rendered themselves to some of the most celebrated modernist aesthetic forms, primarily irony and melancholy. The white settler is haunted by specific incidents connected to the emergency in Kenya, but his visions, dreams, and imaginings come straight from the colonial modernist novel – Conrad and Greene.[9] The great theme in this story is the colonizer's attempt to deal with the challenge of atavism, cultural atrophy, and madness:

> He had heard of rituals in the dark. He had even read somewhere that some of the early European settlers used to go to African sorcerers, to have curses lifted. He had considered these things opposed to reason: but what had happened to him, the visions, surely worked against the normal laws of reason. No, he would exorcise the hallucinations from his system, here, in the dark. The idea was attractive and, in his condition, irresistible. Africa does this to you, he thought as he stripped himself naked. He now staggered out of the car and walked a little distance into the forest. Darkness and the forest buzzing crept around him. He was afraid, but he stood his ground. What next? (*Secret Lives*, p. 74)

Readers of *A Grain of Wheat* do not need to be reminded that the two stories discussed here were to become important subtexts in the novel: Kamau's story of return and betrayal is rewritten in the longer narrative as Gikonyo's elaborate quest for a space in which the dream of nationalism can be reconciled to the hard realities of decolonization; the white settler's narrative of failed "moral ideals in the service of British capitalism" in "Goodbye Africa" (p. 78) is incorporated into *A Grain of Wheat* as Thompson's attempt to rationalize the colonial mission from the vantage point of its failure. What needs to be stressed here is that Ngugi's focus in these stories was not so much the politics of decolonization, but his own attempts to master narrative forms built around the rhetoric of failure which, he had been taught at Makerere College, was the mark of good literature as defined by modernism.

But there is another context for reading *A Grain of Wheat*. This is to be found in Ngugi's first presentation of sections of his novel as autobiography in a piece curiously called "Life in a Village: Memories of Childhood."[10] Ngugi's presentation of a section from his novel as autobiographical was curious because there was no evidence that he was writing about his own life; indeed, it is hard to detect any autobiographical elements as such in *A Grain of Wheat*. It is true that in writing this novel of the last days of colonialism Ngugi was writing about events he himself had witnessed, since he had come of age during the moments of despair, expectations, and disillusionment that are experienced by all the main characters in the novel. But it is also true that Ngugi was well protected from the ruptures and transformations of a dying colonialism by both Alliance High School and Makerere University College. While Ngugi had an intimate understanding of the central events narrated in his novel – the state of emergency in Kenya, the dislocation of communities, and the break-up of families – he was also distanced from them. And this distance needs to be noted because when he finally decided to write the epic of colonialism and decolonization in Kenya, Ngugi needed to confront questions central to novelistic representation: what was the source of his authority as a chronicler of events that were painfully alive at the moment of writing? What kind of language was needed to represent the romance of decolonization without negating its compromised endings? Was Ngugi confident enough to write a novel based on histories that were being contested before his own eyes?

A common response to the last question follows an interesting tactic, one based on Ngugi's mastery of the "great tradition" of the English novel. The gist of this response is that by the time he came to write his third novel, Ngugi had mastered the art of fiction as defined by Leavis and other proponents of the great tradition, but the craft of fiction he had mastered was not one geared toward a representation of the large historical and collective moments he wanted to write about in his novel. After all, the ideal narrative in the Leavisite tradition tended to focus on the moral character of unique individuals struggling against the forces associated with collective entities and desires.

Ngugi's identification with Conrad, whose influence on *A Grain of Wheat* is substantive, has thus come to be seen by numerous critics as his response to the paradox of writing about collective desires in a genre built on the doctrine of a unique bourgeois self.[11] Proponents of this point of view often argue that Ngugi was attracted to Conrad because he could identify with the latter's alienation in relation to the culture of Englishness and empathize with his liminal position inside and outside the central institutions of English literature and culture. Critics such as Peter Nazareth argue that as an émigré novelist, Conrad provided colonized writers such as Ngugi with models of narration in which the unique subjectivity of colonized subjects could be represented in relation to their troubled histories.[12] But while Conrad's influence on Ngugi's literary style cannot be disputed, establishing a parallel identity between the émigré Polish novelist – trying to come to terms with his adopted Englishness – and the postcolonial African writer – struggling to establish a narrative voice outside the culture of colonialism – is more complex than might at first appear to be the case.[13] For Ngugi and his contemporaries, the problem of representing decolonization was compounded by the unexpected way in which the colonial project had ended. In Kenya, for example, no one expected colonialism to end with constitutional compromises. Amidst the violence of colonial rule and resistance represented so vividly in novels such as *Weep Not, Child*, many people could not foresee a quick end to white domination in Kenya. Until the day of independence itself – a moment that was greeted with a sense of uncertainty and disbelief – decolonization could only be talked about in terms of its eschatology, its future promise, rather than its epistemology, its immediate condition of possibility. Deferred in time, decolonization was always represented in its ideality – its prophetic measure, as it were – rather than the constellation of problems it was doomed to carry forward from its colonial past. And yet it was only in its narrative representation, in what Fanon had called its "exact measure," that colonialism could be understood in terms of "the movements which give it historical form and content."[14] *A Grain of Wheat* was Ngugi's first comprehensive attempt to give colonialism and nationalism concrete form and content.

THE PLAY OF ALLEGORY AND IRONY

Ngugi's response to the challenge of giving colonialism and decolonization a historical form and content is adumbrated in the first three chapters of *A Grain of Wheat* where he deploys allegory (the figure that valorizes the authority of ideals) against irony (the figure that calls such ideals into question). As readers of the novel will recall, the narrative opens by calling attention to the crisis of representation that engendered the narrative in the first place:

now that colonialism is over, how is the contested past going to be represented in communal and individual narratives that have yet to clarify the terms of the past they are eager to transcend? What forms will the haunted colonial past take as we move toward the postcolonial future? Initially, these questions seem to invite a certain allegorical response, but as they are placed within the historical context that prompted them in the first place, Ngugi makes an important move toward an ironic discourse. If his nationalist leanings make allegory a tempting linguistic figure for representing the past, taking an exact measure of decolonization seems to force him toward modes of narration that privilege irony as the appropriate form for representing complex, contested, and incomplete histories.

In the first chapter of the novel, for example, Mugo is represented to us as the archetypal subject defined by moral crisis. His relationship to his environment, community, and temporality is one of alienation. At a time when people are supposed to be beginning life anew, Mugo is haunted by what will later be revealed as a complex and opaque past. It is through the prism of this past that the present and future enter his troubled consciousness: "How time drags, everything repeats itself, Mugo thought; the day ahead would be just like yesterday and the day before" (*A Grain of Wheat*, p. 2). A temporal moment that should be defined by rupture becomes one of repetition. In this chapter, as for most of the novel, time is represented from the vantage point of the emergency – the primary referent against which individual and collective desires are measured. Indeed, Thabai, the central locality in the novel, is a creation of the emergency (p. 3); its sense of order is a reflection of the imperial power that created it in order to contain insurgency against colonial rule.

In *A Grain of Wheat*, even people's lives have come to revolve around the emergency which, in the process of narration, is unconsciously elevated to the status of the primal event of late colonialism in Kenya. The stories that the characters in the novel tell each other in an attempt to get a handle on their past revolve around the meaning of their lives during the state of emergency. But, like the state of emergency itself, this telling and retelling of worn out stories is a symptom of the tenuous nature of signification

- and temporality - in Ngugi's novel: is this a novel about the recent colonial past or about the moment of decolonization in which it is set? Why is the central subject of Ngugi's novel also the one man who seems to be most distanced from its central events? How do we explain the structure of time in the novel, especially the paradoxical fact that a hundred-year history of colonialism is contained within a few days before independence? The play of allegory and irony can help us understand the politics of time in *A Grain of Wheat*.[15]

First, we should note that the novel opens by calling attention to an allegorical figure: Mugo is presented to us as the archetypal scapegoat, the representation of the villagers' pain and suffering during the emergency and the depository of their anxieties. At the same time, however, Mugo's allegorical function in the novel is rendered suspect by the tenor of the narrative, which increasingly raises doubts about the social role assigned to him by public opinion and calls attention to his profound dislocation from his immediate context and the norms that define the community. Indeed, while the production of Mugo's character can be seen as evidence of Ngugi's mastery of the bourgeois novel – especially of his ability to create a unique individual defined by his alienation from his self and community – this mastery of form ultimately undermines the desire for allegory in *A Grain of Wheat*. For Mugo's individualism is what sets him apart from his community and his difference is what begins to alert some of his old friends and neighbors to his hidden character – and I would argue, unallegorical – nature and function. Like the hero of the bourgeois novel, Mugo is represented in purely negative terms – "He always felt naked, seen" (p. 5); "he felt hollow" (p. 6) – but without any redeeming moral qualities. The great irony of the novel, of course, is that the Thabai community has come to invest all its desires and aspirations in this naked and hollow man. And part of the reason why Mugo's real character (that of a coward and betrayer) remains inaccessible to his compatriots is because of the allegorical premise on which his subjectivity is built: because he is named after one of the most important Gikuyu prophets (Mugo wa Kibiro), the other villagers cannot conceptualize his nature and role outside their long historical struggle against colonialism. The villagers desperately want Mugo to be the signifier of their authentic temporal destiny.

But the people's attempt to force Mugo to play a allegorical function is haunted by the novel's central irony: *A Grain of Wheat* is the story of the villagers' discovery that Mugo, the man they have anointed as the representative of a heroic past and the conscience of a decolonized future, was the one who betrayed Kihika, the true hero of the struggle for freedom. It is not my intention here to comment on the ironic twists that generate this plot and how the secrets of history are decoded, as it were. What I want to emphasize are the specific ways in which this irony is part of the author's divided intentions discussed earlier. Consider, first of all, that what makes the sanctification of Mugo ironic is that even without the complete story, the reader is aware that the utterances the villagers make about Mugo's role in the struggle for independence are the opposite of what actually happened. Indeed, it is Mugo's discomfort with the role assigned to him by his neighbors that clues us in on his shadowy past.

There is hence a certain complicity between narrator and reader, a complicity that reinforces the gap that separates the realities of the past and the fictions invented to cope with it. In these circumstances, the declarative statements expressing Karanja's guilt – which are, inversely, statements exonerating Mugo – call attention to the cunning reason of irony in the novel: "That Karanja should die on Independence Day seemed just: that he should be humiliated in front of a huge crowd, if he gave himself up, or else be made uncomfortable was only a necessary preparation for the ritual" (p. 155). And in the sentences that celebrate Mugo as the hero of the new nation, we have an excellent example of an irony that develops when semantic expressiveness becomes excessive in regard to its object of description: "Mugo's name was whispered . . . Independence Day without him would be stale; he is Kihika born again" (p. 180).

A Grain of Wheat is perhaps Ngugi's most ironic novel, but whatever authority this irony has depends on its capacity to deconstruct key allegorical moments in the narrative. The constant switches the author makes between allegory and irony generate the energy of this novel; such switches are marked by important temporal transformations. In the second chapter of the novel, for example, the switch from allegory to irony is marked by a calculated shift from the moment of decolonization that opens the novel to the colonial past that many of its subjects would like to avoid. What is interesting about this shift is not its abruptness, but the manner in which the temporality of allegory is swamped by a volatile irony, but still manages to hold its own ground. And we are not concerned with a simple play of tropes here; the shift from allegorical to ironic time is connected to a larger ideological project: the historical past, represented as allegory, is seen, from the vantage point of decolonization, as banal, the subject of mockery; but ironizing history does not abrogate it; irony only changes the historian's terms of reference.

The last point can perhaps be made much better through contrast. In both *The River Between* and *Weep Not, Child*, the history and process of colonization are represented in an almost ecumenical language. Here, for example, is Waiyaki's first lesson on the coming of colonialism in *The River Between:*

"Now, listen my son. Listen carefully, for this is the ancient prophecy... I could not do more. When the white man came and fixed himself in Siriana, I warned all the people. But they laughed at me. Maybe I was hasty. Perhaps I was not the one. Mugo often said you could not cut the butterflies with a panga. You could not spear them until you learnt and knew their ways and movement. Then you could trap, you could fight back. Before he died, he whispered to his son the prophecy, the ancient prophecy: 'Salvation shall come from the hills.' From the blood that flows in me, I say from the same tree, a son shall rise. And his duty shall be to lead and save the people!" He said no more. Few knew the prophecy.[16]

The narrative tries to approximate the language of "tribal" wisdom and prophetic authority; the tenor of Chege's language foregrounds his sacred mission; his discourse is filled with figures drawn from nature and the landscape. This combination of a high moral tone and organic signifiers (trees, animals, and blood) enforces what I have already referred to as allegorical temporality.

The same narrative and a similar set of players reappear at key moments in *A Grain of Wheat*, but now, as the following passage shows, something has happened to the language of prophecy:

Waiyaki and other warrior-leaders took arms. The iron snake spoken of by Mugo wa Kibiro was quickly wriggling towards Nairobi for a thorough exploitation of the hinterland. Could they move it? The snake held on to the ground, laughing their efforts to scorn. The whiteman with bamboo poles that vomited fire and smoke, hit back; his menacing laughter remained echoing in the hearts of the people, long after Waiyaki had been arrested and taken to the coast, bound hands and feet. Later, so it is said, Waiyaki was buried alive at Kibwezi with his head facing into the centre of the earth, a living warning to those, who, in after years, might challenge the hand of the Christian woman whose protecting shadow now bestrode both land and sea. (*A Grain of Wheat*, p. 20)

This version of the story would also like to wear the mask of allegory and to reproduce the figurative language of the prior story (hence the use of the "iron snake" for the railway and "bamboo poles" for guns), but the high moral tone of the original narrative has given way to ironic distance, fragmentation, and uncertainty. Indeed, while important traces of the allegorical stories of Gikuyu deliverance from colonialism remain in *A Grain of Wheat*, such remainders should not conceal the fact that the relationship between this novel and its precursors is one of distance and critique. In *The River Between*, Mugo, the prophet, is invoked as the last defender of Gikuyu culture and political interests; in *A Grain of Wheat*, a traitor is given the name of the prophet as if to mock the prophetic tradition itself.

Now, while such temporal reversals have been interpreted as signs of Ngugi's disenchantment with the narrative of national independence, it is important to note that the theme of disenchantment in *A Grain of Wheat* is not as complete as it first appears and that the allegory which the narrative seems to wish away is central to its overall political objectives.[17] Indeed, the purpose of irony in the novel is to secure the allegorical narrative of national independence at a time when its ideals are threatened at their foundations. Thus, while the first chapter of *A Grain of Wheat* ends by calling attention to the tense relationship between Mugo and his community, the second chapter strives, perhaps without much success, to frame the history of nationalism, somewhere between its beginnings in the 1890s to the eve of independence. The use of an ironic temporality, one defined by dissonance and doubt, allows the author to provide his readers with a trenchant critique of a stillborn decolonization, while his overall ideological commitment is to the ideals of the anticolonial movement.

In contrast, allegory allows Ngugi to secure nationalist ideals because, unlike irony, which always calls attention to the gap between appearances and realities, an allegorical temporality reinforces the homology between textual structures and experiences. In other words, the meaning of an allegorical event is derived from what one may call its spiritual dimension, one which emphasizes connections between the fictional narrative and the continuum of history.[18] Thus, although he is aware of the possibility of national betrayal, old Warui (his name means "the river") recalls the history of nationalism in Kenya, not as a series of ironic configurations, but as a continuum of events in which he was both witness and agent. Significantly, it is by recalling the beginnings of the national narrative that Warui can cope with its setbacks and failures – "When Jomo Kenyatta and other leaders of the Movement were arrested in 1952, Warui recalled the 1923 Procession" (p. 13).

What is the point of all this? Simply that Ngugi asks his readers to enter his novel through two scenes of reading: an allegorical scene in which we are invited to identify with the grand narrative of nationalism and its desires, and an ironic scene in which we are asked to be alert to the discrepancies between the structure of the narrative and the experiences it represents. What makes this schema complicated, however, is that we cannot read *A Grain of Wheat* from one perspective without being cognizant of the other; we cannot read the novel as a radical critique of decolonization without considering its passionate identification with the ideals of cultural nationalism discussed in the previous chapter. Indeed, if *A Grain of Wheat* can be considered as transitional in Ngugi's career – it marks his mastery of the great tradition of the bourgeois novel and his break with it – the most obvious aspect of the transitional character of the novel is its aesthetic attempt to balance the unique history of an individual (Mugo) and that of a collective (the nationalist movement or the emergent Kenyan nation).

Consider the unexpected conjoining of Mugo and Kihika at the end of Chapter Two: Mugo is marked out as a lone individual, an ironic figure, while Kihika, who is constantly compared to Christ

("Kihika lived the words of sacrifice he had spoken to the multitude" [p. 15]) is clearly represented as an allegorical figure. But
when the two characters are brought together in Chapter Three,
over ten years later, we end up with a memorable reversal of the
terminology. In the following scene, Gikonyo is trying to persuade
Mugo to be the "carrier" of Kihika's memory:

"It is like this. The Movement and leaders of the village have thought that
it is a good idea to honour the dead. On Independence Day we shall
remember those from our village and ridges near, who lost their lives in
the fight for freedom. We cannot let Kihika's name die. He will live in our
memory, and history will carry his name to our children in years to
come." He paused and looked straight at Mugo and his next words
addressed to Mugo were full of plain admiration. "I don't want to go into
details – but all know the part you played in the Movement. Your name
and that of Kihika will ever be linked together. As the General here has
said, you gave Kihika shelter without fear of danger to your own life. You
did for Thabai out here and in detention what Kihika did in the forest."
(pp. 23–24)

The villagers consider Mugo to be an allegorical figure – the
means by which Kihika's life and work will be commemorated –
but from the readers' perspective, this representation is ironic
because it is based on a lack of knowledge about the would-be
hero's true activities during the emergency. The ironic implications of Gikonyo's discourse are not as clear at this stage in the
novel as they will become much later, but the narrative has given
us enough evidence to show that Mugo is not exactly what the
villagers assumed he was – he is a dislocated signifier of their
history. The villagers want to invest a rhetorical authority in Mugo
– "You will make the final speech of the day" (p. 24) – but the
reader is fully aware of the hero's linguistic disabilities. The nationalist movement wishes Mugo to be the subject of allegorical coherence and epistemological certainty, but we are privileged enough
to see the difficulties he has comprehending the discourse of
others, or even understanding his own motives and actions.

The process of reversal works the other way too: in his sacrificial
death, Kihika has become the non-problematic figure around
which communal desires – and the narratives that sustain them –
can be organized, but his allegorical function is also based on a

misunderstanding, not so much of his heroic role, but of the fact that the man who betrayed him is supposed to carry his vision into the future. The greatest irony (and allegory) of it all is this: conjoined in their lives and deaths, Mugo and Kihika are all part of a prophecy fulfilled (the achievement of independence); but this is a prophecy which, in its apotheosis and betrayal, is given content and form as much by its utopian propensities as by the series of tragedies and mishaps that bring it about.

HISTORIES, STORIES, AND SITUATIONS

As we have already seen, the stylistic complexity of *A Grain of Wheat* – the deployment of multiple subject positions, interior mono-logue, and the use of different modes of narrative focalization – has often been explained in terms of Ngugi's mastery of the form of the novel in the great tradition.[19] While this assessment is generally correct, it is, nevertheless, important to note the basic connection between the formal complexities that distinguish this novel from Ngugi's previous works and his need to recover a usable past. The author's desire to turn the historic past into what Arjun Appadurai has called (in a different context) a "symbolic resource" is evident at the very beginning of the novel when he makes two historiographical moves: first, Ngugi tries to make his readings comprehend the past through a group of characters who are haunted by repressed histories and "pestering memories" (p. 28).[20] Secondly, he uses these characters' memories – and their remembrance of things past – to play off competing modes of representing the past.

In order to exorcise their haunting experiences under colonial-ism, or turn the contested meaning of the colonial past into a "charter" on which postcolonial identities can be constructed, all the characters in the novel must confront their personal histories and try and transform them into an intelligible source of meaning, a code for explaining their actions in the past and a vehicle for comprehending the difficult choices they have to make on the eve of independence. In the process, the temporality of the novel collapses the distinctions between the past and present that might make a narrative of history more linear and hence easily intelli-gible. Instead of providing coherence and clarity, narratives of things remembered on the moment of decolonization are shown to involve "composition, opposition and debate," and thus end up being circular and unmanageable.[21]

The problem of using the past as a resource or charter is apparent in the community's (and author's) privileging of Mugo in the narrative. For by constructing the moment of independence around the traitor, rather than the sacrificed hero, Ngugi nudges his text – and its readers – to foreground the compromised nature of independence; he uses his novel to show how postcolonial attempts to produce a stable and collective narrative about the past are bound to flounder in the face of competing interpretations, desires, and recollections. The villagers assume that Mugo is the key to understanding the past; they assume that he can be the embodiment of all the heroic values in which they want to dress up the past. But Mugo's relation to this past is ironic; his recollections of the history he is supposed to embody are hazy. The villagers want him not simply to represent the past, but also to bring it back to them through his voice. But when he addresses the crowd, his voice is unable to invoke the past in the rhetorical gestures that his audience requires: "Mugo stood before the crowd. His voice, rusty, startled him. He spoke in a dry monotone, tired, almost as if telling of scenes he did not want to remember" (p. 65). And this voice does not merely speak of events it wants to distance itself from (thus disclaiming the patriotic rhetoric of nationalism); it is disembodied both from the speaker and its referent:

> At first Mugo enjoyed the distance he had established between himself and the voice, but soon the voice disgusted him. He wanted to shout: that is not it at all; I did not want to come back; I did not long to join my mother, or wife or child because I did not have any. Tell me, then, whom could I have loved? He stopped in the middle of a sentence and walked down the platform towards his hut. (p. 66)

There are many attempts to invoke the rhetoric of a heroic past in the novel. These are most notable in those scenes describing Kihika's eloquent speeches about the romance of the Kenyan past and the brave new world to be ushered in by decolonization. The young man's willingness to sacrifice himself in the name of his country and the ancient prophecy of national restoration is celebrated in the novel. But we cannot fail to notice how this rhetoric is imprisoned in the crisis of meaning and the uncertainty about the past and the future that opens and closes the novel. In addition, Kihika's vision of "a heroic past" is recalled through scenes of reading dominated by images of his betrayal and death (p. 88). In seeking the unifying figure of history in the betrayer (Mugo) rather than the martyr (Kihika), the villagers have come to realize, through their collective and individual suffering during the emergency, that the past can only be recuperated through deviations, repressions, and misinterpretations. Ngugi's narrative, then, is one in which the historiographical operation depends on what Michel de Certeau would call "a double-edged effect": by recreating the past from the vantage point of the present, the novel "stages the present time of a lived situation" (it gives us a moment of decolonization clearly distinct from the terrible colonial past); but it produces this past in terms of an absence ("the figure of the past keeps its primary value of representing *what is lacking*") which is disembodied, like Mugo's voice, from the past it represents but which it cannot comprehend outside compromised subjects and events.[22]

The lives of all the characters in the novel are indeed defined by the tension that arises when they try to establish connections or disconnections between the past and their imagined futures. Gripped by anxieties about the inevitable collapse of white power, which has hitherto been the source of his identity and authority, Karanja remains hopeful that he might reconnect his disrupted romance with Mumbi and build a new life. Adopting the new ideology of free enterprise and self-sufficiency, Gikonyo believes he can somehow disconnect himself from the phantom of the colonial past – "He did not let the problems of the heart or anything deflect him from the immediate purpose" (p. 59) – only to discover that the narrative of the future is haunted by repressed histories. Indeed, while Gikonyo stages his postcolonial identity by enforcing the logic of capitalist success, a logic constructed on the belief that the self-made bourgeois subject must break with his antiquity, as it were, the narrative constantly explains his lived situation in terms of the past he would like to renounce. Attempting to map his future in the midst of broken promises and lost expectations, it is to the past that Gikonyo turns as he seeks the code that will explain the meaning of his life in the dark days of the emergency. What he remembers, like all the other characters in the novel, is that singular moment before the declaration of the state of emergency (the train scene) when he met Mumbi: "Gikonyo never forgot the scene in the wood; while in detention, yearning for things and places beyond the reach of hope, he lived in detail every moment of that experience, a ritual myth of a forgotten land, long ago" (p. 98).

So, while Gikonyo is now eager to forget Mumbi and the past she embodies – including the ideals of nationalism and romantic love – he comes to realize that the future cannot be imagined without reckoning with "her feelings, her thoughts, her desires" (p. 247). The main question the novel raises in regard to the past, then, is not whether painful histories can be repressed or be given new value; rather, the most pressing issue for the author and the reader is what character and value this history acquires in its remembering, figuration, and retelling. Here, again, Ngugi does not represent the past as a unified narrative; on the contrary, history is represented in the form of a conflict of interpretations, a conflict that takes three main forms: history as a repressed specter that returns to haunt its actants, the past as an unsayable event, and the act of remembering as a narrative moment of forgetfulness.

There are a couple of ways in which history functions as a specter in the lives of the main characters. For John Thompson and other agents of British colonialism in the novel, the past takes the form of a ghostly revenant; the coming of independence resurrects what he would like to forget most – his role in the killing of political detainees at Rira several years earlier (p. 42). Times may have changed, but for Thompson, the eyes of the library workers at Githima are exactly like those of the prisoners he controlled at the detention camp: "In the men at the library, he had recognized the eyes, the same look" (p. 46). Through the gaze of his undifferentiated others, Thompson confronts the unsayable event, "the wound that had never healed"; a wound which nullifies his past and present because when it was touched "it brought back all the humiliation he had felt at the time" (p. 46). The power of the past depends on the fact that it can no longer be given the same denomination; defined in colonial discourse as atavistic terror, "Mau Mau" is now being turned into a foundational narrative of postcoloniality; deprived of its moral economy, the discourse of settler power in Kenya can only be recalled as trivia – "his mind only dwelt on the past and the trivial side of it: like the dog incident earlier in the day" (p. 48). Here, the specter of the past acquires what Jacques Derrida has called a phenomenality which, at the same time, "comes to defy semantics as much as ontology, psychoanalysis as much as a philosophy."[23] The past returns in the form of a powerful presence that calls into question the language both subjects and readers have developed to contain history (the semantics of time), the personal narratives they have conjured to rationalize their past actions (psychoanalysis), and their causal explanations of the past (philosophy). In this context, the repressed past returns, but it comes back as the negation of the imperial principle that informed it – "the principle of Reason, of Order and of Measure" (*A Grain of Wheat*, p. 53). Indeed, if Thompson seems eager to recall the past he is about to leave behind, it is simply to "exorcise the hallucinations that plagued him" (p. 56).

History returns as a specter in a second way already hinted at earlier in this chapter – in its conception as utopia – the anticipation of a thing that is yet to come, "a thing that is not yet here and may never be there, a thing that is not a thing."[24] This is how the moment of independence is conceived in a remarkable passage toward the end of the novel: "Everybody waited for something to happen. This 'waiting' and the uncertainty that went with it – like a woman torn between fear and joy during birth-motions – was a taut cord beneath the screams and the shouts and the laughter" (p. 203). Before the emergency, nationalists like Gikonyo embraced the struggle against colonialism simply because their narrative was driven by a clear teleology: "Gikonyo walked towards detention with a brisk step and an assurance born in his knowledge of love and life ... The day of deliverance was near at hand" (p. 104). Although his faith in the future is tested by the difficult experiences he undergoes in detention, Gikonyo undergoes hardships and even betrays his oath in the hope of being reconciled with Mumbi, the symbolic mother of the nation: "He only wanted to see his Mumbi and take up the thread of life where he had left it" (p. 113). This is not the way things work out once the future arrives.

Indeed, instead of being a moment of revelation in which the meaning of the past can finally be grasped in retrospect, the day of independence reduces nationalist eschatology into a banal event. In the midst of the crisis of cognition engendered by the coming of independence, for example, Gikonyo comes to see his life story merely in terms of unsayable and unusable histories. The moment of return calls into question the narrative of deliverance itself:

> In the streets, naked and half-naked children played throwing dust at one another. Some of the dust entered Gikonyo's eyes and throat; he rubbed his eyes with the back of his hand (water streamed from his eyes) and he coughed with irritation. He stopped women whose faces he could not recognize and asked them for Wangari's hut. Some stared at him with open hostility and others shook their heads with indifference, making him both impatient and angry. At last a small boy pointed the way to the hut. Walking towards it, Gikonyo wondered what he would do when he stood face to face with Mumbi. Doubt followed excitement; what if Mumbi was at the river or the shops when he arrived. Could he possibly wait for another hour or two before he could see her? (pp. 113–14)

Since none of Gikonyo's precolonial expectations are fulfilled, and since his life story is deprived of its expected ending, his history can be described as belated. And since the meaning of his life (its telos) "was contained in his final return to Mumbi" (p. 116), her ostensible betrayal marks the final collapse of all the dreams – and explanatory systems – nurtured in colonial detention camps.

As Gikonyo's example shows so vividly, the restoration that was expected to justify the whole history of Kenya, especially the suffering people had to endure during the state of emergency, has not come about. And it is in this context that a debate emerges in the novel on whether the past can be more usable in its commemoration or forgetfulness. This debate is important not simply because the kind of profound changes in consciousness which nationalist narratives seek to generate bring with them what Benedict Anderson has called "characteristic amnesias," but also because in postcolonial Kenya, forgetting was an official charter of the government.[25] Furthermore, whether one chooses to forget – "I don't like to remember," says Mugo (p. 67) – or to remember – "I can't forget... I will never forget," cries Gikonyo (p. 67) – forgetting and remembering exist in a chiasmic relationship; they denote a similar relationship with the past, a way of coming to terms with history or of dealing with its haunting.

A Grain of Wheat is a novel written under the strains created by
the ghost of colonialism – "Koina talked of seeing the ghosts of the
colonial past still haunting independent Kenya" (p. 220) – and a
narrative that is keen to institute what we may call an epistemological practice for the postcolonial nation. In other words,
while the novel seems obsessed with the difficulties of finding a
usable history, it posits the act of narration as the process by which
our knowledge of the colonial past is established as a precondition
for establishing a postcolonial future. The novel is certainly interested in the difficulties of establishing the rules of producing new
knowledge in the face of competing claims about the past. The act
of narration thus oscillates between the subjects' imperative to
know and their recognition of the difficulties of establishing meanings in the horror of the emergency: "I was in a strange world,"
says Mumbi, "and it was like if I was mad. And need I tell you
more?" (p. 150). The last phrase is obviously a rhetorical question –
it assumes that the listener already knows and understands the
horrors of a world turned upside down and the madness it generates. But this shared knowledge does not stop Mumbi from recounting her ordeals during the emergency because one of the
many reasons the colonized are brought together on the eve of
decolonization is so that they can tell each other stories of horror,
stories that often echo each other, as one important way of accounting for the past. Telling stories is clearly one way of clarifying
the meaning of the past in order to control its haunting powers.
But as we have already seen, such stories are also occasions to
forget the past.

More importantly, the novel is made up of competing stories, a
mode of contestation that is as much about the colonial past as it is
about the postcolonial future. This situation is further complicated
by the fact that even the identity of the narrator in the novel is
contradictory. For while there are many instances when this narrator adopts a traditional omniscient position and maintains strict
distance from both his or her subject and the reader, there are also
moments when he or she startles us by identifying with both sides
in this narrative contract. Mugo is marked out as the traitor in the
novel, but this does not stop the narrator from identifying with his
predicament in detention (p. 63). The narrator can be impersonal
and empirical – "Kenya regained her Uhuru from the British on

12 December 1963" (p. 203) – but he or she can become part of the same universe of discourse as the narratee: "Many people from Thabai attended the meeting because, as you'll remember, we had only just been allowed to hold political meetings" (p. 64). Furthermore, there are certain discrete moments in the novel when the narrator discards the anonymity of omniscience, acquires a subject position akin to that of the reader, and hence functions as both addresser and addressee (p. 178).

What does this shift in positions of enunciation mean? Does it have a pattern? Does it have any effect on the contextual dimensions of the novel, especially its ambivalent posture toward the politics of decolonization? The best way of responding to these questions is perhaps to expand the range of inquiry here and see the ambivalence of enunciation as a symptom of the complications that arise once the grand narrative of colonialism has collapsed. Without the totality once represented by the narrative of empire, Ngugi's narrators, readers, and characters have to cope with a multiplicity of competing narratives and shifting subject positions.

Let us examine two specific modes of narration which are often in competition in this novel. There is, first of all, a narrative that bears what Joseph Conrad, Ngugi's main influence in this novel, calls "the marks of documentary evidence."[26] This is the narrative that bases its authority on objective historicism, or at least parodies historicism: "Learned men will, no doubt, dig into the troubled times which we in Kenya underwent, and maybe sum up the lesson of history in a phrase" (*A Grain of Wheat*, p. 131). When Mugo's story is told from the perspective of the heterodiegetic narrator, for example, we have a story that is liberated from his neurosis and twisted desires; it is from this perspective that the reader is often clued in on his momentary delusions of grandeur (p. 134.) A great deal of the historical events surrounding the state of emergency in Kenya is also narrated through the documentary method (see pp. 140–41).

But as in Conrad's *Under Western Eyes*, the power of documentary evidence is almost immediately questioned by a second mode of narration, a mode that is not simply subjective, but one whose authority depends, unlike the documentary method, on the reader's engagement with the emotions and desires of the narratees, the presumed audience in the novel. Thus, Gikonyo's and Karanja's narrative of their experiences during the emergency is built around their love and desire for Mumbi; Mumbi's story is in turn constructed around her dreams of romance, heroism, and passion (pp. 136–37). For readers who are inclined to argue that the function of such a subjective mode of narration is to undermine the interpretation of history itself, Mugo's story would appear to be exemplary: his narrative is, as we have already noted, disembodied and fragmented. And yet, there are instances when the documentary mode itself becomes disembodied and fragmented, especially when it adopts the clichéd language of an exhausted nationalist movement.

The point of all this is that the reader is not asked to choose between these narrative modes because they seem to relate the same events with equal power and coherence. This is obvious in those situations where documentary evidence is related in a first-person narrative situation (p. 146), or, as in the following example, in a subtle admixture of the third-person narration and free indirect discourse:

Seeing General R. in the race, she was reminded of what the General had said two days before this. The irony of his words now struck her with her fuller knowledge of the situation. Circumstances had changed since she wrote that note. Then she had not known that the man who had actually betrayed Kihika was now the village hero. How could she tell this to anybody? Could she bear to bring more misery to Mugo, whose eyes and face seemed so distorted with pain? She recalled his fingers on her mouth, the others awkwardly feeling her throat. Then the terrible vacuum in his eyes. Suddenly at her question, he had removed his hands from her body. He knelt before her, a broken, submissive penitent. (p. 207)

In this passage, the final race for Mumbi is seen from her perspective, from that of the omniscient narrator and in a free indirect discourse in which it is not clear who the speaker is ("Could she bear to bring more misery to Mugo?"). It is when they are confronted with these kinds of narrative perspectives that readers are clued in to what I have already called the contested history of decolonization in Kenya.

In fact, the moment of closure in the novel is a masterful working of multiple narrative focalization and is worthy of detailed consideration. This moment of closure is one in which the sense of an ending to the drama of colonialism – the moment of decoloniz- ation – is double-coded by two epigraphs from the Bible: the first epigraph is from the Gospel according to St. John and is based on the proposition that the death of a grain of wheat (its ending or its death) is indeed a new beginning – "if it die it bringeth forth much fruit"; the second epigraph, the one from Revelation, is apocalyp- tic and denotes the end as a radical and unregenerated moment of rupture. And so the question arises, is the end of colonialism the beginning of a new life in Kenya or a millennial passing?

This is clearly a political question, one that comes to obsess Ngugi later in his career, but the best way to approach it is not through his latter-day rhetoric – his critique of decolonization – but the narrative modes he brings to play in the last section of *A Grain of Wheat*. There is, first of all, the documentary mode through which the narrator relates basic historical facts with the detach- ment of a news correspondent: "Kenya regained her Uhuru from the British on 12 December 1963... In the dark, the Union Jack was quickly lowered. When next the lights came on the new Kenya ... band played the new National Anthem and the crowd cheered ... when they saw the flag was black, and red and green" (p. 203). This kind of description represents the moment of independence in quotidian language and refuses to acknowledge the figurative nature of the occasion it describes, a mode of figuration that is apparent in the symbolism of the flags. And if this neutral stance is not enough, the narrator adopts a semantic and syntactical struc- ture that disengages him or her from the objects of representation: "They created words to describe the deeds of Kihika in the forest, deeds matched only by those of Mugo in the trench and detention camps" (p. 204). But this gesture of disengagement – the descrip- tion of the villagers as "they" – is complicated by the fact that the narrator is part of the scene being described: "They mixed Chris- tian hymns with songs and dances only performed during initi- ation rites... And underneath it all was the chord that followed us from street to street" (p. 204). Clearly, the narrator is both inside and outside the drama of independence. He or she identifies with this momentous occasion, but also seeks a neutral position from which to critique the terms of independence.

Thus, the moment of closure in the novel comes to be defined by a series of binary oppositions, binaries that are most manifest in the race between Gikonyo and Karanja: this race is part of the celebration of the newness of independence, but it is also a repetition of the two men's race to the train several years before; it posits a moment in which the act of remembering the past is as important as forgetting it (pp. 208–09); like the moment of independence itself, the race evokes mixed reactions in interested observers such as Mumbi – "She wanted Gikonyo to win, and also prayed that he might lose" (p. 211). In addition, scenes of independence are represented through a commemorative language (it is through common acts of remembering that a new community will be built), but this language is constantly undermined by doubts and ill omens that seem to suggest that perhaps the only way to deal with the past is simply to forget it.

Thus, even as he runs the race of his life to celebrate the coming of Uhuru, Mwaura cannot help but shudder at the unexpected encounter with ghosts from his past: "The ghost had come to eat into his life; the cool Uhuru drink had turned insipid in his mouth" (p. 214). The crowd that comes to celebrate independence makes a harmony, but beneath it all, readers cannot fail to notice that the agency of this harmonization is both a dead and false prophet: "We sang song after song about Kihika and Mugo. A calm holiness united our hearts" (p. 217). And thus the collective narratives that recreate heroic histories and sacrifices (pp. 218–19) become ironic within a context dominated by "the ghosts of the colonial past still haunting independent Kenya" (p. 220).

But how do individual subjects fare in this drama of independence? It is significant that the novel ends with stories built around subjects (Karanja, Mugo, Wambui, and Warui) who call attention to the complex – and undoubtly ironic – problems on which the foundational narrative of independence will be built, and not those characters (Gikonyo and Mumbi), whose allegorical or symbolic function is obvious. Gikonyo will carve a stool to commemorate Mumbi's role as the mother of the nation (p. 247), but such utopian gestures will not resolve the problems embedded in the stories of failure and betrayal associated with people like Karanja and Mugo. For while Gikonyo and Mumbi can confront their individual failings and hence imagine a new associative relationship, they can do so because even in their moments of weakness and betrayal they still operated within the parameters defined by a collective good; it might even be said that their betrayal was done in the name of a certain understandable belief in historical restitution.

In contrast, Karanja's betrayal is premised on an absolute disregard and contempt of collective norms and desires; in betraying his age group for personal gratification, Karanja has committed what the Gikuyu call *Thaahu* (taboo), and as his mother had warned him, "A man who ignores the voice of his own people comes to no good" (p. 226). Within the Gikuyu moral economy, Karanja's betrayal is tantamount to social death; he no longer has the capacity for empathy: "He had gone to see Kihika hang from a tree. He had searched his heart for one ... pity or sorrow for a lost friend. Instead, he had found only disgust; the body was hideous; the dry lips over which a few flies played, were ugly" (p. 230). As he searches for meaning and coherence at the end of the novel, Karanja realizes he has become a hooded self without any history or affiliation; and now, after decolonization, it is this identity of a hooded self that haunts him into an unknown future (p. 231).

Mugo's betrayal of Kihika has similar consequences, for when General R. tells him that his deeds alone will condemn him, he is in effect saying that by betraying a member of his age set, he has indeed killed himself, for as we noted in the introductory chapter, a Gikuyu person has no identity except in relation to his or her cohorts. What complicates this kind of ending, however, is that while it is necessary for Mugo to die so that the culture can be cleansed of the taboo he represents, his death casts a long moral shadow on Independence Day and thus the nationalist struggle. That Wambui and Warui, the oldest people in the long struggle for independence, have to take part in Mugo's killing, indicates the extent of the historical burden the village confronts at what was supposed to be the dawn of a new era. It is not clear whether the elders' acquiescence in Mugo's death diminishes or enhances their moral authority, but it does diminish the meaning of Uhuru: "Wambui was lost in a solid consciousness of a terrible anti-climax to her activities in the fight for freedom" (p. 243). This is how the narrative of decolonization begins and ends – with an anticlimax.

And it could be said that all the novels that Ngugi has written after *A Grain of Wheat* are attempts to figure out why decolonization, which was supposed to will a new nation into being, instead produces cultures and subjects that are held hostage to the colonial past they work so hard to transcend.

CHAPTER 5

The poetics of cultural production: the later short stories and Petals of Blood

Literary critics have never been sure where to locate *Petals of Blood*, Ngugi's epic novel of the culture and politics of neo-colonialism in Kenya. Indeed, as Joseph Mclaren has observed in his detailed discussion of the critical literature surrounding this work, opinion about the novel's effectiveness has tended to be divided along ideological and geographical lines, between different modes of interpretation, and disparate views on the direction in which Ngugi's Marxist politics were pushing his novels in the 1970s.[1] But if the critical literature on *Petals of Blood*, especially during the first two years after the novel's publication had one thing in common, it was the belief that the success or failure of the novel depended on its complex attempt to merge ideology and form. As McLaren has noted, the controversies generated by the novel revolved around two closely related issues: first, the use of realistic devices in fiction and "their validity in voicing political imperatives"; and secondly, "the controversial nature of the political novel and the continued debate regarding art as ideology."[2] And if *Petals of Blood* tended, too often perhaps, to be judged in relation to *A Grain of Wheat*, it was because it seemed to exist both inside and outside the tradition of the European novel. For many of its early critics, the novel seemed to gesture toward familiar patterns of realism popularized by European novelists in the nineteenth century, but it also wanted to go beyond what Ngugi considered to be the limits of this kind of "critical realism," namely the inability of the bourgeois novel to transcend the social and cultural situation it represented and to function as an aesthetic agent of radical change.[3]

The overt politics of *Petals of Blood*, nevertheless, conceal the difficulties Ngugi was facing when he wrote the novel. While it is true that Ngugi conceived this novel as a work that could provide a panoramic view of the neo-colonial state in the process of consolidating its authority, it is also true that he sought to foreground the contradictions of modernity in the postcolony, highlighting the presence of unequal economic arrangements, coercive politics, and a fetishized national culture. At the same time, however, he wanted to create or imagine how, out of the failure of decolonization, literature could create a utopian space beyond the manifest contradictions of what has come to be known as underdevelopment.[4] But beneath its authoritative veneer, its mastery of the postcolonial economy, and its display of narrative totality, *Petals of Blood* was driven by Ngugi's serious doubts about both the possibility of change and the ability of the novel to represent spaces of recuperation and resistance. Returning to Kenya in 1971 after a brief moment of exile, Ngugi had been surprised by the disenchantment he found among ordinary people: "I looked at the tired and bewildered faces of the people: I went to places where people went to drown their memories of yesterday and their hopes and fears for tomorrow in drinking. I visited various bars in Limuru, drinking, singing and dancing trying not to see or to remember ... how could I not see and hear and remember?"[5]

Ngugi started writing the novel as a way of seeing, hearing, and remembering the set of cultural discourses that had willed the postcolonial state into being and the commentaries that were emerging as both ordinary people and intellectuals tried to diagnose what Fanon had characterized as the "pitfalls of national consiousness."[6] The primary problem for the writer, however, concerned not so much the themes that emerged out of these discourses and commentaries – many of these were obvious – but the form which they would take in imaginative narratives. As Frederic Jameson has noted in a suggestive, but controversial, analysis of literary production in the so-called Third World, the passion for "change and social regeneration" that has spawned many political novels such as *Petals of Blood* is inevitably confronted by an aesthetic dilemma or crisis of representation: what are the agents of this change and what form can they take?[7]

WRITING IN AN AGE OF DISILLUSIONMENT

The question of what form was best suited to representing agents of social change appeared so urgent to Ngugi when he started writing *Petals of Blood* in the early 1970s that even as he was working on the novel he was experimenting with a series of short stories based on related themes and characters. Indeed, these stories, collected in the last part of *Secret Lives*, can be read as prototypes of the novel itself. In "Minutes of Glory," for example, the main character, Wanjiru, is an earlier portrait of Wanja in *Petals of Blood*: she functions as an archetypal victim of the neo-colonial *polis* and her consciousness represents what the author considers to be the split between the dream of national consciousness and the empty shell it has become as hopes and expectations give way to cynicism and disenchantment. In other words, Wanjiru's subjectivity marks the split between the form of a decolonized body ("dark and full fleshed") and the unfulfilled dream of independence ("it was as if it [her body] waited to be filled by the spirit"); she is thus compared to "a wounded bird in flight . . . wobbling from place to place."[8] In this story, furthermore, we can begin to see Ngugi's critique of his previous works emerging. For while Wanjiru is like many of Ngugi's heroines in the way she tries to deal with the harsh realities of her life through dreams, her story marks one of the most sustained critiques of the romanticism of landscape discussed in the previous chapters.

Like many of Ngugi's heroines, Wanjiru tries to counter a deracinated urban landscape by investing "the life of her peasant mother and father with romantic illusions of immeasurable peace and harmony," but such longings only sharpen her longing for a childhood world that has become "a distant landscape in the memory": "Her life was here in the bar among this crowd of lost strangers. Fallen from grace, fallen from grace. She was part of a generation which could never again be one with the soil, the crops, the wind and the moon" (*Secret Lives*, p. 86). Faced with what Ngugi conceives to be the absolute hegemony of the emergent African bourgeoisie, postcolonial subjects dream of natal landscape – and ideals in general – only so that they can be mocked or ironized. What makes the culture of the postcolony so tragic, Ngugi seems to be suggesting, echoing Fanon, is that the new ruling class is an illegitimate group without any historical antecedent or authentic identity.

Which raises an intriguing question: how does one represent a class without an authentic identity? In "Wedding at the Cross," Ngugi begins by representing the new African middle-class subject as the perfect image of bourgeois civility:

> Everyone said of them: what a nice family; he, the successful timber merchant; and she, the obedient wife who did her duty to God, husband and family. Wariuki and his wife Miriamu were a shining example of what cooperation between man and wife united in love and devotion could achieve: he tall, correct, even a little stiff, but wealthy; she, small, quiet, unobtrusive, a diminishing shadow beside her giant of a husband. (*Secret Lives*, p. 97)

As soon as the narrator begins to unravel the genealogy of this picture-book family, however, we begin to realize the extent to which the identity and authority of the new African ruling class depends on a very precarious myth of self-making. In this story, the successful merchant is none other than a former bicycle conjurer named Wariuki, who once fell in love with the daughter of a member of the "Christian and propertied class" (p. 99), but could not be accepted by her family because he did not have the credentials of a bourgeois subject. Hurt and humiliated by this rejection, Wariuki escaped to Ilmorog, a frontier town, driven by "the memory of that humiliation in the hands of the rich" (p. 103), but determined to become one of them.

As Wariuki seeks to remake himself as a bourgeois subject he generates a narrative that traverses the landscape of colonial and postcolonial Kenya, touching on the major historical and social events of the time – the Second World War, "Mau Mau," the return of Jomo Kenyatta, and independence. It is within this trajectory that we witness the bicycle conjurer fashioning himself into a member of the new elite. Thus, it is in a moment of deliberate historical forgetfulness that Wariuki, now renamed Livingstone, becomes reunited with his father-in-law and is now accepted as a full-fledged member of the propertied class: "Jones fell on his knees; Livingstone fell on his knees. They prayed and then embraced in tears. Our son, our son" (p. 108). Denied admission into the new ruling class in his youth because he did not even have a basic savings bank account, Wariuki, as Livingstone, is welcomed into the fold like the prodigal son. But in order to be accepted into the new ruling class, Wariuki is forced to renounce every part of his old self; not simply caricature himself, but undergo a form of social death so that whatever self he might have had as a bicycle conjurer is now unrecognizable even by Mariamu, his own wife. Ngugi's concern in this story, as in Chui's narrative in *Petals of Blood*, is the transformation of the African middle class from the defenders of the national interest to caricatures of the departed colonial masters.

Two aspects of Ngugi's last batch of stories in *Secret Lives* need to be underscored as prototypes for *Petals of Blood*: first, there is the author's need to undercut the claim, common in postcolonial Kenya, that the new African middle class is the agent of change and progress; secondly, there is his search for alternative agents of social change in the postcolony. The first task is evident in Ngugi's search for forms of psychoanalyzing the middle class: this is achieved either through the satirical transformation of working-class subjects such as Wariuki in "Wedding at the Cross" or in a comical juxtaposition of working-class characters and elite narrators in a story such as "A Mercedes Funeral." In the latter story, the narrator, fashioned after Marlowe in Conrad's *Heart of Darkness*, functions as a detached commentator and potential critic of the new African elite and also its exemplar. The narrator and his presumed audience are products of the colonial university and its exclusive culture; they remember the past with nostalgia: "you remember our time in Makerere under De Bunsen? Worsted woollen suits, starched white shirts and ties to match" (*Secret Lives*, p. 115). But this narrator is also disturbed by the excess of the new postcolonial culture, an excess manifested in a new economy of representing death itself: "Now I don't know if this be true in your area, but in our village funerals had become a society affair, our version of cocktail parties. I mean since independence" (p. 118).

In "A Mercedes Funeral" in addition, we can see Ngugi's attempt to develop a narrative both within and outside bourgeois culture: as a first-person story, it is told from the perspective of the member of the neo-colonial elite; but the only way the author can delve deep into the psychology of this class is by forcing his middle-class readers to gaze at themselves as one way of understanding their own contradictions. Thus, while the story begins by calling attention to the subjectivity of the unnamed narrator, it quickly shifts its focus to the subject of the narrator's story, a working-class man who dies in the middle of a political campaign and unwittingly becomes the conduit through which bourgeois excesses are played out. Now, the elite narrator and Wahinya, his working-class subject, share a common background: their initial encounter was on the eve of independence, a moment defined not simply by "[B]eautiful dreams about the future," but also the time when it was assumed that divisions of class, caste, and rank would be superseded by the nationalist ideal (p. 121). However, while the narrator and Wahinya had come from a common class background, their lives have diverged: one had gone on to university and postcolonial success while the other had been condemned to social stasis.

In retrospect, however, what subliminally unites the two characters is a deep anxiety about their role as agents of postcolonial change; hence the narrator's claim that "blind chance" had put the two on "different paths" but that they were connected by a common past and the dream of a glorious future. For the narrator, Wahinya's failure to succeed in the postcolonial economy can only be seen as a symptom of the shortcomings of independence; for the worker, however, the narrator is a symbol of what he would have become if nationalism had delivered on its promises. In the end, as Wahinya's dead body becomes the terrain on which false political practices are played out, the middle-class narrator struggles to understand his own location in the new culture; and unable to reconcile his radical critique of independence with his implication in neo-colonial culture, he turns the telling of the story into a sign of his own paralysis (pp. 136-37). And thus for Ngugi, as for his teacher Fanon, the most obvious symbol of the "crack in the national edifice" in postcoloniality is the incapacity of the national middle class to realize the potential represented by the lower classes.[9]

In "The Mubenzi Tribe" (the Mercedes Tribe), the last story in the collection, Ngugi turns his attention, almost with despair, to the ruling postcolonial elite and finds it difficult to derive any narrative of liberation from the beliefs and practices of this class. As a young writer, Ngugi had sought redemption in national (prophetic) narratives; now, in postcoloniality, he can only tell stories about the pejorative identities of the would-be prophets of the new nation. Once driven by the desire for restitution and redemption, the new African ruling class, represented here by another university graduate named Waruhiu, has become a victim of its own egotism, which is also a mark of its insecurity in the new arrangement. In order to secure his identity in this order, Waruhiu had bought into all its insignias – "He had joined a new tribe and certain standards were expected of him and other members. He bought a Mercedes S220" (*Secret Lives*, p. 141).

But for Ngugi, such trappings are masks for what Fanon called "the intellectual laziness of the national middle class . . . its spiritual penury, and . . . the profoundly cosmopolitan mold that its mind is set in."[10] Indeed, like most of the short stories Ngugi produced in the 1970s, "The Mubenzi Tribe" is a narrative of bourgeois failure: it is a story of a member of the new elite struggling to emerge out of imprisonment, bankruptcy, and failed relationships; it is told from the perspective of imminent collapse; the language of the narrative itself, the hesitancy, the ellipses, the lack of direction, is a symptom of this failure. To write about the middle class, Ngugi seems to have concluded, was to be caught in the cultural penury of this class. As he plotted *Petals of Blood*, there was no more urgent question in his mind than how to produce a novel outside the circuitry of a failed neo-colonial culture and its intellectual agents.

THE CRITIQUE OF POSTCOLONIAL MODERNITY

Striving to write a novel beyond the politics of neo-colonialism, and armed with a Marxist ideology that had become central to his aesthetic practice, Ngugi had three alternatives in front of him when he came to write *Petals of Blood*: he could either write a novel representing the psychology of fear and the failure of political expectations in the mode of the bourgeois novel. Or he could write a satirical fable. Or he could try and transform the state of postcolonial crisis and failure into a narrative of change in the tradition of what has come to be known as "socialist realism." Each of these novelistic elements is represented in *Petals of Blood*. The question that needs to be raised, though, is why Ngugi came to identify "socialist realism" as the dominant mode of representing the postcolonial state. To understand this problem, we need to foreground three contexts for this novel: Ngugi's radical and sustained intervention in a political debate that was raging throughout East Africa, a debate on the nature of the postcolonial state and the political economy of underdevelopment; his sense of disenchantment with various forms of the bourgeois fiction, whose mastery he had exhibited in *A Grain of Wheat*; and his desire to write a novel that would overcome the crisis of representation generated by arrested decolonization. A closer examination of all three contexts will enable us to understand both the form and content of *Petals of Blood* as a critique of colonial and postcolonial modernity.

That the novel itself was an attempt to narrate the crisis of underdevelopment in Kenya is not in doubt. Some of its most powerful metaphors, most notably those of drought and decay, are about underdevelopment: throughout the novel, Ngugi makes it clear that if Ilmorog's prosperity in the precolonial past could be explained by the harmonious relationship between its people and nature, then its current (postcolonial) state of decrepitude had arisen from the dislocation of the peasants from their privileged position in the natural cycle. Thus the peasants' impoverishment in both the colonial and postcolonial economy could come to be represented in terms of the drought and the images of death associated with it:

By the end of April it still had not rained. Cows and goats and sheep were skeletons: most herdsmen had anyway moved across the plains in search of fairer and kindlier climes wherein to shelter. They hoped that May would bring rain. But by mid-May which was the last hope for rains which would save them, two cows died; vultures and hawks circled high in the sky and then swooped in hordes, later leaving behind them white bones scattered on stunted and dry grass.[11]

As readers of *Petals of Blood* will recall, the fate of Ilmorog, as it negotiates its identity within the political and moral economy of modernity and modernization, comes to be shadowed by this image of drought, a reminder of this poor community's radical dislocation from what Ngugi, the Marxist, would call a "primitive" mode of production. Simply put, it is through the experience and memory of drought that Ilmorog comes to define and represent itself; even its heroic narrative pales in relation to drought and the stories of famine it generates. In Ngugi's novel, then, the temporality of the postcolonial outpost is measured in terms of the woes associated with drought:

Haunting memories from the past; the year of the locust; the year of the armyworms; the year of the famine of cassava: the Ngigi, Ngunga and Ngaragu ya Mwanga circumcision-groups still bore these names of woe, a witness that uncontrolled nature was always a threat to human endeavour. There was of course another lesson. In 1900, only six years after the year of locusts, the famine was so bad it put to a stop all circumcision rites for the year. No group now carried a name as memorial to the famine of England, so called, because it had weakened people's resistance to the European marauders of the people's land and sweat. (*Petals of Blood*, p. 111)

Here, as elsewhere in the novel, drought is associated as much with "uncontrolled nature" as it is with the advent of European imperialism. While Ilmorog has had its days of glory ("thriving villages with a huge population of sturdy peasants" [p. 120]), it is the region's economic underdevelopment that comes to shape its character; in its impoverished landscape and traditions, the outpost becomes an emblem of the failure of national consciousness. While the metropolis is thriving with new industrial projects, we encounter Ilmorog as a backwater, cut off from the rest of the country in both time and space, available to us only in terms of ruins; it is described as a wasteland; its school "a four-roomed barrack with broken mud walls, a tin roof with gaping holes and more spiders' webs and the wings and heads of dead flies" (p. 5). Forgotten by the rest of the country, its inhabitants live in the shadow of their past, haunted by the ghosts of feudalism and colonialism (p. 6). The story of Ilmorog is that of the warped logic of colonial modernity: "Our erstwhile masters had left us a very unevenly cultivated land: the centre was swollen with fruit and water sucked from the rest, while the outer parts were progressively weaker and scraggier as one moved from the centre" (p. 49).

The first part of *Petals of Blood* is actually an attempt to develop what one may call "a poetics of underdevelopment," a poetics that Ngugi had learnt from Fanon's famous critique of independence. Indeed, it is hard to miss the Fanonist project in the novel. The major events in *Petals of Blood* take place in the "empty shell" of the nationalist dream now transformed into what Fanon would call "a crude and fragile travesty of what it might have been."[12] The principal narrative agents in the novel – Munira, Karega, Wanja, and Abdulla – are defined by their acute awareness of the gap between the promise of independence and the travesty of neo-colonialism. Indeed, what these characters try to narrate is how the dream of national independence has been turned into a post-colonial ruin. As an allegory of the postcolony itself, Ilmorog is transformed, in full view of both narrators and readers, from a community with the potential for autonomy and wealth to a living embodiment of postcolonial decay.

One of the great ironies of the novel is that Ilmorog is destroyed in the process of being modernized and integrated into the national economy. What needs to be underscored here, however, is not so much the irony of progress itself, as Ngugi's complicated attempt to represent the collapse of modernity as the failure of the national bourgeoisie, the class that takes on the responsibility for transforming the community but ends up destroying it. The agents of bourgeois modernity in the novel – Chui, Mzigo, Kimeria – are part of the new postcolonial caste which, in Fanon's memorable terms is "not engaged in production, nor in invention, nor building, nor labor; it is completely canalized into activities of the intermediary type."[13] At the end of the novel, the ruling caste has taken over all of New Ilmorog and transformed it into a mirror image of other metropolitan centers, but they have done so, not by producing goods or inventing institutions, but by buying off what others have produced or built. After all, the economic drive behind Ilmorog's prosperity is the Theng'eta drink that old Nyakinyua perfected, which the bourgeoisie bought off with foreign capital (p. 293).

Now, all these examples of the political economy of underdevelopment in Ngugi's novel are not unique in themselves; as I have already observed, they are part and parcel of a public discourse that was taking place in East Africa at the time, a discourse that is represented in Colin Leys's *Underdevelopment in Kenya*, a book published in the same year as *Petals of Blood*.[14] In addition, underdevelopment had been the subject of several novels by African writers published in the late 1960s, most notably Ayi Kwei Armah's *The Beautyful Ones Are Not Yet Born* and Wole Soyinka's *The Interpreters*. What was unusual about *Petals of Blood*, however, was Ngugi's decision to represent these debates not through the common forms of fable and satire adopted by his contemporaries, but through traditional realism. How do we explain Ngugi's choice of such a traditional mode of representation in the age of the new novel and the avant-garde in African writing?

The choice can be explained by the simple fact that by the 1970s Ngugi had embarked on an important theoretical project, the purpose of which was to try and reformulate the whole idea of literature itself by shifting its locus from the experiences of unique bourgeois individuals, the traditional subjects of fiction, to the social collective. If this project was to succeed, Ngugi argued in an influential essay called "Writers in Politics," it was important for African writers to overcome the traditional separation between aesthetics and politics: "Imaginative literature in so far as it deals with human relationships and attempts to influence a people's consciousness and politics, in so far as it deals with and is about operation of power and relationship of power in society, are reflected in one another, and can and do act on one another."[15] Poking fun at politicians was not the way to go about developing a critique of neo-colonial society, because satire, as Ngugi argued in a rather impatient critique of Soyinka, assumed a measure of superiority over politics. Satire, Ngugi argued, privileged the aesthetic, and with it, bourgeois individualism: "Soyinka's good man is the uncorrupted individual: his liberal humanism leads him to admire an individual's lone act of courage, and thus often he ignores the creative struggle of the masses."[16]

Totality was the operative word in Ngugi's critical lexicon when he was writing *Petals of Blood* – the totality of culture and politics, communal identities, and collective struggle. African writers, he argued, had failed to see "that values, cultures, politics and economics are all tied up together, that we cannot call for meaningful

African values without joining in the struggle against all the classes that feed on a system that continues to distort those very values."[17] *Petals of Blood* was Ngugi's first attempt to represent culture as a totality; it marked his belief in the redemptive power of a materialist aesthetic, its ability to encapsulate cultural forces in terms of the historical contradictions that informed them. It was also his attempt to show that the novel had the imaginative power to move us beyond the rhetoric of failure.

Ngugi had already presented a manifesto for this kind of novel as early as 1966 in his critique of Soyinka's failure "to see the present in the historical perspective of conflict and struggle": "It is not enough for the African writer, standing aloof, to view society and highlight its weaknesses. He must try to go beyond this, to seek out the sources, the causes and the trends of a revolutionary struggle that had already destroyed the traditional power-map drawn up by the colonialist nations."[18] If one were to ask Ngugi what made *A Grain of Wheat* different from *Petals of Blood*, he would most likely say that the former had sought to represent the contradictions of the neo-colony but was unable to project an alternative social system, while the latter took up these contradictions and sought to project a future beyond them.

But in attempting to write a comprehensive novel on underdevelopment in Kenya, Ngugi was caught in a double-bind: he wanted to produce a radical critique of colonial and postcolonial modernity without repudiating its central doctrines – most notably modernization and progress. How could one expose the corrupt ideologies that had emerged out of modernity and modernization while advocating the ideals of these processes? Here, Ngugi was caught up in a narratological and ideological impasse: while he had nothing but scorn for the new middle class and its claim that it was the only proper agent of modernization in the postcolony, and while the modernization of the colonial *polis* had been responsible for the failures he seemed to detect everywhere he turned in the postcolonial landscape, his belief in the necessity and urgency of modernization was unshakable. How could he demonize one form of modernity (the one initiated by the postcolonial state and its agents) and sanction another (the revolutionary modernity demanded by the workers at the end of *Petals of Blood*)?

In essence, Part III of *Petals of Blood*, the part in which Ilmorog gets transformed from a rural hamlet into a modern metropolis, can be read as the author's attempt to simultaneously develop a radical critique of modernity and sanction its redemptive claims. In this part of the novel, we can see how the allegory of the postcolony is enclosed between two forms of modernity – a colonial and postcolonial modernity constructed around the trope of uneven development and the dream of a utopian or socialist modernity espoused by the rising workers. The power of Ngugi's novel, however, lies in its complicated and contradictory representation of the process of change (in modernity) and the diverse responses it triggers among different subjects and classes.

Let us trace this process by observing, as a first step, that the fall of Ilmorog (the outcome of postcolonial modernity) is preceded by a false economic boom that provides Ngugi with an opportunity to reconsider some of the tropes that had driven his earlier works – namely, the associative potential of romantic love, the ideal of a benign nature, and the sanctity of a precolonial past. In this part of the novel, Ilmorog is possessed by what Munira aptly calls "the new motion of things, the new mood of the village after the journey" (*Petals of Blood*, p. 200); it moves to a rhythm that seems oblivious to the political economy of neo-colonialism; and it seeks its temporal authority from the movement of the seasons (pp. 201–02). And when the season of harvest is over, the village makes one final push to celebrate the great rituals interrupted by colonization as if to ward off modernity.

To the extent that the Theng'eta can only be brewed using techniques from the precolonial past, it originally appears to be an emblem of "tradition"; in the end, however, it proves to be a belated attempt to detour colonialism and postcoloniality (p. 204). The festivals and festivities surrounding the harvest and the drinking of the brew propose a future that might be founded on alternative communal histories, marking "a vision of the future rooted in a critical awareness of the past" (p. 198), but this attempt to recover a precolonial past ends up calling attention to the impoverished history of colonial and postcolonial culture in the new nation. In other words, if Theng'eta is a romantic symbol of the African past, a past when the people of Ilmorog existed in a harmonious relationship with nature, it is now recuperated as a signifier of doubt and uncertainty, of the separation between signs and signifiers, of the dream of utopia and the corrupted narrative of decolonization. The romance of the old Ilmorog can only be apprehended from the vantage point of the collapsed grand narrative of colonial conquest and rule, what Karega calls "[t]he past of houses and crops burnt and destroyed and diseases pumped into a continent" (p. 214).

And thus what the Theng'eta spirit seems to promote – an allegorical narrative of a community searching for more meaningful foundations – has to be confronted by another narrative, an ironic narrative that sustains the illusion of a communal story in order to expose its impossibility and failure. Theng'eta is represented as "a dream" and "a wish": it enables the fulfillment of desires but it also creates illusions; it enables the principal subjects to transcend their difficult histories and experiences and thus to valorize the utopian moment in which they can achieve the collective identities that have eluded them for much of the novel (p. 211); but it also calls attention to the historical belatedness of this narrative of communality. Theng'eta promises that the people of Ilmorog will "one day return to a knowledge of themselves and then the kingdom of God and of man will be theirs" (pp. 212–13); but it does not propose how this knowledge will be acquired. Indeed, beneath the allegorical quests implicit in the Theng'eta ceremonies and rituals, there is a clear disjuncture between the desire of the occasion (its evocation of a pastoral world) and its context (colonial displacement).

Like the Last Supper in the Christian tradition, this ceremony seems to provoke narratives that enable the subjects to establish vital connections with one another, but these connections are only made possible by figures of death and loss. Thus a ceremony that began as a celebration of the communal spirit becomes transformed into a ritual of mourning, of commemorating the hitherto unsung and unwept heroes of the past (p. 221). The point to underscore, then, is the essentially ironic nature of the Theng'eta spirit: it brings people together only to push them apart; it evokes the image of an ideal community only to shatter it ("Now it has turned out to be a drink of strife," notes Munira [p. 240]); it conjures the heroic epic of a community in order to turn it into an elegy on the past and a lament on the present.

Where does modernity lie in all this? We can begin to answer this question by noting that in this novel, as in all of Ngugi's subsequent works, the Manichean division that defines the post-colony, a division that is represented almost exclusively in class terms, can only be overcome if all the subjects created by colonialism can, in its aftermath, find comity in the ideals of modernity. This assertion may appear strange for readers who are used to reading *Petals of Blood* as a critique of modernity. After all, one of the novel's primary themes is the collapse of traditional culture or its marginalization in the political economy of colonialism and postcolonialism. In addition, the final collapse of Ilmorog is generated by its radical modernization. This is all true. But there is another dimension to the status of modernity in the politics of Ngugi's novel.

As a Marxist, the author is an advocate of the key ingredients of modernity – the rationalization of culture, the restoration of individual authority, and industrial progress. But as an African – or rather Gikuyu – nationalist he sees modernity as the primary threat to the culture celebrated in the Thenge'ta ceremony discussed above. The result is not only the divided attitude towards modernity that characterizes some of the key sections in the novel, but also a noticeable narrative impasse. Unsure where to take the narrative of decolonization, the author concludes his novel by exposing the hollowness implicit in the ideologies of modernization: "abstracted from the vision of oneness of a collective struggle of the African peoples, the road brought only the unity of earth's surface: every corner of the continent was now within easy reach of international capitalist robbery and exploitation" (p. 262).

And yet, in the dramatic destruction of Mwathi's place, Ngugi also exposes the emptiness that lies at the center of the desire for cultural reversion (p. 266). When modernity arrives with a vengeance, threatening to sweep traditional institutions aside in the name of industrial progress, the people of Ilmorog wait for Mwathi's vengeance, but he never seems to appear, and the elder who was supposed to be the curator of this cultural shrine "had become suddenly deaf and dumb at the sacrilege" (p. 266). The destruction of Mwathi's place is seen as the defeat of traditional knowledge by the cultural forces of modernity. And in reflecting on this defeat, one has the uneasy feeling that in the process of writing *Petals of Blood*, Ngugi was finding it increasingly difficult to represent modernity as both an ideological necessity and as the source of the forces that were destroying institutions and values he considered vital to an African cultural and economic renaissance.

Beneath Ngugi's faith in the redemptive power of culture and the aesthetic – and this is another important context for understanding *Petals of Blood* – was his own uncertainty about the efficacy of the Anglophone novel. If writing *Petals of Blood* had proven to be "a hard day's journey," as he was to note later, it is precisely because the novel had foregrounded the emerging disjuncture between the author's ideological commitment and the tradition of the novel he had inherited through a colonial education.[19] Ngugi understood, perhaps better than any African writer, that the novel was, in both a positive and pejorative sense, a bourgeois genre. As we saw in the previous chapter, he had deployed, in *A Grain of Wheat*, the best aspects of this form – the representation of subjectivity, a sense of temporal dislocation, and the use of the interior monologue – to represent the process of decolonization. And it was because *A Grain of Wheat* was centered on the experiences, psychology, and consciousness of unique subjects, that Ngugi had been able to capture individual and discrete reactions to the drama of decolonization in memorable ways. The ending of the novel, as we have already seen, had reduced the allegory of the nation to the drama of individual subjects trying to come to terms with their repressed pasts. The novel had proven useful as a tool of understanding and narrating the psychology of colonialism.

And yet, the place of the novel genre in Africa was ambiguous: it was bound up with the culture of colonialism; it was an alienated and alienating genre in the sense that it was at odds with Ngugi's notion of society and culture as collective entities. This alienation manifested itself in three respects: first, if the whole purpose of writing in a neo-colonial situation was to mobilize the social collective for change, the "readerly" assumption made in Ngugi's earlier novels – the assumption that the narrative was a private transaction between a learned writer and a privileged reader – was not going to work: "After I had written *A Grain of Wheat* I underwent a crisis," Ngugi was to note later. "I knew whom I was writing about but whom was I writing for?"[20] Secondly, there was an obvious gap between the bourgeois form of the novel, which was bound up with the interest of an educated middle class, and the world Ngugi wanted to write about – the world of workers and peasants. If the novel was to serve as a catalyst for social change, it needed to persuade its middle-class audience to recognize a national interest beyond their own economic and political interests. Thirdly, Ngugi's limpid ideology of culture in the 1970s was in conflict with the major sectors of the postcolony; keenly aware that his notions of culture were at odds with the ideology of the Kenyan ruling class (a subject I will explore in the next two chapters), Ngugi had embarked on an important intellectual project, one whose goal was simply to rescue the idea of culture itself from both colonialism and nationalism.

As far as Kenya was concerned, Ngugi was fighting a war on three fronts: he was fighting against the Arnoldian and Leavisite idea of culture inherited from the colonial school (the idea that culture represented the rarified values of the elite); he was fighting against the cultural nationalists' investment in a romanticized African culture, an idea that had turned this past into an erotic subject that was now being performed for tourists by governmental organizations; and he was trying to go beyond the Fanonist notion of culture as the crystallization of nationalism toward the Marxist claim that culture constituted a superstructure, one overdetermined by economic forces. While it is now easy to assume that Ngugi's preferences were obvious (the essays written during this period seem to celebrate the orthodox Marxist dogma about base and superstructure), the situation was much more complicated. In spite of his vociferous pronouncements, Ngugi could not rid himself entirely of his previous (liberal) idea of culture not only because it had been so crucial to his early career, but also because it was an integral part of the social landscape he was trying to represent.

We can understand this point better if we examine the ways in which multiple cultural scenarios are played out in *Petals of Blood*, sometimes promoting ideologies that run counter to authorial intentions. A case in point: Ngugi's representation of Ilmorog before it is overtaken by the forces of modernity seems to emerge from the Marxist blue book on a primitive mode of production. At its beginning, Ilmorog moves to the rhythms of nature, undisturbed by outside forces, thriving in its "common labour," secure in its organic culture (p. 120). The image of precolonial Ilmorog fits Ngugi's theory on political economy elaborated in *Decolonising the Mind:* the "level of development of productive forces" is low and the people are dominated by "an incomprehensible nature" knowable only "through ritual, magic and divination"; but this nature is contained "through a collective response and a cohesive social order."[21]

From an ideological perspective, there is no doubt that Ngugi prefers the world of modern rationality to this primitive culture. And yet, beneath the novelist's rather patronizing view of precolonial African culture, *Petals of Blood* is a novel driven – unconsciously perhaps – by Ngugi's desire to locate and recuperate an organic Gikuyu culture and mode of knowledge amidst the debris of postcoloniality. Consider, for example, how mystical forces constitute the center of Old Ilmorog, how Mwathi's place, rather than the rational forces of progress, embodies the soul of the community. As Munira learns soon after arriving in the village, the mysterious sage, Mwathi wa Mugo (the names signify both shepherd and prophet) functions as "the spiritual power over both Ilmorog ridge and Ilmorog plains, somehow, invisibly, regulating their lives" (p. 17).

Ngugi, the Marxist, may not be a champion of the culture that has been produced by the "low productive forces" overseen by Mwathi, but clearly, the passing of the past, the destruction of Mwathi's place by the willful machinery of progress, is one of the most painful scenes in the novel and perhaps the most obvious indictment of modernity and modernization. As we witness the destruction of Mwathi's place, we realize that something wrong has taken place since we first encountered Ilmorog as a wasteland, a land ravaged by drought and the incomprehensible forces of nature. Simply put, as the old community is destroyed by the more advanced forces of industrial capitalism, the novel tries, sometimes with desperation, to secure the spirit of the old world; in an attempt to salvage something out of the destructive forces of modernization, Ngugi performs, or ritualizes, Gikuyu culture (or his understanding of it) as if to ward off the triumphant forces of modernity as they move toward their apogee. This explains the language of nostalgia and romance that the author uses to represent Nyakinyua's brewing of the Theng'eta (pp. 205–10).

But in examining the significance of the rituals surrounding this brewing, we need to remember, first of all, that until this moment, the Theng'eta had been outlawed by colonial authorities and that the art of brewing itself had been lost except to the oldest members of the community; the brew is the purest symbol of a precolonial past. Thus, recuperating this symbol and the past it embodies becomes a religious rite ("They started work on the idea with a playful religious fervour" [p. 205]), a rite whose primary tropes are those of rebirth and renewal (Theng'eta first appears in the form of seedlings). But the brew is also part of a larger cultural drama, a rite of communal affirmation, the highlight of which is what the narrator calls "the opera of eros" (p. 207). The erotic dance enacted here is important because, as I suggested in Chapter Two, it is through such eroticism that Gikuyu individualism is often expressed, and this in the name of the "organic" or "tribal" community.

What is particularly striking about the erotic dance that Nyakinyua initiates is the note of historical belatedness that hovers over the whole performance. The overt subject of the opera is communal unity: performers are invited to forget their loneliness and through "an erotic war of words and gestures and tones" (p. 208) become part of the mythic rituals of their ancestors, recreate the first marriage which was the foundation of their community (the opera is really a Gikuyu wedding song). But as this attempt to recapture the past moves toward a climax, it collapses under the strain of the recent history of Ilmorog:

They listened to Nyakinyua as she sang Gitiro. At first it was good-humoured, light-hearted, as she commented on those present to a chorus of laughter... But suddenly they were caught by the slight tremor in her voice. She was singing their recent history. She sang of two years of failing rains; of the arrival of daughters and teachers; of the exodus to the city.

She talked of how she had earlier imagined the city as containing only wealth. But she found poverty; she found crippled beggars; she saw men, many men, sons of women, vomited out of a smoking tunnel – a big, big house – and she was afraid. Who had swallowed all the wealth of the land? Who? (pp. 209–10).

What does this admixture of eroticism and a critique of colonialism mean? We can perhaps find the answer to this question by recalling another moment in the novel in which the eroticism of Gikuyu song is featured prominently. I am thinking here of the scene in the middle of the novel when Munira accidentally stumbles into Chui's house and witnesses a group of upper-class men and women singing "a few native songs," reveling in "the juicy sections of songs normally sung at circumcision" (pp. 149, 150). Now, if Ngugi the cultural nationalist had momentarily been attracted by the eroticism of a precolonial culture (and there are numerous instances when he posits this as perhaps a way out of the ruins of the postcolony), he is quick to realize how traditional culture itself has become commodified. One may be seduced by the romance of the past, but as the events following the Theng'eta ceremony ultimately prove, "native culture" can only be recuperated either as a commodity or as an aesthetic object disconnected from its realities. It is the discovery of this double-bind that triggers Karega's melancholy after the Theng'eta ceremony: "It was really very beautiful. But at the end of the evening Karega felt very sad. It was like beholding a relic of beauty that had suddenly surfaced, or like listening to a solitary beautiful tune straying, for a time, from a dying world" (p. 210).

It is important that the historical belatedness of traditional culture is echoed by Karega, because of the main subjects in the novel, he is the one most attuned to the politics of cultural production in the postcolony; he is the one character who is continuously cognizant of the pitfalls of all the cultural programs enumerated in the novel. He is as skeptical of the romance of traditional culture as he is contemptuous of the liberal ideology of the new ruling class. Karega can see through the facade of national culture because, as a student, he had witnessed Chui the nationalist become transformed into a replica of Fraudsham, the custodian of colonial Englishness (p. 171). The main point, then, is that those critics of

Petals of Blood who have been too quick to read it as a "Marxist novel" driven by a clear ideological agenda need to consider the competing notions of culture it presents.[22] It is perhaps in the form of the novel that these competing interests are manifested.

CULTURE AND THE IDEOLOGY OF FORM

Of the many important formal innovations Ngugi makes in *Petals of Blood*, none is as striking as his use of various dialogic forms and related techniques. The author has provided the best explanation for the use of dialogism in the novel in *Decolonising the Mind*: "*Petals of Blood* had taken a stage further the techniques of flashbacks, multiple narrative voices, movement in time and space and parallel biographies and stories. The technique allowed me to move freely in time and space through the centuries and through all the important landmarks in Kenya's history from the early times and back to the twelve days duration of the present of the novel."[23] From a temporal perspective, the novel can indeed be divided into three sections: the twelve days when the principal characters are interrogated by the police for the murder of Chui, Mzigo and Kimeria (the mystery story); the years of independence, which the characters recall as they try to explain their fate in the New Ilmorog (the postcolonial narrative); and numerous stories that dramatize, often from an omniscient perspective, the history of Kenya from the prehistoric period to the 1970s (the key landmarks here are the original settlement of Ilmorog and the assassination of the lawyer).[24] Ngugi intends these narratives to complement one another: while the different stories are told in differing styles and from different perspectives, they are supposed to inform each other as the author tries to capture the totality of the postcolony and its antecedents. Each of these narrative modes, however, presupposes a certain politics of form, a politics that might at times be at odds with the ideologies that drive them and, in some instances, with the author's intentions.

There is another way of presenting this problem. Ngugi desires to capture the totality of a culture that is no longer organic, a culture in which the essential forces of society and even nature are immanently at odds with each other and the relation between subjects and their worlds is defined by radical dissonance. Perhaps we can understand the challenge the novelist faces here by recalling Georg Lukács's famous definition of the novel as a genre in search of an absent totality: "The novel is the epic of an age in which the extensive totality of life is no longer directly given, in which the immanence of meaning in life has become a problem, yet which still thinks in terms of totality."[25] Ngugi's primary referents – the colony and postcolony – are some of the most obvious symbols of the collapse of the immanence of meaning in life in modern Africa: both the colony and postcolony are brought into being through the radical disruption and reorganization of traditional societies, their modes of production, and basic identities. In the absence of the kind of organic community that makes immanent totality possible, Ngugi, like most writers of epic novels seeks, to borrow Lukács's words, "to uncover and construct the totality of life" through the form of the novel.[26] In a world in which men and women are alienated from their histories and traditions, the novel seeks to create its own structures of totality.

In other words, while most of *Petals of Blood* is about the destruction of individuals and communities, Ngugi's style seems intended to rise beyond this contingent situation. Against the narratives promoted by bourgeois historiography, the author seeks to recover the authority of "tribal" historians: "there are many questions about our history which remain unanswered . . . Just now we can only depend on legends passed from generation to generation by the poets and players of Gichandi, Litungu and Nyatiti" (*Petals of Blood*, pp. 67–68). The current history of Ilmorog is one of deracination and reification, but beneath it all, the narrative tries to recapture the organic past through legends and rituals whose origins lie in what the Gikuyu call "Agu na Agu, Tene wa tene" (p. 68) – the epoch of epochs, the past before the past. Even though the process of colonization engenders a violent disruption of rituals of community (pp. 68–69), it too is represented as a continuous process as the author tries to harness the stubborn process of time to the organic community.[27] Even the conversion of the colonized to Christianity (the process that marks their alienation from the ancestral past) becomes, as in the case of Waweru (Munira's father), part of a teleology, the fulfillment of a prophecy (p. 89). In addition, in a novel where highly subjective stories and experiences are preponderant, the reader cannot fail to notice the significant spaces occupied by the collective voices of addressers (we) and addressees (us); almost without exception, the individual narrators are defined as outsiders who become part of "us" in the process of sharing "their" stories.

What conclusion can we draw from these examples? The most obvious one is that Ngugi's goal is to capture the totality of colonial and postcolonial Kenya by providing us with multiple narratives that reinforce each other; the sum of the parts constitutes the desired whole. But there is something else taking place here: Ngugi's ambition is nothing less than the representation of the totality of epic forms and the worlds they represent. Indeed, the definitive and transformative moment of the novel is the narration of "the epic journey across the plains" (p. 143), the journey the villagers take to claim their place within the economy of colonial and postcolonial modernity. The description of the journey as epic is not simply a descriptive gesture; it is an attempt by the author to establish a crucial utopian moment in the novel, a moment that lies at the very heart of Ngugi's politics of form in this work.

Once again, Lukács provides a useful perspective on the relation between epic and journey, between old epics and novelistic ones:

The totality of [Dante's] world is the totality of a visual system of concepts. It is because of this sensual "thingness," this substantiality both of the concepts themselves and of their hierarchical order within a system, that completeness and totality can become constitutive structural categories rather than regulative ones: because of it the progression through the totality is a voyage which, although full of suspense, is a well-conducted and safe one ... In a novel, totality can be systematised only in abstract terms, which is why any system that could be established in the novel – a system being, after the final disappearance of the organic, the only possible form of a rounded totality – had to be one of abstract concepts and therefore not directly suitable for aesthetic form-giving.[28]

Lukács's argument on the nature of epic can be broken down into several elements. In the traditional epic, the totality of the world is represented in terms of visual and sensual systems that are an inherent part of the world they represent; the sense of totality we recognize in these epics is constitutive of this world and is not a set of devices developed by poets or bards to organize this world and control our perception of it; the voyage that presents this totality to us is well conducted in the sense that it is not subject to ironic twists or contingent circumstances. In the modern novel, by contrast, the sensual images that represent the world are not inherently part of it, but have been constructed by the writer to create a rounded totality in a situation in which the organic world has disappeared; figures of totality in the novel thus come to be seen as abstract concepts rather than an integral part of the world represented.

Ngugi is both a good and a bad student of Lukács: he recognizes that the world of his novel has lost its organic unity, but he seeks to represent its desire for totality in concrete rather than abstract terms. Let us examine this process as it is played out in the epic journey to the city. Let us begin by recalling that the people of Ilmorog embark on their epic journey out of a sense of frustration with their isolation and marginalization and their recognition that their organic world has disappeared under the uneven forces of progress (*Petals of Blood*, p. 115). Clearly, the journey is not posited as a return to the past – Nyakinyua's speech makes clear that this world is gone forever. What the journey seeks to establish, on the contrary, is a new community of political and economic interests. And it seeks to do so by appealing to a set of moral codes and concepts that colonial and postcolonial modernity has tried to destroy. In thematic terms, the epic journey to the city is the process by which, to use Lukács's words, "completeness and totality can become constitutive structural categories" of Ilmorog's present and future.[29] Indeed, if the first part of the novel is characterized by a poetics of underdevelopment, as I argued earlier in this chapter, the second part is an attempt to perform the totality of culture itself, to "forge a community spirit" that will make the villagers agents in the narrative of progress, or as one of them puts it, to recover Ilmorog's "stolen heart" (p. 116).

The most important point, though, is that the epic journey to the city initiates a significant shift in Ngugi's novel: it elevates Ilmorog from its previous identity as a place of escape, isolation, and loss, and endows it with a historical aura (pp. 120–24). If the first part of the novel is dominated by the characters' sense of abjection and the community's decrepitude, as I argued earlier, the new Ilmorog has become a sensual place in which individual subjects can rise beyond their *angst* and alienation and reconstitute or reimagine themselves as part of an organic body. Within the aura provided by Ilmorog's recovered past, Karega imagines himself as Ndemi, the founding father, and uses this imagination to overcome the pain engendered by Mukami's suicide and his expulsion from Siriana (pp. 124–27). Within the aura of a recovered tradition, Wanja seeks redemption and virtue (p. 126), Abdulla relives the romance of his heroic past (p. 134), and Munira "felt for a time freed from the overwhelming sense of always being on the outside of things" (p. 139).

Ngugi is a good student of Lukács because, as we can see from the above examples, he knows how to invent totality in a voyage of suspense. And there is no better example of this totality than that scene in which Abdulla single-handedly maims two antelopes with a catapult and stones and provides meat for the hungry multitude; in this act, the ex-freedom fighter becomes transformed "into a very extraordinary being whom they had never really known" (p. 139). More significantly, in this episode, Abdulla not only reveals his real self but brings the history of anticolonial resistance, which the new ruling class has tried to repress, into sharp focus; the present journey provides an occasion for recalling and commemorating journeys that had hitherto been buried in selves that would rather forget than remember the past of anticolonial struggle (p. 142). The epic journey generates a space in which fragmented lives are reconnected through narrative:

Abdulla's story had made them aware of a new relationship to the ground on which they trod: the ground, the murram grass, the agapanthas, the cactus, everything in the plains, had been hallowed by the feet of those who had fought and died that Kenya might be free: wasn't there something, a spirit of those people in them too? (p. 143)

Satisfied that this narrative moment has established the spatial and temporal connections which the people of Ilmorog were lacking earlier in the novel, the narrator smugly describes it as "the peak of the epic journey" (p. 143). But it is precisely in the representation of the connective episodes here as immanent and constitutive that

Ngugi proves to be a bad student of Lukács. For who can fail to see how fabricated such scenes of connection and redemption are, how they are created not so much to represent Ilmorog as it really is – a postcolonial wasteland – but to create an illusion of totality and utopian hope when it is most lacking? Scenes such as "Abdulla's feast" (p. 143) can be described as abstract in a Hegelian sense – they represent "the nostalgia of the characters for utopian perfection, a nostalgia that feels itself and its desire to be the only true reality."[30] But this does not mean that Ngugi's novel is imprisoned in this nostalgia; indeed, those critics who have tended to dismiss the novel as a political tract have failed to recognize how the author affirms his characters' nostalgia (and thus his own ideological preferences), but also subjects them to rigorous critique.[31]

The truth is, the epic of community in *Petals of Blood* is constantly undermined by an ironic bourgeois narrative centered on the crisis of individual subjects. The epic narrative discussed above may seek to affirm the power of community and collective action, but the careful reader cannot fail to notice how the illusion of a unified Ilmorog is built on "the mutual relativity of elements essentially alien to one another."[32] The totality of the novel is nothing more than the collection of disparate and antagonistic individual relationships connected to one another by shared experiences and memories but disunited by the same. Readers are hence put in a situation in which Ilmorog is the space that brings people together, but engenders their alienation from one another. For example, Munira's narrative is compelled by a deep desire to recover his unspeakable past, but what initially appears to be a very private story soon gets projected onto other characters: he may want to tell his story in order to understand "the beginning of his death" (p. 27), but the value of his narrative can only be measured against the actions of others. It is against Chui's ascendancy, for example, that Munira's failure to succeed in the neo-colonial economy can be understood; it is only against Karega's activism that his politics of withdrawal can be understood.

Narrating one's unique individual experience (the essence of the bourgeois novel) is an attempt by Ngugi's subjects to simultaneously separate and conjoin themselves to one other. The same process can be detected in Wanja's narrative: she tries to recall her past in order to understand her unique self – what she calls her "maimed soul" (p. 78) – but also to establish connections with other such souls. In the process of telling each other stories about their unique pasts the principal characters function as both narrators and narratees. By narrating the story of his expulsion from Siriana, for example, Munira touches a "chord" in Wanja's past and prefigures Karega's experiences at the institution; it is through such stories that "shadowy connections" are recovered (p. 46). What began as a series of unconnected events is transformed into a narrative of common suffering and shared desires. The people who inhabit Ngugi's novel might be divided by background, history, class interests, and political commitments, but once we have recuperated their pasts, we have to concede that the antagonisms that divide the victims (Munira, Karega, Wanja, and Abdulla) from their victimizers (Chui, Mzigo, and Kimeria) emerge from their mutual connections in the past.

How do we explain the mutual past and temporal coincidences that unify these characters? Munira remembers such connections and coincidences from a totalized apocalyptic perspective – "The coincidence ... must have struck him as having a God-ordained significance" (p. 99). Placed within the context of the whole narrative, however, the episodes and events in which the characters recognize the intersection of their life stories can best be described as ironic – they are part of the author's attempt to transform inadequate relations "into a fanciful yet well-ordered round of misunderstandings and cross-purposes, within which everything is seen as many-sided, within which things appear as isolated and yet connected, as full of value and yet totally devoid of it, as abstract fragments and as concrete autonomous life, as flowering and decaying, as the infliction of suffering and as suffering itself."[33]

In spite of Ngugi's attempt to transform his characters' connections in the past into an epic narrative, the motor that drives *Petals of Blood* is nothing less than "the romanticism of disillusionment."[34] After all, the story is told from the perspective of three narrators and narratees who have few things in common except an overwhelming sense that their utopian desires have been "crushed by the brute force of reality" and that "defeat is the precondition of [their] subjectivity."[35] Consider, then, the meaning of these narrators and narratees' names: Munira is a stump; Karega connotes a rebel, but a rebel in Gikuyu society is also one confined to the margins of his community; and Wanja is the outsider. So all three subjects are defined by their marginality, a state of existence into which they have been forced by brutal circumstances but which they must now transform into the basis of their identity. As both narrators, narratees, and subjects, these subjects live and relive experiences defined by a radical chasm between the utopian desire for belonging and totality and the brutal realities that have brought them to Ilmorog.

Let us examine this chasm more closely as it is represented in Munira's story: of the principal subjects in the novel, Munira is the only one without manifest utopian desires; he arrives in Ilmorog to escape from such desires, and when he narrates his experiences ten years later, he goes out of his way to repress the utopian nature of his quest. Indeed, Munira can only reflect back on his Ilmorog sojourn from a dystopic – even apocalyptic – point of view. It is only from this apocalyoptic perspective that Munira can make sense of his past. It is hence not by accident that when the police come for him at the beginning of the novel, he "had just returned from a night's vigil on the mountain" and was reading "the Book of Revelation" (p. 2) True, Munira represents Ilmorog's history as teleological, but he plots the community's narrative as a movement toward apocalypse, a moment toward ruin and destruction which, nevertheless, is the vanishing point in which he achieves ultimate knowledge about the human condition (p. 333). Since it is from this apocalyptic perspective that Munira tells his narrative, it is easy to get the impression that his long sojourn in Ilmorog has not changed him; indeed it is easy to argue that the Munira who arrives in the village driven by his sense of failure in the post-colonial economy and by an overriding desire to escape communal ties, is the same one we encounter ten or so years later.

But Munira's subjectivity – and hence his location at the center of the novel – is more complicated than this view might suggest. Defined by defeat and detachment, like many heroes of the bourgeois novel, Munira is caught between being and belonging. Although we are constantly reminded of his need to detach himself from the rhythms of life in Ilmorog, we cannot fail to notice the melancholy that emerges every time he reflects on the peasants' productive relationship with their landscape: "He walked or cycled to his house, an outsider to their activities on the land, and he felt sad and a little abandoned" (p. 20). Most significantly, like the heroes of Ngugi's earlier novels, Munira's journey is a quest for a lost romantic ideal, the ideal of what Raymond Williams, echoing Hegel, calls "an organic community."[36] Although Munira's stance appears to be strictly apolitical, the keen reader cannot fail to notice the ways in which his failure and disillusionment serve as one of the most salient indictments of decolonization which, in producing subjects incapable of fulfilling themselves in the new world, has collapsed on its foundations. Munira is indeed represented as the prisoner of both the colonial past (described as "that long night of unreality" [p. 88]) and of postcolonial deception.

This then is the paradox represented by Munira: he dominates the novel because it is only through him that Ngugi can narrate the crisis of national consciousness and foreground the failure of the postcolonial *polis*; but because he has turned this failure into the condition of possibility of his identity, he cannot be trusted to present us with a coherent critique of decolonization and its consequences. This paradox explains the presence of Karega and Wanja in the novel: like Munira, they have suffered through the monumental events of postcolonial failure; but unlike him they have sought to transcend the failures embedded in these events. If Munira is the most obvious symbol of Ngugi's education in the form of the bourgeois novel, Karega and Wanja are his first attempts to create the allegorical heroes of socialist realism. My main interest here, then, is not what these subjects represent (their names are transparent indicators of their allegorical functions), but the ways Ngugi deploys these characters as he tries to make them agents of a radical politics. It is in this context that gender becomes an important category in the novel.

As we have already observed, in the short stories published in the early 1970s, Ngugi had began to think about the potential represented by women as agents of political transformation. He seemed to believe that since men dominated the neo-colonial *polis*, women represented certain forces that could be harnessed and turned into agents of subverting the bourgeois order. It is within this context that women such as Wanja come to stand for both absolute maginalization and radical subversion in Ngugi's later novels. But in trying to account for the role of women in the postcolony, Ngugi begins with the rather sexist premise that as a woman, Wanja is the depository of passions and deep mysteries; introduced as "the new object of our gossip" (p. 31), she is constantly represented as both liberated and constrained, talking freely about a world larger than Ilmorog, but rarely revealing her inner self: "She talked feelingly about all these things as if in every place she had been she had immersed herself in the life there: otherwise she rarely discussed her personal life, or talked about herself" (p. 33).

Against the background of postcolonial atrophy, Wanja is depicted as the source of "boundless energy and enthusiasm," and these forces are manifested in the effect she has on the men around her: "She had a way of making a man's heart palpitate with different emotions and expectations at the same time" (p. 41). When her power is not represented in terms of passion, Wanja is allegorized as the temptress, sure of "her power over men" – "she knew how they could be very weak before her body" (p. 56). For a brief moment in the novel, Wanja tries to overcome her reputation and tries to "make something of herself" (p. 126), but haunted by her past in the form of Kimeria, and often asked to sacrifice herself for the sake of the new Ilmorog, she ends up functioning as a stereotypical Jezebel, plotting her revenge on the men who ravaged her for years. And it is because of this stereotyping that many readers of the novel might fail to see how Ngugi has tried to turn Wanja's energies into instruments of political insurgency. The point to underscore, however, is Ngugi's consistent suggestion that in her multiple roles in the novel – as a prostitute, a granddaughter, entrepreneur, or community organizer – Wanja is interpellated and imprisoned by the logic of the neo-colonial culture and economy. But Wanja is an important point of counter-distinction to Munira because in the end, in spite of her suffering, she is able to imagine a utopian moment in which the problems narrated in the novel might be overcome (p. 338).

The same can be said about Karega. In many ways, the young

rebel's experiences mirror those of Munira and there are crucial instances in which his rebelliousness conceals the kind of romanticism of disillusionment discussed earlier. But in the end, Ngugi seems to suggest that Karega's disenchantment, perhaps because it is so radical, opens up spaces in which alternative narratives and communities can be imagined. One way of exploring this problem is to compare the different narrative roles Ngugi assigns to Munira and Karega. As we have already seen, Munira's narrative is driven by what we may call an apocalyptic – the desire to establish a vision that rises above "the corrupt laws of a corrupt world" and thus consolidate a transcendental order based on "higher laws, pure, eternal, absolute, unchanging" (p. 296). Munira may be a lost soul, his world may be fragmented, his self may be at odds with his past, his family, his world, but the story he tells seeks to establish connections, to overcome gaps, and to assert the totality of the world he seeks to destroy at the end of the novel. In contrast, Karega's story is driven by uncertainty; gaps and ellipses mark the very language of his most personal narrative:

I do not understand it, the whole thing. The beginning so clear . . . or was it an illusion? And the end so hazy that the beginning and the idea behind the beginning were buried in a mist of bitterness, the recrimination and cruel, blind vengeance. Massacres of hopes and dreams and beauty. The bright beginning . . . the bitter end. For a time I was determined to make it. I had after all a good school certificate. I said: Chui and the school can eject me . . . but the country: there is room for all of us at the meeting point of a victorious struggle. Fruits of Uhuru. You do my bit . . . I do my bit . . . we move a mountain . . . why not? There was the big city. I walked from office to office and everywhere, it was the same. No Vacancy. (pp. 103–04)

Although the final scenes of the novel seem, in a rather melodramatic fashion, to insist on the young rebel's coming to revolutionary self-consciousness, and although the author wants to end his novel by conjuring a utopian scenario in which the problems that plague the postcolony can be overcome through a reinforced national consciousness and the solidarity of workers awakening to their historic role, Karega is as much a prisoner of his doubts as of the Kenyan state. As he contemplates his fate in prison, Karega connects his fate to the peasants who in the past had mapped out the path to freedom in Kenya; he visualizes a future in which workers and peasants will seize power to "overturn the system" and "bring to an end the reign of the few over the many, the era of drinking blood and feasting on human flesh"; and for a moment he is carried "on the waves of this vision and of the possibilities it opened up for all the Kenyan working and peasant masses" (p. 344). But in spite of this revolutionary rhetoric, *Petals of Blood* is a novel preoccupied with the presence of a political impasse; Karega's vision is just that, an unfulfilled dream: "Tomorrow ... tomorrow..." (p. 345). It is in these ellipses – the gaps left open by the narratives of colonialism and postcoloniality – that Karega can imagine a future in which the dream of independence might be fulfilled. But these gaps also call attention to the failure of the old dream of freedom and national consciousness. This is how the future comes to be represented in a revolutionary aphorism – "Tomorrow ... tomorrow" – which is also a sign of doubt and uncertainty. In this doubt and uncertainty, readers can detect how even in its revolutionary message, *Petals of Blood* replicates the complicated and ambivalent endings in Ngugi's first three novels.

CHAPTER 6

Performance and power: the plays

My basic argument up to this point is that Ngugi's career has been defined by a systematic attempt to master the form of the European novel and to see how its techniques can be brought to bear on the complicated cultures and histories of colonial and postcolonial Africa. I have argued that this engagement with the novel as an aesthetic object is as important as his evolving political ideology in the 1960s and 1970s. And yet, in spite of his numerous attempts to move the novel beyond its European bourgeois heritage – a heritage in which the genre is driven by the need to account for unique individual experiences for isolated and privileged readers – and turn it into an instrument of mass culture and collective change, Ngugi was, for most of this period, the archetypal intellectual writing about the experiences of "the people" from the sanctuary of the university. As we have already seen, the author's sense of his own alienation from his objects of representation, his awareness of the gap between the subjects of his novel (often peasants and workers) and the rarified mode of novelistic expression, became for him a source of artistic *angst* and ideological soul-searching in the 1970s. In these circumstances, Ngugi's occasional turn to drama was one way of dealing with the crisis that this African writer had to confront when he attempted to represent subjects and cultural situations that were at odds with the language and aesthetic ideology of his inherited novelist tradition.

THE USES OF PERFORMANCE

Ngugi cannot be considered a major African playwright, but it is in his drama that he has found ideal opportunities for bringing the work of art (the aesthetic object) face to face with the *Lebenswelt* (the world of everyday life). For if Ngugi's panoramic novels of the postcolony end up being representations of very subjective experiences, as the example of *Petals of Blood* exemplifies so well, his plays provide the space in which he can fulfill his dream of turning artistic production into a communal enterprise. Indeed, if the performance of Ngugi's first Gikuyu play, *Ngaahika Ndeenda*, is now heralded as a radical development in his writing career, it is not because the writing of the drama marked the first time he had produced work in his native tongue; rather, this play was to mark a turning point in the author's aesthetic ideology because it enabled him to overcome the boundary separating him from his audience and his text from its context. For Ngugi, the collective generation of this play pointed a way out of the prisonhouse of European languages and culture, and thus of his own education, experience, and vocation: "Although the script was drafted by Ngugi wa Mirii and I, the peasants and workers added to it, making the end product a far cry from the original draft. Everything was collective, open and public, and it was fascinating to see a unity gradually emerge virtually rubbing out distinctions of age, education, sex and nationality."[1] In addition, if Ngugi's political ambition in the 1980s was to turn his art into an instrument of overcoming the class divisions that plagued the postcolony, clearly the very production of the play in collaboration with workers and peasants could be seen as an attempt to will a new national community into being.

Now, Ngugi has wondered, as have many of his readers, why his plays have often gotten him in trouble with state authorities in both Kenya and Uganda: what kind of threat does his drama pose to established power?[2] And why are the same institutions of state power less threatened by his novels, which deal virtually with the same themes and issues? These questions go beyond the relationship of the writer and the state; they are good indices of the ways in which dramatic texts provide both a counter-discourse to the ritualized mechanisms of state control and perform alternative conditions of being, situations which call into question the symbolic economy of state power but also subvert the "inflated rituals" of governance and domination that have been defined as the essence of postcolonial culture and politics in Africa.[3] Ngugi's plays attest to the fact that it is in performance, rather than mere writing and reading, that the compromised narratives of state power are contested and discredited.

In regard to Ngugi's own work as a playwright, three strategies of using performance against the institutions of power can be identified. First, Ngugi has consistently conceived his plays as forms in which art can resist the hegemonic performances and rituals of state power, the social dramas associated with the new African ruling class, and political ideologies that promote the government's control over modes of communication and entertainment. For this reason, each of Ngugi's major plays was written as a specific intervention into local cultural and political debates on the pressing question of power in the postcolonial era. For example, *The Black Hermit* was written in "celebration" of Uganda's independence in 1962. The new leadership in Kampala wanted a cultural text that would signify "a break with the past" and Ngugi was keen to produce a play to meet this desire for newness, for historical rupture. But by calling attention to the pathologies of colonialism, of the dangers facing a stillborn African independence, and a divisive rhetoric that constantly militated against the ideal of black unity, Ngugi's play caused so much discomfort to the new rulers that its run at the Uganda National Theatre was short-lived. In a similar vein, *The Trial of Dedan Kimathi* was written as Ngugi's response to what David Cohen has called "the economy of debate" on the meaning of the Kenyan past:

Since the midst of the Mau Mau experience of the 1950s, what Mau Mau was, what it means, how it was individually and collectively experienced, whether its ideals and objectives were abandoned or carried on, and by whom for what ends have been the most captivating questions in Kenyan political life, theater, and literature. In the early 1980s, the debates had reached the point where lawsuits were being filed among combative Kenyan historians. By the 1990s it had become clear that the question of "whether or not Mau Mau was betrayed" has since the 1950s been the core motor of production of Kenyan historiography joining questions of social justice with debates arising from the inspection of fresh layers of material from archives and memoirs.[4]

Because of its attempt to intervene in the debate on the historiography of Kenya, this play, too, was to encounter a multitude of political problems and obstacles.

On another level – and this is the second important shift represented by Ngugi's dramatic works – plays could, perhaps more than novels, perform a more immediate epistemological function. We can understand the relation between performance and epistemology by recalling the argument made in the last chapter: that by the 1980s Ngugi had come to define literature as a means of formulating and sharing knowledge about the post-colonial condition. But because novels were read in private, there was no guarantee that the act of reading would itself lead to radical change. Now, it is true that readers have the ability, in the words of Michel de Certeau, to "invent in texts something different" from what the author intended,[5] but in Ngugi's case, this did not simply mean that novels could be expected to fulfill their author's ideological intentions. Ultimately, the radical political intentions evident in works such as *Petals of Blood* could not count on anything more than the goodwill of privileged readers; but for writers committed to producing alternative knowledge about the post-colony, the epistemological function of narratives could not be left to what Johannes Fabian has called "cover-all protestations of goodwill"; what was needed was a way of spelling out in as much detail as possible "what actually happens when we communicate and engage in dialogue."[6]

Ngugi's professional turn toward drama can hence be read as a rethinking of the epistemology of literary expression, the search for forms in which political action could be represented through what Fabian calls "action, enactment, or performance"; in the process of mediating knowledge through "acting," the author could redefine his relationship with ordinary readers.[7] Conceived as a cultural instrument of change, drama, more than the novel, could be formalized to overcome the historical and social gap between intellectuals and workers, between popular culture and elite forms of artistic expression. *Ngaahika Ndeenda* (*I Will Marry When I Want*) was indeed an invitation, from some Kenyan workers to some Kenyan intellectuals, to redefine the nature of culture and knowledge in the postcolony.

Thuutha wa ndeereti, amwe a kamĩtĩ ĩyo ya mĩikarĩre makĩũrio maandĩke ithaako rĩa ngerekano rĩa kũonania mĩtũrĩre ya mũingĩ. Ithui

Ngũgĩ eerĩ tũkĩgwĩrwo nĩ mũrigo ũcio. Wandĩki wa ithaako rĩĩrĩ ria ngerekano wambĩrĩiirie hau.[8]

(After a long discussion, some members of the cultural committee were asked to write a play to examine the way of life of ordinary people. We, the two Ngugis, took on this responsibility. That is how the writing of this play began.)

But how could the two Ngugis, university-based intellectuals, begin even to comprehend the inner or spiritual lives ("ũhoro wa mũoyo") and struggles of people whose experiences were so different from the lives of the privileged elite? Could intellectuals produce a play that was charged with enacting the practice of everyday life without privileging "the productive apparatus" of drama as high culture? This was to prove to be a vexing question for Ngugi and his co-author:

Rĩrĩa twerirwo twandĩke ithaako rĩrĩ, nĩ twathĩnĩkire mũno tuĩgikaamenya ha kwambĩrĩria. No nĩ geetha tũhote kwandika ũria arĩmi-anyiinyi na aruti-a-wĩra matũũraga, nĩ twaririe na o mũno na tũkĩmahooya ũtaarĩ igũrũ ria rũthiomi rwitũ, mĩĩkarĩre iitũ, nyĩmbo ciitũ, na mathĩĩna maitũ. o na ta mũrimi ũmwe mũnyiinyi ũtooũ i kana e nũ we watuungire rwimbo rũothe rwa gitiiro. Kwa ũguo, kũna ithaako rĩrĩ nĩ maciaro ma ngwatanĩro ya andũ aingĩ, na makĩria ya arĩmi-anyiinyi na aruti-a-wĩra a Kamĩrĩĩthũ. (*Caitanni Mutharaba-ini*, p. 5)

(When we were asked to write this play, we had serious problems trying to figure out where to start. And in order to be able to represent how they lived, we had long discussions with peasants and workers as we tried to learn more about our language, our traditions, our songs, and our problems. Indeed, a peasant who could not read at all composed the lyrics for the Gitiiro dance. As a result, this play is the result of a communal effort, especially of peasants and workers from Kamĩrĩĩthũ.)

Ngugi's hope was that in this artistic collaboration between intellectuals and peasants, the character of the productive apparatus itself could be changed.

But performance presented Ngugi with a third strategy for rethinking the poetics of cultural production in the postcolony – it forced him to take oral traditions and popular culture seriously and to seek ways of incorporating them seriously into his aesthetic ideology. If drama had become important to Ngugi at precisely the moment he seemed unsure about the capacity of the novel to effect social change, it is perhaps because it could enable him to incorporate what he would call, in the preface to the Gikuyu edition of *Ngaahika Ndeenda*, "ūhoro wa moyo ya aruti-a-wīra na arīmi-any-iinyi" ("the soul of peasants and workers") (p. 5). His assumption was that this soul would be best represented in an idiom that was closer to the lives of the workers and peasants he wanted to write about.

What, then, was new in Ngugi's drama? We shall address this question later when we examine *Ngaahika Ndeenda* in detail. For now let us make a distinction between literary and popular culture as two distinct modes of political practice: in the former, the author could incorporate components of popular culture such as songs into his writing, but so long as these elements were produced in languages and genres that were only available to privileged readers, who were in turn construed as the only true interpreters of the crisis of the bourgeois state, their popularity was still contained by what de Certeau calls "the interpretation given by *socially* authorized professions and intellectuals"; as a result, literal meaning would continue to be "the index and the result of a social power."[9] But in a situation where the parameters of writing are set by the practices of everyday life, as was the case with *Ngaahika Ndeenda*, popular culture would acquire a different dynamic; instead of being merely a response to questions and conditions, popular culture would acquire a more activist role; in Fabian's words, the text of popular culture "*asks* questions and *creates* conditions."[10] And it was because Ngugi's new play was asking forbidden questions and creating alternative conditions for discussing politics in postcolonial Kenya that the government felt compelled to destroy the Kamīrīīthū theatre on March 12, 1982, accusing the author and his collaborators of "teaching politics under the cover of culture."[11]

But what was wrong with this public discussion of postcolonial politics? Why did the government of Kenya feel threatened by a play that contained materials and views that Ngugi had already expressed publicly in his essays and novels? In its drive to ensure that it had a monopoly on politics, the Kenya state had sought to make fundamental distinctions between pure culture, which it considered to be ahistorical and apolitical, and political utterances, which were allowable only through the medium and institutions that the state itself had authorized – the universities, the established press, and literature in European languages. Since the postcolonial state was engaged in elaborate performances of its own – as the most active producer of images and discourses on radio and television – popular theatre presented counter-performances that threatened the government's monopoly of spectactorship and hence power. This is the lesson Ngugi eventually learnt when he was arrested at the end of 1977 and detained without trial for one year. But it had taken him twenty years of writing sometimes bad plays to get to this point.

DRAMA AND POSTCOLONIAL IDENTITIES: THE EARLY PLAYS

Ngugi's early plays, most notably the *Black Hermit* and the scripts collected in *This Time Tomorrow*, are closer in theme and structure to his short stories than to his novels. From both the cast of characters and the dramatic situation that is his primary concern in the early drama, it is evident that Ngugi's concern in these early plays is the conflict between the "modern" subject emerging from colonial institutions such as the university and the church, striving to reconnect with old traditions, only to discover that more often than not, the ideas of nationhood are at odds with "tribal" affiliations and practices. The theme and structure of these plays is often simple: we encounter the modern subject in a state of crisis, a crisis manifested in his or her attempt to reconcile cosmopolitan nationalism and the nostalgia for a lost world of childhood and youth. These symbolic fields (the modern and the traditional) are represented by the figures of two types of women, one connecting the hero of the drama to the past and the other pulling him toward the future. And since the crisis of culture and identity embedded in the hero's affiliation with these women cannot be resolved, it is through the death or departure of one or both of the women that a space is created for interrogating postcolonial identities.

Clearly, part of what appears to be the simplicity of Ngugi's early drama can be explained by the binary opposition around which his early plays are constructed. In the *Black Hermit*, for example, the cast of characters can be divided between modernists in the city and traditionalists in the village. The play is structured by the hero's movement from the city to the village; its language associates each locality with a distinctive set of values, with the villagers speaking in verse and proverbs and the cosmopolitans using ordinary prose. But on closer examination, the play is more complicated than these predictable binaries might suggest. True, the city is associated with movement and activity while the country is the depository for a certain kind of nostalgia; but it is hard to tell which set of values the author prefers. For while the language spoken by people in the countryside would seem to gesture toward the pastoral (the verse seems to want to underscore this aspect of traditional life), this language is marked by a sense of loss or lack. The country folk often speak in poetic incantations that are, nonetheless, subverted by the contents of the speech acts: "Of a truth, / This world is really bad / Not the same as the old / When sons still gave respect to parents, / Honoring claims of motherhood."[12] Thus the play opens with an old woman trying to assert the authority of motherhood – the synecdoche of tradition – and a wife trying to make claims for the romance of the hearth: "I can't do without a husband, / Without a man to warm my bed" (*The Black Hermit*, p. 3). But such claims for the authority and values of tradition are like signs without a signifier; indeed, they are apostrophic gestures in the sense that they seem to be directed at absent figures. What initiates this drama, after all, is the heroes' ideological – and semantic – displacement from the traditional values the women who open the play embrace.

Furthermore, these women's appeal to the authority of the past and the hearth only calls attention to the absence of the son and husband who was supposed to secure old traditions: "Remi was once a God-fearing child, / Obedient to me and his father, / Always desiring to do the right thing" (p. 6), notes the hero's mother. But for the elders of the village, Remi's alienation from his native land began even before he was born, when his father became converted to Christianity. The first act of the play, then, is not so much about the hearth, or the efficacy of old traditions in the world of postcolonial modernity, but a sustained attempt by the author to call attention to the emptiness of the space which

Remi, the would-be nationalist, was supposed to occupy. For as we
saw in previous chapters, while the moment of independence,
which is also the setting of this play, constitutes the cusp that
separates the colonial past and the decolonized present, it is also an
important occasion for reflecting on the gap that separates the
keepers of tradition and their Westernized progeny.

The debate in the first act is thus as much about the place of the
old ways in the moral economy of modernity as it is about Remi's
role as the subject who might bridge the historical gap, in Gikuyu
cultural discourse, between the *karing'a* (the cultural purists) and
kirore (the educated ones):

> ELDER: We knew him once for a good son
> He acceded to our wishes
> And married this woman,
> A daughter of the tribe,
> Instead of a white-skinned woman.
> We were happy.
> Remi was not the husband of Thoni, alone.
> Remi was also the new husband to the tribe.
> Through his big education,
> He would have bound us together.   (p. 8)

In this passage alone we can identify the set of problems and
paradoxes Ngugi's early plays try to mediate. Remi's tragedy arises
from his paradoxical role in his community: on one hand, he is
considered to play the role of the good son who accedes to the
traditions of the "tribe" and marries his brother's widow; on the
other hand, he is asked, because of his education, to perform a
modernizing function at odds with his people's wishes.

Many of the people watching this play when it was performed at
the National Theatre in Kampala on the occasion of Uganda's
independence could clearly recognize their own cultural dilemmas
in Remi's futile attempt to perform these multiple functions. In this
sense, we should read Ngugi's play as an attempt to create a
performative space in which the character and affinities of the new
postcolonial subject can be interrogated and one in which an
immanent postcolonial disenchantment can be enacted. Indeed,
the question of Remi's failure to live up to the expectations of his
people – "Remi refused to go to Nineveh, / He fled to the City of

idolatry" (p. 21) – is explicitly connected to postcolonial disenchantment (pp. 28–29).

When we finally come face to face with Remi in Act II of the play, we immediately recognize that above and beyond the political problems which the play foregrounds – nationalism and modernity – it is also about a more subjective crisis: who and what is Remi? Although he is first presented to us in the city – the common symbol of culture and enlightenment – he is located in a nightclub surrounded by darkness (p. 23), "brooding over something" and his "eyes fixed in space" (p. 25). In this dark setting, the man who was educated to lead his people to the New Jerusalem is haunted by his past; indeed, it is because he feels "trapped by the tribe " that he has "escaped to the city" (p. 31). Clearly, if the "tribe" sees Remi's marriage to his brother's wife as the bond that ties him to his roots, the young man sees the woman as "a wound" that refuses to heal (p. 32). In refusing to accept the validity of this marriage, Remi has rejected the authority of the group and asserted his own unique – and hence modern – identity; but in asserting his modern identity, Remi has to come to terms with displacement and the pain it entails: "I shall not go home. I will never go home," he cries early in the play (p. 36).

What appears to be Remi's declarative intention – his eager embrace of exile – is his awareness of a triple dilemma that is also the enabling condition of his postcolonial identity and subjectivity. On one hand, the act of willing into being a new national identity demands that Remi renounce his "tribal" roots and his private self; for this reason, his departure for the city and his desire for an cosmopolitan identity, are represented as part of "our nationalist fervour" (p. 41). By the same token, however, he is aware of the tenuousness of a public identity severed from the private life: "Surely a man's public life is given meaning only by the stability of his private life," he declares (p. 41). In the end, a return to the hearth, of the kind elaborated in the first act of the play, does not resolve the problems that modernity raises; indeed, Remi's dilemma is very similar to Waiyaki's in *The River Between*, a novel written at about the same time as *The Black Hermit*: how can one be a modern subject within the traditionalism celebrated by the nationalism?

Remi's return to his village in Act III is an attempt to resolve this problem. But as he discovers soon enough, the categories that mediate the terms of the cultural debate – modernity and tradition included – are themselves very tenuous. The Christians in his village see themselves as the guardians of a tradition of religious conversion; they are hence determined that Remi should be "kept away from politics, / Away from the influences of tribal elders" (p. 58). And yet the grammar the Christians use, the language of restoration and purity, is borrowed from the precolonial culture. In a similar vein, the elders see Remi as the man who will restore their culture to its precolonial standing, but they speak of his return in the messianic language of Christianity and modernity:

> 1ST NEIGHBOUR: The elders meet.
> So many of them.
> People've come from afar,
> From ridges around and beyond
> They pour into the meeting ground.
> They dance and sing.
> Hark!
> You can hear the drums.
> They carry branches.
> And sing old songs of war
> When we, Mama, used to be a tribe,
> Before the white-man came.
> Now they sing of another coming,
> After the going of the white-man.
> They sing of a new man,
> To restore the tribe to its land,
> To its old ways.   (p. 59)

No wonder Remi speaks of his cultural mission of synthesis in such confused ways; no wonder he wants to return home, to the hearth, in order to crush "the shackles of custom," unaware that he speaks within a discourse that custom – in all its varieties – has authorized or enabled. In short, Remi's tragedy – and that of his generation – arises from the fact that questions about custom and tradition, which are also questions about the country's destiny, can only be mediated by what Ross Chambers, writing in a different context, has called the "suicide tactic."[13] The strange thing about the "suicide tactic" in *The Black Hermit* is that its practitioner – and victim – is Thoni, the woman whom Remi has rejected and, in the process, transformed into the symbolic ground on which the destiny of the nation is fought.[14]

It is, of course, now a little difficult to understand why the conflict between tradition and modernity seems to dominate Ngugi's early plays. Indeed, given the convulsions that the post-colonial state in Africa has undergone in the last half-century, and given what appears to be the reversal of the very terms of this debate, it is hard to understand why this question should have dominated most of the drama Ngugi produced in the 1960s. But to restate a point already made in my discussion of Ngugi's early novels, the act of writing, on the eve of decolonization and after, was conceived as an instrument of rethinking colonial notions of subjectivity and especially of interrogating the divisions that were the consequences of conquest and rule. What this meant, among other things, was that like many African authors of his generation, Ngugi saw himself as both an advocate of enlightenment in the postcolony – "the educated are very few and the great illiterate mass looks up to them for leadership and guidance," he was to argue in a 1962 essay – and of the preservation of "the African way," a way defined by "the community in all its manifestations."[15] At the same time, however, Ngugi was honest enough to admit that culture itself could not resolve rifts rooted in historical and economic circumstances. Many of his early plays are attempts to rehearse, as it were, these problems and their imagined resolutions.

Indeed, some of the plays from this period are very provisional in character; they are improvisations on themes that were to be elaborated in the novels. But while Ngugi's early novels were concerned with the fate of individuals within the parameters established by communal ideals, his short plays were predicated on the actions of individuals resisting communal identities and functions. In the aptly titled *The Rebels* for example, the drama pits an educated son against both his community and father; the point of dispute is, as so often in Ngugi's plays, a woman. The elders have chosen a wife for Charles in the belief that this kind of "communal" marriage will ensure his affiliation with his community – "it is the custom and tradition on this our ridge," he is told.[16] Charles disrupts the old order of things when he brings home his "foreign" fiancée, thus asserting his free will against what his father considers to be the old ways. Two issues raise this simple play to a level beyond the banal confrontation between father and son. First, what is at issue in such private questions as betrothal and marriage is nothing less than the mandate of the imagined community of the nation: by his willingness to marry a girl from another ethnic group, Charles is performing the drama of nationhood and questioning old axioms of social organization – "She is not, as you can see, of our tribe. But what is tribe?" (*This Time Tomorrow*, p. 8). By insisting on the right to choose a wife for his son, the father is insisting on his authority as the custodian of custom – "Custom must be maintained. It is a sacred law. We don't want rebels in our midst" (p. 9).

Secondly, the terms of this whole debate seem mixed up: Nauru may present himself as the defender of custom, but we have already been informed that in his youth he rebelled against his own father and left his home "under a curse" (p. 5); given this family history, there is no compelling reason for Charles to renounce his love and vision or to sacrifice himself and his convictions "for blind custom and tradition" (pp. 12–13). In fact, given his education and commitment, Charles has every good reason to free himself from what his fiancée calls "the burden of our separate pasts" (p. 13). What is unusual in this play – as in the rest of the scripts collected in *This Time Tomorrow* – is the way the characters who would seem best equipped to transcend what Ngugi sees as old and outdated customs use them as a mask for their own indecisiveness, their own lack of agency as it were. Charles sees his curse as that of the modern African: "Torn between two worlds. I wish I were not myself. Then I would not have to choose between a father's curse, a tribe's anger, and the anguish of a betrayed heart" (p. 13). But as in *The Black Hermit*, Charles is released from the obligation to choose sides by the suicide of the woman his father wanted him to marry (p. 15).

As we have already noted, it is now easy to dismiss the themes and structures of Ngugi's early plays as simplistic attempts to diagnose the crisis of the modern African. But such retrospective perspectives should not negate the fact that when these plays were produced – at the cusp between the end of colonialism and the beginning of decolonization – the modern African's location in a symbolic field in which vestiges of old traditions were often in conflict with the desire for modernity was the source of immeasurable anxiety. This anxiety is evident in many of the columns Ngugi wrote in the *Sunday Nation* in 1962 and 1963, the critical years of Kenya's transition from colony to postcolony: educated people were experiencing a conflict between Western and "tribal" ways, he would argue, and there was the need for a national ideal that would synthesize these forces; the Kenya he wanted was one freed from the shackles of customs which had outlived their purpose.[17] The plays from this period are hence centered on the crisis of a decolonized African subject asked to carry out the project of modernity without the civilizational authority of Englishness.

Where does Englishness fit into this equation? We are now so used to seeing Ngugi as a radical defender of African languages and traditions that we forget that at the beginning of his career he was an advocate of the liberal values acquired from the masters of colonial enlightenment. Like these masters, Ngugi recognized the significance of the folk and the "tribal" as a source of aesthetic materials, but he still posited the individual endowed with taste and civility as the guarantor of culture, that is, "sweetness and light." But as the postcolonial landscape began to unravel – or rather to assert its new character – Ngugi's plays began to shift from the vision of liberal humanism toward a radical critique of postcoloniality itself.

Thus in a play like *The Wound in the Heart*, one of the greatest themes in the literature of decolonization – the ideal of return and restoration – is ironized in ways that recall some of the most memorable scenes in *A Grain of Wheat*. The setting of the play is the moment of decolonization itself: the state of emergency is over, and Ruhiu the nationalist is about to return home from prison to fulfill his dream of freedom. But what was supposed to be a celebratory moment is surrounded by a rhetoric of doubt: "The whole dark Emergency has left an incurable wound in the country, which might go on bleeding for a long time to come" (*This Time Tomorrow*, p. 21). The drama of decolonization thus comes to be performed in an ironic structure and rhetoric, one that calls attention to the failure of nationalism and to the gap between the dream of nationalist restoration and the reality of betrayal. Simply put, Ruhiu is publicly celebrated as a prophet and a leader, but privately everyone in his village knows that his wife has had a child with "a white man, my enemy," in his absence (p. 26). Once again, a double suicide is seen as a dramatic solution to the problems of wounds that refuse to heal, of pasts that fail to go away.

Now, while Ngugi may use such death scenes as melodramatic resolutions to the intangible problems his plays raise, there is a sense in which such denouements are symptomatic of his characters' inability to temporize the space between the end of colonialism and the beginning of decolonization. Even in 1967 when he wrote *This Time Tomorrow* for the BBC, Ngugi was still unsure about the temporal connection between an immediate past marked by tangible historical events such as the state of emergence and the as yet uncharted landscape of postcoloniality. He was equally unsure about his own ideological response to the set of conflicts he was observing in this new landscape. The aporetic ending of *This Time Tomorrow* is a clear sign of Ngugi's ideological uncertainty:

WANJIRO: I am old enough to look after myself. I am going – now. Asinjo is waiting for me. Goodbye, mother.

NJANGO: Wanjiro! Wanjiro! Don't go away. Don't leave me alone! What shall I do without you? *(Silence, then quietly.)* I am a useless old woman. *(Kiongo enters. But Njango does not hear him).*

KIONGO: Hurry up! Hurry up! You there! Woman! What are you doing? Hurry up! *(He runs out still shouting orders.)*

NJANGO: They are herding *us* out like cattle. Where shall I go now, tonight? Where shall I be, this time tomorrow? If only we had stood up against them! If only we could stand together! *(Then bulldozer whine to crescendo, and resultant crash as hut is pushed down. Then silence.)*

(This Time Tomorrow, p. 50)

This ending is distinctive for the way it departs from the semiotics of closure in Ngugi's other plays from this period: instead of a suicide tactic (killing oneself to escape a terrible social situation), we have a woman rejecting the authority of the parent and running away with her "alien" lover; we have young people refusing to live in the prisonhouse of tradition. But this gesture of individual revolt is not matched by any collective revolt; on the contrary, the slum dwellers are herded away like cattle, wistful about their stillborn power, but unable to do anything about their situation. Ngugi's pessimism in 1967 provides a startling contrast to the rhetoric of revolution in the plays published ten years later.

PERFORMING POSTCOLONIALITY: THE LATER PLAYS

Compare the above scene with the following memorable ending to Ngugi's last play in English, *The Trial of Dedan Kimathi*, co-written with Micere Mugo:

People's Song and Dance:
Male and Female soloists recommended.

SOLOISTS:	Ho-oo, ho-oo mto mkuu wateremka!
GROUP:	Ho-oo, ho-oo mto mkuu wateremka!
SOLOISTS:	Magharibi kwenda mashariki
GROUP:	Mto mkuu wateremka
SOLOISTS:	Kaskazini kwenda kusini
GROUP:	Mto mkuu wateremka
SOLOISTS:	Hoo-i, hoo-i kumbe adui kweli mjinga
GROUP:	Hoo-i, hoo-i kumbe adui kweli mjinga
SOLOISTS:	Akaua mwanza mimba wetu
GROUP:	Akijitia yeye mshindi
SOLOISTS:	Wengi zaidi wakazaliwa
SOLOISTS:	Hoo-yea, hoo-yea Umoja wetu ni nguvu yetu
GROUP:	Hoo-ye, Iloo-ye umoja wetu ni nguvu yetu
SOLOISTS:	Tutapigana mpaka mwisho
GROUP:	Tufunge vita na tutashinda
SOLOISTS:	Majembe juu mapanga juu
GROUP:	Tujikomboe tujenge upya.[18]

A summary of the song in English will help us elaborate its ideological message: both the soloists and group sing of the movement of a big river that flows from east to west, north to south; they are part of this river, which is posited as the symbol of the revolutionary movement which the colonial enemy, by condemning the hero to death, has unwittingly created. The singers note that by killing the firstborn in the African family (the revolutionary leader, Dedan Kimathi), the enemy has ironically created more revolutionaries; the new movement now vows to fight to the very end using hoes and machetes to liberate itself, determined to build a new future. Clearly, compared to the pessimism in the plays discussed above, this song is symptomatic of the revolutionary rhetoric that characterizes Ngugi's later plays. My concern here, however, is with the changes that had taken place in the author's politics – and aesthetic ideology – since the mid-1960s.

We can start by noting that after a decade of writing plays centered on the struggle of postcolonial subjects to transcend the destructive authority of tradition, an authority often vested in the "tribe," Ngugi's ideological message has shifted significantly in the 1970s, moving away from individual anxieties to collective desires. It is notable that at the end of *The Trial of Dedan Kimathi*, individuals (the soloists) and the collective (the choral group) sing the same song and help reinforce the same message. The central symbol of the drama – and indeed its architecture – is not the binary opposition between an enlightened individual and the masses, but the usurpation of individual identity by the enlightened collective will. *The Trial of Dedan Kimathi* is perhaps not a good play in an aesthetic sense, but it is the drama that enables Ngugi to finally make the transition from the liberal ideology of Makerere to the Marxism that produced works such as *Petals of Blood* and *Devil on the Cross*. This shift is most apparent in the way Ngugi organizes the dramatic space which, in his works, must be considered to be a metaphor of society itself.

One of the dramaturgical features which Ngugi's early plays seem to share is the way the stage is organized in a binary opposition between the figures of tradition, often a group of elders or villagers, and the ambivalent hero, a university-educated subject caught between the demands of his or her community and history which are at odds with his or her desires. The dramatic architecture of *The Trial of Dedan Kimathi* also relies on binaries, but the terms of opposition have changed in telling ways. Consider the cast, for example: the subjects deployed in the play can be divided into two camps, with Kimathi the revolutionary hero pitted against the symbols of colonial authority (the soldiers, the prosecutor, and the judge), and each side supported by a cast of their ideological kin. But from the very beginning – and most of the movement of the drama confirms this – Ngugi and Micere Mugo have also foreseen the need and possibility of ironic shifts and chiasmic reversals; they have created situations in which one character can play different roles and where the crossing from one political camp to the other is part of the complexity of narrating the history of colonialism in Kenya.

This is not to imply that the ideological preferences of the authors are not clear. Ngugi and Mugo want to produce a drama in which the audience cannot be left in doubt as to the identities of the heroes against colonial conquest and rule and those who collaborated with the enemy. Indeed, one of the primary motives of writing the play, the authors tell us in their introduction, is to rectify what they see as a shameful misrepresentation of the history of colonialism in Kenya and the absence of "the heroes and heroines of our history" in the work of imaginative artists. Their play is, in fact, an angry response to Kenneth Watene's play, *Dedan Kimathi*, which Ngugi and Mugo considered to be part of an intellectual industry "busy spewing out, elaborating and trying to document the same colonial myths" as imperial texts (*Trial*, Preface). The architecture of the play is hence intended to make sure that the lines that separate the heroes and villains will not be blurred.

At the same time, however, *The Trial of Dedan Kimathi* was written and produced in a postcolonial situation in which the terms that had come to shape the heated debate about the Kenyan past – and indeed the reality of postcolonialism – had shifted significantly. Simply put, the question of who was the hero and what actions constituted emancipatory practices in the immediate past had been complicated by the rhetoric of independence in two important respects: first, because the new ruling class in Kenya was made up mostly of those who had collaborated with colonialism, it was hard to convince audiences that the values of those who had died during the struggle for independence – and had been forgotten since – were worth pursuing. Secondly, since the postcolonial elite (including intellectuals and writers) had continued to demonize the people Ngugi and Mugo considered to be the real heroes of independence, it was difficult to force the middle-class audience that came to see the play to reappraise what seemed to be their dogged determination to forget the past. A simple binary opposition between heroes and villains could simply not do because it could easily reinforce the fears and prejudices of this middle-class audience. By creating a fluid set of characters, the authors could compel their audience to enter the world of the play without firm presuppositions. Indeed, many of the new strategies of representation adopted in the play seemed calculated to call Aristotelean dramatic unities into question and to destabilize the audience's sense of time, place, and character.

With regard to the question of time, for example, the play was presented in movements rather than acts. The assumption here is that while movements, like acts, are a series of actions connected together on a temporal level, they are defined by disjuncture, or a play of irresolvable contradictions. The play produces knowledge through the dramatization of temporal conflicts. In the first movement, we have a play of images of darkness and light which is also about two movements in African history: since the past of "Black people's struggle" is concealed in darkness, its enactment on the stage which Ngugi and Mugo have provided constitutes the lifting of this veil of darkness (pp. 4–6). And while the trial of Kimathi in a colonial court is the focal point of the play, there is no doubt that the postcolonial regime that has failed to live up to the ideals that the hero died for is itself on trial here. As the following exchange illustrates, enacting the past is one way in which characters and audiences can be asked to rethink their past as a way of questioning their present:

WOMAN: Sit down and eat slowly... If I were your mother, I would have you wash your filthy hands thoroughly, mend your clothes, wash them and teach you how to eat properly.
BOY: I have no mother.
WOMAN: You?
BOY: Yes. She died during childbirth.
WOMAN: And father?
BOY: Father was driven away from Mbari land in Nyeri by one of his relatives who worked as a court interpreter. Now that man is a big government chief and a big landowner. (*maliciously*): But I will never forget the day Kimathi's men burnt down his homeguard post. That post used to be the people's grave!
WOMAN: And don't I now know the man you are talking about?
BOY: H'm. The man was clever at court cases and bribed the magistrates.

(p. 18)

In this scene, there is an almost subliminal movement from the time when the action is set (the 1950s) and the period in which the play was performed (the late 1970s). First, the tenses being used here begin by confusing temporality; the linguistic exchange or the prepositional content of the scene refuses to distance it to a past that can easily be contained. In other words, the language used in this scene is designed to call attention to the presentness of the past: the father who lost his land during the emergency has obviously not regained it in the postcolonial period, and the relative who deprived him of the land (and was made a colonial chief in the bargain) has been further rewarded by the new government instead of being punished for his "sins" under colonialism. Secondly, when the woman says that she knows the man the boy is talking about, she is calling attention to one of the deepest anxieties of the ruling class in Kenya – the fear that too much discussion of this haunted period in the country's history might question the legitimacy of the new elite or that it might be "fingered" for its defense of colonialism.

In spatial terms, there is notable fluidity in the physical setting of the play and the meanings associated with different localities. We can understand this fluidity if we recall that in Ngugi's earlier plays, settings are clearly metaphorized: the city is a metaphor of postcolonial modernity while the country is associated with either pastoral values or intransigent traditions. In *The Trial of Dedan Kimathi*, on the other hand, settings are in the form of montages: a street scene quickly changes to the court scene (pp. 22–23); the encounter between the fruit-seller fades into Kimathi's cell (pp. 30-31); and the action in the third movement takes us from a street scene in Nyeri, to the Nyandarua forest, and back to the courtroom. During these movements and transitions, the play tries to both uphold and complicate different forms of social and cultural encounters. In one such encounter at the beginning of the play, for example, what is set up as the radical difference between the moral authority of the *matria* (in the person of the fruit-seller who is described as "*a mother, a fighter*" [p. 8]), and an African soldier fighting to maintain British rule, is suddenly turned into a site in which the two can mediate their mutual identity: "We are only ants trodden upon by heavy, merciless elephants" (p. 14). Similarly, in a memorable confrontation between a white settler and

Kimathi in court, the former is represented both as the index of colonial power and as a pathetic symbol of the failure of white authority in Kenya (pp. 28–29).

There is a remarkable spatial transition in the symbolic economy of the theatrical space itself: at the beginning of the play, as we have already observed, the court is organized around what Fanon has popularized as the Manichean allegory of colonial geography:[19]

In the court, blacks and whites sit on separate sides. It is as if a huge gulf lies between them. The air is still and tense. To break the tension, people on both sides try to make conversation in low voices. The clerk orders them to keep quiet – meaning the blacks more than the whites, but really to no people in particular. One of the settlers walks to the clerk and holds him up by the collar. (p. 23)

The writers provide this visual representation of the culture of colonialism in detail because they do not want its import to be missed: the colony is divided between Africans, who are poor and repressed and hence apt to identify with Kimathi's ideals, and powerful and prosperous white settlers who barely conceal their contempt for blacks and their loathing for the hero, whom they see as the embodiment of all the evils that threaten their privileged world.

In the course of the play, however, this Manichean organization of the stage – and, by implication, colonial society – is steadily undermined in two ways: first, it is exposed as a function of class, rather than racial relations, and is explicitly connected to the narrative of capitalism and acquisition. A case in point: when Henderson reminds Kimathi that the two share a common childhood background (pp. 34–35), he is suggesting that the huge gulf that separates them is not a natural one but the product of historical forces. Secondly, without racialism and discrimination (p. 45), the solidarity of the Africans is undermined by their different class backgrounds and interests: the African business executive, politician, and priest want the war to end for the same reasons as the settlers – it threatens their economic interests. And thus at the end of the play, the force of the Manichean allegory has been attenuated: *"Courtroom. But now the white people's side is joined by Politician, Business Executive, Priest, Banker, Gati, Gatotia, Hungu, Gaceru,*

Mwendanda – who occupy a bench at the very back and not proper chairs like the whites. The judge is in the chair. Kimathi is still in chains and heavily guarded as in the former court scene" (p. 79). The basic power relationship has not changed – the judge and Kimathi occupy unchangeable places in the power structure – but on another level, the gulf that separated Europeans from Africans has been narrowed, and in the process the terms of debate have shifted. Indeed, if the beginning of the play, by emphasizing racial divisions, made it palatable to a postcolonial elite because it was addressing the past in which they did not have any power, its ending, by deflating the significance of racial categories, has brought the debate up to the present that they dominate.

There is one area, however, in which *The Trial of Dedan Kimathi* operates within the conventions of traditional drama: the whole set of ideological conflicts dramatized in the play, and the numerous shifts in time and space discussed above, are stabilized by the presence of the hero and the ideals he represents. The figure of Dedan Kimathi is, in fact, Ngugi's point of entry into the debate on postcoloniality in Kenya; the drama is motivated by the authors' need to discover the "real" Kimathi beneath the mythologies and debates in the postcolony and to perform his identity and idealism as a way of mediating a complex set of questions about power and ideology in Kenya:

We agreed that the most important thing was for us to reconstruct imaginatively our history, envisioning the world of the Mau Mau and Kimathi in terms of the peasants' and workers' struggle before and after constitutional independence. The play is not a reproduction of the farcical "trial" at Nyeri. It is rather an imaginative recreation and interpretation of the collective will of the Kenyan peasants and workers in their refusal to break under sixty years of colonial torture and ruthless oppression by the British ruling classes and their continued determination to resist exploitation, oppression and new forms of enslavement. (Preface)

There is a very revealing contradiction in this statement of purpose: Ngugi and Mugo want to rescue a real Kimathi from the mythologies of colonial writers, but they also want to go beyond the mimetic function this process entails. They do not want to reproduce the heroism of Kimathi as it emerges in "reality" at the "farcical" trial in Nyeri; on the contrary, they want to go beyond this reality and discover a collective identity in the heroic. In representing Kimathi's trial, they hope to turn his personal anguish into something larger than the individual figure. And thus, it is in the process of performing the hero's individual struggles that the authors hope that the collective will can be recreated and interpreted. But how do you turn the hero – inherently defined as a unique individual – into the symbol of collective desires and intentions? What is the status of the historical in *The Trial of Dedan Kimathi*?

One way of responding to these questions is to argue that the authors' representation of Kimathi is part of their attempt to produce a heroic individual who can symbolize the aspirations of the nation in its moments of trial and also fulfill the audience's desire for a narrative that will help them to understand their repressed history. This is the way David Cook and Michael Okenimkpe have read the play:

Mythologizing is not falsification. Selected images, events, speeches and individuals embody certain needs of a people. Myths draw upon history. But writers who develop national myths are using history as part of a continuing process that can help determine and shape the future by encouraging certain possibilities in society and perhaps discouraging others. To such writers history is not static, but is material out of which social and economic realities have created the present, providing various openings for the future. The historical Kimathi is important to Ngugi and Micere Mugo as a man whose work must be projected into the future. So their play selects facets of his life-story which can inspire an audience to action in the present. Thus his ideas and what he stood and stands for must be re-interpreted by the writers in terms of the different circumstances of the present time.[20]

But much more than mythologizing and social projection is going on in this play: the authors are also attempting to deconstruct the Kenyan national mythology and to provide an alternative view of the past at the same time. These two functions explain how Kimathi is represented on stage as both the icon of the anticolonial struggle and the phantom that haunts the official narrative of the past. The Kenyan audience certainly comes to see the play with the preconceived image of Kimathi as both a mythological figure (a national hero) and the symbol of the postcolony's inability to come to terms with its harrowed past. As a result, the more vexed question that the play raises is how the figure of Kimathi can be made to represent the postcolony's complex – imaginary – relationship with the past. This complexity is indeed part of the thick description that surrounds the play: it is evident in the portrait of the hero on the cover of the published play, a portrait that all the actors playing the part of Kimathi fashioned themselves after, a portrait that many in the audience remember from colonial era newsreels and newspaper pictorials. Presented by the colonial government as the face of the unrepentant terrorist, this image is now appropriated as a symbol of defiance and courage, an irresistible part of the national iconography.

What needs to be interrogated further is not the ideological message of the play – this is banal even in its best moments – but the condition of reception of this drama. For ultimately the authority of this play depends on how Kimathi connects or disconnects readers and viewers to Ngugi's version of Kenya's recent past. In the authors' view, the figure of Kimathi in chains is a sign of his defiance against the colonial machinery of oppression: "To a criminal judge, in a criminal court, set up by a criminal law: the law of oppression. I have no words" (*Trial*, p. 25). But how does this claim appear to a primarily middle-class audience that is still apprehensive of the powerful forces Kimathi represented a generation ago? It is highly likely that members of the audience will identify with, and applaud, Kimathi's defiance so long as it is directed at tangible symbols of colonial oppression. So long as Kimathi is portrayed and received as the embodiment of a symbol of black defiance against white racism, the only people who would be threatened by the play are the last remnants of settler power in Kenya. Indeed, when the play was produced at the National Theatre in Nairobi in 1976, opposition toward it did not come from the Kenyatta government, but from established settler interests who tried to stifle it using their powerful connections in the office of the Attorney General.[21]

But so long as Kimathi was portrayed or perceived in racialist, anticolonial terms, the authors were failing in their primary objective to turn the figure of the hero into a dramatic symbol of the

failure of the postcolonial Kenyan government to live up to the
ideals of the liberation. Aware of this danger, the writers tried to
preempt it through two devices. The first device was the representation of oppression in colonial Kenya as determined by class
rather than racial interests. The challenge facing the authors here
was how to make sure that what had taken place in a courtroom in
Nyeri (in 1956) could be represented as an event that could speak
to the postcolonial present (1976). Here, a useful device was the
universalization of Dedan Kimathi – his presentation as the symbol of oppressed people everywhere, a free-floating signifier in
time and space. The most obvious symbol of this universalization
was the representation of Kimathi (on stage) as a Christ-like figure,
a man subject to temptations, like Jesus in the wilderness, often
struggling to rely on the strength of his people to compensate for
his own weaknesses, and yet often "sitting on hot coals of trials and
temptations" (p. 44). Like Jesus on trial, Ngugi's Kimathi is torn
between conflicting demands and needs; filled by hopes and expectations, his soul is often in chains (p. 45). While Kimathi, like
Jesus, is finally able to put his doubts behind him it is in the process
of doing so that he is revealed as both man and superman: he is
ordinary because, like us, he has desires, doubts, and false hopes;
but he is more than us because he has been able to overcome the
temptations of betrayal.

And yet, one of the most complex aspects of the play is the way
Kimathi's individuality is underscored at the very moment he is
asked to play a messianic role. This is evident toward the end of the
play when Ngugi and Mugo call attention to some of the most
contentious aspects of the hero's private life even as they foreground his mythical status. In the last scene in the Nyandarua
forest, for example, Kimathi is shown to be a sentimental man,
attached to his family and fighting-men and women, and imprisoned in childhood nostalgia (pp. 75–78); but he is also shown to
be a tough and – perhaps – merciless commander ready to have
those who have deviated from the path of his movement executed
(p. 79). What is significant, however, is how both his strengths and
weaknesses are framed by some powerful insignias of deification;
these include "The Song of Kimathi," which recalls the transfiguration of Jesus, and Kimathi's final valedictory speech, which

reminds us of Jesus before Pontius Pilate (pp. 82–83). It is in this evocation of a familiar Christian grammar, rather than through Marxist slogans, that the authors try to connect the events on the stage with a larger community of workers and peasants.

PERFORMANCE IN THE POSTCOLONY

With the writing and performance of *I Will Marry When I Want* in 1978, Ngugi was finally able to achieve his aesthetic ambition – to overcome the gap that separated his art and his politics. More than any of Ngugi's previous works, this play was going to function as something other than the depository of knowledge about the postcolonial situation, a knowledge that would be presented to a passive audience by an elite writer; on the contrary, the author and his collaborators were now seeking a form in which knowledge could be produced through enactment.[22] This shift from "observation" to "action" was implicit in Ngugi's critique of his previous works, including *The Trial of Dedan Kimathi*, considered to be one of his most radical plays:

> In 1976 I had collaborated with Micere Mugo in writing *The Trial of Dedan Kimathi*. In the preface to the published script we had written what amounted to a literary manifesto calling for a radical change in the attitude of African writers to fight with the people against imperialism and the class enemies of the people. We called for a revolutionary theatre facing the consequent challenge: how to truly depict "the masses in the only historically correct perspective: positively, heroically and as the true makers of history." We had gone on to define good theatre as that which was on the side of the people, "that which, without masking mistakes and weaknesses, gives people courage and urges them to higher resolves in their struggle for total liberation." But we never asked ourselves how this revolutionary theatre was going to urge people to higher resolves in a foreign language?[23]

What is important in this self-critique is not so much Ngugi's dissatisfaction with the language of theatre (although this was becoming crucial to Ngugi's cultural project), but the recantation of what the author had previously seen as the foundation of his writing, namely his claim that ideology, or content, was the most important thing in representation, and that form was secondary.

For what Ngugi was discovering, as he and his associate set out to script *I Will Marry When I Want* for the peasants at Kamĩrĩĩthũ, was that a work could not have an ideological effect except in performance. He had also come to realize that the essence of a work of art was not to be found in mimetic representation (the "historically correct perspective"), but in its reading or reception.[24]

A true revolutionary theatre, Ngugi had come to realize, was one that invited what he considered to be the "true makers of history" to become participants in the interpretation and representation of this history. If the postcolonial state had developed elaborate performances of control and rule, alternative performances like the ones that took place at Kamĩrĩĩthũ between 1977 and 1982 had the potential to disturb the way power was mediated in Kenya far more than the elaborate revolutionary tropes in novels such as *Petals of Blood*. Indeed, after Ngugi was arrested and imprisoned at the end of 1977 – an act that was intended to stop the production of *I Will Marry When I Want* – many of his readers wondered why he was being jailed for a work that did not contain anything he had not stated in *Petals of Blood*, which had been published only the year before. If the subversion of the work did not lie in its ideological message, surely it had something to do with its form. Our primary concern, then, is the formal aspects that made this a different kind of work.

We can begin by examining the function of the stage as a space of performance. Like Ngugi's earlier plays, the stage in *I Will Marry When I Want* aspires to the traditional Aristotelean unities of time, place, and character; but it goes beyond this formalized idea of the play as the representation of character in several respects: first, the play establishes a temporal unity which it then seeks to qualify. In other words, while the immediate action is set in postcolonial Kenya, the play moves back in time and space precisely because it is only in terms of such retrospection that the present can be understood. Now, this kind of movement is not unusual in itself (there are equally impressive flashbacks in Ngugi's earlier plays); what is significant is the way in which the play shifts the locus of causality. While the use of flashbacks in the earlier plays serves to explain the present and is hence secondary to it, the retrospective moment in *I Will Marry When I Want* is endowed with greater historical and political value.

Another way of presenting this problem is to note that although the play is about political and social problems that plague the postcolony, these problems are quite quotidian; the play speaks of issues which occupy everyday discourse – unemployment, marriage, corruption – and is thus not original in any sense of the word. Indeed, all the play does is reproduce on stage what everyone knows or does, and repeat discourses of everyday life that do not match the original experiences of the workers and peasants who are asked to put their lives on public display. It is in acknowledgment of this gap between experience and performance that the Gikuyu version refers to drama as "ithaako rĩa ngerekano" (which translates as both "let's pretend" and "a parable"). Whether it is considered a "let's pretend" or " a parable," a performance claims verisimilitude only momentarily; as soon as it is over, we are back in the real world where the issues the play has raised are real and obsessive.

In its retrospective moments, however, the play brings back memories and experiences which, because we do not experience them on an everyday basis, are bound to be more disturbing and subversive. Let us look at the subversive dimension of the play by examining a seminal scene in Act 1. The scene opens with a bold declaration of its political message through Kĩgũũnda's invectives against the postcolonial condition: in the forceful exchange between the peasant and his wife, daughter, and neighbors, the most obvious problems of the postcolonial condition are displayed – corruption, unemployment, landlessness, and the influence of foreign cultures and religions. The play would hence seem to present a familiar pattern in Ngugi's drama – its conflict emerges out of an opposition between the "haves" and "have nots"; its ideological message is going to be presented through a conversation that takes place on stage, one in which the audience is not involved. But the exchange between Kĩgũũnda and other subjects on the stage is not the gist of the performance. Indeed, from the perspective of the audience of peasants who came to see the play, this exchange has no value because, as I have already suggested, it is a banal representation of their "real life" experiences.

The real value of the performance lies in the flashbacks that follow Kĩgũũnda's invective, for his "going back in time" is not simply a recollection of his childhood and youth, but the recovery of the past which the postcolonial state has worked so hard to conceal and repress. Several points can be noted about the cultural grammar in which this recollection is presented: the past comes back to Kīgūūnda in the form of the songs and dances which colonial culture had banished as uncivil and subversive; the tone of the dialogue ranges from nostalgia to defiance, two emotions that connect the players and the audience to a time that many people in Kenya would prefer to forget; "the remembrance of things past" (*I Will Marry*, p. 26) is the performance of memory against the silence promoted by the state; the "habit of thinking too much about the past" (p. 29) is an emotive weapon against the official culture of silence.[25]

There is a second way in which this play is different from Ngugi's earlier works, including the texts Ngugi produced in the 1970s: it uses language as "a system in action" and makes oral forms of expression central to this system.[26] Let us examine these two aspects of the play by noting, with Fabian, that the performativity of a text does not depend on its ability to express "something in need of being brought to the surface, or to the outside"; rather performance is "the text in the moment of its actualization (in a story told, in a conversation carried on, but also in a book read)."[27] Our attention, then, should be focused on how the play actualizes the quotidian in the postcolony. It does this in some memorable ways. There is, for example, the elaborate presentation of interiors, decor, and costume. The play opens in Kīgūūnda's home:

Kīgūūnda's home. A square, mud-walled, white-ochred, one-roomed house. The white ochre is fading. In one corner can be seen Kīgūūnda's and Wangeci's bed. In another can be seen a pile of rags on the floor. The floor is Gathoni's bed and the rags, her bedding. Although poorly dressed, GATHONI is very beautiful. In the same room can be seen a pot on three stones. On one of the walls there hangs a framed title-deed for one and a half acres of land. Near the head of the bed, on the wall, there hangs a sheathed sword. On one side of the wall there hangs Kīgūūnda's coat, and on the opposite side, on the same wall, Wangeci's coat. The coats are torn and patched. A pair of tyre sandals and a basin can be seen on the floor. (I Will Marry, p. 3)

This description is remarkable for the way it actualizes the life of the Kenyan (or Gikuyu peasant) without using the romanticized or allegorical language in Ngugi's earlier plays; indeed, this scene draws its force of meaning from the way in which its ordinariness performs its symbolic (political) function. The walls and size of Kĩgũũnda's home are easily recognizable as signs of abject poverty in the postcolony, a point reinforced by the rags on the floor and the torn and patched coats. When we encounter the other protagonists of the play a little bit later, their livery indicates their class and social position: "AHAB KĨOI and JEZEBEL are dressed in a way that indicates wealth and wellbeing. But the NDŨGIRE family is dressed in a manner which shows that they have only recently begun to acquire property" (p. 42). In its setting, the play displays the obvious; there is no need for us to go out of our way in search of a deeper meaning.

In the moral economy of the postcolony, property and propriety are closely connected. Thus, in the third act of the play when Kĩgũũnda has temporally acquired some money, his change in social status is marked by the transformation of the interior of his house:

Kĩgũũnda's home. The interior is very different from what it was in previous scenes. A new dining table with chairs. On the table is a big suitcase, also new. New plates, cups, basins and so on. A suit hangs on the wall where Kĩgũũnda's old coat used to hang. On one wall hangs a picture of Nebuchadnezzar exactly like the one in Kĩoi's home. On the other wall, exactly on the spot where the title-deed used to be, now hangs a board with the inscription: 'Christ is the head ... etc," again like the one in Kĩoi's house. The title-deed is not now anywhere in the house. (p. 91)

It is through the insignias of wealth and class, rather than ideological utterances, that power relations are mediated and ultimately represented. Since the beginning of land consolidation in Kenya in the 1950s, an individual's claim to land ownership has been determined by the existence of an official title-deed which has come to be displayed – and valued – as an insignia of one's power and sense of identity. As Kĩgũũnda reminds his wife early in the play, the title-deed is the essence of his identity as a man and head of household (p. 14). But as the play progresses, the audience discovers that the title-deed has a double meaning and function: on the one hand, it is a representation of Kĩgũũnda's entitlement to his plot of land and a sign of what the Gikuyu edition refers to as "ũgĩmaru ngoro" – the maturing of mind and soul. On the other hand, however, the title-deed is a fetish in the Marxist sense of the term – it represents the subject's illusions about his own sense of power. It is this illusion that threatens to collapse every time peasant and bourgeois confront each other on stage:

As KĨOI and his group enter moving close to one wall of the house to avoid contact with the GICAAMBAS, one of them causes the title-deed to fall to the ground. They don't pick it up. And because of their worry about seats and the excitement at the arrival of the KĨOIS, KĨGŨŨNDA and his wife do not seem to have their minds on the fallen title-deed. GĨCAAMBA walks to the title-deed and picks it up. All eyes are now on GĨCAAMBA and they give way to him. GĨCAAMBA looks at the title-deed, then at the KĨOI group then at the KĨGŨŨNDA family. He hangs the title-deed back on the wall. GĨCAAMBA and NJOOKI go out. (p. 42)

Here, the representatives of two classes are brought together on stage and are asked to negotiate their relationship through the title-deed, the sign of the land whose ownership they contest. The theme of class conflict here is a familiar one in Ngugi's works; what has changed, however, is the grammar in which the working-class struggle is represented, for unlike in *The Trial of Dedan Kimathi*, the two sides cannot easily be divided into heroes and villains. Desiring the same object and seeking to occupy the same territory, neither Kĩoi nor Kĩgũũnda can claim the moral or ideological high ground; the title-deed hangs precariously between them, or falls on the ground as if to elude them; and Gĩcaamba stands between them as the hero of the play who is, nevertheless, relegated to its margins.

One of the most innovative aspects of the play is the way in which the authors ultimately reject the Aristotelean conflict on which the weight of their ideological argument was supposed to be built. The play opens by setting up a conflict between two forces or classes representing opposed moral and political interests. The allegorical separation of these two forces is most apparent in the setting of the stage and the names and demeanor of the principal characters: the stage directions make it clear that from their first encounter the Kĩoi and Kĩgũũnda families will be seen as "representing two opposing groups in the house" and that their attire will mark them as occupying different class positions (pp. 42–43). For the Gikuyu audience, this opposition is already apparent in the names the authors have given their principal characters: Kĩoi is the aggrandizer and the glutton while Kīgūūnda is a man of the soil, a simple peasant (p. 42). As the play progresses, the relationship between the opposing groups is complicated by their mutual desires, ambitions, and illusions. By the beginning of Act III, the Kīgūūnda home has become a poor imitation of the Kīoi household (pp. 91–92). But it is precisely at this moment of merging that the deep antagonism between the two classes is clarified as the network of relationships established in Act II is now shown to be fraudulent. After their brief moment of glory, the Kīgūūnda family has been beaten back to its ground zero: *"most of the new things are no longer there. The house is very much like the way it was at the beginning of the play except for the picture of Nebuchadnezzar and the board with the inscription 'Christ is the head' which still hangs from the walls as if in mockery"* (pp. 103–04).

At this stage in the play, it would appear as if the peasantry has been beaten back by the bourgeoisie. But this is not exactly the case, for what happens, in dramaturgical terms at least, is that both Kīoi and Kīgūūnda are evacuated from the scene of performance to create a space for Gīcaamba, who, having hovered around the opposing camps like an apparition, becomes the moral center of the play and the conscience of the betrayed national consciousness (p. 113). Now, Gīcaamba's ideological pronouncements at the end of the play may appear familiar to the readers of Ngugi's earlier plays, as does the call and response performance that brings everything to closure, but this should not make us oblivious to the formal innovations Ngugi and his co-author make in the conclusion to *I Will Marry When I Want*. For beneath Gīcaamba's call for heroic struggle and the response that takes up themes of revolution and renewal, the play as a whole is an attempt to represent complex relationships that arrested decolonization has engendered. This is a play about class struggle. But it is also a play on the conflicts between parents and their children, between generations and genders, all struggling to make sense of the postcolony and its phantasms. And in trying to make sense of this world, these subjects deploy a set of conflicting languages and cultural codes. It is in an attempt to represent this world on stage that Ngugi turns to orality and popular culture.

The significance of this play to Ngugi's *œuvre* is to be found not so

much in his decision to write in Gikuyu, but how in writing about –
and for – a Gikuyu audience he is able to capture the multiple
idioms, axioms, and registers through which common people
make sense of postcoloniality. One way of understanding this turn
to the oral and the popular is to examine both how particular
idioms and registers are deployed in the play and how characters
shift from one cultural grammar to another and, more importantly, how their use of language transforms old notions about oral and
popular forms. Consider, for example, the use of proverbs in the
play. As in many African texts, proverbs are evoked in *I Will Marry
When I Want* as insignias of traditional wisdom and are thus often
used to buttress arguments against the vices of modern society,
such as alcoholism (p. 5) and excessive individualism (p. 13), or to
celebrate virtues such as prudence and thrift (pp. 17, 18). Such
examples are spread throughout the text. So are "sayings" that
promote caution (pp. 21, 33) or seek to regulate conduct (p. 73).
Many original readers of the play will recognize these proverbs
and sayings either because of their poetic quality or linguistic
structure, and they will easily see how they enable the characters to
negotiate individual and communal relationships and make sense
of the postcolonial universe. Proverbs and sayings enable the
characters – and by extension the audience – to have a grasp of
their increasingly complex world. But for Ngugi's immediate audience, these two figures of discourse have a more urgent function:
they are recognizable as figures of speech that come directly from
the established corpus of Gikuyu proverbs; many of the sayings
belong to a genre attributed to the founding father of "the Gikuyu
nation."[28]

The continuous use of songs in the play offers an interesting
contrast to the traditionalism of proverbs and sayings, for it is truly
in the range and genre of songs used in the play that the multiplicity of idioms is manifested. Indeed, the contestation of the national
space between different classes and sects is rehearsed and performed through song and dance. Let us examine a few examples
briefly: first, there is the deployment of song and dance as an
expression of nostalgia and longing: overwhelmed and dislocated
by the political culture of the postcolony, Kĩgũũnda recalls the
Mĩcũũng'wa dance of his youth, which is in turn performed by

"actual dancers," to capture the awakening of Gikuyu youth to the nationalist dream (pp. 11–13). What is intriguing, however, is the way the song moves beyond the character's nostalgia to represent the collective longing of what has come to be known as the generation of the 1940s in Central Kenya, a longing that expresses this generation's rejection of colonial rule in elegiac tones:

> *Mother ululate for me,*
> *For if I don't die young I'll one day sing songs of victory.*
> *Oh, yes, come what come may*
> *If I don't die young I'll one day sing songs of victory.* (p. 12)

Secondly, songs and dances function as important instruments of historical commentary. Indeed, if the primary theme of the play is that the failure of postcolonial culture can be explained by the betrayal of national consciousness, it is through songs and dances that this culture is confronted by its historical repressed. The dances and songs that are foregrounded in the play – dances such as Nyaangwicu and Mwomboko – are the dances of youthful self-assertion, which are now recalled within a context of failure, betrayal, and a sense of loss. Thus, mesmerized by "memories of their past youth" (p. 22), or "engrossed in memories of the past," Kĩgũũnda and Wangeci resort to songs and dances from the past to indict the present.

Finally, the language and tone of these songs is intended to provide a counterpoint to the rhetoric of forgetfulness promoted by the postcolonial state and its cultural institutions.[29] The official discourse insists that the painful past must be transcended if the country is to move forward into a brave new future; it insists that the roles played by different actors during the colonial period must be repressed for the sake of a common ideology of nationhood. In contrast, the popular songs in the play are about self-conscious remembering; they enact the act of memory itself. By valorizing "bitter memories" such songs encourage the "habit of thinking too much about the past" (p. 29), which is the habit of cultural vigilance: "*Where is Waiyaki's grave today? / We must protect our patriots / So they don't meet Waiyaki's fate*" (p. 28). I consider these songs to be the key to understanding the ultimate political function of Ngugi's play because as popular, or well-known songs, they invite the audience to participate in the performance, to connect the experiences of everyday life with the aesthetic object (the drama) on stage. And in abrogating the separation of the aesthetic object and the lived experience, such songs – and the play as a whole – come to challenge the dominant discourse of the state. In the process, they set a new pattern for Ngugi's subsequent works.

CHAPTER 7

The prisonhouse of culture: Detained *and* Devil on the Cross

Sometime in 1977, a few days after Ngugi was promoted to the position of Associate Professor of Literature at the University of Nairobi, the first African to hold a position that had been left unfilled since the departure of the last group of British expatriates in the department, Okot p'Bitek, the Ugandan poet and one of the strongest advocates of popular culture in East Africa, expressed the fear that the novelist had finally become a member of the intellectual establishment. Okot p'Bitek's fear was that now that Ngugi had been accepted by the institutions of education and power in Kenya, he could no longer be interested in incorporating popular and oral culture into his work or the literature curriculum.[1] But these fears were soon proven unfounded, because precisely at the time that he was being invited into the inner sanctuaries of University governance, Ngugi was embarking on the theatrical experiment at Kamĩrĩĩthũ discussed in the previous chapter. And as throngs of workers, peasants, and students boarded buses and trucks to see the performance of *I Will Marry When I Want*, p'Bitek was impressed enough to declare the experiment at Kamĩrĩĩthũ the most important event on the African literary and cultural scene in the postcolonial period. For the first time, p'Bitek told an Oral Literature Seminar at the University of Nairobi, intellectuals had taken culture to the people and the people were teaching them the terms by which they understood and represented cultural experiences and expressions.[2]

Reflecting on the impact of Kamĩrĩĩthũ on his own aesthetic practice in *Decolonising the Mind*, Ngugi described the changes that were taking place in his thinking and writing as nothing short of "an epistemological break."[3] What did this claim imply? What kind of revolution was taking at Kamīrīīthū and how did it affect the direction of Ngugi's literary career? While it is true that the works immediately preceding *I Will Marry When I Want* had advocated revolutionary political change in postcolonial Kenya using the language of Marxist-Leninism, what was happening in Kamīrīīthū was a revolution of a different kind: it was foregrounding not the philosophy or theory of change, nor valorizing the programs under which change would take place, but imagining change in a more immediate and assessable form. The choice of language and audience had helped Ngugi overcome the gap between history as an experience and object of analysis and its status as an everyday experience; as the writer put it succinctly, by making the victims of colonialism actors in their own history, there was now "no barrier between the content of their history and the linguistic medium of its expression."[4] If the elaborate critique of postcolonialism in Ngugi's monumental works in English, most notably *Petals of Blood*, had struck readers as unreal and alienating, the language of *I Will Marry When I Want* was the language of everyday rituals, conversations, and politics. As I have already noted, the drama itself was actually not imaginative or original; its title, like many of its motifs, came directly from the cultural grammar of workers and peasants. Its political force lay in its ability to give this grammar – and the political disenchantment it bore – a stage on which it could be expressed publicly. In providing a platform for airing disenchantment, the author and his collaborators were turning the literary experience into a systematic critique of the culture of postcoloniality and were thus posing a direct threat to the political authority of the state.

THE WRITER IN POLITICS

Here is Ngugi's account of how the Kenyan state struck back at the country's most famous writer in the last two days of 1977:

It was at midnight on 30–31 December 1977 at Gitogoothi, Bibirioni, Limuru. Two Land-Rovers with policemen armed with machine-guns, rifles and pistols drove into the yard. A police saloon car remained at the main gate flashing red and blue on its roof, very much like the Biblical sword of fire policing the ejection of Adam and Eve from the legendary

Garden of Eden by a God who did not want human beings to eat from trees of knowledge, for the stability of Eden and his dictatorship over it depended on people remaining ignorant about their condition. Behind the saloon car were others which, as I later came to learn, carried some local administrative officials and the local corps of informers... Armed members of the special branch who swarmed and searched my study amidst an awe-inspiring silence were additionally guarded by uniformed policemen carrying long range rifles. Their grim determined faces would only light up a little whenever they pounced on any book or pamphlet bearing the names of Marx, Engels or Lenin.[5]

The scene of Ngugi's arrest is a classical representation of the "nervous condition" of the postcolonial state and its performance of power as a counterpoint to its ideological poverty; the power of the state lies not so much in the actual manifestation of power, but its fictional representation or performance of its presumed supremacy.[6]

It is a familiar scene in the postcolony: the state appears to the writer in the middle of the night like a ghost endowed with the authority of the law. The symbolic identity of the state emerges as much from its capacity to arrest and imprison one of its subjects without cause and due process as its willingness to flaunt its instruments of death. The state manifests itself in the ideological masks it wears, masks that derive their power from their inscrutability and their existence beyond law and reason.[7] The imaginary power of the state is also represented in both the nervousness of the agents of power – the police, administrative officials, and informers – and their "awe-inspiring silence." In the midst of it all is the figure of the writer, the representative of bourgeois heroism, standing up against the tyranny of power, reflecting on the performance of terror from the security of romantic irony: "I could not help musing over the fact that the police squadron was armed to the teeth with guns to abduct a writer whose only acts of violent resistance were safely between the hard and soft covers of literary imaginative reflections," Ngugi notes (p. 16).

In *Detained*, Ngugi's memoir of his arrest and imprisonment, there is a clear opposition between state power and writing, or rather, aesthetic reflection. Indeed, one of the primary themes of this memoir and *Devil on the Cross*, the novel Ngugi wrote during his imprisonment, is the power of art to unmask the state by exposing its moral bankruptcy; writing is here presented as one of the most potent instruments against "the culture of silence." The writer's survival against the elaborate labyrinth of deception and the chain of oppressive institutions is celebrated as the triumph of the human spirit against all forms of tyrannical power. If one then accepts the basic ideological and formal chronology I have presented in this study – a chronology that sees Ngugi's career as beginning with a problematic acceptance of the liberal ideology of culture promoted by the high priests of the great tradition, which is ultimately rejected in favor of the Marxist doctrine of culture as a weapon of ideological struggle – the two works under discussion here present us with a series of difficult questions: did Ngugi's celebration of the artist's triumph over adversity in both *Detained* and *Devil on the Cross* mean that he was revalorizing the aesthetic as an autonomous category with values that could be pitted against those of political economy? Were his new works now to be read as attempts to rethink the doctrine of collective action and struggle enunciated in *Petals of Blood* in preference to the action of heroic individuals such as himself (in *Detained*) or similar artistic figures such as Wariinga and Gatuiria in *Devil on the Cross?* Did Ngugi's strenuous sensitivity to formal issues mean that he had abandoned or qualified the operative maxim in his Marxist heyday, the belief that content was the overdetermining category in the shaping of a literary work?[8]

We can approach these questions as they emerge in *Detained* by calling attention to an often forgotten aspect of Ngugi's prison memoir: his use of the space of incarceration, the prison and the cell, as a site of self-reflection and as an occasion for establishing affiliation with the tradition of literary resistance as it is represented in the genre that Barbara Harlow has called "prison literature."[9] Ngugi characterizes his memoirs as a series of notes, suggesting that they are somehow spontaneous reflections on his imprisonment and the set of issues it raises for him as a person, as a writer, and as an intellectual. But this foregrounding of the fragmentary and disconnected is deceptive, not only because the whole memoir is concerned with states of historical and cultural continuity, but also because what might appear to be random notes are structured by the presence of the body of the writer, a body which, because its very survival is under threat, acquires moral authority in the process of writing. What gives the memoir coherence, then, is the presence of the writer as a human being rather than a narrator; what makes this memoir an authoritative statement on the fetishism of the state is that the author's painful prison experiences are recalled from the vantage point of his release, what he presents as his triumph over adversity. Another way of presenting this problem is to note that the political arguments Ngugi makes in his memoir depend as much on their theoretical cogency as on his ability to gain empathy from his readers. Ngugi now writes about state power, not as something read in texts on authoritarianism, but from his own personal experiences in the dungeon of postcoloniality. Above all, he places his own subjectivity and survival at the center of the narrative. "I am not trying to write a story of sentimental heroism," Ngugi writes as if to disclaim the argument I am making here. "I am only a stammerer who tries to find articulate speech in scribbled words" (*Detained*, p. 97).

And yet what we have in this document is not stammering but eloquence, and this eloquence has two important consequences for the meaning and shape of the memoir of imprisonment and the novel that came out of this experience. First of all, since the state, in imprisoning the writer, had sought to silence him, it is in this prison that Ngugi faces the test – and temptation – of the culture of silence. As the author notes in his preface to *Detained*, certain influential forces in the Kenyan government had argued for his detention in order to teach him "a lesson in submission, silence, and obedience" (p. xi). The memoir is thus both a testimony to the author's resistance to the culture of silence and a weapon in the discursive wars in the postcolony, which are ultimately rhetorical battles over the territory of representation and interpretative authority. In his preface to *Detained*, and in key moments in the memoir, Ngugi insists that he saw his adversaries not as individuals but as representatives of "certain social forces"; by the same token, he casts his ideological and interpretative position in class and social terms:

I have, therefore, tried to discuss detention not as a personal affair between me and a few individuals, but as a social, political and historical phenomenon. I have tried to see it in the context of the historical attempts, from colonial times to the present, by a foreign imperialist bourgeoisie, in alliance with its local Kenyan representatives, to turn Kenyans into slaves, and of the historical struggles of Kenyan people against economic, political and cultural slavery. (*Detained*, p. xi)

But no sooner has Ngugi evacuated what one may call the subjective interest from the discursive wars of the postcolony than he is forced to acknowledge the ways in which class positions and personal backgrounds intertwine in the saga of his imprisonment. The attacks launched on the author by Charles Njonjo, the influential Attorney General and theoretician of the Kenyatta regime, are clearly cast in terms which are as class-based as they are personal; in the culture that colonialism built, it is difficult to speak about one category (class) except in terms of the other (the self): "There was, of course, every reason to make Charles Njonjo attack me, even while I was in detention. It is not merely a question of background (he is the son of a colonial chief while I am the son of a peasant) but more of a difference in the perception of our roles vis-à-vis the struggle of Kenyan national culture against foreign imperialist cultures" (p. xxi). Ngugi had tried to write about his prison experiences in the most objective way – in the context of a "social, political and historical phenomenon" – but as the reaction to *Detained* was to show, this memoir was to become his most subjective work and was always in danger of being read as a "personal affair" between him and those who had imprisoned him.

My contention, of course, is that rather than deny this subjectivity, which is inherent in the genre of the memoir, we should see it as the key to understanding *Detained* as an integral part of Ngugi's *œuvre*. I would like to suggest that it is precisely because of the centering of the self in the narrative of imprisonment that Ngugi is able to allegorize his own experiences and turn them into fables of the class struggle in the postcolony and the imcomplete history of decolonization. Everything revolves around the moral authority that detention bestows on the writing self. In this respect, the memoir begins by posing an intriguing question about the space of writing: "What are the limits of the sphere of an author's operations?" (p. xx). This is perhaps the question that haunts him most during his detention and after, as he tries to justify the choices he has had to make as an author writing against the instrumental culture of the state.

Haunted by doubts about the choices he has had to make and the consequences he had to bear, Ngugi looks around his cell and wonders how the writing self can maintain its integrity in chains and outside its normal spheres of operation. And if writing now seems to have an urgency it did not have before, if it appears to be a question of survival rather than social commentary, it is because the fate of the writing self can no longer be taken for granted. In his first day in prison Ngugi finds himself turned into someone other than what he had always assumed himself to be, deprived of the name that had made him internationally famous, and stripped of an identity nurtured and protected in his writings. In Kamiti Maximum Security Prison, his country's most infamous prison, where the bones of his beloved "Mau Mau" hero Dedan Kimathi are interred in an unmarked grave, Ngugi is reduced to a number: "12 December 1978: I am in cell 16 in a detention block enclosing eighteen other political prisoners. Here I have no name. I am just a number in a file: K6,77. A tiny iron frame against one wall serves as a bed and a tiny board against another wall serves as a desk. These fill up the minute cell" (p. 3).

If we think of the implications of this erasure of self – what does it mean for an author to exist without a name? – we can begin to understand why liberal categories such as individualism become central to Ngugi's struggle to survive in prison. The writing self is quarantined from the world that has hitherto provided it with raw materials for fiction; the writer's body has been denied the movement and space in which narrative thrives, the privacy in which poetic language is produced, and the freedom that makes self-expression possible (p. 6). Imprisonment is here represented, in typical bourgeois terms, as a systematic threat to the integrity of selfhood. The state seeks to imprison the soul and to destroy his imagination and cultural capital: "Despite the efforts of my fellow detainees, the feeling of being alone would often steal into me and I would be seized with the momentary panic of a man drowning in a sea of inexplicable terror" (p. 21). In order to resist this feeling, Ngugi privileges his own subjectivity – and his voice – as the condition of possibility of being and becoming; writing is the only

guarantee that the self and its voice cannot be repressed (p. 11).
And thus, everything that happens in the world of the prisoner
becomes a symbol of the forces that help the self in its struggle
against social death.[10] The child who is born when the father is in
prison is seen as "A message from the world. A message of hope. A
message that somewhere outside these grey walls of death were
people waiting for me, thinking about me, perhaps even fighting,
with whatever weapons, for my release" (p. 12). Such messages of
solidarity appear, to "a person condemned to isolation," like
"Joshua's trumpets that brought down the legendary walls of
Jericho" (p. 27).

A second point follows from the above celebration of the integrity of selfhood: it has to do with Ngugi's celebration of his identity
as a writer and a reader, of his self-conscious deployment of the
literary text as one way of breaking down the psychology of
imprisonment. The memoir proper opens with a defiant invocation of a fictional character – "Wariinga ngatha ya wĩra"
(Wariinga heroine of labor [p 1]) – that presages Ngugi's claim,
much later in the book, that his creation *Devil on the Cross* under
conditions of imprisonment was his mark of triumph against the
state). Throughout the memoir, the act of writing is posited as the
ultimate defiance against state terror. But even more important is
Ngugi's location of himself in his new prison community as a
writer and a reader; his anchor remains literature, or rather, the
literary canon of postcolonial writing in Africa.

There is another way of presenting this location of the writer in
the politics of state terror. From the very beginning of the memoir,
readers of African prison literature cannot fail to notice the important role intertextuality plays in *Detained*; it is through the
intertext that Ngugi links himself to other writers in the African
postcolonial scene. Indeed, Ngugi's experiences of prison is not
original because it has, by his own reckoning, been represented for
him in prior texts by Kwame Nkrumah, Dennis Brutus, Wole
Soyinka and Abdilatif Abdalla (p. 6). This turn to literature is
noticeable as much for its pragmatism as for its irony. Consider the
fact that before his imprisonment, Ngugi was a radical lecturer in
African literature who was known to be dismissive of writers like
Brutus and Soyinka for their bourgeois individuality and senti-

mentality.[11] Now, as he seeks literary guides through the labyrinthian world of Kamiti prison, he is forced to reread these writers anew: "I used to teach Dennis Brutus' book of poems, *Sirens Knuckles Boots*, but I never really understood the title. Now I do. I read his *Letters to Martha* more avidly. His opening letter captures very accurately the emotions of a new political prisoner" (p. 144).

Rereading other African writers' experiences of imprisonment, Ngugi develops the means of understanding and representing his postcolonial interdictors. Indeed, scenes of imprisonment in this work are often presented in a figurative language that belies the harsh realities of prison life. In the first part of the memoir, in particular, Ngugi is keen to represent the act of political detention in its "exemplary ritual symbolism": the huge prison gates open "like the jaws of a ravenous monster" (p. 19), its walls "still dripped with the blood of the many Kenyan patriots who had been hanged there for their courageous Mau Mau guerilla struggle against British imperialism" (p. 19); the "petty and childish" rituals of imprisonment are followed to the letter "by bemedalled officers and decorated warders" (p. 19). As the following description of the prison chaplain shows, the banality of postcoloniality can only be captured in its perverse irony and *bêtise*:

He was in a prison officer's uniform of khaki trousers and jumper-coat lined with aluminum buttons and a decoration of two or three stones on the shoulder flaps. He also carried the hallmark of all prison officers and warders – a cord over the left shoulder carrying a whistle hidden in the breast-pocket. But underneath these symbols of oppression, he wore the holy uniform of a reverend: a black cloak ending in a white collar round the neck. He appeared to me, at the moment, the very embodiment of an immense neo-colonial evil let loose over our beautiful Kenya. (pp. 22–23)

Ngugi's romance of the Kenyan nation, a romance built on such archetypal tropes as patriotism and identification with the motherland, meets its ultimate test in prison; unprotected by the *matria* and no longer able to invoke his patriotism because the emotive identification with the motherland can no longer be justified, the imprisoned writer seeks to understand the failure of nationalism by psychoanalyzing the national body.

The second chapter of *Detained* sets out to interrogate the culture of postcolonial tyranny by tracing it to its colonial antecedents.

Here, Ngugi seeks to establish the cause of the "pitfalls of national consciousness" and to locate the origins of the disease that has afflicted his beloved nation without tarnishing the ideals of decolonization. The psychoanalysis of the national body is cast in the form of a dialectic. The culture of colonialism is, first, represented as the site of vacuity and negation; narratives of anticolonial resistance are recuperated as the antithesis of colonial emptiness, but they are also shown as disabled by both colonial and anticolonial power. The Kamĩrĩĩthũ project is then seen as the return, as it were, of the nationalist repressed, presenting us with a site in which the questions left unanswered by decolonization are flushed out into the open.

With regard to the first movement, Ngugi makes the assumption that the English who settled in Kenya during the colonial period did not create a culture worthy of note; even the works of Elspeth Huxley, the most popular settler writer in Kenya, do not amount to anything more than "anaemic settler polemics": "Beyond the title and the glossy covers, there is only emptiness, and emptiness as a defence of oppression has never made a great subject for literature" (p. 30). The settler class flaunted its mastery of the theatre as a mark of its civility and continued to fight for exclusive rights to the Kenyan National Theatre well into the 1980s, but what was presented as the last refuge of Western civilization and bourgeois civility in the colony, argues Ngugi, was itself a sign of the cultural bankruptcy of the settler class: "Their theatre, professional and amateur, never went beyond crude imitation and desperate attempts to keep up with the West End or Broadway. This theatre never inspired a single original script or actor or critic" (p. 30).

In his attack on the cultural bankruptcy of the settler class in Kenya, Ngugi seems to be arguing against one of the most persistent claims in postcolonial studies – the claim that colonialism was ultimately about culture and cultural production – and to scorn any idea that a dominant class could produce affirmative culture.[12] The lasting images of colonial governance are not manifested in aesthetic ideals, but in insignias of brutality and oppression – "The rickshaw. The dog. The *Sjambok*. The ubiquitous underfed, wide-eyed, uniformed native slave" (p. 32). Rethinking the culture of colonial settlement from behind bars, and rereading the annals of conquest and rule, Ngugi is able to make a logical link between the culture that decolonization was supposed to have transcended – the culture of silence and fear – and the postcolonial economy of terror (pp. 34–43).

In order to deal with this inherited terror, however, Ngugi is impelled to a second discursive movement, one that privileges African resistance to colonial rule as the ultimate moment of cultural production in Kenya. In some of the most lyrical passages in his memoir, Ngugi both commemorates and affiliates himself with the insurgency against colonial rule and the counter-discourse it generates. If settler culture was symbolized either by its emptiness or its organs of oppression, the narrative of resistance emerges from the ashes of history in the form of its heroic figures, the phoenixes of anticolonial struggle, as it were. The romance of resistance moves us against the arbitrary logic of colonial laws and jails. Demonized as a witch in the colonial text, Me Kitilili, the Giriama resistance leader, is transformed by Ngugi into an icon of the purest ideals of nationalism – vision, courage, and patriotism. Arrested and deported to the Kenyan highlands, Me Kitilili nevertheless rises from her prison to haunt the colonial machinery of power:

And now comes an even more remarkable feat from this woman. On 14 January 1914, Me Kitilili and her fellow detainee escaped from prison and with help from friendly patriots of the other Kenyan nationalities, they walked all the way back to the coast to continue the resistance. Rewards were announced for any person or persons who would assist in the recapture of this brave Kenyan. She was eventually caught on 7 August 1914, and detained. But she remained proud, defiant and unrepentant to the very end. Me Kitilili had rejected the colonial culture of fear and the slave consciousness it sought to instill in Kenyans. (p. 48)

Now, while Ngugi's version of these histories of resistance has been contested by Kenyan historians writing from a different ideological perspective, the issue raised by his discourse here concerns not so much the veracity or authenticity of his narrative of history but the effect he seeks to provoke in his readers as he tries to locate himself in the postcolonial landscape. Indeed, these narratives are not useful for what they tell us about the Kenyan past, but in their attempt to provide a handle on the present. In addition, while Ngugi creates a clear bipolar opposition between the culture of colonialism and figures of resistance against it – an opposition in which the pedantic grammar of colonialism is no match for the poetry of patriotism – there is no doubt that, viewed from the vantage point of decolonization, both positions prove inadequate. Why? Perhaps because both colonialism and nationalism are incomplete projects. Colonialism is most apparently incomplete because it has lost its absolute power and aura. True, Ngugi's main argument in the memoir is that beneath the veneer of independence, the postcolonial state has taken on the oppressive mantle of colonialism. The law that allows for his detention without trial, to cite one prominent example, has had a continuous history that runs from the 1897 Native Courts Regulation to the Public Security Regulations of 1966; what lies between the two events is just "sweet semantics" (p. 51).

And yet, for the postcolonial government such "sweet semantics" were central to the political and cultural legitimacy of the postcolonial elite in Kenya because, although the first Kenyatta government did not abolish many settler laws or institutions, it went out of its way to denounce the discourse of racial discrimination and to get rid of the insignias of settler hegemony – the rickshaw, the dog, and the *Sjambok*. In cultural terms, nothing allowed the postcolonial elite to consolidate its position more quickly than its ability to argue that it was an instrument of "true" nationalism and to celebrate African culture as the most obvious symbol of independence. Although the project of decolonization appeared incomplete when one saw the extent to which pro-British loyalists dominated the Kenyatta government, the most vivid reminder of the cultural transformations taking place in Kenya was the way the government promoted some aspects of African culture, especially so-called traditional dances, that had been banned by the colonial authorities.

In his memoirs, however, Ngugi wants to locate the spirit of "true" nationalism outside the activities of official nationalists such as Kenyatta, in the practices of earlier figures of resistance against colonial rule whom history seems to have forgotten; it is in such figures that he finds the virtues of patriotism and the romance of the *patria*. But the discourse of resistance he celebrates in figures such as Me Kitilili is also incomplete for the simple reason that this discourse could neither outlive colonialism nor be sanctioned by postcolonial culture. If Ngugi's narrative turns melancholic when he reflects on the resurrection of the "colonial Lazarus" (p. 62), it is because, against the background of a great "historical betrayal," he is aware of the belatedness of the romance of heroism.

Detained is a utopian memoir because it seeks to resurrect the heroes of Kenyan nationalism who are out of place in the post-colonial order of things. Its material and psychic condition of production, however, calls into question the efficacy of such efforts. Ngugi's desire for a romance of national resistance is overwhelmed by the feeling, shared by his fellow detainees, that "something beautiful, something like the promise of a new dawn had been betrayed, and our presence and situation at Kamiti Maximum Security Prison was a logical outcome of that historical betrayal" (p. 63). Betrayal generates melancholia and "bitter reflections"; in order to beat back the "devil of despair" (p. 65), the imprisoned self elects "another history, a beautiful history, a glorious history" (p. 64). But the prisoner soon discovers that the history of insurgency is a beleaguered history, surrounded by temptations and the weaknesses of the soul. As he reflects on the history of resistance to colonialism in Kenya, Ngugi either commemorates the heroic dead (and creates some powerful elegiac prose), or comes face to face with figures of insurgency, such as Harry Thuku and Jomo Kenyatta who had, in his view, given in to the ghost of colonialism.

The third movement in Ngugi's dialectic emerges when he tries to hollow a new space of resistance and cultural expression beyond a dead colonial culture and an atrophic moment of radical change. Thinking about the implications of the Kamĩrĩĩthũ project, for example, he is comforted by the belief that culture can still function as a countervailing force against hegemony. What he sees represented in Kamĩrĩĩthũ are the two images, the two cultures of the postcolony, struggling to occupy the same space. But the Kamĩrĩĩthũ experiment has become more than a place, a stage; it has begun to be associated in the author's imagination with both the romance of high nationalism and the reality of colonial terror.

He remembers Kamĩrĩĩthũ, the village, through the prism of
adolescence and youth, of initiation and rites of passage, and of the
destruction of the hearth, cultures and memories (pp. 74–76). We
are reminded that Kamĩrĩĩthũ has, under different guises, been a
central locality in Ngugi's prior works and the source of some of
the deepest emotions of return and betrayal in his *œuvre* (p. 74).

Reduced to a place of imprisonment under a colonial state of
emergency, and abandoned as a ruin by the postcolony, this
village becomes the site where the history of colonialism and
resistance can be enacted and then transcended in the name of an
alternative future (p. 77). This is the place where the repressed
spirit of "true" nationalism is brought alive to exorcize the ghost of
the colonial Lazarus (pp. 78–79). And so the imprisoned self holds
on to the figure of Kamĩrĩĩthũ as the sign of its own redemption:

I would never, for as long as I lived, and for as long as I was sane, disown
the heroic history of Kenyan people as celebrated in *Ngaahika Ndeenda*, or
be a conscious party to the historical betrayal mourned and condemned
in the same drama. My involvement with the people of Kamĩrĩĩthũ had
given me the sense of a new being and it had made me transcend the
alienation to which I had been condemned by years of colonial education. (p. 98).

Out of this political conviction emerges a renewed investment in
the instrumental function of the art object, for in order to save
himself, preserve his sanity in prison, and overcome the pain,
humiliation, and despair of incarceration, Ngugi feels compelled
to write a novel that would constitute his way out of the prisonhouse of postcolonialism. If the logic behind his detention was to
silence him, the novel would become "my most important weapon
in the daily combat with the stony dragon" (p. 156). Let us turn to
this novel.

BEYOND DISENCHANTMENT: *DEVIL ON THE CROSS*

Devil on the Cross, the novel Ngugi wrote in prison in order to defeat
the "the stony dragon" of postcolonial terror, is a work defined by
two paradoxes: given the circumstances in which this work was
produced, it is clearly informed by strong emotions and deep

personal feelings. These are the feelings and emotions that run through the imprisoned Ngugi's body and mind – and the last two pages of *Detained* – as prison warders confiscate the rolls of toilet paper on which he had written the work: "It is only a writer who can possibly understand the pain of losing a manuscript, any manuscript. With this novel I had struggled with language, with images, with prison, with bitter memories, with moments of despair, with all the mentally and emotionally adverse circumstances in which one is forced to operate while in custody – and now it had gone" (p. 164). These emotions of loss and pain are only matched by the exhilaration that Ngugi expresses when the new Superintendent of the Prison hands him back his manuscript: "'Thank you!' was all I said, but he will probably never know the depth of the emotion behind those two words. Nor perhaps what his action meant for the birth of a new literature in Kenya's languages" (p. 165).

Two paradoxes are evident in the above statements: first, Ngugi describes *Devil on the Cross* as a novel loaded with – and surrounded by – the emotions of imprisonment; and yet few readers and critics of the novel would characterize it as affective in the familiar terms of the bourgeois novel; indeed, this work is not emotive or sentimental in the same way as Ngugi's early novels, nor does it contain the collective emotions generated by his major plays. Are terms such as emotion and sentiment being redefined here, or is the novel simply incapable of sustaining the emotion behind it? Had Ngugi turned to *ostreinane* (estrangement) because he now wanted "his audience to comprehend the action intellectually,"[13] as Alamin Mazrui has argued, or was evacuating emotions from *Devil on the Cross* a way of repressing the subjective and – in Ngugi's lexicon – the bourgeois aspect of the novel as a genre?

The second paradox emerges from Ngugi's questionable claim that *Devil on the Cross* inaugurated a new literature in Kenyan languages. As an astute student of Kenyan history and culture, Ngugi was fully aware of the long tradition of imaginative works in Kenyan languages, most notably in Swahili. So, why did he seem eager to claim the authority of beginnings for his first novel in Gikuyu? One of the central issues Ngugi had to confront in producing a novel in Gikuyu was not simply the problem of

audience and novelistic tradition, but of his own prior investment
in the ideals of the bourgeois novel as a genre. As I will argue more
explicitly in the next two chapters, the problem of language
brought Ngugi face to face with his own alienation in the institutions of literary production in the European languages and generic
traditions. His deepest anxiety – what kind of form would a novel
in Gikuyu take? – arose because he had spent a good deal of time
mastering the European novel and he did not know how to let go
of what he had mastered. As a result, *Devil on the Cross* would appear
to be something manifestly new in his *œuvre*, but also something
quite familiar: it would mark his major turn to orality – or what he
calls "the appropriation of the novel into the oral tradition"[14] –
but the structure of the novel and the ideas informing it, not least
the Faustian theme as it appears "in several works of European
literature: Marlowe's *Faustus*, Goethe's *Faust*, Thomas Mann's *Dr.
Faustus*, and Bulgakov's *The Master and Margarita*,"[15] are borrowed
from the European tradition.

If literary critics now seem confused about the place of *Devil on
the Cross* in Ngugi's *œuvre* – is it to be grouped with his earlier works
or does it really mark a break from his past practices? – it is simply
because the genealogy of the novel is schizophrenic.[16] It is a work
that wants to maintain its generic identity as a novel in the
European sense of the word while rejecting the central ideologies
that have made this form what it is, including the assumption of an
elite audience. Read against this background, the novel is central
to an understanding of Ngugi's troubled relationship with his
British liberal education and Gikuyu cultural nationalism. More
importantly, the double identity of the novel as a work that draws
both on Gikuyu traditions and the European concept of the novel
points us in two important directions which culminate in the
writing of *Matigari*, a work now considered to be Ngugi's most
successful attempt to transform the nature of the novel in Africa.
First, it leads to Ngugi's rethinking of the place of the reader in the
production of narrative; second, it initiates a rethinking and rerep-
resentation of the postcolonial space beyond the discourse of
disenchantment that dominated African writing from the middle
of the 1960s to the end of the 1970s.

From its opening pages, the novel goes out of its way to make
the reader an important part of its discursive universe and it does

so by appealing to the authority of the oral tale and the community of listeners it presupposes. This appeal to the oral tale is most apparent in the overture to the Gikuyu edition that was, most unfortunately, omitted from the English translation. This preface is aptly titled "Uga iitha!" which, as the formulaic opening to all Gikuyu folktales, calls for undivided attention from the audience and sets the scene for the narrative exchange. In the latter regard, the overture is intended to establish the narrative contract – the relationship between addresser and addressee, teller and listener. The overture sets the terms in which the story is exchanged between these two sectors of the narrative exchange. The overture begins with a caution – "Rugano ruuru ni rwa kiiriu" (This is a contemporary story) – and then presents *Devil on the Cross* as a story, as a fictional tale, which is, nevertheless, based on contemporary or real events.[17] The overture then goes on to comment on the circumstances in which the story was produced – the banning of *I Will Marry When I Want*, the imprisonment of the writer, and Ngugi's determination to produce a novel in the Gikuyu language. More than mere background, then, the history of the production of the novel becomes an occasion to institute a relationship between the novelist and his audience.

The language used in this overture seeks to establish intimacy between writer and audience by invoking a common grammar and set of values. This is the intimacy evoked by the language of proverbs and the aura surrounding them, and the story teller's final invocation for the reader to give in to the spell of the story, to overcome the distance between the narrator and the reader: "Kiuge iitha riu nguganire" (say *iitha* so that I can tell you a story). The key in the last phrase is the word *iitha*, which is defined as the "response interjected by the listeners after each clause, sentence, or passage in the recital of folk-stories, yes! go on!"[18] Simply put, this interjection is the story teller's demand for assent from the listeners, an assent that endows the story with communal cultural authority. By the same token, by giving their assent, the listeners become important agents in the making of the story and its effectiveness. The narrative contract, then, depends on a dialogical relationship between addresser and addressee, now conjoined by the oral tradition they are supposed to share.[19]

But if orality is what authorizes both story teller and listener in this novel, one must hasten to add that one of the reasons why *Devil on the Cross* is defined as a modern tale is the simple fact that its oral resources came from three distinct sources: Gikuyu oral discourses, biblical narratives, and contemporary urban stories. Indeed one of the most remarkable features of the Gikuyu version is the extent to which it takes the close connection between these discourses for granted, shifting from one to the other regardless of the different historical and ideological circumstances that produced them, and oblivious to the assumed opposition between tradition and modernity in African literature. The novel opens with a fragment with three clear biblical referents: words are identified as the source of the light and truth that some people want to hide under a bushel; the incantatory language used by the narrator echoes the Sermon on the Mount ("Happy is the man..."); and the call for the crucifixion of the devil "who would lead us into the blindness of the heart and into the deafness of the mind" reminds one of Paul's evangelicalism in many of his epistles.[20]

If the narrative voice in the first fragment seems to be that of a fervent Christian, the section that follows seems to locate the speaker elsewhere: the speaking voice is now explicitly that of a Gicaandi player, a prophet of justice, a diviner, and a teacher.[21] Thus, the novel opens with a binary structure that it also calls into question: the evangelical speaker and the Gicaandi player are separated by time, space, and ideology, but they also speak the language of apocalypse and revelation. Indeed, in order to discover who he really is, the Gicaandi player, like Jesus in the wilderness, goes through a period of fasting and introspection before he speaks to us in the language of the biblical prophet on the advent of a long-awaited apocalypse:

And after seven days had passed, the Earth trembled, and lightning scoured the sky with its brightness, and I was lifted up, and I was borne up to the rooftop of the house, and I was shown many things, and I heard a voice, like a great clap of thunder, admonishing me: Who has told you that prophecy is yours alone, to keep to yourself? Why are you furnishing yourself with empty excuses? If you do that, you will never be free of tears and pleading cries. (*Devil on the Cross*, p. 8)

The interplay between the Gikuyu acolyte and the biblical prophet takes a slightly different turn in Chapter Two when the devil appears to Jacinta Wariinga as the manifestation of her recent misfortunes. The story that is told in this chapter – of landlords and thugs "wearing dark glasses" (p. 10) and the Devil "clad in a silk suit" and carrying "a walking stick shaped like a folded umbrella" (p. 13) – is a familiar one in East African urban lore, it belongs to a popular genre associated with rumors and vampire stories.[22]

And thus in reading orality in *Devil of the Cross*, readers should constantly be aware of the intermixture and interplay of different genres and traditions, and the author's self-conscious decision to switch from one idiom to another regardless of the temporal setting of his novel. For what Ngugi seems to recognize, after several works built on Manichean oppositions, is the difficulty of making distinctions between oral traditions derived from Gikuyu culture and the biblical traditions imposed during colonial rule. Indeed, in many cases, there appears to be an important affinity between Gikuyu oral culture and the narratives of the Old Testament: the incantations, voices, and visions of the Gicaandi prophet are similar to those of biblical prophets. Proverbs and sayings are often used in the novel to secure or evoke the authority of traditional wisdom, but they perform the same role in the Bible; Gikuyu rituals and ceremonies are important in Ngugi's search for a new language of representing the postcolonial landscape, but so are Catholic rituals (p. 190). Commentators on the function of orality in the novel have called attention to the significance of songs or music in general as "the inseparable component of the enactment (performance) of contemporary Kenyan history."[23] What has not been emphasized enough are the multiple traditions of these songs. For while in the end Ngugi's desire, like that of Gatuiria in the novel, is to rediscover the disappearing songs of the Gicaandi genre, the path to this process is marked by popular "radio" songs (p. 19), "Mau Mau" songs (p. 39), and urban "Congolese" music (p. 93).

We can draw two conclusions from this admixture of idioms: first, it is intended to call attention to the complexity of the politics of everyday life in the postcolony; the mixture of idioms shows how the culture of the postcolonial state can no longer be seen in terms of the opposition between tradition and modernity. Some readers might dismiss Ngugi's desire to rediscover older cultural forms as an expression of his nostalgia for old Gikuyu traditions, but such readers will inevitably fail to notice how this novel, written in Gikuyu, but intended to be a deconstruction of the alliance between a Gikuyu comprador class and foreign capital, contains a harsh critique of the function of tradition in the discourse of postcoloniality. This deconstruction of tradition is most obvious in the grotesque competition that dominates the middle of the novel, a competition to identify the most greedy capitalist in Kenya. Now, while the competition is cast in biblical and Faustian terms – it opens with the parable of the sower (p. 82) and is focused on stories about souls given up in return for gold – its most obvious ironic moments are those in which the contestants cite Gikuyu proverbs and sayings to endow their pan-capitalist testimonies with the aura of tradition (pp. 99–101). So we have a situation in which the authority of tradition is claimed by both radicals (Muturi) and conservatives (Mwireri wa Mukiraai).

Secondly, the mixture of idioms in the novel cannot be discussed outside its dialogical intentions. The narrative opens by complicating the identity and authority of the narrative voice and then proceeds to establish a multiplicity of stories; above all, it insists on the interaction of narrators and interlocutors; the narrative exchange takes place between narrators and listeners within the fictional world of the novel, and real readers are often reduced to eavesdroppers. In addition, one of the most important functions of orality in the novel is to create, or perform, the dialogical, not simply by introducing languages and genres that challenge the monolithic assumptions of the novel as a genre, but also by creating narrative exchanges or dialogues that invite the reader to participate actively in the novelistic world.[24] The latter function is most vividly represented in the performance of the Gitiro (operatic) song in *Devil on the Cross* (pp. 46–51): Mwaura begins to sing a common evangelical song about beating back the devil, but the theme of the song is transformed by Muturi into something else, maintaining the original tune but carrying a different subject; then Muturi and Wangari form a duet that pushes the political message of the song even further. Similarly, the function of the song gets changed as it moves from one set of singers to another: Mwaura starts the song as an expression of his irrelevance, but Muturi and Wangari perform it as a signifier of their patriotism; the song then becomes a metacommentary on the politics of the postcolony. There is something even more important about these songs: whether they come to us from the past (p. 54) or the present (p. 50), they are songs that are familiar to Gikuyu readers, who are invited to sing them together with the fictional characters and thus become part of their universe and to reflect, as Gatuiria does, on their meaning and implication (p. 58). It is through songs and related genres that heteroglossia comes to occupy an important position in Ngugi's novelistic discourse.[25] There are many instances in *Devil on the Cross* when two voices coming from different directions hold a conversation either to challenge or affirm each other's positions. An example of this kind of dialogical relationship is the three-way conversation between Mwaura, Muturi, and Wangari, cited earlier, or the "verse-chanting competition" between Gatuiria and Wariinga (p. 128).

It is important to note that the kind of formal experimentation discussed above is part of Ngugi's sustained attempt to go beyond the politics of disenchantment which had come to dominate the African novel since the collapse of the postcolonial state in the early 1970s. In other words, Ngugi was using formal experimentation to rethink the politics of everyday life in contemporary Africa in terms other than the disintegration, decline, and failure valorized by avant-garde writers such as Ayi Kwei Armah and Wole Soyinka. In this novel, as in *Matigari*, Ngugi locates his narrative within the same discourse of disenchantment as Soyinka and Armah (this is the social reality his characters have to confront), but he also tries to transcend it through the use of oral forms.

Another way of thinking about the question of writing beyond disenchantment is to reflect on the relationship between the two journeys that structure *Devil on the Cross*. The first journey is akin to a secular pilgrimage through the charred landscape of the postcolony: "Matatu Matata Matamu Model T Ford, registration number MMM 333, was like a church; the passengers were deaf to the noise of the vehicle as it waddled along the *TransAfrica Highway*, bearing them towards Ilmorog, the seat of the great competition in modern theft and robbery' (p. 81). The motif of the journey used here might appear to be a parody of John Bunyan's *Pilgrim's Progress* – the voyage toward salvation and self-understanding – but the allegorical meaning and import is similar. The six characters in the taxi are cast as representations of different classes and sectors of the population. Mwaura literally means one who makes off with other people's things, a thief; Muturi is a blacksmith, a worker; Wangari is a mother, named after one of the daughters of Gikuyu and Mumbi, the mythical parents of the Gikuyu people; Wariinga means a woman in chains, while Gatuiria is the seeker of truth; Mwireri wa Mukiraai is one who thinks only of himself. But even more important than the characters' allegorical names is the shifting roles they play in the drama of postcoloniality, a drama which, as we have already seen, is played out in competing – and yet dialogical – languages, idioms, and modes of signification. And the point to underscore is simply this: the characters in the taxi represent a set of meaning and interests that are at once opposed and united by their location in the drama of national independence.

Opposed to the utopian possibilities of the journey in the taxi are the unspeakable horrors of the competition in theft and robbery that takes place in the cave. Here we are not in Bunyan's paradise but deep in Dante's cave, in a hell without any redemptive qualities, a world of disembodied voices and social cannibalization. If the language in the taxi is designed to encourage debate and dialogue even when there are fundamental disagreements among the characters, the language in the cave is designed to alienate; if the people in the taxi seek some common humanity across class differences, the principal participants in the competition of thieves and robbers have the features of predatory animals. What we might consider to be the redemptive qualities of the first journey would hence appear to be negated by the predatory nature of its destination; instead of securing the sense of community sought by some of the travelers in the taxi, the pilgrimage has led the reader to the despicable bottom of postcolonial failure.

And if what makes postcolonial disenchantment bearable is its utopian possibilities, Ngugi's novel seems to be dominated by the image of an unanthropomorphic world that seems to confirm the apocalyptic tone that opens the novel. Gatuiria's final vision of the cave captures this world succinctly:

"I wish it were a dream," Gatuiria replied. "Kimeendeeri wa Kanyuanjii was certainly there, but it was difficult to tell whether he was a human being or a fat, hairy worm with a beak. *Anyway*, Kimeendeeri had just finished his monologue (monologue or verbal diarrhoea? you might ask). He started by giving us details of his wealth. then he bragged about how he wanted to set up an experimental *farm* to investigate the feasibility of exporting the labour of our workers to foreign countries through pipe-lines, and to discover whether their bodies could eventually be made into fertilizer to ensure the continued productivity of rich people's farms here and abroad. And suddenly I saw all the people in the cave open their mouths, and they looked at me with eyes that seemed hungry and thirsty for human blood and human flesh, and fear seized me, and I desperately started looking for an escape route." (p. 196)

This is where the allegorical journey ends – at the bottom, at the pits of national consciousness.

The second journey, two years later, seems to want to take place as if the events that preoccupy at least two thirds of the novel were not important, as if the space in between has willed a new world into being. The most obvious shift in the narrative exchange in the second journey is the absence of Wangari and Muturi, who were the sources of our notions about the ill-fated birth of the post-colony and the moral consciousness of the novel. The evacuation of these elders from the center of the narrative has important implications for both the form and ideology of Ngugi's novel.

Let us explore the displacement of the moral center of the story by noting that while Wangari and Muturi, like the older gener-ation in *Petals of Blood*, are celebrated as the heroes of a nationalist dream that has survived the ravages of postcoloniality, they are also associated with nostalgia and historical belatedness. This does not mean that the two characters are not important to the ideo-logical scheme of the novel; on the contrary, postcolonial culture appears to be morally bankrupt when it is contrasted to the ideals the elders continue to uphold. And yet, so long as postcolonial culture is judged from the idealistic vista and the ethical position presented by this generation, the "unspeakable horrors" of the postcolonial city can only be represented in the elegiac language of failure and betrayal. Wangari can only speak of her involvement in the struggle against colonialism from her own bitter understanding and experience of its betrayal: "But these legs have carried many bullets and many guns to our fighters in the forest ... and I was never afraid, even when I slipped through the lines of the enemy and their home guard allies. Our people, today when I recall those things, my heart weakens and I want to cry!" (p. 40). Similarly, Muturi can only narrate his story of trade union radicalism from its defeat by powerful state institutions (p. 73).

What seems to be happening in the novel, then, is a crucial generational and generative shift: in the first journey, Wariinga and Gatuiria seem trapped in parataxis, eager to narrate their individual and collective stories, but unable to find a language for representing the unspeakable "world." They find it difficult to turn their individual disenchantment into an allegory of their generation's betrayal. Of the many things the two young people discover they have in common, none is more important than their coming to consciousness about their alienation from the histories and traditions that should have anchored them in the national space, the grand narrative of nationalism represented by Wangari and Muturi's memories. Gatuiria's rhetoric is one of doubt about cultural genealogies and etymologies: "Where are our national languages now? Where are the books written in the alphabets of our national languages? Where is our own literature now? Where is the wisdom and knowledge of our fathers now? Where is the philosophy of our fathers now?" (p. 58). His research project is continuously undermined by the lack of a living tradition of thought and reflection: "The centres of wisdom that used to guard the entrance to our national homestead have been demolished; the fire of wisdom has been allowed to die; the seats around the fireside have been thrown on to a rubbish heap; the guard posts have been destroyed; and the youth of the nation has hung up its shields and spears" (pp. 58–59). The tragedy of his generation, he avers, is that it has nowhere to go "to learn the history of our country" (p. 59).

But Gatuiria is an important figure in the novel for something more than the questions he raises: he is the best representation of a type of character who is indispensable to Ngugi's aesthetic project

– the bourgeois subject defined simultaneously by its longing for a national ideal and its radical alienation from the nation. Readers will recall that the travail of such figures – figures who occupy almost every Ngugi text all the way from Waiyaki in *The River Between* to Karega in *Petals of Blood* – is manifested in their romantic relationship with women, who, as we saw in earlier chapters, are represented as the custodians of the desired traditions of the national community, or of its ultimate betrayal. The question that arises here, then, is this: is Wariinga a "new woman" in Ngugi's works, a sign of the increasing significance of gender (and the empowerment of women) in his works, as some critics have claimed, or does she belong to that familiar national allegory in which women function as "the territory over which the quest for (male) national identity passed, or, at best . . . the space of loss and all that lies outside the male games of rivalry and revenge"?[26]

The significance of Wariinga in the novel perhaps lies in the ways she operates within and outside the national allegory. For a start, she appears to us not as the familiar woman in the national romance (the custodian of tradition), but as an archetypal figure of loss, alone in the city, ashamed of her body (p. 11), and haplessly abused by men. She is introduced to us as an individual in an acute state of crisis, contemplating suicide. She can then be described as a new kind of woman because she is not asked to perform a symbolic function in the national narrative: she is an individual struggling to make ends meet in the city. But no sooner has Wariinga's individual identity been established than it is undermined by the stories she tells or hears. Indeed, Wariinga undermines her own individuality when she transforms her struggle for survival in the city into an allegorical narrative about other beautiful women ("Mahua Kareendi") who find themselves lost in the labyrinthine world of the postcolony (pp. 17–26).

And thus the question arises: who is Wariinga? A unique female subject who defines herself against the nationalist narrative, or a symbolic figure in the national romance? She tells a painful story of individual desire and disappointment, but she tells it as the story of another, detached from it, yet emotionally invested in its outcome. She appears to us as a victim of male games of rivalry and power, but unlike other famous Ngugi women, most notably

Wanja in *Petals of Blood*, she does not give in to the malevolent (male) forces around her, but embarks on the journey to Ilmorog as a novice, eager to learn and to find a new language of self and a new relationship to her community. Furthermore, in her relationship with Gatuiria, she is not represented as "the territory" in which male identity passes, but as a kindred spirit driven by the same desires and plagued by the same doubts. Indeed, the two characters emerge out of the cave connected in powerful and subliminal ways, engaged in an incantation whose apostrophic language expresses their sense of betrayal and patriotic longing (p. 128).

Wariinga and Gatuiria are also engaged in a common intellectual project: Gatuiria's quest, as he constantly reminds the reader, is for "the music of my dreams" (p. 59), which is also the quest for an uncontaminated path to national culture. He is haunted by the cacophony of postcolonial separation and loss and enchanted by the possibility of a unified national voice, what he calls "a choir of heavenly angels proudly celebrating the heroic deeds of the nation" (p. 60); against the "morning frost that blights the shoots of patriotic love," his ultimate desire is to compose "music that expresses the soul and the aspirations and the dreams of our nation" (p. 132). Wariinga's project is to break out of the prison-house of self-hate and victimization and to assert her identity outside the culture and economy of arrested decolonization.

In the last part of the novel, in the second journey Wariinga and Gatuiria make, the former is presented to us as a woman who has broken the chains of patriarchy and rejected "the temptations of Satan" (p. 215). If the Wariinga we met at the beginning of the novel could only speak about herself and her experiences through displacement, the new one has found the language to represent this self by differentiating it from its former identity:

No, this Wariinga is not that other Wariinga. This Wariinga has decided that she'll never again allow herself to be a mere flower, whose purpose is to decorate the doors and windows and tables of other people's lives, waiting to be thrown on to a rubbish heap the moment the splendour of her body withers. The Wariinga of today has decided to be self-reliant all the time, to plunge into the middle of the arena of life's struggles in order to discover her real strength and to realize her true humanity. (p. 216)

Even within the logic of the national allegory, Wariinga has acquired agency; instead of functioning as an object of male desires, she has become a figure of female insurgency against postcolonial patriarchy, a true "daughter of the Iregi rebels!" (p. 222).

And yet – and this is the paradox that many commentators on the role of gender in this novel have missed – Wariinga's coming into consciousness as an independent woman, that is, her allegorization as the new woman, is also the process that imprisons her in the discourse of nationalist patriarchy. She develops enough strength to celebrate her body, and yet the beauty of this body is measured in terms of its appeal to Gatuiria (p. 224); she is a very successful mechanic, but she acquires value in the novel as a catalyst for her fiancé's national symphony (pp. 226–27); she is memorable for her ability to break into the male public sphere, but on the day of her betrothal, she is placed on a pedestal as the incarnation of the romance of "the Gikuyu way" (p. 242). Wariinga is hence located in a difficult juncture in postcolonial cultural discourse: she expresses the author's desire for radical transformation and utopian resolution, but she is also a symptom of the arrested nature of such desires and longings. Indeed, what appears to be the radical difference between her first and second journeys is also a sign of their troubled conflation.

On the surface of things, it would appear that the second journey differs from the first both in terms of the conditions under which it is undertaken and the different destinations: in the first journey, Wariinga really has no choice about her mode of transportation or her destination; in the second journey, she appears to have such a choice because her engagement to Gatuiria is entered into willingly and under the promise of a happy and equal partnership. But as the ending of the novel confirms, the second journey, like the first one, is a forced encounter with the devil Wariinga thought she had renounced at the end of the first journey; for this reason, what was designed to be a new beginning becomes a confrontation with old histories, tragedies, and betrayals.

By killing Gatuiria's father, the man who had abused her as a young woman, Wariinga would appear to have begun a new revolutionary life, but this new life is called into question by two important formal features in the last section of the novel. The first feature is what appears to be the ironic or mock parodic celebration of Wariinga and Gatuiria's journey to Nakuru: "It is true that their journey to Nakuru was pleasant ... Gatuiria and Wariinga's journey was pleasant as they walked through the gates of the homestead" (p. 246). The prose is intended to create anticipation, but for those readers who will recognize this description of the journey as the vulgarization of a "Mau Mau" battle song, the journey to paradise is filled with dangers and threats.[27] The song forewarns us of such dangers.

The second formal feature concerns the omniscient narrator's stance: in spite of the radical transformation of both Wariinga and Gatuiria, the omniscient narrator (the Gicaandi player) returns at the end of the narrative still preoccupied with the same doubts as the ones that opened the novel, as if nothing much has changed. Wariinga has finally taken care of the devil from her past, but what does this mean in terms of her own life and that of the ravished national body? The narrator refuses to address this question and ends the story with ellipses: "Wariinga walked on, without once looking back ... But she knew with all her heart that the hardest struggles of her life's journey lay ahead ..." (p. 254). The ellipses that end the novel are clearly ambivalent and can be interpreted in either of two ways: they can be seen as space in which the reader can provide an aftermath for Wariinga's story as it moves into the future; or they can function as the most visible sign of the author's uncertainty about the future. It is to *Matigari* that readers must turn for a possible resolution of these moments of doubts and crisis.

CHAPTER 8

The work of art in exile: Matigari

Of all Ngugi's major works, none seem to have generated as much ideological and theoretical debate as *Matigari*. This debate has revolved around the identity of this novel in relation to the author's stated intentions, its place in the changing canon of African literature, and the way it forces us to rethink cultural production in the postcolonial state. Reaction to Ngugi's major novels has always been strong and contentious, but the most remarkable thing about the debates revolving around *Matigari* is that they have not been concerned with the author's personality and his politics, but with a specific set of formal questions: does the overt and consistent use of allegory in the novel represent a new form of didacticism or does it lend itself to linguistic creativity? Is Ngugi's concern with the everyday politics of the postcolonial state a continued search for, and refinement of, techniques of realistic representation, or is the site of everyday culture one of experimentation, in the tradition of what has come to be known as the left-wing avant-garde? Is the powerful religious language of the novel an abdication of Marxist secularism, or is religion deployed in the name of an aesthetic ideal and ideological ends? And what is the meaning of Ngugi's appropriation of Gikuyu oral narratives – does it constitute a significant move away from the tradition of the European novel, or is orality a mark of his embrace of post-modernism?[1]

Whichever way one approaches *Matigari*, it opens up a set of complicated questions in relation to Ngugi's aesthetic ideology and the tradition of the novel in Africa. As I will be arguing in this chapter, part of the power of the novel is generated by its profound political ambivalence and its valorization of a set of fictions that seem to call into question Ngugi's well-known position on the novel as an art form, the politics of everyday life, the language of African literature, nationalism and culture, and even modernity and modernism. *Matigari* seems to be a novel that simultaneously falls back on the most traditional notions of story telling (it seeks to recreate the aura of the communicative exchange between the story teller and his or her listeners), and to depend on some notable aspects of the modernist aesthetic (apparent in its rejection of determinist meanings and its privileging of representation over experience).[2] But the novel even makes this kind of separation of traditional and experimental form difficult because it constantly switches from one register to the other: we are asked to read Matigari's quest as an allegorical journey modeled on a famous Gikuyu folktale – thus located in a specific culture and tradition – and as a universal narrative, that is, one beyond time and space, specific geographies and temporalities. We are encouraged to read Matigari's experiences as specific responses to familiar signs of postcolonial failure, framed by recognized historical and political signposts; but then we are discouraged from giving credence to this history and context because, as we are warned early in the novel, this is, after all, an imaginary story without a fixed time or space.[3]

Some prominent critics of the novel have expended a lot of effort trying to show why it must be located centrally within a tradition of realism, and while the evidence adduced for such readings cannot be discounted, it is still important to begin with a simple question: if Ngugi is still attracted to realism, why does he seem to go out of his way to deconstruct it in *Matigari?*[4] Three possible answers to this question will go a long way to providing a context for reading the novel and recognizing its boldness both in Ngugi's *œuvre* and African (postcolonial) fiction. The first point to note in this regard is that *Matigari* was written out of the author's (unacknowledged) exhaustion of realism. By the early 1970s, Ngugi had argued that one of the problems facing African literature in the postcolonial era was that the writer "was in danger of becoming too fascinated by the yesterday of his people and forgetting the present."[5] Echoing Fanon's claim that such an obsession with the past turned the author away from "actual events," Ngugi had turned to realism (as defined in the Marxist tradition) as his point of entry into the drama of everyday life in the postcolony.[6] The result was *Petals of Blood*, Ngugi's magnificent and problematic tribute to "socialist realism." This turn to high realism was intended to fulfill Fanon's claim that "the native intellectual who wishes to create a work of art must realize that the truths of the nation are in the first place its realities" and that it was out of such realities that "the learning of the future" would emerge.[7]

But in his zeal to establish a Marxist aesthetic whose goal was nothing less than the representation of the realities of the nation beyond bourgeois surfaces, Ngugi had also missed Fanon's key qualifier to the dictum that revolutionary literature could only emerge out of "actual events." While literature needed to establish connections with the drama of everyday life, Fanon cautioned, it could not afford to be reduced to the reality it sought to represent; indeed, the search for "true" realism was itself a mark of the artist's alienation from his cultural roots: "Before independence the native painter was insensible to the national scene ... After independence his anxiety to rejoin his people will confine him to the most detailed representation of reality. This is representative art which has no internal rhythms, an art which is serene and immobile, evocative not of life but of death."[8] How could an art committed to the detailed representation of reality become serene, immobile, and deathly? Ngugi would perhaps argue that works such as *Petals of Blood* had, through the evocation of "actual events" played out the dynamic epoch in which, to quote Fanon again, "the people are treading out their path toward history."[9] Furthermore, Ngugi would argue, what distinguished "critical realism" (which was "serene and immobile"?) from socialist realism, was the latter's attempt to transcend the actual event and project how the narrative of the future would emerge.

And yet, whatever name it bore, realism had to be considered lacking in an area which Ngugi had come to consider imperative to the political function and cultural effect of his works – the relation between the novelist, his postcolonial culture, and his ideal or intended audience. The aesthetic effect of realism depended on its ability to turn "actual events" into art works, and in this transformation "realities" were abstracted into categories that could not be identified simply with their sources or referents. *Petals of Blood* worked well for those readers who could connect its numerous narrative abstractions (stories) with actual events (histories), or who could read palpable aspects of Kenyan history (for example the 1975 murder of J. M. Kariuki) into its narratological equivalent (the death of the lawyer in the novel). For readers without the ability or resources to make such transference, history could indeed appear immobile and distant.

The second reason why realism appeared wanting in the 1980s was because Ngugi's priorities had changed after the Kamĩrĩthũ experiment and his subsequent imprisonment. If his earlier works had sought to represent the history of the postcolony and the everyday events that dominated life in it, his later works were increasingly concerned with creating an alternative to the bourgeois public sphere inherited from colonialism and perpetuated in postcoloniality. His focus now was not simply what was real, but the sites in which meanings and realities were "articulated, distributed, and negotiated."[10] If novels such as *Petals of Blood* and *Devil on the Cross* were concerned with ways in which European conventions of realistic representation might be applied to a postcolonial setting, *Matigari* was a novel that sought to reconceptualize the relation between art and reality; its major success as a novel would come to depend on its capacity not merely to represent reality but to create it.[11] It was by problematizing the nature of reality, by turning the "real" into a shifting and subjective category, that Ngugi was able to dramatize the textual economy through which the state established its political and cultural hegemony and the discursive mechanisms through which deterritorialized sectors in society, such as the urban poor, were making sense of the contested politics of everyday life.

THE USES OF ALIENATION

Matigari is perhaps distinguished from Ngugi's prior novels by its complete evacuation of the authoritative narrative voice. In its contingency and irony, and in its celebration of alienation, the novel sets out to transcend the conditions that enabled it in the first place; it exists both inside and outside the politics it seeks to represent. One might argue, then, that the third reason why realism was not going to work for Ngugi was that in order for the novelist to return to the dynamic sources of his culture, to use one of his favorite phrases borrowed from Amilcar Cabral, he needed to acknowledge his own estrangement from the people he had chosen as the subject of his work of art.[12] Critics have been so eager to celebrate Ngugi's return to the sources of his culture – Gikuyu oral traditions, Kenyan urban legends, and the King James Bible – that they have sometimes forgotten that *Matigari* is as much a novel about alienation and exile as it is about *retour* and *Heimat*. Ngugi himself was never in doubt about the conjunction between notions of home and return, and those of alienation and exile. In his introduction to the English edition of the novel, he went out of his way to remind his readers of the two most salient features of *Matigari* – its indebtedness to Gikuyu folktale and its production in exile.

My argument here is that the link between the return to Gikuyu oral sources and the trope of exile is more profound than many cursory readings of the notions of home and return which dominate the novel might suggest. Indeed, if Matigari had not been written in exile, it could not have taken the form it did, not simply because the author's alienation from his country made him nostalgic for the oral tales of his childhood, but because in exile, Ngugi was able to free himself from the anxieties of the European novel and its conventions, which were also anxieties about history and nation, realism and language. Writing in exile, he did not feel the pressure of representing the historical realities of the postcolonial state in Kenya; on the contrary he wanted to use local sources to produce a universal narrative on repression and the search for freedom.

We can perhaps understand this shift better if we recall that the realistic novel has traditionally been associated with the ideal of the nation and the discourse of nationalism. As a student of the European novel, Ngugi understood how realism had emerged as a formal category in order to represent the coming into being of the new nation and its bourgeois subject; as a teacher and critic, he was attracted to the realist novel because of its capacity to represent the totality of historical (national) experiences.[13] During the heated debate on language that Ngugi initiated in Kenya just before his imprisonment, some of his political opponents and critics had tried to discredit him by arguing that in choosing to write in Gikuyu, the novelist's political commitment had increasingly moved away from nation to region or ethnicity.[14] What these critics missed was how Ngugi remained committed to the "truths" of the nation long after they had been discarded by other postcolonial writers, and how what appeared to be his turn to region or ethnicity was his desperate attempt to secure a center for national identity in an age of antinationalism.

Ngugi was increasingly referring to the ethnic group as a nation not because he had embraced a newly fashioned and mangled brand of identity politics, but because he still needed to hold on to the ideals of nationhood and the metaphysics of progress it entailed. He needed to hold on to these ideals because cultural identity and the ideals of national community on which they were predicated were the heart and soul of his writing. The category of the nation – and its referent – would change several times in the course of Ngugi's career, but so long as the national ideal remained the base of all forms of identity, he could continue to argue that his works were attempts to realize these ideals. Once it had become clear that the postcolonial nation was not the agent of such ideals, Ngugi, like many writers of his generation, had to search for them elsewhere – in local communities, in African languages, in stories of nostalgia. This search would continue even in exile. Indeed, it could be said that in exile, the political value and cultural capital of nationhood had become even more important.[15]

But exile also provided a space of rethinking the terms of identity. Between London and New York, liberated from the vagaries of the nation and the burden of its everyday realities, Ngugi could begin to rethink the three categories that the nation and the novel had brought into being – geography, time, and subject. As a novel produced in exile, and thus the furthest removed from its subject, *Matigari* could be interpreted as a work that reflects its author's self-consciousness about his distance from his cultural sources, his language, and his intended audience. It is sometimes tempting to read the novel as Ngugi's way of coming to terms with his heritage, his language, his culture, but as we shall see in a moment, Matigari's narrative quest is driven by what he both lacks and needs – a household.[16] The most modernist element of the novel, then, is to be found in its acceptance of its alienation, its acquiescence to the simple fact that it cannot be authorized by the land it speaks about, by the language it deploys, or the homeland it desires. *Matigari* is a narrative of return which, to borrow Michel de Certeau's memorable terms, is generated by a sense of loss and historical obligation. Unlike the novels of revolution Ngugi produced in the 1970s, *Matigari* is a story of loss and longing.

I want to argue, then, that *Matigari* is best read as a novel generated by doubts about personal and collective identity, the authority of temporality, and the reader's ability to recuperate stable meanings from the narrative of a belated postcolonial history. After all, the narrative begins by urging its readers to reject the determinacy associated with fixed temporal entities; it begins by granting readers the license to locate it in a country, time, and space, of their choice; and it is inaugurated through a rhetorical gesture that disclaims determinism.[17] As if this abrogation of narrative authority were not enough, Matigari's narrative is represented as allegorical (thus endowed with specific ecumenical meanings and intentions), and as contingent (surrounded by doubts about its identity and materiality). Who and what is Matigari? This is the question the novel raises at strategic moments, and the multiple answers it provides add to the layers of ambiguity surrounding Ngugi's hero. Is Matigari a modern revolutionary or a conservative, a traditionalist? Is he a figure from Christianity or Gikuyu mythology? Is he the prophetic figure that will usher us toward a future beyond neo-colonial decay or is he a relic from the past we would prefer to forget?

The reader's first encounter with Matigari only complicates notions about his identity and his or her own location and relationship to this story. Matigari is presented to readers as the representation of multiple and often contradictory fictions and functions: he is first presented to us, in apocalyptic terms, as a man at the end of an epoch ("It was all over now"), preceded by the riderless horse that signifies death; and yet he is haunted by memories of times past and is hence motivated by nostalgia ("It felt so long ago"

[*Matigari*, p. 3]). And so almost as soon as he is introduced to us, the question of Matigari's temporality is raised to complicate our relation to him and the history that produced him: does he belong to the future or to the past? Is he of our present time or of that period of pain and suffering that we have worked so hard to forget?[18]

What, indeed, is the relation of his time to our time? This is the problem surrounding Matigari's history and identity at the beginning of the novel. His first gesture on return is to bury his revolutionary past; but he cannot do so without coming to terms with the culture of his youth, his initiation into manhood (p. 4); he sets to gird himself with "a belt of peace," determined to go and "rebuild my house" (p. 5), but his actions, his character, his very materiality, are surrounded by doubts about origins and identities. We are asked to read Matigari as a subject of history, even as he speaks a language that deflects our attention away from what one may call his social determinants or even his historicity. As a human being, Matigari is represented in the most banal language – "He was middle-aged and well-built" (p. 3). He is almost impatient with his corporeality and the burden of history and the human condition: "What trials one had to endure on this earthly journey" (p. 5). His target is often described as a house, but he visualizes this as something more than a dwelling: Matigari's "home on top of the hill" is clearly intended to recall Jerusalem. His mission is described in the familiar rhetoric of patriotism and nation restoration ("I must rise up now and go to all the public places, blowing the horn of patriotic service and the trumpet of patriotic victory" [p. 6]); but his celebratory language is qualified by the apostrophic grammar of melancholy ("So many traps, oh so many temptations, in the way of the traveller of this earth" [p. 6]). The narrative, in short, begins by complicating the central categories of social identity – time, subject, and self.

If the Kenyan government set out to arrest the fictional Matigari, whom it mistook for a real-life revolutionary, it could only do so by misreading Ngugi's novel, by assuming that ideological intentions in the novel were intelligible and determinate. The novel itself promotes such interpretative errors. Ngugi is very careful in his presentation of ambivalence as the essence of

Matigari's subjectivity and of his complicated relation to the post-colonial world. Indeed, it can be said that questions and doubts about the postcolonial subject's identity are the motors that drive this narrative, setting up and undermining its competing centers of meaning. In fact, Matigari's radical difference from Ngugi's recent revolutionaries, such as Karega in *Petals of Blood* and Gatuiria in *Devil on the Cross*, can be found in the way he is made to eschew a hermeneutical function: he is not associated with a radical rejection of the narrative of nationalism nor with a systematic search for an alternative explanation for the postcolonial experience; isolated from such events by his "long time in the forest," he is associated with "the fatigue of many years," social naiveté, and historical amnesia. What appears to be Matigari's lack of political inhibitions or rather his indifference to the postcolonial culture of silence is often represented as a reflection of his misunderstanding of the history of postcolonialism; against the discourse of power and capital, his appeal to universal history is possible because he has not been a witness to the history of postcolonial disenchantment (p. 45).

Clearly, only hasty readers can fail to notice that Matigari's moral authority, unlike that of prophetic figures in Ngugi's earlier works, does not depend on an eschatological premise or promise; on the contrary, the central irony in the novel is that his words and ideas carry weight because of his capacity to remind people of ideals long repressed. Speaking the language of cultural nationalism, a language that is couched in biblical rhetoric, Matigari forces his interlocutors to embrace these ideals even if it means establishing a nostalgic relationship with history: "His words seemed to remind them of things long forgotten, carrying them back to dreams they had had long before" (p. 56). And thus Matigari becomes an important agent against the culture of forgetfulness that has engendered the postcolonial nation.[19] But he is only able to perform this function because of the ambiguity surrounding his character and the indeterminacy of his life story: who is this Matigari who smuggles food into prison or makes jail walls open? His fame and moral authority spread in the absence of concrete answers to his identity: "He became a legend. He became a dream. Still the questions remained: Who *was* Matigari ma

Njiruungi?" (p. 66). In the absence of a determinate answer to the puzzle of Matigari's identity, and with the license granted to them by urban legends and evangelical mythologies, people invent their own versions of Matigari; out of such inventions, the narrative acquires even a greater momentum.

Consider, then, how questions about Matigari's identity are linked to the overall indeterminacy of meaning in the novel. At the beginning of the second part of the text, the children in the city dumpster listen to Muriuki tell the story of how Matigari saved Guthera from the police dog and the resulting narrative exchange transforms the actual event into a fantasy: "Muriuki added salt to his story. Their thoughts grew wings" (p. 69). When it is prised away from the actual event, Matigari's story fulfills a communicative function in the postcolonial culture; it gives both narrators and listeners the license to tell their own stories to counter the phantasmic narratives promoted by the state. There is a craving for an alternative phantasm: "Muriuki, tell us! Who is Matigari ma Njiruungi?" (pp. 70–71). In his weaving of a story about the mysterious stranger, Muriuki acquires the very agency the state has tried to deny him; in listening to the resulting narrative, the dispossessed become active players in the politics of everyday life: "The children spread the news. They took it to the people, who were in any case thirsty for such a story" (p. 71).

Throughout the novel, the narrator discourages both fictional and real readers and listeners from seeking a systematic and empirical narrative in Matigari's life and experience. No sooner do readers think they are closer to Matigari's real identity than they are seduced by the lure of the fictional or even the fairy-tale. The hasty reader might assume that the fictional tale has become the opium of the people because it provides them with "something dramatic, something that livened up their otherwise drab lives" (p. 71); but this notion is quickly disabused when we realize that in a situation in which the oppressive apparatus of the state has colonized reality and truth, they cannot be sought in the realm of the real but in the idiom of spectacle and stories. Indeed, one of the most important political functions of the stories and fantasies surrounding Matigari's identity and actions is how they reopen and recontextualize the history that the state has sought to repress in the name of truth. This is especially the case when rumor about Matigari's identity begins to touch the sore spot of the country's recent history:

"What events?"
"Haven't you heard?"
"Heard what?"
"This strange news?"
"If I had heard it, would I be asking you to tell me about it?"
"Those who went have come back!"
"Which ones?"
"Must you really have everything spelt out? Can't you guess who Matigari ma Njiruungi are?"
"But those are fairy-tales surely? Are they still living?"
"Rumor has it that they have come back with flaming swords in their hands!"
"Flaming swords?"
"Yes! To claim the products of our labour."
"Just a minute! Say that again."
"The country has its patriots."
"Have you actually seen him, or are these rumours?"
Everyone anxiously waited for an answer. Who was Matigari? What did he look like?
At that moment, Matigari appeared before them. He stood about two paces away from them and greeted them.
They all turned towards him.
"My friends! Can you tell me where a person could find truth and justice in this country?"
They looked at him disapprovingly. Some made wordless noises of disapproval. They turned their eyes away from him.
"What is this man asking? Let's first hear stories about Matigari ma Njiruungi! Have you set eyes upon him? What does he look like? How big is he?" (pp. 71–72).

This exchange is remarkable for at least three reasons: first of all, it is an example of Ngugi's mastery of Gikuyu orality and everyday speech. The passage, borrowing from the Gicandi oral genre, presents us with an encounter between friends and proceeds to develop a series of coded commentaries on the political implications of Matigari's return. This coding is itself necessitated by the contingent political situation – the culture of silence and fear enforced by the state – but its overall significance lies in the effect the dialogue generates. In a subtle way, the passage opens with a series of rhetorical questions through which the speakers avoid responsibility for what they are saying, but it is through avoidance that they subvert the culture of silence. The second point, then, is that in talking about an enigma – Matigari – in enigmatic terms, the speakers communicate what would be considered to be a subversive message about the possible return of old revolutionaries and are able to get away with it. The language of this exchange affirms the truth of the event by disclaiming the truth value of the speech act: the story of Matigari's return is described as a fairy-tale or as a rumor. When the point is finally made – "The country has its patriots" – it is done in an almost innocuous way.

The third reason why this passage is remarkable supports the argument I have been presenting so far: that the political agency of the narrative depends on its disclaimer of the real. Stories about Matigari have more cogency and power than the personality and character of the man himself. Like the body of Christ, the figure of Matigari acquires meaning through the struggle over its interpretation: he can be read as "the One prophesied" (p. 81), as the fictional figure in old folktales (p. 127), as the performer of miracles (pp. 157–58), or as a revolutionary, the worst nightmare of the ruling class (pp. 169–70). But all these instances provide readers with a common pattern: no sooner has an interpretative community laid claim to this figure than the narrator intervenes to assert its inderminancy. Through a series of rhetorical questions, Matigari is positioned between his materiality and figuration, between his realism and allegorism: "Was Matigari a man or was he a woman? A child or an adult? Or was he only an idea, an image, in people's minds? *Who Was He?* (p. 158); "Is he real or just a figment of people's imagination? Who and what really *is* Matigari ma Njiruungi? Is he a person, or is he a spirit?" (p. 170). Matigari's elusive identity, his appearance and disappearance on the post-colonial landscape, shifts this narrative constantly from its overt theme – its meditation on the nature of home and patria after decolonization – to the question generated by its conditions of production: what does it mean to be a postcolonial subject displaced from home, history, and culture?

INSIDE AND OUTSIDE REALISM

Ngugi's novel is deliberately frustrating to those who seek a definitive identity and meaning for Matigari and for the history he engenders. This problem is complicated by the fact that Ngugi makes the search for a deep hermeneutics of history one of the primary themes of his novel: he wants to make the important point that in order to understand postcolonial culture and what is seen as its betrayal of nationalist ideals, those who have lived the nightmare of colonialism must dig up its repressed histories and subjects. In this respect, doubts and questions about Matigari's identity only reinforce the urgent need to establish his elusive character and the tortured history that produced it. Indeed, toward the end, the tone of the novel suggests that the question of Matigari's identity has become so central to understanding the betrayal of nationalism that the narrator is being begged to solve this puzzle and provide answers to the historical riddle before it is too late. At the same time, however, the whole movement of the narrative – and its moment of closure – relies on energies derived from our inability to solve the riddle: the hero's moral authority depends on his mysterious identity.

A similar paradox is presented by Matigari's world: he moves in an easily identifiable political and cultural landscape and invokes familiar histories and traditions; the narrator may tell us to locate this narrative in the country of our choice, but Ngugi's immediate readers know where it takes place and who it is talking about. Like the dwellers of the postcolonial city who follow Matigari's magical acts almost religiously, such readers can read between the lines, as it were; in reading between the lines, they create a new world for the novel, outside its bound pages. So, if the problem of realism has become one of the main points of critical debate about this novel, it is because Matigari's quest is both motivated by an urgent desire to understand and represent "contemporary social reality" and to liberate it from the symbolic economy of postcolonialism; reality must be represented and deconstructed at the same time.[20] What this means is that that Matigari throws himself, as it were, into the immediate material world he needs to understand (this is where the realism of the novel resides), but is immediately disenchanted by this world, which he now seeks to transcend (herein lies the motivation for modernism in the novel). While I agree with F. O. Balagoun's claim that the novel mixes genres and methods, I reject his desire to privilege its realism. On the contrary, I want to argue that while Ngugi may still desire realism as the highest form of representation, *Matigari* marks the limit of this desire and perhaps its impossibility; the novel demonstrates that because the history of the postcolony represents the failure of the central categories of modernity – the nation as the basis of a unified identity, a rational, self-reflective bourgeois subject, an intelligible reality, and a progressive history or temporality – it cannot be encapsulated in the narrative economy we have come to associate with realism.

One does not need to read far into Ngugi's novel to see how quickly modernity and realism fail as ideological and methodological entities. One cannot, for example, claim that the unnamed nation in the novel is the object of any kind of patriotic love or affiliation; associated with a disembodied, yet tyrannical voice, the nation is no longer the object of love and desire that was apparent in Ngugi's early novels, or the subject of radical critique as in the middle novels; it is now represented as an alien and alienating object, inscrutable, obtrusive, and repressive. One may then proceed to argue that one of the reasons why Matigari and his aura seduce people is because the individual subject has become the representative of the best ideals and values of his community, in essence its moral center. But this privileging of subjectivity is called into question by Matigari's alterity, the fact that he is otherworldly and cannot hence function as a site of identification. The novel is full of the material signs of the colonial landscape, but it is not patient with the language of verisimilitude: if people seem to be unimpressed with the materiality of Matigari and to be enchanted with his romance, it is because this romance is also associated with a utopian site where old ideals can be secured and be represented. For if the novel were to privilege the language of the social, it would be a victim of the official discourse that has colonized everyday life in the postcolonial state. In a significant shift from his obviously realistic novels, most notably *Petals of Blood*, Ngugi produces a narrative that is located in a specific time and space but seeks to transcend both of them.

Consider, for example, Guthera's story. It is a familiar one in Ngugi's works: a young woman devoted to her church and her father is made to make the difficult choice between her virtue and vice, love and self-betrayal (pp. 33–37). We have seen variations of this story in Ngugi's works over the years: it is the story of women such as Muthoni and Nyambura in *The River Between*, Mwihaki in *Weep Not, Child*, Mumbi in *A Grain of Wheat*, Wanja in *Petals of Blood*, Gathoni in *I will Marry When I Want*, and Wariinga in *Devil on the Cross*. In these earlier works, the struggle between virtue and vice is gendered in terms that are clearly nationalist, for these women are asked to help readers choose between personal and patriotic love and define the true nature of nationalism and patriotism.[21] These women are certainly associated with individual acts of heroism, but in the face of betrayal and treachery, their real virtue is revealed through their ability to overcome their wounded past and give up excessive desires so that the male protagonists can plot out the ideal *polis* of nationalist literature.[22]

The Guthera story presents us with a similar story but with major qualifications and differences in means and ends: the language so highly allegorized that what would in normal circumstances be a very personal story reads like a parable from the Bible ("Long ago, there was a virgin" [p. 33]). In order to acquire its universal meaning, the story is distanced in time. Denied its specificity, the story loses its aesthetic effect (it does not move us because it does not conceal its parabolic function or its artifice), but gains another (it is a parable that speaks to us across cultures and contexts). Now, while Wariinga's story in *Devil on the Cross* was presented to us as the everyday story of an everyday girl (a Kareendi), Guthera represents herself as a "*muiriitu gathiraange*" (a pure woman) which is translated as "a virgin" but is loaded with a double symbolism since it brings to mind the sacrificial virgin and the Virgin Mary. In this respect, Guthera's story is not typological in the realist tradition as defined by critics such as Lukács, but is allegorical in the biblical sense.[23] While Wariinga's story was intended to foreground the everyday experience of a woman lost in the city, Guthera's story seeks to transport readers beyond this immediate point of reference.

And so the question persists: if Ngugi's intention in the novel is to capture social reality, why do his central figures function, in their names, meanings, and narrative functions, as allegorical vehicles? The most immediate reason that comes to mind is that the opposition between realism and allegory proposed here is a false one, that allegory helps the author capture social reality in a deeper sense by estranging readers from the banal discourse promoted by the state. This is perhaps true for the novel as a whole, but the Guthera story contains another explanation: that allegory enables Ngugi to transcend the failed economy of nationalism and thus realism. Evidence for this claim can be found embedded in the simple fact that Guthera and her narrative do not serve the functions which Ngugi had assigned women in his earlier novels: given the choice between the love of the father (and thus nation and patria) she chooses her heavenly father (p. 36); more significantly, in spite of her name, she is not turned into an agent of an ideal national identity; instead of being presented as a victim of the system or as a heroine, she is located somewhere in between the two roles. Clearly, the form of woman can no longer be turned into what Jean Franco has called "the territory of domestic stability" in the name of the nation nor can it be the agency through which the narrative of an ideal national identity "holds out its lure."[24]

From the vantage point of postcoloniality, the nation is no longer the guarantor of identity and its lure and its ideals have been exposed as unattainable. At the end of her story, Guthera provides a clear explanation why she does not sleep with policemen: she associates them with the death of her father and her own betrayal. In response, Matigari falls back on the old language of nationalism, trying to make a distinction between patriotic and treacherous soldiers: "There are ... two types of soldiers. Some are there to protect the people, others to attack them" (p. 37). Guthera's rejoinder is instructive: "I have never seen even one of them protecting the people," she says (p. 37). For those who have lived the social reality of postcoloniality, the language of patriotism is banal, its ideals far removed from everyday life. Without the nostalgia to compensate for this lack, people like Guthera are not absolute victims of the system (because they have found ways of surviving in it), but they are not eager to take on heroic roles either (they have no models of the kind of selfless action on which pure heroism is constructed). Indeed, while Matigari – and the author – encourage us to read the hero's journey or quest as one generated by the desire for the ideals of truth and justice, it is not hard to see how such ideals are represented, from the outset, as unattainable in the politics of everyday life. Ngugi tells us that his novel is based on an oral story about a man who undertakes the search for a man who can cure his illness; he also tells us that the man's journey is plotted, as it were, by the elusiveness of the would-be curer; what he does not note is how the cure itself may be non-existent. In any case, what begins as a straightforward search for an ideal (a cure) is complicated by everyday life and nature.[25]

The quest motif is not, of course, new in Ngugi's novels: as it is deployed in both *Petals of Blood* and *Devil on the Cross*, it is essential to the political message of his novels; it is in journeys that they undertake that Ngugi's political heroes both seek to escape the deracinated postcolonial landscape and to reach a socialist utopia; it is in the process of making such journeys that the hero's political commitments are transformed or solidified. Now, Matigari's quest is also transformative in the sense that it is in the course of his journey through the postcolonial landscape that he becomes convinced that the cause of nationalism has been betrayed. What is different, however, is that Matigari's journey is not cast, in utopian terms, as an act of restitution in which the quest enables one to overcome historical fragmentation and initiate social and individual change. While Matigari's journey begins as an act of *retour* – to the household, to the community, and the unalienated self – his *Erfahrung* (quest) is marked by loss, rupture, and an inability to negotiate the effects of arrested decolonization.[26]

Beneath Matigari's aura lies his alienation. This alienation is apparent from the beginning of the novel where, as we saw before, Matigari is introduced to us as a self divided, a self caught between two temporalities. His journey is propelled by two time frames in conflict: he yearns for the future promised by decolonization, a future symbolized by his imaginary house on the hill, but he cannot wrest himself from memories of childhood and youth, memories that can only return him back to a time of colonial rule and terror symbolized by Settler William. Matigari's nostalgia and melancholy are clear evidence of his suspension in time and space (p. 6). What of his alienation and loss? They can be found in his romance of the nation: for against the harsh reality of postcolonial terror, Matigari speaks the language of restitution which, in the circumstances, cannot be read as anything more than an expression of his naiveté.

Matigari may be the last custodian of nationalist or socialist ideals, but it is significant that his romance of nationhood is represented in an ironic discourse that distances him from both the narrator and the reader. This kind of irony is evident in that scene at the beginning of the novel when Matigari first encounters the shanty town children outside a leather factory. This scene is first loaded with familiar Christian symbolism. Like Jesus in St. Matthew's Gospel, Matigari sees children as the manifestation of the kingdom of heaven or, in this case, the nationalist utopia; so when he sees a battalion of children running in the middle of the street he believes, if only momentarily, that he has found his children and his return must be complete.[27] The Gikuyu text captures the play of anticipation and doubt well: "Togukorwo ciana imwe ciakwa iri ..." ("Maybe some of my children are ..."). The assertion is one of anticipation, but the ellipses open up a space of uncertainty and doubt. Matigari's desire for *retour* is balanced by the narrator's awareness of the gap between the nation's longing for a future of freedom and prosperity and the perverted form that decolonization has taken. The Gikuyu text valorizes this gap much better than the English translation:

Akiigua aathera ngoro. Akihiũha na kũria karaagita na ciana cierekeire, ngoro yaake ĩtuumatuumage ... reke hiũhe ngameere nĩ ndaacooka ... matige mbũrũũrũ ... tuinũkanie ... tũingire nyũmba hamwe ... twakie mwaki hamwe ... kai ndaakinyagira kii tiga nyũmba yaakwa ... mũcii ... kihuurũko ... ciana ithaakagire githakuinĩ kana nja nyekinĩ ... mbooco yagwa thĩ tukeenyũrana ... gikeno kiingi thũũtha wa thĩĩna mũingĩ ... heho ... ng'aragu ... njaga ... kwaga toro ... mĩnoga ... na gikuũ kũhũũraga huti kaingi? ... gũtiri kĩega kiumaga heega ... Gũtirĩ utukũ ũtakia. (p. 10)

(He felt his heart cleansed. He hurried toward the direction of the tractor and the children, his heart thumping. Let me hurry and tell them I have come back ... so that they can stop the rumbling ... so that we can go home together ... light the fire ... what else was I seeking except my household ... home ... a place of rest ... with children playing under the eaves or on the grass outside ... sharing a bean which has fallen on the ground ... much happiness after a lot of strife ... cold ... famine ... sleeplessness ... fatigue ... and death always coming up to the fence ... no goodness comes from a good place ... there is no night that does not eventually turn into day.)

In order to fully appreciate Ngugi's use of ironic discourse in a passage like this one, we need to emphasize that what we have here is a scene of misrecognition: unaware of the realities of neo-colonial poverty, Matigari remains focused on his ideals; his language conjures images of a precolonial homestead whose restoration is justified by years of pain and struggle. As a result, Matigari's language, the language of national romance, is cast in the form of a wish or a dream; his "cleansed" heart hankers for visions beyond the crude materiality of the factory and its waste; he imagines his children playing in a pastoral yard, under the eaves or on the grass. What makes this language ironic are two closely related factors: first, Matigari's interior monologue, rather than being connected to any recognizable reality, is alienated from its referents; second, the narrator refuses to endorse the hero's desires because he or she knows, as does the reader, that they contain images that cannot be sanctioned by the reality before us. Indeed, the sentence that follows – "Aakorire uriru muthenya barigici" ("he met a scene of horror in broad daylight") – is a reminder of how far Matigari's vision is removed from the postcolonial scene represented here by a garbage dump in which vultures, dogs, and children fight for food (p. 11).

Matigari's journey into this landscape only serves to underscore the radical division between the ideals of national restoration and its ill-fated history in decolonization; as a result his quest, rather than affirming the ideals of national restoration, becomes a journey in which even the basic grammar of nationalism is pushed to the limit and idealism is dislocated. This dislocation is most apparent in the three movements, or structural divisions, of the novel:

Matigari's awareness of the marginality of the national romance in the postcolonial economy (part one), his rethinking of the project of decolonization (part two), and the ambiguous establishment of a new narrative of identity (part three). Let us examine these movements in turn.

In the first part of the book, Matigari's journey can be read as a kind of quest, not as mere adventure or experience, but a journey that implies, to borrow Miriam Hansen's words, "both a temporal dimension, that is, duration, habit, repetition, and return, and a degree of risk to the experiencing subject."[28] Matigari's journey is one in which the temporal dimension (the hero's return) is defined by a degree of risk. Displaced from the real experience in the postcolony, Matigari has to depend on others for his education in the ways of the new world. The characters who educate him have names which, at first sight, appear to confirm Matigari's ideals and expectations: his new companions are Muriuki (the resurrected one), Ngaruro (the sign of transfiguration), and Guthera (the pure one). But we cannot read Matigari's education in the hands of these subjects without noticing the apparent irony – they live in a world in which the ideals their names represent are negated. What lessons can Matigari learn from these degraded subjects of postcolonial modernity?

One could, of course, reverse the terms involved in any discussion of Matigari's education and argue that he is the teacher in this situation. But what lessons can Matigari teach those who have lived through the disenchantment of decolonization? What knowledge does he bring to the banality of postcolonial life? It is important to note that contrary to the motif of quest indicated by the structure of the novel, Matigari does not see himself as an agent of change when he first returns from the forest. In the first part of the novel, for example, he simply assumes that the ideals of decolonization have been fulfilled and his task has been completed: he has returned home to rest. Others may interpret his actions in mystical and messianic terms, but as far as Matigari is concerned, the beginning of the narrative is actually its ending. At the beginning of the novel, then, Matigari sees himself standing at the end of time: "It was all over now" (p. 3). The riderless horse that welcomes him is a familiar sign of death – of the end. But even as he embarks on what he assumes is the moment of closure, Matigari is well aware of the risks involved: "It was all over now, but he knew he still had to be careful" (p. 3).

And before the end of the first part of the novel, he has confronted all the risks that have come to define postcoloniality – economic decline, the abuse of political power, and the crisis of culture. The overriding question for him now is how he can meet the challenge posed by these unexpected experiences. How does Matigari meet the risks posed by arrested decolonization? He appeals to the moral authority of a traditional African community: "you've dared to raise a whip against your own father?" he asks Boy. "You're not my father!" Boy shouts back (p. 48). The conflict here involves more than mere semantics: Matigari falls back on the language of tradition in which the father and son relationship is determined by the age grade system. Boy defines paternity strictly in terms of biology. The crisis of language is also a crisis of moral values.

The second part of the novel is concerned with the search for moral or ethical values, most notably, truth and justice. Confronted by the failures of the grand narrative of nationalism, Matigari embarks on a journey whose goal is nothing less than the restitution of "things long forgotten" (p. 56). Is this a journey into the past or the future? It is both, for Matigari has now become the subject of what the Gikuyu text aptly calls "*Uhoro*," which means both an event and a discourse: as an event, he is a symbol of the past, of history; but as a figure of discourse he belongs to the present, the moment of enunciation. It is significant, then, to see Matigari as generating a historical narrative defined by his own mystical character and his doubleness (his commitment to a decolonized future is predicated on the recovery of old values). More significantly, in order to speak about Matigari as "*Uhoro*" (an event), people are forced to simultaneously invoke the past and present and thus judge the experiences of the latter against the ideals of the former. The song the people of Trampville compose for Matigari is emblematic of the temporal doubleness I have in mind here: it is supposed to be an original composition, but in reality it is a mere replica of an old song in a Gikuyu folktale; but the song is composed and performed in a context that is so different that it no longer has an essential connection with the old song (p. 71). And as I argued earlier, it is telling and retelling this *"Uhoro"* that the workers of Trampville are able to recover narratives, ideals, and experiences which the postcolonial dictatorship has foreclosed.

In his journey through the postcolonial landscape, Matigari forces a rethinking of the culture and economy that has emerged after decolonization (p. 72). In the first part of the novel, as we saw earlier, Matigari is educated in the ways of the world when his ideality is confronted with the realities of postcolonial power; in the second part of the book, this pedagogical motif is reversed in fascinating ways: now, it is the populace of the postcolony that are educated when the logic of their quotidian life is confronted by ideals long forgotten or negated. As Matigari goes around the country asking people where he can find truth and justice, he makes these values, rather than power and property, central to the discourse on nation and identity. As I argued earlier, people seem more interested in the stories surrounding Matigari rather than his concrete existence, but this does not mean that his fiction has no political function. On the contrary, the more people become absorbed in Matigari's fiction, the more it becomes an indispensable counterpoint to official discourse; in being able to talk about the phenomenon of the strange man seeking truth and justice, the populace are able to overcome the culture of silence sanctioned by the state.

Telling stories about Matigari becomes the vocal point of public discourse. Again, the Gikuyu text captures this function well: "Guothe caai wahoraga andu mathikiriie ngoga iria iri cama gukira uuki kana cukaari" (p. 67) ("Everywhere the tea went cold as people listened to astonishing stories which were sweeter than honey or sugar"). In the end, as these stories are repeated over and over again, they deprive the state of its monopoly of discourse and call its version of the national narrative into question. By the end of the second part of the book, it has become apparent that what appears to be the narrative locus – Matigari's quest for truth and justice – is not as important as the way this quest is received or interpreted; the defining question is no longer who Matigari is, but his capacity to undermine official discourse by presenting a narrative of virtue as an alternative to the empty rhetoric of state power (pp. 123–25).

The final part of the novel is ostensibly about Matigari's disenchantment, his recognition that the "belt of peace" he has been wearing is useless when confronted by the ruthless machinery of power. But Matigari's abandonment of his peaceful quest and his resort to armed resistance should not conceal an even more radical shift in Ngugi's narrative, for the novel has moved us from its initial preoccupation with a linear and univocal narrative of return (part one), to a dual quest for the meaning of both past and present (part two), to a polyvocal narrative in which different voices are competing for moral and discursive authority (part three). Matigari is still the focus of the last part of the narrative, but his story is broken up into montages and other forms of dispersed lexical units, each denoting a set of values and series of meaning in competition with one another. This break-up of forms echoes Matigari's ultimate hermeneutical discovery: "The world is turned upside down, but it must be set right again. For I have seen that in our land today lies are decreed to be the truth, and the truth is decreed to be a lie" (p. 137). Matigari's knowledge is not so much a coming to consciousness, as is often the case in the bourgeois novel, but a recognition of the irony that defines his relationship with the world he seeks to change. The final movement of the novel can actually be read as Matigari's performance of his newly acquired irony: While at the beginning of the novel he had sought to recover his house by appealing to his natural and social rights, he now realizes the significance of ironic strategies and thus arrives at the house disguised as a "dignitary" (p. 164).

While Matigari's return was intended to bring the question of colonialism to an end, it has, ironically, reopened it. More importantly, while the novel ends by affirming the familiar themes about revolution and change, such affirmations are made against the background of doubt and uncertainty triggered by Matigari's mysterious identity which the ending of the novel confounds rather than resolves: "Everywhere in the country the big question still remained: Who was Matigari ma Njiruungi? Was he dead, or was he alive?" (p. 174). And it is precisely because of the mysteriousness of his self and his actions that Matigari can function as a sign of resistance and identity. Without a thorough knowledge of who he is and the forces he represents, the state cannot imprison him; and because he has no knowable or fixed character, the populace can transform him, in their imagination, into an agent of social change. At the end of the novel, it is clear that what is more important than the ostensible realities represented in the novel are the discursive forces at work in the narrative and the different fictional genres that Ngugi has deployed – the language of Christian deliverance and apocalypse, the American Western, and the urban tale. In this novel, reality has become secondary to the forms in which it is represented, and this marks an important development in Ngugi's career.

CHAPTER 9

Writing freedom: essays and criticism

Ngugi first called attention to the close relation between his non-fictional and fictional works in the preface to *Homecoming*, his first collection of essays, where he noted that although his critical prose and literary works were differentiated by genre and the protocols and conventions of writing and reading, their conditions of production were similar. Many of the essays in this collection, he reminded his readers, were written at about the same time as his first three novels and were thus products of "the same moods"; they also touched "on similar questions and problems."[1] But even as he laid out the common ground occupied by his novels and essays, Ngugi was eager to separate their political function, and in this separation we can begin to understand the unseen ideological and aesthetic forces that have shaped his art and thought from the beginning of his artistic career as a student at Makerere University College to his preeminence as an African writer in exile. The creative writer, Ngugi reminded the readers of his first collection of essays, was "immersed in a world of imagination that is other than his conscious self. At his most intense and creative the writer is transfigured, he is possessed, he becomes a medium" (*Homecoming*, p. xv). Creative writing, Ngugi seemed to suggest, emerged out of an unconscious world (of drives and desires) and the novelist or poet was a genius in touch with higher creative forces. In contrast, the act of writing critical essays was motivated by the need to rationalize the author's "beliefs, attitudes and outlook" in a more "argumentative form" (p. xv). The fictional works had a symbiotic relationship to the critical essays, but the two could not be conflated.

What is interesting about Ngugi's separation of the unconscious

imagination of fiction and the argumentative form of the essay is
the way it calls attention to the ideological and aesthetic paradox
that explains his writing career and several important ruptures in
his works. This contradiction takes two closely related forms: on
the one hand, Ngugi's career has been one sustained attempt to
show how the literary imagination is connected to a certain set of
political and social interests; he has been consistent in his belief
that literature does not grow out of a vacuum but is "given
impetus, shape, direction, and even area of concern by social,
political and economic forces in a particular society" (p. xv). From
the very beginning of his career, as a student of English at
Makerere University in the early 1960s to his exalted position as
the high Marxist guru of African literature at the University of
Nairobi in the 1970s, Ngugi has defined the character of literature
in terms of its overdetermination by political economy. What has
changed over time is the nature of this overdetermination, or
rather the structural relation between the text and its historical
context.[2]

On the other hand, however, Ngugi has always granted the
aesthetic a measure of autonomy from the political. Because it
seems to be overshadowed by Ngugi's desire to promote the
political function of literature, this notion of aesthetic autonomy is
easy to ignore; but it has been at the very center of his thinking
about literature and culture in one form or another. Indeed, what
has changed over time is not Ngugi's claim that art has a social
function that cannot be reduced to simple politics, but the nature
and degree of the dialectical relation between the two realms of
social experience. Even in the preface to *Homecoming*, which was
written when Ngugi had fully embraced a Marxist aesthetic ideology that seemed to subordinate the art object to productive forces,
he would still insist that literary works could neither be abstracted
from, nor subsumed in, political economy: "Literature is of course
primarily concerned with what any political and economic arrangement does to the spirit and the values governing human
relationships" (p. xvi). In thinking about the different claims Ngugi
has made about the nature of art and its relation to politics, it is
apparent that the two cannot be separated entirely nor be collapsed into each other. To do so would mean missing the most subtle

elements in his critical work. For even as he increasingly espoused materialist theories of art and strove to privilege the base structure over the superstructure, Ngugi could simply not let go of the central liberal notion that art was about the human spirit, individual and collective values, and social relationships. This liberal notion of art was, of course, inherited from Matthew Arnold and F. R. Leavis via the Makerere school of English. It was a notion built on the belief that while art could not be entirely separated from political and cultural forces, its value lay primarily in its subjective, spiritual, and moral character; it was an idea built on the claim that art, more specifically literature, provided security from the violence associated with radical change.[3] This was the central creed in Ngugi's early essays. His interest in "Mau Mau," he told Dennis Duerden in a 1964 interview, was not generated by an ideological necessity – the need to rehabilitate and represent this important historical event – but the artistic need to show the effect it had on ordinary people and its "destruction of family life, the destruction of family relationships."[4] Of the many writers he had read as an undergraduate at Makerere University College, Ngugi told his interlocutors in the early 1960s, the ones who influenced his art most were modernists like D. H. Lawrence, who had "a way of entering into the spirit of things," and Joseph Conrad, who impressed the young writer by his mastery of "the morality of action" and the represention of human suffering.[5]

By the time he came to write his more mature theoretical essays, Ngugi had stopped foregrounding such subjective questions as morality and spirituality, but he could not entirely expunge the grammar of liberal culture from his thinking about art. Even in his most radical essays written in the 1970s and collected in *Homecoming*, most notably "Literature and Society," art was still defined by what we may call a metaphysics rather than an ideology: literature was part of "man's artistic activities"; it was characterized as "a symbol of man's creativity, of man's historical process of being and becoming" (p. 6). True, literature had a social character and could not thus be abstracted from its context, which was in turn defined by a complexity of historical forces; but it could not be considered to be "just a mechanistic reflection of social reality" (p. 6). During his high Marxist period Ngugi was a harsh critic of "the general tendency" to see literature as something belonging to a "surreal world, or to a metaphysical ethereal plane"; but he adamantly insisted that while it emerged from "man's historical process of being and becoming," literature was something more than the process that produced it: literature was an "artistic activity," a symbol of "man's creativity"; it could not transcend historical forces but neither could it be reduced to these forces (p. 6).

THE WRITER IN A COLONIAL SITUATION

I begin by calling attention to the uneasy relationship between Ngugi's well-known materialist view of history and cultural production and his lesser-known insistence on the semi-autonomous nature of the work of art for two reasons: first, to underline a certain continuity in his thinking on art and literature even in the midst of his many declarations about the epistemological ruptures that characterize his career. Secondly, to foreground his troubled relation to the colonial culture that had created him as a writer and from which he has been trying to escape ever since. One way of thinking about these problems is to recall a point that I have been making throughout this study: that apart from his own experiences growing up under colonialism in Kenya and maturing as a writer in the culture of arrested decolonization, Ngugi's aesthetic foundation was not in Marx or Fanon, whom he discovered later in his career, but in the doctrines of Englishness associated with Matthew Arnold and F. R. Leavis and promoted in the imperial sphere by colonial schools and universities. Carol Sicherman has provided us with a systematic analysis of Ngugi's imprisonment in the colonial library and aesthetic.[6] It is an imprisonment that began in the prestigious Alliance High School where Ngugi was a model student product of the colonial culture represented by E. Carey Francis, the headmaster of the school.

Carey Francis was a colonial missionary in every sense of the world: he believed that the African could be educated into the ways of Christian virtue and faith which were, significantly, also the ways of Englishness. Run on the lines of an English grammar school, Alliance sought to reproduce the African as a perfect colonial subject. And even in the midst of "Mau Mau" and the political crisis in Kenya in the 1950s, Carey Francis was eager to draw attention to the way some Africans could be educated into the ways of Englishness:

The school is run on the lines of a grammar school in this country [i.e., England] but with everything simpler; no matrons and no frills. The boys wash their own clothes and keep the place clean. We engage in much the same activities: games, dramatics (we have produced a full Shakespeare play each year for the last three years), singing, Scouting and innumerable societies. Boys have a background poor in the things of European civilization: they know nothing of wireless and motor bicycles and little of money, and few of them come from homes where there is intelligent conversation or where books or even newspapers are regularly read. Yet they are essentially the same as English boys. They would bear comparison with those of the European schools in Kenya, or with a good school in this country, in intelligence, in athletic prowess, in industry, courtesy, courage and trustworthiness, and as gentlemen.[7]

Carey Francis, the product of Cambridge and the imperial spirit, was the replica of Thomas Arnold in the colonial sphere. Above all, he knew his Africans well, knew where they had come from and where they were going. His African students had not inherited the finer things of European civilization and its material culture, but they could be educated into civility through games, work, and Shakespeare.

Although he was perhaps one of the most brilliant mathematicians of his generation, Carey Francis did not seem to believe that science was central to the project of educating the African: sports and English were more in tune with colonial thinking on such matters. Those who mastered English, Ngugi was to recall later in *Decolonising the Mind*, were accorded a special place in the colonial order of things.[8] As one of the strongest adherents of this creed, the young Ngugi arrived at Makerere University eager to master English and Englishness – its moral tone, its manners, and its literary texts. And later at Makerere University College, as Sicherman has reminded us, he would join an English Department cast in the Arnold and Leavis mold, one that promoted "'universal' moral values, interiority, and individualism."[9]

Ngugi's journalist writings from the early 1960s provide clear evidence of the hold colonial culture had on his generation even on the eve of decolonization: these essays are minor in Ngugi's larger project, but it is not by accident that they all advocate the liberal values of colonial culture, values such as self-restraint, moral judgment, and the cultivation of civility. Though written on the eve of Kenyan independence, these essays were not concerned with the political project of the time – a project driven by the desire to redefine the relation between the colonizer and the colonized. Ngugi's attitude toward nationalism was skeptical not so much because he had foreseen the pitfalls of arrested decolonization, but because he feared that a nationalist ideal that promoted collective interests above individual desires would end up becoming a cultural prison that was as bad as colonialism. The end result of nationalism, he argued, in an early review essay collected in *Homecoming*, "should be man ultimately freed from fear, suspicion and parochial attitudes," not man chained to collective interest and identities (p. 24). Individuality had to be promoted and defended because the collective forces that had brought the new nation into being had the potential of denigrating the self; culture needed to be protected from anarchy.[10]

As a good product of liberal colonial culture, Ngugi could not see how the great ideas of liberalism – individualism and liberty – could be conceptualized without the terminology he had inherited from his masters. It is a mark of the hold the ideals promoted by Carey Francis had on the young writer that the colonial headmaster would be represented in both *The River Between* and *Weep Not, Child* as a benevolent figure without prejudice and malice.[11] And it is a mark of Ngugi's awareness of his indebtness to the colonial creed that when the ghost of Carey Francis was to reappear in *Petals of Blood*, fifteen years later, it would take the Dickensian form of Cambridge Fraudsham, the colonizer of the African mind, the agent of a deformed bourgeois civility, the sham and fraud that Cambridge produced. What had taken place between 1964 and 1977? How did Saint Francis become the devil incarnate?

The common response to this question is to argue that Ngugi was liberated from the colonial ideology by his discovery of Fanon and Marx when he was a graduate student at Leeds University, where the liberal Englishness of F. R. Leavis had given way to the

English Marxism of Arnold Kettle.[12] This is true to the extent that
Fanon and Marx provided Ngugi with an alternative ideology and
methodology at a time when, as he was to note later in *Moving the
Centre,* formerly colonized peoples "were demanding and asserting
their right to define themselves and their relationship to the universe from their own centres in Africa and Asia."[13] A greater
revolution, however, was taking place in Ngugi's own relationship
to his aesthetic theory and practice. Having begun his writing
career as a firm believer in the ideals of the great tradition, ideals
anchored in Arnold's influential claim that culture had a value that
was greater than that of material production and Leavis's notion
that the essence of literature lay in its moral claims, Ngugi was now
seeking ways of shifting his aesthetic ideology from morality and
sensibility to history and epistemology.

Rejecting the great tradition as his frame of reference, Ngugi
affiliated himself with other African, Asian, and Caribbean writers
as they sought, he noted in *Moving the Centre,* "the right to name the
world for ourselves" (p. 3). The interesting point, though, is that *A
Grain of Wheat,* the novel in which he sought to reject the great
tradition, was the one in which he displayed his mastery of the
forms of the European novelistic conventions. And it is perhaps
out of his own awareness of the power of inherited forms and
aesthetic ideologies that Ngugi was prompted to turn more and
more, in the essays and reviews written in the late 1960s and early
1970s, to a set of problems closely associated with the nature and
function of a literary tradition.

Take, for example, Ngugi's difficult attempt to redefine culture
in a postcolonial situation. Many of the essays written in the 1960s
and early 1970s were really attempts to think about culture and its
relation to the social forces which the Arnoldian/Leavisite tradition had denigrated or excluded from the aesthetic sphere. But in
order to explore the relation of culture to society, Ngugi had first to
come to terms with the tradition of cultural nationalism which had
occupied a prominent place in his early novels, but one which had
presented a dilemma of sorts to his critical thinking. This dilemma
arose from a temporal or theoretical cauldron: Ngugi had celebrated nationalism in his novels, but his critical essays had consistently warned against the threat of nationalism to bourgeois

individualism. By the time his thinking had changed enough to allow him to endorse the national project, it was quite clear that the promises of independence were being forgotten and the narrative of national consciousness could only be generated by an awareness of its failure and abortiveness; and at the same time, however, it did not make sense to deconstruct the nationalist project without first endorsing it.

The major essays in *Homecoming* are conscious attempts to work out this dilemma, to understand the nationalist project from the (paradoxical) vantage point provided by its failure. The inaugural question here, as Ngugi was to recognize in an essay appropriately titled "Toward a National Culture," was about interrogating the liberal idea of culture itself; and this involved, among other things, a radical rethinking of the place of traditional African culture in intellectual discourse and its bearing on the character of the new nation: "Is culture something which can be preserved, even if this were desirable? Is there such a thing as an original culture?" (*Homecoming*, p. 4). Ngugi accepted a basic premise borrowed from Melville Herskovist's anthropology – that African culture was not lost in the process of colonization, but had actually retained important "survivals" which might be considered to be the basis of a new national culture. But he had serious doubts about whether the aspects of African culture that had survived colonialism were the right ones. How could traditional culture, which had been the basis of the African nationalist project, be reconciled to the needs of a modern world? These problems run through his early works. Indeed, the conflict in *The River Between* is between a Gikuyu culture that represents itself as pure and a Gikuyu culture that prides itself on its mastery of colonial modernity.

Ngugi's theoretical reflections on culture in a postcolonial situation were further complicated by the fact that he was writing at a time when it was difficult for an African writer to celebrate the idea of a national culture without being associated with a new ruling class that had wrapped itself around the romance of the past and turned culture into what Fanon had called "a religious cult."[14] In order to legitimize itself while masking its continuous commitment to the colonial project, the new Kenyan state, under Jomo Kenyatta, had become adept at performing "national culture" as part of its spectacle of power.[15] Against this background, Ngugi needed to provide a critique of the state's use and misuse of African culture: at the same time, however, he had come increasingly under the influence of Fanon and one of the central doctrines in the latter's thought was how culture, which was once at the center for the struggle of African independence, had increasingly become an instrument of neo-colonial social and economic relationships. In 1959, at the Congress of Black Writers and Artists in Rome, Fanon had argued that among "the cultured individuals" of the colonized countries, the idea of culture was concomitant with the politics of decolonization: "For these individuals, the demand for a national culture and the affirmation of the existence of such a culture represent a special battlefield. While the politicians situate their action in actual present-day events, men of culture take their stand in the field of history."[16]

At a time when Ngugi was still espousing the doctrine of an individual identity pitted against the nation, Fanon had recognized the centrality of culture in the political economy of colonialism: because colonial rule and conquest had sought to empty "the native's brain of all form and content" and distort, disfigure, and destroy his or her past, the work of rehabilitating national culture was imperative.[17] What made culture so important in the narrative of liberation, argued Fanon, was its location in the field of history, which was nothing less than the body and the heart of the colonized; the very "legitimacy of the claims of a nation" depended on the colonized subjects' ability to recover and celebrate the value of their denigrated history.[18]

Taking his cue from Fanon, Ngugi turned his attention to the question of history in African literature in a 1968 essay called "The Writer and His Past." In this essay, a signature piece in *Homecoming*, Ngugi began his reflections on the writer's relationship to the past not by affirming the essential historicity of literary production, or the significance of history to postcolonial literature, but by noting how the narrative of history and the historical events associated with colonization continued to haunt the African writer. Ngugi presented this haunting of history as inherent in the novel as a genre: the novelist is haunted by a sense of the past, he argued, because of the generic imperative that he (or she) must

come to terms with history and sensitively register "his encounter
with history, his people's history" (p. 39). History gave novelists
authority because it connected them to the "mainstream" of
collective dramas. But the presencing of history in fiction also
exposed the author's tenuous relation with time, for the invocation
of temporality did not necessarily provide the novelist with
answers to the most troublesome question about the status of the
historical event in a fictional narrative; alienated from the histories
they represented, novelists were often forced to ponder the value
of their works to the future of their nations (p. 40). Ngugi traced the
haunting of the novelist by history to questions of locality and class:
produced in the "emptiness" of colonialism, colonial subjects were
detached from the mainstream of history; their identity was the
effect of a misdirected temporality.

And yet in order for the novelist to live up to what Ngugi
considered his or her social mission, he or she had to come to terms
with the past: "What the African novelist has attempted to do is
restore the African character to his history. The African novelist
has turned his back on the Christian god and resumed the broken
dialogue with the gods of his people" (p. 43). Such acts of restitution did not, however, ameliorate what Jacques Derrida has come
to call the "hauntology of history,"[19] for if the writer became too
fixated with the past, history could become a fetish, an act of
forgetfulness rather than commemoration. The African writer
who became too fascinated with history and the need to correct his
disfigured past became detached from what Ngugi considered to
be the urgent concerns of the contemporary period. History
haunted the novel in its paradoxical imperative: only a recounting
of the past enabled the African to overcome the alienation engendered by colonial culture; but the representation of African society
in its pastness could easily become a form of renunciation of the
dynamic forces driving postcolonial society.

Writing on national culture ten years after Fanon, Ngugi had
the advantage of witnessing the dialectic of national culture transformed into postcolonial mysticism and romance; his task, then,
was to demystify the idea of national culture by restoring its
dialectical force. The tactic he adopted was a simple one. He
rejected the liberal notion of culture as a product of individual

talent and called attention to the dialectical and historical process that enabled social practices. This was the cultural work of the essays he had brought together in *Homecoming*:

Culture, in its broadest sense, is a way of life fashioned by a people in their collective endeavour to live and come to terms with their total environment. It is the sum of their art, their science and all their social institutions, including their system of beliefs and rituals. In the course of this creative struggle and progress through history, there evolves a body of material and spiritual values which endow that society with a unique ethos. Such values are often expressed through the people's songs, dances, folk-lore, drawing, sculpture, rites and ceremonies. Over the years these varieties of artistic activity have come to symbolize the meaning of the word culture. Any discussion of culture inevitably centres around these activities, but we must bear in mind that they are derived from a people's way of life and will change as that way of life is altered, modified, or developed through the ages. In our present situation we must in fact try to see how new aspects of life can be clarified or given expression through new art-forms or a renewal of the old. (*Homecoming*, p. 4).

In this passage from the 1972 introduction to *Homecoming*, Ngugi had made the first move toward a Marxist definition of culture. What stood out in this passage was his determination to call attention to factors which, in his view, the official definition and practice of African culture was trying to repress: the fact that culture had a collective character and that it was a product of the dialectical relationship between human beings and nature. At a time when political leaders in African were fetishizing culture and using it to control political dissent, Ngugi was careful to represent the function of culture in the new African nation as one tied to radical political interests: "Political and economic liberation are the essential condition for cultural liberation, for the true release of a people's creative spirit and imagination" (p. 11).

At this point, we need to recall that while Ngugi's (theoretical) notions of culture had been inherited from colonial liberalism and transformed by postcolonial Marxism, his early novels had been premised on the romance of African or Gikuyu culture popularized by nationalists in Kenya since the 1920s. Neither his Makerere liberalism, nor his Fanonist Marxism could exorcize the romance of culture that had created such a powerful work as *The River Between*. This idea of culture as the representation of the romantic spirit of a people could, in fact, find a place in his evolving, materialist notion of cultural production in the 1970s. It explains the claim, in the introduction to *Homecoming*, that what distinguished African art from its European counterpart was its instrumentality – African art "was not, as it is in modern Europe, severed from the physical, social and religious needs of the community" (p. 6); it had an "integrative function" (p. 7). It did not occur to Ngugi that his evidence for this view of culture was coming from the same authorities who were being accused of having turned national culture into a mystical instrument of state power or the colonial library.

Ngugi's dilemma here was simple: how could he distance himself from the cultural nationalists, who were now in power in Kenya and elsewhere in Africa, without negating their ideals and ideologies which, as we saw earlier in this study, were crucial to his own authority as a writer? His solution was equally simple: he could harness the symbols and events of cultural nationalism and append them to Fanonist Marxism and in the process rewrite the history of nationalism in Central Kenya. A case in point: while Ngugi's early novels had dramatized the process by which cultural nationalists sought to appropriate and nativize colonial institutions, Ngugi, writing on national culture in *Homecoming*, would claim that the anticolonial struggle in Kenya had been marked by a rejection of "the missionary colonial institutions" and it was out of this negation that new art forms had emerged (pp. 11–12). In order for Ngugi's art and thought to emerge out of what he himself was later to characterize as a crisis, he needed to rewrite the history of colonialism and nationalism so that he could rethink his own relationship with the past and re-evaluate his project within the political and symbolic economy of neo-colonialism.

There is, in addition, a way in which Ngugi was using his essays on national culture to question his own identity as a colonial subject and a former adherent to the liberal ideologies of the Makerere school. The confrontation between the new Ngugi – Marxist and agnostic – and the old Ngugi – faithful Christian and cultural nationalist – took place when the novelist addressed the

Fifth General Assembly of the Presbyterian Church of East Africa (PCEA) at Nairobi on March 12, 1970. This gathering was important for reasons which might not be apparent to many readers. The PCEA was perhaps the most influential Protestant church in Kenya. As the Church of Scotland Mission it had been closely associated with colonial culture, and had been at the vanguard of many debates on cultural and social policies, most notably those relating to education and health. It had educated many members of the new African elite, including Jomo Kenyatta, the president of Kenya in the 1970s, and Ngugi himself. The values promoted by this church – hard work, thrift, and education – were central to the ethic promoted in Ngugi's early works. Clearly, Ngugi had been invited to address the church because of his close social and cultural affinities with it. Indeed, Ngugi was a close intellectual ally of the Reverand John Gatu, the liberal Moderator of the Presbyterian Church of East Africa.

Knowing how closely he was associated with Christianity in Kenya, Ngugi must have felt it imperative to begin his address with a renunciation of his own Christianity: "I am not a man of the Church. I am not even a Christian" (*Homecoming*, p. 31). As Ime Ikiddeh was to note in his introduction to *Homecoming*, this renunciation of Christianity and the established church was considered by the delegates attending the PCEA meeting to be heretical:

He had hardly ended his address when a wiry old man visibly choking with anger leapt to the floor, and, shaking his walking-stick menacingly towards the front, warned the speaker to seek immediate repentance in prayer. The old man did not forget to add as a reminder that in spite of his shameless denial and all his blasphemy, the speaker *was* a Christian, and the evidence was his first name. Ngugi had never given serious thought to this contradiction. Now it struck him that perhaps the old man had a point, and the name James, an unfortunate anomaly, had to go. (p. xi)

What is remarkable about this scene of renunciation – and Ngugi's whole address to the Presbyterian Church of East Africa – is that the old man was right on the mark when he described the novelist's denial of Christianity as shameless. For leaving the issue of the name aside, the evidence of the novelist's Christianity was to be found in his fictional works and his whole stream of thought.

Indeed, the essay that came out of this address, "Church, Culture and Politics" (one of the key pieces in *Homecoming*) was a display of Ngugi's mastery of the Christian idiom. True, the subject of the essay was the way in which the church had been implicated in the colonial project in Kenya and how it had repressed the nationalist movement, but the register that Ngugi adopted to make this argument was clear evidence of his own intimate knowledge of the discourse he was renouncing. True, Ngugi was presenting his Christian audience with narratives and signs of their own failure to support nationalism, and their willingness to secure cultural alienation, but he was also trying to convert his listeners to a new gospel of Christian charity wearing the mask of socialism.

Indeed, if the triumph of Christianity in Kenya could be explained by its uncanny ability to translate seminal African values and cultural practices into the idiom of the early Christian church, Ngugi's task was similarly that of translating socialist values into the grammar of African Christianity:

I believe the Church could return to (or learn lessons from) the primitive communism of the early Christian Church of Peter and also the communalism of the traditional African society. With this, and working in alliance with the socialist aspirations of the African masses, we might build a new society to create a new man freed from greed and competitive hatred, and ready to realize his full potential in humble co-operation with other men in a just socialist society. Remember that Book of Revelation: "I saw a new heaven and a new earth" . . . Yes, but the cry of the psalmist in the Old Testament is more apt to our situation: "How shall we sing the Lord's song in a strange land?" I believe that Christians, together with members of other organizations which avow humanism, could help in the struggle to move away from the strange land of capitalism, neo-colonialism and western middle-class culture. For this we may very well need to destroy the old temple to build a new, different one. (p. 36)

In rejecting the Christian tradition that had been central to his identity as a writer, however, Ngugi had created the space in which he could turn Marxism into a constitutive element of his future work as a novelist and a critic. In the essays collected in *Writers in Politics* and *Barrel of a Pen*, Ngugi began a project whose goal was not simply to change the way students and scholars in

Kenya talked about literature, but one in which literary culture could no longer be confined by the colonial traditions of Englishness inherited at independence. As he noted in the preface to *Writers in Politics*, his concern in the 1970s and 1980s was not so much how an African literary culture had emerged out of colonialism, but larger questions of literature's relevance to life and its capacity to intervene in contentious debates on the meaning of culture, education, and language. But what was provoking such debates? Why did literature seem to be more central to debates about culture and national identity than other disciplines in the humanities and social sciences? And why did Ngugi – the Marxist and hence internationalist – seem to be obsessed with questions about national language and literature?

The literature debate in Kenya in the 1970s, a debate that was ostensibly about what kind of literary texts needed to be taught in Kenyan schools after independence, was ultimately about the status of English and Englishness in the postcolony. In other words, the teaching of literature had become central to discourses on national identity and autonomy in Kenya because English literature, as a discipline, was the last to be decolonized. Indeed, when Ngugi wrote his essay "Literature in Schools" (the center piece of *Writers in Politics*) for a national conference on literary education in Kenya in 1976, what appeared to be the colonized status of the discipline manifested in the simple fact that the Inspector of Literature in the Ministry of Education was still an Englishman and the curriculum was still Anglocentric. For almost twenty years after independence, the Ministry of Education had resisted all attempts to appoint an African as the Inspector of Literature in English. And if the colonial cultural apparatus seemed to have chosen literature as its last battleground, nationalists of all ilks could be forgiven for believing that literary studies was the key to a postcolonial identity.

Indeed, if the whole basis of English education in the colonies was the Arnoldian and Leavisite idea that literature was the medium through which the character of the nation was expressed, then the nationalists felt impelled to defend the decolonized polis from its colonial inheritance. This was the assumption Ngugi made at the onset of his essay on literature in Kenyan schools:

The current debate about literature in our schools has shown that we Kenyans are very concerned over the literary diet now being ladled out to our children. This is as it should be. For education is "a mirror unto" a people's social being. It has been a major ideological battlefield between the economic, political and cultural forces of oppression and the forces for national liberation and unity. Hence, the education system of us Kenyans was one of the first national fortresses to be stormed by the colonial spiritual policemen preparing and subsequently guarding the way for the permanent siege of the oppressed by all the other occupation armies of British imperialism.[20]

Education was central to Ngugi's critique of postcolonial society in the 1970s for a number of reasons: he considered it to be woven into the social being of the formerly colonized body and mind; it was at the center of the ideological struggle over the control of the colonial infrastructure. Indeed, Ngugi often suggested that education (especially literary education) was more than a superstructural element of social production and reproduction in the traditional Marxist sense: it was a key category in the whole configuration that had tried to turn Africans into bourgeois subjects. Thus, Ngugi's concern in the essays collected in *Writers in Politics* was not simply education as a social category; more specifically, he was thinking of the place occupied by literature in the educational system. In this regard, he still accepted the Arnoldian view that literature was the mark of the spiritual character of the nation. While the gist of Ngugi's essays on the teaching of literature in the postcolony was his critique of the continuing hegemony of English in Kenyan schools, he was not troubled by the fact that his view that literature reflected "the life of a people" in words and images was, in effect, an endorsement of colonial Englishness.

At the same time, however, Ngugi went beyond the Arnoldian and Leavisite assumption that literature reflected the spiritual life of a people by introducing a materialist dimension to the idea of culture: literature, he argued, reflected, in images and words, "a people's creative consciousness of their struggles to mould nature through co-operative labour and in the process acting on and changing themselves" (*Writers in Politics*, p. 35). Since colonial Englishness had tended to represent peoples and their traditions and spiritual lives as abstract or ahistorical entities valued for their contribution to the mythology of a unified national culture, Ngugi was now calling attention to the dynamic nature of culture and literature: literary expression provided us with representations of a people's consciousness, but this was a consciousness that emerged out of their struggle with the environment and their efforts to create social life out of nature. In this sense, literature bore its historicity boldly – it contained "people's images of themselves in history and of their place in the universe" (p. 35). Ngugi's primary complaint against the literary curriculum in postcolonial Kenya was that it was deliberately intended to repress the historical nature of Kenyan culture and thus to alienate students from their histories and everyday experiences. If the best kind of literary education was intended to bring students to consciousness, as it were, neo-colonial education was alienated and alienating in its texts and methods:

> Thus the teaching of only European literature, and mostly British imperialist literature in our schools, means that our students are daily being confronted with the European reflection of itself, the European image, in history. Our children are made to look, analyse and evaluate the world as made and seen by Europeans. Worse still, these children are confronted with a distorted image of themselves and of their history as reflected and interpreted in European imperialist literature. (p. 36)

Ngugi chastised the educational bureaucracy for subscribing to the notion that "the European imperialist bourgeois experience" was "the universal experience of history"; he was convinced that literary education could only engender "a critical mentality" if it was centered on the literature of African peoples (p. 38). But he had yet to confront the question of language.

WRITING AND THE POLITICS OF LANGUAGE

In July 1979, several months after his release from political detention, Ngugi presented a talk called "Return to the Roots: National Languages as the Basis of a Kenya National Literature and Culture" to the National Press Club of Kenya. While most of the members of the press assembled on this occasion were primarily interested in Ngugi's political pronouncements and his troubled relationship with the Kenyan state, intellectuals and cultural workers welcomed his address as a rare opportunity for the novelist to address and clarify some issues that had been troubling them since the Kamĩrĩĩthũ experiment and the writer's imprisonment at the end of 1977. For many of them, Ngugi's cultural practice and theoretical reflections, especially on issues pertaining to national identity and language, had crossed an important, but as yet unexplained threshold. In his decision to write and produce *I Will Marry When I Want* in Gikuyu, Ngugi had finally begun to address an audience of workers and peasants who had served as central subjects in his novels and plays, but for whom his writing remained inaccessible as long as he continued to produce it in English.

The implications of this step had, however, been obscured by Ngugi's detention at the end of 1977 and the questions that he had left unanswered. Did his decision to write in Gikuyu mean that he would now be producing one literature addressed to a local Gikuyu-speaking audience and another addressed to an English-speaking elite in the metropolitan centers? Was he rethinking the whole discourse on national identity in Kenya, a discourse which, in its most tendentious form, assumed that a viable sense of national identity demanded the suppression of regional and ethnic languages and cultural practices? Did Ngugi's decision have theoretical implications for his politics, especially his decade-long embrace of Marxism and his espousal of a materialist mode of cultural production? If so, how could Ngugi reconcile his apparent celebration of ethnic languages with the Pan-Africanism and internationalism inherent in his Fanonist and Marxist ideologies?

In his speech "Return to the Roots," later to be one of the essays collected in *Writers in Politics*, Ngugi set out to redefine African literature in terms of its ideology and language. Aiming to establish a direct connection with his linguistic past (as if to bypass the years during which he had built his reputation as an African writer in the English language), he began by rephrasing the problem first raised by Obi Wali in 1962: "Whose language and history will our literature draw upon? Foreign languages and the history and cultures carried by those languages? Or national languages – Dholuo, Kiswahili, Gikuyu, Luluba, Kikamba, Kimasai,

Kigiriama, etc. – and the histories and cultures carried by those languages?" (p. 61). At the end of his speech, Ngugi restated the answer presupposed by his questions: "Only by a return to the roots of our being in the languages and cultures and heroic histories of the Kenyan people can we rise up to the challenge of helping in the creation of a Kenyan patriotic national culture that will be the envy and pride of Kenyans" (p. 65).

This declaration marked Ngugi's radical departure from two of his earliest doctrines on language: first, the claim in his juvenilia that English had advantages over African languages because it had a larger vocabulary (p. 57); and second, the belief that the identity and function of African literature depended on appropriating the colonial language to represent the African experience. What some observers might have missed in Ngugi's speech was its contradictory position on the ideology of language. As the title of his speech suggested, writing in African languages implied the capacity of literature to recover a collective ethos and to bear a national history and memory: "Literature as a process of thinking in images utilizes language and draws upon the collective experience-history embodied in that language" (p. 60).

But this nativist or idealist notion of language was yoked to a Marxist or materialist theory of language that Ngugi had been espousing for over ten years: the assumption that language was a social phenomenon arising out of historical necessity; that linguistic practices reflected the struggle between human beings and nature and the division of labor; that in its representational and ideological function, linguistic practice embodies both continuity and change in historical consciousness. But if language was a product of different generations and social classes, how could it transcend historically engendered social divisions to become the signifier of a unified nation and its many voices? Indeed, how could the materiality of language be reconciled with Ngugi's romantic conception of literary language as a special dimension of a *Sprachgeist?*

Although Ngugi's address did not answer such questions, it did present the broad outlines of a program that he was later to elaborate in *Decolonising the Mind.* At the heart of this program were fundamental assumptions about the nature of language and its relation with being, and about the collective character of Africans as users of language. Ngugi's organic notion of language – the belief that a national language represented inalienated being – was predicated on his investment in an ahistorical notion of a precolonial African past in which speakers existed in harmonious relationship with their environment. The imposition of colonial rule on African societies, Ngugi argued, had separated speakers from their language, alienated them from their environment, and colonized their minds. And while the literature of nationalism and decolonization sought to articulate a new African identity through the Africanization of the European languages, this literature was already imprisoned in the categories carried by these languages. Attempts to resolve the conflict between African peoples and the colonizing structures without negating the European language as the carrier of an oppressive value system were hence doomed from the start.

Far from being a mere question of language choice, then, Ngugi's linguistic program was grounded in a set of theoretical assumptions that called into question the prevailing doctrines on the function of European languages in the production of African literatures. Ngugi's intervention in the language debate was part of his own attempt to re-examine the relation between language, ideology, and modes of production, a relation which was at the heart of his high Marxist aesthetic. The ostensible cultural nationalism that had impelled Ngugi to write in Gikuyu could be predicated on an unquestioning embrace of European notions about nationhood and tradition, but we need to pay closer attention to the discursive formation that allowed him to claim that, in switching languages, he was also making "an epistemological break" with his past.[21] Amidst the heated debates that Ngugi's views on language were to generate it was easy for readers to forget that the problem of language had always been at the center of his aesthetic ideology, that his evolution as a novelist and literary critic has been motivated by his obsession with the role of language as a structuring category of culture, thought, and experience.

In his "liberal" phase, for example, Ngugi conceived his use of language as a way of "entering into the spirit of things" and of establishing communion with his environment; he admired D. H.

Lawrence for his capacity to "enter into the soul of the people, and not only of the people, but even of the land, of the countryside, of things like plants, of the atmosphere."[22] While reading Lawrence provided the young Ngugi with the language that would enable him to capture the essence of things, the novels of Joseph Conrad proffered a vivid example of how an acquired language could be used to interrogate such essences. In his search for a language for his fiction, Ngugi was sensitive to the specific historical context in which these fictions were grounded, but his linguistic practice was predicated on a metaphorical view of language according to which human essences were as important as the historical references.

Although the novelist could not escape the force of history in his early works, historical contexts were seen as a means to a more profound end – a universal human culture. In 1964, Ngugi would complain that his historical situation had forced him to deal with "the geographical or racial situation" which "adds a special problem which makes it even more difficult for the African writer to really confess what is in his heart of hearts"; African writers in Kenya, he would add, were handicapped by their inability "to stand a little bit detached; and see the problem, the human problem, the human relationship in its proper perspective."[23]

While Ngugi's early novels resonate with the contradictions of the history of colonialism in Kenya, the theory of language promulgated in the essays written in the early 1960s seems to posit language as the vehicle toward an ahistorical – maybe transcendental – realm of freedom. In one of the earliest essays collected in *Homecoming*, for example, the novelist asserts that what enabled good writing was not political, but individual, freedom; the end of this freedom, he asserted was "man ultimately freed from fear, suspicion and parochial attitudes: free to develop and realize his full creative potential" (*Homecoming*, p. 23). Beneath this yearning for a universal language of human essences, however, the novelist was haunted by what he referred to as the language of "real life"; he had to live and struggle with the knowledge that "in the Kenyan scene of the last sixty years you cannot separate economics and culture from politics. The three are interwoven. A cultural assertion was an integral part of the political and economical struggle" (p. 26).

What do these contradictory positions tell us about Ngugi's emerging politics on language and culture? Ngugi was a university graduate – an heir to the European liberal tradition – struggling to come to terms with his native Gikuyu culture which, in the 1950s, spoke the language of nationalism and political struggle. As a result, his emerging views on language were shaped both by his desire to credentialize himself within "English" as a discipline of study and his attempts to claim African cultural nationalism as a generative force in his fiction. Even when he embraced materialist theories of language in the mid-1960s, he was still attempting to reconcile the specific historical circumstances of his texts with his desire to gain access to a universal language of freedom. In addition, his famous renunciation of "English" as an academic discipline was an attempt to reconcile his newfound international-ism with its dreaded enemy – nationalism. In both cases, language provided the indispensable *raison d'être* for ideological shifts and transformations. Indeed, while many of the essays in *Homecoming* and *Writers in Politics* reflect Ngugi's self-conscious attempt to break with Makerere liberalism, they also show the extent to which he was haunted by the problem of representing African history at a time when he was struggling with the possibility of articulating a theory of culture and language capable of transcending the anxie-ties of history.

In "The Writer and His Past," a *Homecoming* essay on the writer's relation to history discussed earlier, Ngugi observed that the African novelist was "haunted by a sense of the past. His work is often an attempt to come to terms with 'the thing that has been,' a struggle, as it were, to sensitively register his encounter with history, his people's history" (*Homecoming*, p. 39). In this assertion, Ngugi seemed to have made a decisive move toward a material conception of history; but he also acknowledged the difficulty of reconciling the historical with the act of writing, which he con-tinued to regard as transcendental. Ngugi's ambivalent relation with history generated some interesting tensions in his early works precisely because he feared that the historical (which had provided the subject for his works) might also be a source of contamination. Indeed Ngugi began his reflections on the relation between the writer and the past by invoking the Aristotelean distinction between the historian and the poet; when he declared that "one describes the thing that has been, and the other a kind of thing that might be," Ngugi was reaffirming the need for the poet to transcend the materiality of history (p. 39). His assumption was that the poet could use history as a launching pad to attain an imaginative realm beyond history, for only when the historical imperative was transcended could imaginative writing become possible. Within this context, Ngugi's anxieties about language arose from the realization that, for the African writer, a return to the past was an inevitable confrontation with the alienating tendencies of colonial history.

At this stage in his career, Ngugi wanted to encounter the past so that he could contain it and thus transcend its troubled terms of representation. Although he felt that African languages could play an important role in the development of an African narrative of history, he was more concerned with escaping from the liberal (Arnoldian) definitions of culture and literature he had inherited through his colonial education. Toward this goal, he made a shift from his previous ideal definitions of literary language and affirmed that literary practice had no life outside its material conditions of production. This was his manifesto as it was elaborated in *Homecoming*: "Literature does not grow or develop in a vacuum; it is given impetus, shape, direction and even area of concern by social, political and economic forces in a particular society" (p. xv). It is only within the totality of the productive forces that language and literature produce ideology; political and economic liberation are "the essential condition for cultural liberation, for the true release of a people's creative spirit and imagination" (pp. xv, 11). During most of the 1970s, Ngugi's primary concern was not with language as the defining principle of African literature, but with the ideology of language. His primary goal was to articulate a more coherent materialist theory of linguistic practice and to Africanize the colonial language so that it could help liberate African culture from the surviving institutions of imperialism.

Although Ngugi's discourse on language was avowedly internationalist at this point, his ideological concerns were predominantly nationalist. The nation, which he had described as the coming together of different ethnic and linguistic groups, was now redefined in *Homecoming* as a national community within "a socialist context" (p. 46). For Ngugi, a national literature was predicated not on the use of any particular language, but on the relevance of a literary work's content to the contemporary political situation, the ability of its narrative forms to carry this content, and the appropriateness of its ideological orientation. Ngugi's conception of a national literature that sustained a national ethos was central to these essays which constituted his intervention in the Nairobi debate about the uses of literature.

By 1979, Ngugi was no longer defining national consciousness in terms of the ideological implications of language, the content or form of literary practice, or even the function of literature in the pedagogical apparatus; the languages African writers used had now become the primary determiner of what constituted "patriotic" and "authentic" African literature. As he asserted in *Writers in Politics*, it was only "by a return to the roots of our being in the languages and heroic histories of the Kenyan people [that we can] rise up to the challenge of helping in the creation of a Kenyan patriotic national literature and culture" (*Writers in Politics*, p. 60). From this point onwards, Ngugi's theory of literature would be anchored by a model of language defined by a paradox: language had both a material, historically determined function and a metaphysical, or spiritual dimension. From a materialist perspective, the meaning and function of language depended on its conditions of production; but as a metaphysical force, language represented the innate nature of beings and communities.

Ngugi's challenge in *Decolonising the Mind* was to explain how writing in an African language could enable him to perform these functions at the same time. How could language be both a medium of representing historical change and an immutable storehouse of collective memories and communal identities? The basic problem readers are bound to encounter in analyzing theories of language as they emerge in *Decolonising the Mind* concerns the rationale behind Ngugi's linguistic "conversion": did he decide to write in Gikuyu for pragmatic or philosophical reasons? The question of language choice, he argued, was settled for him the moment he was invited by peasants in his village to write a script for their community center: "It was Kamiriithu which forced me to turn to Gikuyu and hence into what for me has amounted to 'an epistemological break' with my past" (*Decolonising the Mind*, p. 44). Simple necessity, then, provided the incentive for a philosophical and ideological transformation which would, in Ngugi's view, resolve the crisis of writing in English he had been experiencing since 1967 (p. 72). When he was arrested in 1978, the need to defy "the intended detention of my mind and imagination" forced Ngugi to chose a new language – "I would attempt a novel in the very language which had been the basis of incarceration" (p. 71).

But Ngugi was not entirely content with this explanation, for he found it necessary to activate a whole barrage of rhetorical devices to justify his linguistic choice. Furthermore, while the choice of Gikuyu might have settled the language problem that had haunted Ngugi for years, it also reopened the difficult issue of literary tradition: did his new writings belong to the world of Gikuyu literary expression, or were they novelistic or dramatic genres in the European tradition? Clearly, choice of language had not resolved all of Ngugi's theoretical problems. Indeed, while his decision to write in Gikuyu had initiated an important *rapprochement* between Ngugi and his audience, it foregrounded three theoretical problems that he needed to resolve if he hoped to regenerate his writing and to sustain its function as a mode of social critique. First, he had to confront his unquestioning belief in the efficacy of the nineteenth-century European novel, its conventions of realism, and its modes of linguistic representation. Second, he had to resolve the tension between his materialist theory of language and his nationalist inheritance of language as an instrument of nativism. Third, he needed to propose a new program that would mediate the ambivalent relation between language and national identity – a program that would answer a question that continues to haunt cultural production in Africa: does the nation depend on a single unifying language to sustain its identity, or is the national space inherently polyglot?

Ngugi's "epistemological break" was intended to generate a concept of language that would enable him to continue writing fiction after he had lost faith in the tradition of the "realist" European novel as a mode of social critique. Before this time, one of the central ironies in Ngugi's literary practice was his unquestioning faith in the capacity of European novelistic techniques – in the "critical realist" mode – to represent history in all its panoramic and dialectical fashion. He himself retrospectively read the technical shifts in his *œuvre* as attempts to perfect the mimetic function of the novel, a function whose ideological and formal apotheosis would be an ideal marriage of form and content. As a writer, teacher, and critic, he had expressed his faith in the orthodox Marxist claim that form is determined by content. In writing for a "worker/peasant readership," Ngugi concluded, "the most important thing was to go for a subject matter, for a content, which had the weight and the complexity and the challenge of their everyday struggles" (*Decolonising the Mind*, p. 78).

But if the introduction of new forms depended on changes in the social conditions or ideology, as he had been arguing up to this point, there was nowhere for him to turn after writing *Petals of Blood*. According to his own model, the epic form of this novel and its engagement with the history of Kenya could only have arisen under the pressure of ideological necessity – in this case, the Fanonist notion of a collapsing national consciousness. Because the objective historical conditions that had given rise to Ngugi's masterpiece were not going to change in the near future, he would be compelled to renounce his ideology, to reject traditional notions of realism, or to stop writing novels altogether. His decision to write in Gikuyu provided an escape route out of this dilemma, for it enabled him to reject realism without renouncing it, and to experiment with modernist and postmodernist forms without acknowledging their legitimacy. In short, Ngugi's recourse to Gikuyu oral traditions (especially in *Matigari*) allowed him to accept a hitherto unrecognized affinity between modernist and postmodernist forms and African oral traditions.

But because Ngugi was profoundly influenced by the Lukácsian doctrine that modernism constitutes a negation of historical reality, he needed to develop a new theory of language to reconcile the representation of history with formal experimentation. For this reason, as the essays collected in *Decolonising the Mind* articulate so clearly, he now came to see language, rather than history or culture, as the key explanatory structure for human life and as the enabling condition of human consciousness: "The choice of language and the use to which language is put is central to a people's definition of themselves in relation to the entire universe. Hence language has always been at the heart of the two contending social forces in the Africa of the twentieth century" (*Decolonising the Mind,* p. 4). In Ngugi's new epistemology, language – rather than military conquest or appropriation of land – had come to be conceived as the most important instrument of imperialism, "the most important vehicle" for sustaining colonial power (p. 9). This shift from political economy to language has an important ideological implication: it marks Ngugi's break with his Marxist past and its materialist theories of language and allows him to bolster his case for language choice by positing a theory of identity and social consciousness which, in its nativism, ignores historicity and social agency.

In an autobiographical context, he even describes his own childhood and youth in terms of a trajectory that moves from linguistic harmony with his African community to a disjunctive relationship under the grip of the colonial language. According to this model, the native tongue promotes a view of the world that is shared by all members of the linguistic community. When children from Gikuyu peasant families attend the colonial school, the sense of harmony between them and their environment is lost; language and literature become instruments of alienation, "taking us further and further from ourselves, from our own world to other worlds" (p. 12). But if the young Ngugi spoke Gikuyu in all the spheres of social life, and if the colonial system used education and language to alienate him from his cultural environment, several questions need to be posed. Did the Gikuyu linguistic community share a common interest in spite of class, cultural, and regional differences? Did the emerging Gikuyu landowning class of colonial chiefs and traders have the same harmonious relation with the environment as Ngugi's *ahoi* (squatter) family? Did the Gikuyu language used to instruct students in the missionary schools promote the same ideology as the Gikuyu language used in the independent schools that Ngugi attended?

The truth is, despite Ngugi's search for a theory of language that can define communities and structure experiences, no language can exist independently of the social condition of its speakers or the ideological presuppositions behind the institutions in which it is taught. Thus, missionary schools used the Gikuyu language to promote Christian and European values. The Bible in Gikuyu was the central text in colonial education in Central Kenya. The Gikuyu *kariing'a* (pure) schools, established to give pedagogical sustenance to the nationalist movement, used the Gikuyu language and the Bible for a different ideological purpose – the promotion of cultural nationalism and African values. Yet the *kariing'a* college at Githunguri (under the leadership of Jomo Kenyatta and Mbiyu Koinange) could still use English as a self-willed entry into the discourse of history dominated by the colonizer. Against all historical evidence, then, Ngugi proposes a theory of language that allows him to reconcile three conflicting perspectives on language: the materialist, the romantic, and the phenomenological. But even if one rejects this forced harmonization of conflicting opinions one has to accept the fact that the real value of Ngugi's discourse on language lies in its reconceptualization of national identity and of the institutions of literary and cultural production as vehicles of this identity.

THE RETURN TO ENGLISH

In *Decolonising the Mind*, Ngugi made two powerful statements that were going to dominate the nature of his critical and cultural work in the 1980s and 1990s: he claimed that his decision to write fiction in an African language constituted an epistemological break; he also argued that the essays collected in this volume signified his "farewell to the English language as a vehicle for any of my writing" (p. xiv). For a brief period in the late 1980s, Ngugi was so determined to fulfill his pledge to abandon English that he even made conference presentations in Gikuyu and published a significant critical essay in his mother tongue in the prestigious *Yale Journal of Criticism*.[24] But soon after the publication of this essay, Ngugi returned, without explanation, to his familiar role as a critic of imperial European languages writing in English. By the time he took up a senior professorship at New York University in the mid-1990s, it was clear that Ngugi's effort to use Gikuyu as the language of both his fiction and critical discourse had been defeated by the reality of exile and American professional life.

Ngugi tried to keep Gikuyu as an important part of his intellectual and literary work through *Mũtiiri*, a journal he founded and edited through New York University, but in reading the critical and fictional work that he was presenting through this publication, one could not help noticing that his work was being haunted by the pressures of producing knowledge in an African language within the limits and demands of Western institutions of knowledge. What did it mean to produce a journal in Gikuyu when Ngugi was separated from his immediate readers and what he would consider to be the vital linguistic resources of an African language? What dictated the themes and cultural grammar promoted by a Gikuyu journal produced in the heart of the most cosmopolitan city in the world?[25]

In regard to the first question, Ngugi's efforts to produce a professional journal in an African language were impressive. The first volume of *Mũtiiri* offered essays on specialized topics in fields – such as sociolinguistics, computing, and social theory – that had rarely been taken up in African languages. At the same time, however, there was no doubt that Ngugi saw the function of the journal not simply as communicative (the sharing and dissemination of knowledge within a community of readers united by a certain set of experiences and interests), but also vindicative (it wanted to prove that an African language could perform certain linguistic, philosophical, and scientific functions as well as European languages). And thus even in its concern with things Gikuyu or African, the journal seemed to function under the anxieties created by its conditions of production and distribution.

In regard to the second question, then, the very professionalism of the journal, its impressive list of contributors and choice of subjects, reflected a desire, among its publishers and editors, to both "Africanize" the practice of producing knowledge within the Western academy, but also "westernize" Gikuyu discourses on subjects ranging from love to multiculturalism. *Mũtiiri* was an important project in Ngugi's critical discourse not because it embodied the kind of epistemological rupture he had sought when he "broke" with English, but because it seemed, momentarily at least, to provide the editor and his associates with a space in which the cultural project initiated at Kamĩrĩĩthũ could be continued in exile. If the concerns of the journal seemed provincial then, it was not because it had a limited repertoire of subjects, readers, or contributors; rather, instead of perpetuating or rethinking the significance of the Kamĩrĩĩthũ project – its challenge to the bourgeois public sphere and its reconceptualization of the role of audiences in performance – the journal tended to be a forum for representing the cultural disenchantment of a Gikuyu émigré intellegentsia struggling to recover a "national" culture for metropolitan Gikuyu readers distanced from Kenyan concerns. In addition, if the issues in the first volume are to be considered representative, *Mũtiiri* was being driven not so much by the concerns of Gikuyu or Kenyan workers and peasants, but the rhetoric of American identity politics. The peasants and workers whom Ngugi had invited into the institutions of cultural production during his Kamĩrĩĩthũ phase seemed to have disappeared in a project produced in their own language.

Did the language of *Mũtiiri*, then, make any difference to the kind of topics it seemed to favor or the discursive economies it seemed to promote? What did it mean to produce literature and theory in an African language according to the protocols established by American and European institutions? These questions were made more urgent by what appeared to be Ngugi's sudden – and unaccounted – return to the English he had loudly rejected in *Decolonising the Mind*. This return was apparent in *Moving the Centre*, Ngugi's interregnum work, his revised edition of *Writers in Politics*, and more decisively in his Clarendon Lectures published as *Penpoints, Gunpoints, and Dreams*. Ngugi's "return" to English was perhaps not surprising given the difficulties of working and living in exile; the more complicated problem for students of his works is how to explain this return in the context of Ngugi's politics of language and to account for his theories and practices as they were being shaped, not by the peasants and workers of Kenya, or even African institutions of higher learning, but by the very Western institutions whose policies he had previously attacked.

On the surface, *Penpoints, Gunpoints, and Dreams* would appear to be the continuation of one of Ngugi's oldest intellectual projects – an attempt to understand the relationship between the artist and the state in Africa. But this choice of subject, especially the emphasis on the relationship between art and power, represents both continuity and discontinuity in Ngugi's critical practice. The continuity is apparent in Ngugi's concern with the institution of art, most specifically literature and performance, in a context dominated by questions of power. It is not hard to understand why the question of power has been so central to Ngugi's critical discourse: he came of age under the domination of the colonial state in Kenya at one of its most violent phases, the state of emergency in the 1950s; he matured as a writer in that unfortunate phase in African history when the liberal postcolonial state adopted the oppressive mechanisms of its colonial predecessor. But beneath the author's relentless concern with how power affects artistic production, there is a less apparent mode of discontinuity in his thinking about the sociology of literature. This discontinuity is to be found in his shift in focus from writing, more specifically the novel, to performance; there is also a more significant change in the author's substitution of the state, as a social and analytical category, for the notion of society that had dominated his earlier works.

Of these two shifts, the first one is the easiest to explain. After his experiences at Kamīrīīthuī – the rethinking of the place of the audience in the making of drama – Ngugi seems to have recognized the power of performance as a force of social change. What he discovered, as he constantly argues throughout *Penpoints, Gunpoints, and Dreams*, was that the site of performance represented a unique example of how practitioners of the theatre could break down the barrier between producers of art and its recipients. His basic claim, then, is that when it was opened up to the world outside its own spatial confines, theatre would turn audiences into active social agents. And it was because it recognized the subversive potential of the performative space, Ngugi argued, that the state had historically sought to either control or destroy performance. This was the most important lesson learnt at Kamīrīīthū and Ngugi was determined to spread the message even further. And although he continued to define himself as a novelist, it was quite apparent that he was no longer content with forms of art that were restricted to individual and privileged bourgeois readers. This shift from the scriptural economy to orality is already apparent in the performative dimension of *Matigari;* it also explains Ngugi's serious investment in theatre and cinema during the early days of his exile.[26]

The question of Ngugi's shift from the problem of literature in society to the conceptual category of the state is far more complex. It is made much more complicated by a set of closely related factors: as an African working in Europe or North America, Ngugi was no longer producing works that were, strictly speaking, being determined by the postcolonial state. In exile, the questions that had made the state the overwhelming presence in the production of Ngugi's art – censorship, imprisonment, and the culture of silence – were no longer as important or urgent. At the same time, however, the notion of society that Ngugi had deployed in his earlier essays seemed to have been overtaken by historical events – the end of the cold war and the "triumph" of capitalism. Remember, after all, that in his early essays Ngugi's understanding of society as a social and analytical category had been intimately connected to Marxist ideology and aesthetic. In Ngugi's Marxist essays, for example, society was seen as a product of the relationship between "men" and their productive forces; social relations were mediated by the notion of class struggle; and history was defined by a teleology that led from primitive production, through the crisis of capitalism, toward a classless society. This narrative, borrowed from Marx's *Grundrisse* and the *German Ideology*, was the engine driving the essays and fiction Ngugi produced in the 1970s. Similarly, the socialist aesthetic in these works was premised on a very specific understanding of the relation between society and the subject and form of literature.

Except for those instances when Ngugi provided his readers with trenchant critiques of specific postcolonial regimes and their unsavory practices, the Marxist essays did not seem to be interested in the state as a theoretical category. This disinterest in the problematic of the state was itself a direct product of the Marxist theory that Ngugi had inherited, albeit indirectly, from Hegel and Lenin. Marxism's residual Hegelianism, for example, could not enable him to conceive the state, in its revolutionary phase, as anything other than an idealized, albeit abstract, guarantor of rights. This investment in the role of the state as an agent of freedom was also apparent in the Leninist belief that the revolutionary state had a crucial role to play in the construction of socialist society (the idea of revolution was, after all, dependent on the ability of radical forces to control the state apparatus).[27]

Against this background, *Penpoints, Gunpoints, and Dreams* provides a startling shift in Ngugi's theoretical concerns even when it seems to rehearse familiar positions. None of these concerns is more pressing and troublesome than Ngugi's totalized conception of the state as the enemy of art, his valorization of performance as a genre that is inherently subversive, and the ultimate disappearance of society as a theoretical category in his critical works. Indeed, the power of Ngugi's thesis in *Penpoints, Gunpoints, and Dreams* – that art consolidates its identity and function in opposition to "the state's terror and paranoia" – depends on his conception of the totalized identity of the state and its irrationalism.[28] Ngugi's basic premise is that the state has a universal history, character, and function. In order to make the claim that art acquires its political identity in the human community as an oppositional force, it seems almost imperative for him to build his case on examples that take the universality of both his objects of analysis (the state and art) for granted. Thus, lessons drawn from Gikuyu oral culture are brought into direct comparison with stories in the Old Testament, which intersect with dialogues from Plato's *Republic*, which are in turn drawn into a dialogical relationship with more recent victims of postcolonial terror such as Nawal el Sa'adawi.

There is something attractive in this method of analysis: Ngugi interprets local cultures for their international implications; he analyzes specific instances of cultural production (such as the struggle for control of the national theatre in Kenya) for their global meaning. In addition, his delineation of the relationship between art and the state is notable for its clarity of expression and vision, its cognizance of how local and global knowledge provide similar points of reflection. At the same time, however, Ngugi's argument – his primary claim that art is conceptualized in opposition to state power – is disappointing in its refusal, or inability, to confront its own contradictions and to account for its exclusions.

There is, for example, his basic premise that art has a "godlike" aspect reflected in the fact that it is celebrated by different cultures around the world as a mode of creation (*Penpoints, Gunpoints, and Dreams*, pp. 10–12). Ngugi begins by reading what appears to be the worship of art and the artist in "traditional" society as the basis of its oppositional beginnings, then he moves on quickly to contrast the diachronic nature of art with what he sees as the synchronizing function of the state. Ngugi's broad and consistent claim is that "a state, any state, is conservative by its very nature as a state" (p. 13).

Indeed, the opposition between a conservative and destructive state and radical and redemptive art forms is the conceptual cornerstone of *Penpoints, Gunpoints, and Dreams:*

It would seem to me, taking all the four aspects of art and their opposites in the state into account, that the state, when functioning to its logical conclusion as the state, and art functioning as art are antagonistic. They are continuously at war. The state in a class society is an instrument of control in the hands of whatever is the dominant social force. Art, on the other hand, in its beginnings was always an ally of the human search for freedom from hostile nature and nurture. (p. 28)

But this kind of claim only invites more vexed questions: can the state ever be an agent of social good, as both liberals and Marxists have argued over the last two centuries, or is it inherently evil? Is the power and function of art ensured by its inherently redemptive quality or is the association between the work of art and freedom adscititious? And if we are to take the polarization between art and the state seriously, what are we to make of the argument, often made in regard to the cultural institutions of European fascism, that theories of the aesthetic had a logical connection to the cultural politics of the fascist state?[29] Ngugi might argue, in response to the last question, that what was happening in Nazi Germany or Fascist Italy was an instance of the state misusing art for its destructive ends. Still, it is hard to dismiss the argument that certain ideologies of art helped legitimize fascism.

Similar problems are discernible in Ngugi's exploration of what he calls the "Socratic" aspect of art: "Art has more questions than it has answers. Art starts with a position of not knowing and it seeks to know" (p. 15). The problem here is not so much the claim that art has an interrogative rather than epistemological function; rather, in his generalized reading of the kinds of questions art raises, questions he traces all the way from Plato to Nietzsche, Ngugi avoids the more difficult question in this discourse: what are the conditions in which certain questions are raised and not others? Plato's Socrates is not merely interested in questions; he is involved in a philosophical project whose goal is to secure the idealism of the state or the authority of the moral order. As is well known, Plato banishes art from the ideal Republic because it promotes a mode of knowledge that contravenes the idealism of the moral order, an order that is guaranteed by the state. For Nietzsche, on the other hand, the failure of art is implicit in its classical association with idealism; he asks questions whose goal is to break down the logic of art, or rather its association with rationality.

Plato sees art as dangerous because it has no capacity for truth while Nietzsche attacks art for being imprisoned in rationalism. The two philosophers pose their questions about art in specific circumstances in the history of Western thought – Plato at the beginning of the state and at the inaugural moment of poetic reflection, Nietzsche at what is seen as the end of both processes. Do Old Testament and Gikuyu sages pose the same question? Is the colonial and postcolonial state in Africa identical to Socrates' Athenian state? The problem with the theory of art in *Penpoints, Gunpoints, and Dreams*, then, is not that Ngugi fails to provide the kind of qualifiers that the above assertions seem to demand. Indeed, he is fully aware of "the complexities of history and social formations" that make it impossible for us to posit the function of either art or the state as "logical absolutes" (p. 28). The problem is much more elementary: the positing of art and state as conceptual and moral absolutes and opposites.

The arguments presented in *Penpoints, Gunpoints, and Dreams* are much successful when Ngugi turns to the specific relation between power and the politics of performance (chapter 2); language, democracy, and globalization (chapter 3); and the challenge of orality to theories of art built on the unquestioned primacy of writing (chapter 4). What is impressive about these chapters is not their power of critique or theoretical reflection, but Ngugi's ability to link his own observations and experiences as a practitioner of the theatrical arts to some of the issues that have come to dominate debates about performance. In discussing the problem of space in the theatre, for example, Ngugi restates or slightly revises the dominant view in the field of performance studies – the claim that the power of the theatrical space depends on its openness and/or enclosure – but he then moves on to reflect on his own encounters with the politics of performance in Kenya. In drawing on his experiences at both the National Theatre in Kenya and Kamĩrĩĩthũ, Ngugi presents a series of arguments that are as much about space as they are about imprisoned bodies. He argues, for example, that the struggle for the National Theatre in Kenya, a struggle that pitted radical artists against the remnants of "settler power," was much more than an attempt to deploy the space of performance toward different ends; it was also the struggle between two historical traditions: patrons of European performances at the National Theatre in Nairobi saw them as evidence of culture and civilization in the postcolony; in contrast a nationalist performance such as *The Trial of Dedan Kimathi* stood for a different tradition, one "celebrating the Mau Mau heroism and its centrality in bringing about independence for Kenya" (p. 49). Advocates of "white theatre" saw their task as one of maintaining the continuity of colonial culture in postcolonial Kenya by maintaining control over the space of performance; their belief was that "the only people who could ensure that continuity were British white"; in opposition, the nationalist project was "linking itself to the culture and aesthetic of resistance developed by the Mau Mau activists as they fought in the mountains . . . as they called for a new Kenya and a new Africa" (p. 49).

Two important observations emerge out of this discussion: first, in reflecting on the nature of power and performance in Africa, Ngugi recognizes and calls attention to the role of prisons and other institutions of control as "the enclosure in which the state organizes the use of space and time in such a way as to achieve what Foucault calls 'docile bodies' and hence docile minds" (p. 58). Secondly, he notes that the openness of the performance space terrifies "those in possession of repressive power" (p. 63) in very concrete terms. When the Kenyan government set out to destroy

the Kamĩrĩĩthũ theatre in 1982, Ngugi notes, it had already identified the physical space of performance as the bearer of symbolic
meaning beyond the ideologies of the performers and their works.
But how exactly does the space of performance come to function as a site of opposition to political power? Ngugi is sensitive to
the different ways in which power engages with the open space
and he presents some compelling examples from colonial and
postcolonial Africa. The most revealing of these examples are two
in which he was personally involved: the dispute surrounding the
production of *The Trial of Dedan Kimathi* at the National Theatre in
Nairobi in 1976 and the banning of the production of *I Will Marry
When I Want* in 1977. In the former instance, he recalls, the state
was unhappy with the ideological message of *The Trial*, a work that
challenged the legitimacy of the postcolonial state by calling attention to its decidedly colonial foundations; but the state did not
consider this threat strong enough to ban the production of the
play. In contrast, *I Will Marry When I Want*, a work that bore the
same ideological message and structure as *The Trial*, was considered such a threat to the national security interest that it was banned
after only a few months of performance and its author was subsequently imprisoned. How do we explain these diverse reactions by
state power to the work of art?

Ngugi explains the difference in spatial terms: produced at the
National Theatre in Nairobi, *The Trial* was a subversive play, but it
was being performed within the space authorized by the Kenyan
state and bourgeois culture; in contrast, Kamĩrĩĩthũ was a space
developed in opposition to the authorized institutions of the theatre. Ngugi's emphatic claim is that the "open space among the
people is the most dangerous area because the most vital" (p. 68).
But in this conclusion – as in the spatial terms that precede it – we
can detect what I consider to be the weakness of the grammar of
performance studies that Ngugi adopts in *Penpoints, Gunpoints, and
Dreams*. Surely the issue here goes beyond the nature of the space of
performance; what is at work here, is a complex network of
political interests and paranoia which, it seems, the space of
performance appears to foreground. In the case of Kamĩrĩĩthũ, for
example, the Kenyan state was involved in a larger political drama
than the one contained in the space of performance. On the

contrary, the state was involved in a political drama that was about the practice of power itself, namely the postcolonial Kenyan state's growing insecurity in the late 1970s over the question of the Kenyatta succession. It was involved in a struggle over radical politics (Marxism was acceptable so long as it was confined to bourgeois institutions such as the National Theatre and the university). Above all, the Kenya state could not conceive of a play in an African language outside its own paranoia about class and ethnicity: the Kenyatta government was frightened by the possibility of an alliance between a radicalized intelligentsia and a disgruntled peasantry, while the Moi regime lived in fear of a resurgence of a Gikuyu nationalism that had often used culture as its most powerful mode of insurgency. What made a performance space open or closed, then, had to do with a configuration of all these political forces and the desires of the real and projected audience.

But knowing that the author is perhaps one of the best students of cultural politics in Africa, one cannot help wondering why the grammar of performance seems to take precedence over culture and politics or what the earlier Ngugi would consider to be the ideological imperative. Is there a paradigmatic shift here? If so how can we explain it? One could try and explain Ngugi's move away from ideology in terms of his location within an American institution in which the language of disciplines seems to be more important or intelligible than critical practices whose points of reference are located in distant countries and communities. He would then be accused of being interested in power as an abstract rather than a social practice. In addition, one could argue that Ngugi is trying to represent African cultural practices in the familiar language of performance criticism in order to connect with his American and European readership. Alternatively, one could argue that Ngugi's affinity for the universal language of space emerges from the exiled artist's alienation from "the space which nourishes his imagination," an alienation which he tries to overcome by occupying "the global space" (pp. 61–62). *Penpoints* does not resolve any of these questions or problems; indeed, the book seems to raise difficult questions of Ngugi's status as an émigré African writer: how is his location or dislocation in America, his concurrent centering of global space, and the adoption of a universal language of art and performance going to affect his fictional writing, now condemned to be produced in places far removed from his beloved East Africa?

Conclusion

In taking stock of Ngugi's career to date, and as we ponder the effects of exile on his fictional works, three questions need to be addressed: Where does he stand in the canon of African writing? What influence have his works had on the shaping and reshaping of this tradition of letters? Can we pass any useful judgments on the aesthetic or cultural values of his major novels and plays?

In response to the first question, it is important to note that Ngugi started writing at a time when many African countries had become independent and in a period when African writing, though not wholly institutionalized as a field of study, was no longer a novelty. What this meant, among other things, was that unlike the first generation of modern African writers, most notably Peter Abrahams, Camara Laye, and Chinua Achebe, Ngugi's literary beginnings were marked by the reality of decolonization, the inevitable end of the narrative of colonization that had dominated African writing for at least two centuries. Colonialism was no longer the central facet of African life when Ngugi started writing his major works. On the contrary, the narrative of independence dominated the context in which his works were produced, the emergence of new nations in which, it was hoped, autonomy and freedom would be instituted on the continent. Ngugi's postcolonial identity explains both his relation to – and difference from – the pioneering generation of African writers of whom Achebe is the best Anglophone example.

Like Achebe and the first generation of modern African writers, Ngugi was interested in a fairly coherent set of questions and ideas – the process of colonization and its effect on African selves and cultures; the efficacy and limit of old traditions in the constitution

286

of new African identities; the imperative for decolonization; and the failure of national consciousness. In addition, Ngugi's project was similar to that of his precursors in its engagement with the difficult question raised by the English tradition he had inherited through his colonial education: could a literature committed to decolonization be produced in European languages and literary conventions? Although Ngugi is now famous for his brief break with English later in his career, his position on the question of language and literary tradition was fairly close to that espoused by African writers such as Achebe: he had been given the language and he was going to use it toward different ends.[1] In addition, while Ngugi may have arrived on the literary scene several years after Achebe, Abrahams, and Laye, he was, like them, a product of three powerful cultural institutions whose appeal and influence were to outlive official colonialism: the Christian missions, the colonial school and university, and the European literary canon.

Ngugi's relationship to these institutions – and through them the history and process of colonization – was, nevertheless, marked by subtle distinctions and an altered mode of displacement that should remind readers of important local differences in what sometimes appears to be the universal story of colonization and decolonization in Africa. Several points, which ultimately explain Ngugi's literary standing and influence in postcolonial writing, are worth some reflection here: first, the process and nature of colonialism in Kenya was made different from, let us say Achebe's Nigeria, by the existence of a substantial settler population, the expropriation of large tracts of African land, and the dominance of a racialized colonial culture defined by what Frantz Fanon would call "the principle of reciprocal exclusivity."[2] As we saw in the first three chapters of this study, relations between the colonized and colonizer were often mediated through violence and radical protest.

While one cannot argue that colonialism appears more violent than in Achebe's works, it is fair to say that in Ngugi's narratives, this violence is more immediate, perceived in a subjective language that can easily be contrasted with what one critic has called "Achebe's cool, dispassionate style."[3] The language of *The River Between* and *Weep Not, Child*, the works Ngugi produced in the aftermath of the "Mau Mau" uprising and the harsh colonial response, bears the scars of this violence; spatial and human relationships in these works are overdetermined by the colonial attempt to force Africans into submission and compliance.

But the oppressive nature of colonial rule in Kenya has had an unintended effect on Ngugi's works, one that goes to the very heart of the narrative language of his first novels: against the acute sense of loss generated by the expropriation of African lands, these narratives are memorable for their romantic invocation of the landscape, which is associated with individual and collective loss and desire. As Ngugi has succinctly noted, this attachment to landscape is one of the defining characteristics of East African writing: "the natural landscape dominates the East African literary imagination. This awareness of the land as the central actor in our lives distinguishes the East African literary scene from others in the continent and it certainly looms large in my own writings from *The River Between* to *Matigari*."[4]

While Ngugi's writing is overdetermined by the reality of British imperial rule in Kenya, it is equally attuned to local resistance to the culture of colonialism. In his engagement with the emergence of independent schools in Kenya (see chapter 2) and local attempts to interpret colonial culture from the vantage point provided by African narratives of prophecy and restoration, Ngugi's works are closer to the discourse of cultural nationalism than what we now consider to be the first narratives of decolonization, represented by works such as Achebe' s *Things Fall Apart* or Laye's *L'Enfant Noir*, works more notable for their special pleading for the African's place in modern culture than for their radical self-assertiveness. But the primary reason why Ngugi's early works seem to reflect the spirit of nationalism, and to be more attuned to the radical politics of decolonization, is because they are produced after decolonization and are preceded by texts such as *Things Fall Apart* and *L'Enfant Noir*.

In other words, Ngugi became a writer at a time when the authority of African cultures – and debates about African traditions – had all been assured by the independence of Ghana and Nigeria. As a result, his works are not characterized by the kind of defensiveness about African cultures and traditions we find in the works of his predecessors. At the same time, if Ngugi's novels take the existence of an African culture for granted, it is precisely because of the existence of the novels by Achebe and Laye which, in addition to clearing the space in which African literary culture flourished in the 1950s and 1960s, also engaged with colonial mythologies about African subjects and cultures in what appear to be definitive ways. In short, by the time Ngugi started writing in the early 1960s, defending African cultures and traditions was no longer a political or literary imperative because his precursors – ranging from the Negritude poets to proponents of the African image – had already accomplished this task.

The best way of responding to the second question – what has been Ngugi's influence in the shaping and reshaping of the post-colonial tradition of letters? – is to reflect on the methodological and theoretical challenges presented by his works. Three of these challenges have, in fact, determined the kind of strategies adopted in this reading of Ngugi's *œuvre*, namely, the problem of reading texts and contexts, a rethinking of the function of authors and readers in the interpretation of literature, and the nature of oppositional writing in general. As is apparent in my introductory chapter, Ngugi's works underscore the complex, ambivalent, and dialectical relationship between texts and contexts in general and in postcolonial cultures in particular. As we saw in the first chapter, Ngugi's novels demand a kind of reading that both rejects and affirms one of the central tenets in poststructural and postmodern theory – the disclaimer of a stable historical referent and process.[5] In their thematic concerns, language, and structure, Ngugi's novels demand particular attention to the historical events that are also their condition of possibility.[6]

Indeed, it is hard to understand the spatial structure of *The River Between*, the trope of education in *Weep Not, Child*, the use of interior monologue in *A Grain of Wheat*, the epic dimension of *Petals of Blood*, or the use of the discourse of gossip and rumor in *Matigari*, without being cognizant of the specific historical events that frame the narrative contract between Ngugi and his readers. Such historical events as "female circumcision," "Mau Mau," postcolonial betrayal, and the state's use of terror to control its subjects are constitutive of the form of these novels. But as we also saw in our reading of specific contexts in Ngugi's novels and plays, these texts are not passive conduits for a history that predates them. Indeed, Ngugi's works have been most influential in their intervention in controversial debates about Kenyan pasts; not only have his novels functioned as agents of a certain radical historiography, but also as the vehicles through which two generations of Kenyan readers have been able to access their past or, more modestly, to see their history as a key factor in the shaping of postcolonial cultures and identities.

Ngugi's influence in challenging the role of readers and authors in the shaping of literary meaning is not unique in itself (it is perhaps a characteristic shared by almost all postcolonial writers); but because of what I have already characterized as the immediacy of the historical events in his works – in addition to his forceful presence as a literary critic and theorist (see Chapter Nine) – there is a sense in which Ngugi foregrounds the writerly function in his works much more strongly than his contemporaries. And thus against the poststructuralist desire to remove the presence of writers from their texts, Ngugi makes the writing self one of the nodal points of his writing. As we saw in Chapters Six and Seven, the author's reflections on the imprisoned writer's ability to produce a text is not simply a response to his own circumstances, but a statement on why we should not take the writer in postcolonial writing for granted.

The question of the reader's function in Ngugi's writings can be directly related to the oppositional ambitions of his works. This study gives readers a central role in the production of textual knowledge in a colonial and postcolonial situation. In doing so, my intention has not been to define Ngugi's *œuvre* as a series of texts built around a reader-centered aesthetic; rather, it is to call attention to how practices of reading can be construed, in John Frow's terms, "as determinate social practices within a specific historical regime."[7] There is no better example of this process than the reading, or what Ngugi sees as the misreading, of *Matigari* upon its publication in Kenya in 1987:

Matigari, the main character, is puzzled by a world where the producer is not the one who has the last word on what he has produced; a world where lies are rewarded and truth punished. He goes round the country asking questions about truth and justice. People who had read the novel started talking about Matigari and the questions he was raising as if Matigari was a real person in life. When Dictator Moi heard that there was a Kenyan roaming around the country asking such questions, he issued orders for the man's arrest. But when the police found that he was only a character in fiction, Moi was even more angry and he issued fresh orders for the arrest of the book itself. That's why, in February 1987, in a very well co-ordinated police action, the novel was seized from all the bookshops and from the publisher's warehouse.[8]

It is important to note that Matigari (the character and the novel) had acquired political agency in the process of being read; it was through the interpretative strategies they applied to the novel, that readers came to determine its political practice. This bears out John Frow's seminal conclusion about the process of reading in determining the effect texts have in the social sphere: "the regime of reading is what allows readers to do work upon texts, to accept or transform readings offered as normative, to mesh reading with other social practices and other semiotic domains, and indeed to formulate and reformulate the categories of the regime itself."[9]

In regard to the question of value and judgment, it is up to individual readers to decide which of Ngugi's texts are important to them, not simply because of the vexed nature of the problem of objective value in aesthetic theory, but also because in the course of his career, the author has produced novels and plays that seem to affect readers, in different times and places, in a variety of ways. The plurality of response to Ngugi's works addressed in the course of this study is perhaps the best measure of his success and importance as an artist. More important than the preferences of individual readers is the changing aesthetic ideology in each of the works studied here and the shifting narrative strategies Ngugi adopts as he tries to come to terms with a violent colonial history and what sometimes appears to be an inscrutable postcolonial condition.[10]

This work has sought to trace this aesthetic ideology and the forms it generates all the way from the trope of landscape in *The River Between*, the colonial *Bildungsroman* in *Weep Not, Child*, the complex deployment of modernist epic forms in *A Grain of Wheat* and *Petals of Blood*, to the decisive turn to orality in *Devil on the Cross* and *Matigari*. In spite of their different forms and ideologies, these works are united by their humanistic vision and concern. For, at home and in exile, Ngugi continues to believe that in its search for "a genuine homecoming," African literature "will truly reflect the universal struggle for a world which truly belongs to all of us."[11] This study is intended to reflect the same spirit in the criticism of his works.

Notes

I. INTRODUCTION: READING TEXTS AND CONTEXTS

1 The most comprehensive historical and bibliographical background to Ngugi's works can be found in two books by Carol Sicherman: *Ngugi wa Thiong'o: A Bibliography of Primary and Secondary Sources 1957–1987*, London: Hans Zell, 1989 and *Ngugi wa Thiong'o: The Making of a Rebel, A Source Book in Kenyan Literature and Resistance*, London: Hans Zell, 1990.

2 See especially G. D. Killam, *An Introduction to the Writings of Ngugi wa Thiong'o*, London: Heinemann, 1980; C. B. Robson, *Ngugi wa Thiong'o*, London and New York: St. Martins Press, 1979; and David Cook and Michael Okenimpke, *Ngugi wa Thiong'o: An Exploration of His Writings*, London: Heinemann, 1983.

3 Ngugi has encouraged this tendency to represent the history of his works as a series of epistemological breaks. See, for example, chapter three of *Decolonising the Mind*, London: James Currey, 1986.

4 Ngugi wa Thiong'o, *Homecoming: Essays on African and Caribbean Literature and Politics*, Westport, CT: Lawrence and Hill, 1972, p. 47.

5 Michael Taussig, *The Nervous System*, London and New York: Routledge, 1992. p. 44.

6 *Ibid.*, p. 44.

7 *Homecoming*, p. 47.

8 *Ibid.*, p. 39.

9 For an extensive analysis of the historical imagination and historiographical styles, see Hayden White, *Metahistory: The Historical Imagination in Nineteenth-Century Europe*, Baltimore: Johns Hopkins University Press, 1973, pp. 1–41. For a discussion of colonialism and its effects on the shaping of modern history and culture see, for example, Nicholas Dirks, "Introduction: Colonialism and Culture," in *Colonialism and Culture*, ed. Nicholas Dirks, Ann Arbor: University of Michigan Press, 1992, pp. 1–25.

10 *Homecoming*, p. 40.

11 *Ibid.*, p. 48.
12 For a discussion of emotions in Ngugi's works, see Simon Gikandi, "Moments of Melancholy: Ngugi and the Discourse of Emotions," in *The World of Ngugi wa Thiong'o*, ed. Charles Cantalupo, Trenton, NJ: Africa World Press, 1995, pp. 59–72.
13 Tabitha Kanogo, *Squatters and the Roots of Mau Mau*, London: James Currey, 1987, pp. 119–20.
14 Frank Furedi, *The Mau Mau War in Perspective*, London: James Currey, 1989, p. 80.
15 *Homecoming*, p. 45.
16 Ngugi wa Thiongo, *Secret Lives*, London: Heinemann, 1975, preface.
17 As Prime Minister Jomo Kenyatta informed the new Kenyan nation on October 20, 1964, the foundation of the future would lie in the theme of "forgive and forget"; the contested past needed to be forgotten in the name of an imagined community: "There have been murmurs here in Kenya about the part played by one set of people, or another set of people, in the struggle for Uhuru. There has been talk of the contribution made, or refused, by this group or that. There has been – at times – vindictive comment, and a finger of scorn has been pointed at some selected race, or group, or tribe. All this is unworthy of our future here." See Jomo Kenyatta, *Suffering Without Bitterness: The Founding of the Kenyan Nation*, Nairobi: East African Publishing House, 1968, p. 241.
18 See Tom Conley, "Translator's Introduction" in Michel de Certeau, *The Writing of History*, New York: Columbia University Press, 1988. Ngugi makes the connection between silence and the postcolonial state's attempt to contain history in *Barrel of a Pen: Resistance to Repression in Neo-Colonial Kenya*, Trenton, NJ: African World Press, 1983, pp. 7–32.
19 Ngugi wa Thiong'o, *Moving the Centre: The Struggle for Cultural Freedoms*, London: James Currey, 1993, p. 137.
20 Quoted in Sicherman, *Ngugi wa Thiong'o: The Making of a Rebel*, p. 392.
21 *Moving the Centre*, pp. 138–39.
22 See Georg Lukács, *The Theory of the Novel*, Cambridge, MA: MIT Press, 1971, p. 88.
23 Frederic Jameson, "Third World Literature in the Era of Multinational Capitalism," *Social Text* 15 (Fall 1986), 65–88.
24 Ngugi presents this argument forcefully in the essays collected in *Writers in Politics*, London: Heinemann, 1981.
25 *Ibid.*, p. 7.
26 "Third World Literature," 67.
27 *Ibid.*

28 For some excellent discussions of history and the problem of representation in Ngugi's novels, see David Maughan-Brown, *Land, Freedom, and Fiction: History and Ideology in Kenya*, London: Zed, 1985 and Abdul JanMohammed, *Manichean Aesthetics: The Politics of Literature in Colonial Africa*, Amherst, MA: University of Massachusetts Press, 1983, pp. 185–225.

29 See the interview in *African Writers Talking*, ed. Dennis Duerden and Cosmo Pierterse, London:Heinemann, 1972, p. 123.

30 *Homecoming*, p. xvi.

31 *Writers in Politics*, pp. 5–6.

32 JanMohammed's *Manichean Aesthetics* was pioneering in this regard, but his focus was on the politics of Ngugi's novels not their aesthetic form.

33 Terry Eagleton, *The Ideology of the Aesthetic*, Oxford: Basil Blackwell, 1990, p. 3.

34 *Ibid.*

35 *Ibid.*

36 *Ibid.*, p. 2.

37 This book departs from the common approach, exemplified by Cook and Okenimpke, which represents Ngugi's career in terms of phases of growth in his "philosophy of life." See Cook and Okenimpke, *Ngugi wa Thiong'o: An Exploration of His Writings*, p. 13.

38 John Frow, *Marxism and Literary History*, Cambridge, MA: Harvard University Press, 1986, p. 171.

39 Ngugi's relation to Gikuyu nationalism became a political issue when he started writing in his native tongue in the late 1970s. Some of the pertinent questions in this debate are raised by Ali Mazrui in "The Detention of Ngugi wa Thiong'o: Report on a Private Mission," reprinted in Sicherman, *Ngugi wa Thiong'o: The Making of a Rebel*, pp. 33–36. My concern here, and elsewehere in this book, is not Ngugi's politics of identity, which are much more complex than his adversaries are willing to acknowledge, but the trope of cultural nationalism as it was developed in Central Kenya from the 1920s to the "Mau Mau" period.

40 For a general history of the Gikuyu in the colonial period, see Godfrey Muriuki, *A History of the Kikuyu, 1500–1900*, Nairobi: Oxford University Press, 1974. A discussion of some of the ways in which Gikuyu identity emerged as a response to the economy of colonial conquest and rule can be found in the chapters by John Lonsdale in Bruce Berman and John Lonsdale, *Unhappy Valley: Conflict in Kenya and Africa*, vol. II, London: James Currey, 1992, pp. 265–468.

41 See *ibid.*, especially pp. 315–22.

42 For a general discussion of the "colonial situation" as a theoretical

concept, see Georges Balandier, *The Sociology of Black Africa: Social Dynamics in Central Africa*, trans. Douglas Garman: New York: Praeger, 1955, 1970.

43 *A History of the Kikuyu*, p. 165.

44 Ngugi wa Thiong'o, *The River Between*, London: Heinemann, 1965.

45 See Berman and Lonsdale, *Unhappy Valley*, p. 2 and Robert L. Tignor, *The Colonial Transformation of Kenya: The Kamba, Kikuyu and Maasai from 1900 to 1939*, Princeton: Princeton University Press, 1976, p. 226.

46 L. S. B. Leakey, *The Southern Kikuyu Before 1903*, vol. 1, London: Academic Press, 1977.

47 *The River Between*, p. 20.

48 See Tignor, *The Colonial Transformation of Kenya*, p. 10 and Berman and Lonsdale, *Unhappy Valley*, p. 20; a far more complex history of Gikuyu expansionism in the colonial period can be found in Kanogo's *Squatters and the Roots of Mau Mau*.

49 Tignor, *The Colonial Transformation of Kenya*, p. 32.

50 See Jomo Kenyatta, *Facing Mount Kenya*, New York: Vintage (1938), 1965. For an excellent discussion of the relationship between African writers, the national imagination, and the European literary tradition, see Abiola Irele, "African Letters: The Making of a Tradition," *Yale Journal of Criticism* 5.1 (1991), 69–100.

51 Marshall S. Clough, *Fighting Two Sides: Kenyan Chiefs and Politicians, 1918–1940*, Boulder: University Press of Colorado, 1990, p. 162.

52 Quoted in *ibid.*, p. 164.

53 See, for example, the "Mau Mau" songs collected in Gakaara wa Wanjau, *Nyimbo Cia Mau Mau*, Karatina, Kenya: Gakaara Press, no date and Maina Kinyatti, *Thunder from the Mountains: Mau Mau Patriotic Songs*, London: Zed, 1980.

54 Clough, *Fighting Two Sides*, p. 164.

55 A theoretical discussion of the role of culture in the colonial project can be found in Dirks, "Introduction: Colonialism and Culture," p. 3.

56 See *ibid.*

57 Samuel G. Kibicho, "The Continuity of the African Conception of God Into and Through Christianity: A Kikuyu Case-Study," in *Christianity in Independent Africa*, ed. Edward Fashikole-Luke, et al., Bloomington: Indiana University Press, 1978, pp. 370–88.

58 W. Scoresby Routledge, *With a Prehistoric People: The Akikuyu of East Africa*, London: Frank Cass (1910), 1968, p. 154.

59 F. B. Welbourn, *East African Rebels: A Study of Some Independent Churches*, London: SCM Press, 1961.

60 The background to these events can be found in Carl Rosberg and John Nottingham, *The Myth of "Mau Mau": Nationalism in Kenya*, New

York: Meridian, 1966, pp. 105–35.
61 *Facing Mount Kenya*, p. 306.
62 See Rosberg and Nottingham, *The Myth of "Mau Mau,"* especially chapters 3, 4, and 5.
63 Welbourn, *East African Rebels*, p. 141.
64 Rosberg and Nottingham provide the essential background to "Mau Mau," but their work needs to be read together with the works by members of the movement or its sympathizers, most notably Donald I. Barnett and Karari Njama, *Mau Mau from Within*, New York: Monthly Review Press, 1966; Bildad Kaggia, *Roots of Freedom, 1921–1963: The Autobiography of Bildad Kaggia*, Nairobi: East African Publishing House, 1975; Josiah Mwangi Kariuki, *Mau Mau Detainee*, London: Oxford University Press, 1963; Gakaara wa Wanjau, *Mau Mau Author in Detention*, trans. Ngugi wa Njoroge, Nairobi: Heinemann, Kenya, 1988; the "guild historians" are represented by Robert Buijtenhuijs, *Essays on Mau Mau: Contributions to Mau Mau Histogriography*, Leiden: African Studies Center, 1982; Kanogo, *Squatters and the Roots of Mau Mau*; Furedi, *The Mau Mau War in Perspective*; Gert Kershaw, *Mau Mau from Below*, Oxford: James Currey, 1997. The "official" colonial perspective on "Mau Mau" can be found in F. D. Corfield, *Historical Survey of the Origins of Mau Mau*, London: HMSO, 1960; and L. S. B. Leakey, *Mau Mau and the Kikuyu*, London: Methuen, 1952.
65 I borrow the concept from Taussig, *The Nervous System*.
66 Ngugi wa Thiong'o, *Weep Not, Child*, London: Heinemann, 1964, pp. 116–17.
67 This is the gist of the argument presented by Lonsdale in *Unhappy Valley*, pp. 378–423.
68 For "Mau Mau" and the postcolonial debate about the Kenyan past, see Frederick Cooper, "'Mau Mau' and the Discourses of Decolonization," *Journal of African History* 29 (1988), 313–20; and David William Cohen, *The Combing of History*, Chicago: University of Chicago Press, 1994, pp. 59–64.
69 For Ngugi's position in the debate on "Mau Mau" and its historiography, see *Barrel of a Pen*, pp. 7–31.
70 *Secret Lives*, pp. 45–46.
71 Carey Francis's contribution to this debate can be found in Sicherman's *Ngugi wa Thiong'o: The Making of a Rebel*, pp. 390–96.
72 *Secret Lives*, p. 54.
73 See *Moving the Centre*, p. 97.
74 I am idebted to Biodun Jeyifo for this expression. See "The Nature of Things: Arrested Decolonization and Critical Theory," *Research in African Literature* 21.1 (1990), 46.
75 This episode is narrated by Rosberg and Nottingham in *The Myth of*

"*Mau Mau*," p. 123.

76 *Homecoming*, p. 29.

77 *Barrel of a Pen*, p. 10.

78 See Frantz Fanon, *The Wretched of the Earth*, trans. Constance Farrington, New York: Grove Press, 1968, especially the chapter titled "The Pitfalls of National Consciousness."

79 Quoted in P. Wastberg, *The Writer in Modern Africa*, Uppsala, Scandinavian Institute of African Studies, 1968, p. 25.

80 Fanon, *Wretched*, p.148.

81 *Ibid.*, p. 149.

82 *Ibid.*, pp. 157, 165, 166.

83 On the Makerere school and its connection to Arnold, Leavis, and the "great tradition," see Carol Sicherman, "Ngugi's Colonial Education: 'The Subversion ... of the African Mind,'" *African Studies Review* 38.3 (December 1995), 11–41.

84 Ngugi wa Thiong'o, *A Grain of Wheat*, London: Heinemann, 1967, p. 107.

85 *Ibid.*, p. 342.

86 *Moving the Centre*, p. 68.

87 *Ibid.*, p. 71.

88 Colin Leys, *Underdevelopment in Kenya: The Political Economy of Neo-Colonialism 1964–1971*, London: Heinemann, 1974, p. 247.

89 *Ibid.*, p. 247.

90 Ngugi wa Thiong'o, *Petals of Blood*, London: Heinemann, 1977, p. 181.

91 *Writers in Politics*, pp. 53–54.

92 See Achille Mbembe, "The Banality of Power and the Aesthetics of Vulgarity in the Postcolony," *Public Culture* 4.2 (1992), 1–30.

2. NARRATIVE AND NATIONALIST DESIRE: EARLY SHORT STORIES AND *THE RIVER BETWEEN*

1 The appropriate background to Ngugi's location within the colonial educational system can be found in Carol Sicherman, *Ngugi wa Thiong'o: The Making of a Rebel, A Source Book in Kenyan Literature and Resistance*, London: Hans Zell, 1990; and "Ngugi's Colonial Education: 'The Subversion ... of the African Mind,'" *African Studies Review* 38.3 (December 1995), 11–41.

2 On the Gikuyu first encounters with colonialism, see Godfrey Muriuki, *A History of the Kikuyu, 1500–1900*, Nairobi: Oxford University Press, 1974.

3 For a theological examination of the *Athomi* and their beliefs, see Samuel G. Kibicho, "The Continuity of the African Conception of

God Into and Through Christianity: A Kikuyu Case-Study," in *Christianity in Independent Africa*, ed. Edward Fashikole-Luke, et al., Bloomington: Indiana University Press, 1978, pp. 370–88; for a brief discussion of the Gikuyu within colonial culture, see Simon Gikandi, *Maps of Englishness: Writing Identity in the Culture of Colonialism*, New York: Columbia University Press, 1996, pp. 32–37.

4 The strongest proponents of this idea of tradition among the Gikuyu were perhaps Jomo Kenyatta and Louis Leakey. See Jomo Kenyatta, *Facing Mount Kenya*, New York: Vintage (1938), 1965; and L. S. B. Leakey, *The Southern Kikuyu Before 1903*, London: Academic Press, 1977.

5 The idea of organic community is borrowed from Raymond Williams, *The Country and the City*, London: Oxford University Press, 1973, p. 195.

6 See *ibid.*, p. 195.

7 For a discussion of literary beginnings and the theoretical problems they pose, see Edward Said, *Beginnings: Intention and Method*, New York: Basic Books, 1975.

8 The standard assumption about what made literature great at the beginning of Ngugi's career can be found in Leavis's majestic introduction to *The Great Tradition:* the really great writers "are significant in terms of the human awareness they promote; an awareness of the possibilities of life"; they have an intense understanding of tradition and "an intense moral preoccupation." See F. R. Leavis, *The Great Tradition*, New York: New York University Press, 1973, pp. 1–27.

9 For a systematic account of the Makerere English course, see Sicherman, "Ngugi's Colonial Education."

10 "Mugumo," in Ngugi wa Thiong'o, *Secret Lives*, London: Heinemann, 1975, pp. 2, 15. Further references to this edition will be made in the text in parenthesis.

11 A writer's greatness, argued Leavis, depended both on the ability to embrace a tradition and to transcend it; an author's originality depended on an ambivalent relation to the notion of tradition itself. See *The Great Tradition*, p. 5.

12 The original version of the story, called "The Fig Tree," can be found in David Cook, *Origin East Africa: A Makerere Anthology*, London: Heinemann, 1965, pp. 70–76.

13 My discussion of the relation between reproduction and nationalism, eros and politics, relies heavily on the work of Doris Sommer. See *Foundational Fictions: The National Romances of Latin America*. Berkeley: University of California Press, 1991, especially chapter 1.

14 Michel Foucault defines heterotopias as countersites, spaces where all the other sites to be found in a culture "are simultaneously

represented, contested, and inverted." See "Of Other Spaces," *Diacritics* 16 (1986), 24.

15 See Sicherman, "Ngugi's Colonial Education."

16 The exception is perhaps Abdul JanMohammed in *Manichean Aesthetics: The Politics of Literature in Colonial Africa*, Amherst, MA: University of Massachusetts Press, 1983.

17 Ngugi wa Thiong'o, *The River Between*, London: Heinemann, 1965, p. 1. Further references to this edition will be made in the text in parenthesis.

18 This is Fanon's classical definition of colonial geography. See *The Wretched of the Earth*, trans. Constance Farrington, New York: Grove Press, 1968, pp. 39–40.

19 John Lonsdale, "The Prayers of Waiyaki: Political Uses of the Kikuyu Past," in *Revealing Prophets: Prophecy in East African History*, eds. David M. Anderson and Douglas H. Johnson, Oxford: James Currey, 1995, pp. 240–91.

20 Charles Ambler, "'What is the World Coming To?' Prophecy and Colonialism in Central Kenya," in Anderson and Johnson, *Revealing Prophets*, p. 222.

21 See Jomo Kenyatta, *Facing Mount Kenya*, pp. 133–37.

22 The relationship between romantic love and patriotism, sexual attraction and social formation, is discussed by Sommer in *Foundational Fictions*, pp. 30–40.

23 Benedict Anderson, *Imagined Communities: Reflections on the Origin and Spread of Nationalism*, London: Verso, 1991, p. 41.

24 JanMohammed, *Manichean Aesthetics*, pp. 206–07.

25 Nicholas Dirks, "Introduction: Colonialism and Culture," in *Colonialism and Culture*, ed. Nicholas Dirks, Ann Arbor: University of Michigan Press, 1992, pp. 1–25.

26 While the process of codifying cultural practices into a social system reaches its apotheosis in the nationalist period, it seems to be concurrent with the foundation of the colonial state in Kenya; indeed, some of the earliest anthropological studies of the Gikuyu are produced by anthropologists who were active in the early stages of establishing a British colony in Kenya. See, for example, W. Scoresby Routledge, *With a Prehistoric People: The Akikuyu of East Africa*, London: Frank Cass (1910), 1968.

27 Fanon's memorable claim was that the art of decolonization could not be produced simply by representing the people's past; on the contrary, the condition of possibility of a postcolonial art was the fluctuating moment when the whole colonial formation was called into question: "Let there be no mistake about it; it is to this zone of occult instability where the people dwell that we must come; and it is

there that our souls are crystallized and that our perceptions and our lives are transfused with light." See *The Wretched of the Earth*, p. 227.

28 John Frow, *Marxism and Literary History*, Cambridge, MA: Harvard University Press, 1986, p. 171.

29 This attitude is summed up by Kenyatta at the end of *Facing Mount Kenya*: "If Africans were left in peace on their own lands, Europeans would have to offer them the benefits of white civilisation in real earnest before they could obtain the African labour which they want so much. They would have to offer the African a way of life which was really superior to the one his fathers lived before him, and a share in the prosperity given them by their command of science. They would have to let the African choose what parts of European culture could be beneficially transplanted, and how they could be adapted" (pp. 305–06).

30 Mary Douglas, *Purity and Danger: An Analysis of the Concepts of Pollution and Taboo*, London: Routledge, 1988.

31 Hence Kenyatta's assumption that once autonomy had been established, Africa would have access to a modern (European) life guaranteed by "a command of science." See *Facing Mount Kenya*, p. 306.

32 See The Gospel According to St. Luke, 6:17.

33 Anderson, *Imagined Communities*, p. 193.

34 Sommer, *Foundational Fictions*, p. 6.

35 *Ibid.*

36 This point has been noted by Abiola Irele in "African Letters: The Making of a Tradition," *Yale Journal of Criticism* 5.1 (1991), 69–100.

3. EDUCATING COLONIAL SUBJECTS: THE "EMERGENCY STORIES" AND *WEEP NOT, CHILD*

1 Frantz Fanon, *The Wretched of the Earth*, trans. Constance Farrington, New York: Grove Press, 1968, p. 40.

2 *Ibid.*, p. 40.

3 Ngugi wa Thiong'o, *Homecoming: Essays on African and Caribbean Literature and Politics*, Westport, CT: Lawrence and Hill, 1972, p. 22.

4 Biodun Jeyifo, "The Nature of Things: Arrested Decolonization and Critical Theory," *Research in African Literatures* 21.1 (Spring 1990), 33–46.

5 *Secret Lives*, London: Heinemann, 1975, p. 15. Further references to this edition will be made in the text in parenthesis.

6 Patricia Seed, *Ceremonies of Possession in Europe's Conquest of the New World, 1492–1640*, Cambridge: Cambridge University Press, 1995, pp. 1–15.

7 For the notion of the "unhomely," see Homi Bhabha, *The Location of*

Culture, London and New York: Routledge, 1994, pp. 9–18.

8 For a superb discussion of the relation between suicide and narration, see Ross Chambers, *Room for Maneuver: Reading (the) Oppositional (in) Narrative*, Chicago: University of Chicago Press, 1991, p. 105.

9 For the intricate politics of violence, land, and the colonial situation, see the studies by David Maughan-Brown, *Land, Freedom, and Fiction: History and Ideology in Kenya*: London: Zed, 1985; Abdul JanMohammed, *Manichean Aesthetics: The Politics of Literature in Colonial Africa*, Amherst, MA: University of Massachusetts Press, 1983; and John Lonsdale, "The Moral Economy of Mau Mau: Wealth, Poverty and Civic Virtue in Kikuyu Political Thought," in *Unhappy Valley: Conflict in Kenya and Africa*, ed. Bruce Berman and John Lonsdale, London: James Currey, 1992, vol. II, pp. 315–467.

10 Kenyatta had, of course, argued that the land was the visible bond of kinship and the basis of social organization in Gikuyu culture; it was also the key to understanding the Gikuyu political culture and moral system. See *Facing Mount Kenya*, New York: Vintage (1938), 1965, pp. 298–99.

11 Quoted in Carol Sicherman, *Ngugi wa Thiong'o: The Making of a Rebel, A Source Book in Kenyan Literature and Resistance*, London: Hans Zell, 1990, p. 18.

12 Ngugi wa Thiong'o, *Weep Not, Child*, London, Heinemann, 1964, p. 13. Further references to this edition will be made in parenthesis in the text.

13 Jonathan Culler, *Flaubert: The Uses of Uncertainty*, Ithaca, NY: Cornell University Press, 1974, p. 28.

14 The point I am making here is not that colonialism was more benign toward women than men; rather, I am calling attention to the ways in which African nationalist literature presents the emasculation of the father by colonial forces as the source of the tragic disintegration of the familial and communal space. The exemplary text in this regard is Chinua Achebe's *Things Fall Apart*.

15 Fanon, *Wretched*, p. 39.

16 *Ibid.*, p. 225.

17 Culler, *Flaubert*, p. 147.

18 This is the argument made by Gilles Deleuze and Félix Guattari in *Kafka: Toward a Minor Literature*, Minneapolis: University of Minnesota Press, 1972.

19 For an excellent discussion of the relationship between romance and reification, see Frederic Jameson, *The Political Unconscious: Narrative as a Socially Symbolic Act*, Ithaca: Cornell University Press, 1981, pp. 206–80.

20 Chambers, *Room for Maneuver*, p. 108.

21 *Ibid.*, pp. 108–09.

22 This is Chambers's assertion in full: "Getting back at the world is what suicide is frequently all about; and biographically speaking, both Nerval and Aquin ended their lives (as did Benjamin). Their deaths are speech-acts, rhetorical performatives speaking to us, still, of the social and political extremities to which, as individual humans, they found themselves reduced." See *ibid.*, p. 109.

4. REPRESENTING DECOLONIZATION: *A GRAIN OF WHEAT*

1 For more information on Ngugi's discovery of Fanon, see Carol Sicherman, "Ngugi's Colonial Education: 'The Subversion . . . of the African Mind,'" *African Studies Review* 38.3 (December 1995), 11–41.

2 Frantz Fanon, *The Wretched of the Earth*, trans. Constance Farrington, New York: Grove Press, 1968, p. 148.

3 Ngugi wa Thiong'o, *A Grain of Wheat*, London: Heinemann, 1967, epigraph. Further references to this edition will be made in parenthesis in the text.

4 Ngugi's reflections on the politics of decolonization can be found in the essays he wrote at the end of the 1960s and early 1970s; these are collected in *Homecoming: Essays on African and Caribbean Literature and Politics*, Westport, CT: Lawrence and Hill, 1972.

5 *Wretched*, p. 149.

6 For a theoretical study of the politics of time in literature, see John Frow, *Marxism and Literary History*, Cambridge, MA: Harvard University Press, 1986; the best study of the relation between endings and narrative meaning is perhaps Frank Kermode, *The Sense of an Ending*, Oxford: Oxford University Press, 1966.

7 See Peter Nazareth, *Literature and Society in Modern Africa: Essays on Literature*, Nairobi: East African Literature Bureau, 1972.

8 See *Secret Lives*, London: Heinemann, 1975, p. 46. Further references to this edition will be made in parenthesis in the text.

9 For a discusson of Ngugi's debt to Conrad, see Ben Obumselu, "'A Grain of Wheat': James Ngugi's Debt to Conrad," *The Benin Review* 1 (1974), 80–91.

10 This piece can be found in P. Wastberg, *The Writer in Modern Africa*, Uppsala: Scandinavian Institute of African Studies, 1968, pp. 99–111.

11 It is not by accident that many readings of the novel try to approach the social and historical questions it raises through a reading of its main characters. See, for example, David Cook and Michael Okenimpke, *Ngugi wa Thiong'o: An Exploration of His Writings*, London: Heinemann, 1983, pp. 69–89.

12 See Obumselu, "'A Grain of Wheat.'"

13 Ngugi's honors paper at Makerere University was on Conrad. As Sichermann aptly notes, Conrad's appeal lay "in his examination of alienation, self-betrayal, and heroism." See "Ngugi's Colonial Education," p. 17. On Conrad's appeal to postcolonial writers in general see Peter Nazareth, "Out of Darkness: Conrad and Other Third-World Writers," *Conradiana* 14. 3 (1982), 173–87.

14 *Wretched*, pp. 36–37.

15 My discussion here is indebted to Paul de Man's seminal essay on irony and allegory, "The Rhetoric of Temporality." See Paul de Man, *The Rhetoric of Temporality*, Minneapolis, University of Minnesota Press, 1983, pp. 187–228.

16 Ngugi wa Thiong'o, *The River Between*, London, Heinemann, 1965, p. 20.

17 This is the view asserted quite strongly by Cook and Okenimpke, who described *A Grain of Wheat* as "a fierce passionate examination of heroism and treachery." See *Ngugi wa Thiong'o*, p. 69.

18 This problem is explored in Ross Chambers's *Room for Maneuver: Reading (the) Oppositional (in) Narrative*, Chicago: University of Chicago Press, pp. 237–41.

19 As we shall see in the next chapter, the harshest critics of *Petals of Blood* considered the novel to have failed to master the formalism Ngugi had exhibited in *A Grain of Wheat*.

20 See Arjun Appadurai, "The Past as a Scarce Resource," *Man* 16 (1981), 201; see also Michel de Certeau, *The Writing of History*, trans. Tom Conley, New York: Columbia University Press, 1988, pp. 56–113.

21 Appadurai, "The Past as a Scarce Resource," 202.

22 For a general discussion of narrative, memory, and identity, see de Certeau, *The Writing of History*, p. 23.

23 Jacques Derrida, *Specters of Marx: The State of Debt, the Work of Mourning, and the New International*, New York: Routledge, 1994, p. 6.

24 *Ibid.*

25 Benedict Anderson, *Imagined Communities: Reflections on the Origin and Spread of Nationalism*, London: Verso, 1991, p. 204. In one of his major speeches as the prime minister of Kenya, Jomo Kenyatta made the forgetting of the past a cornerstone of his postcolonial government in memorable terms: "It is the future, my friends, that is living , and the past that is dead." See *Suffering Without Bitterness: The Founding of the Kenyan Nation*, Nairobi, East African Publishing House, 1968, p. 241.

26 Joseph Conrad, *Under Western Eyes*, Harmondsworth: Penguin, 1979, p. 351.

5. THE POETICS OF CULTURAL PRODUCTION: THE LATER SHORT
   STORIES AND *PETALS OF BLOOD*

1 Joseph McLaren, "Ideology and Form: The Critical Reception of
   Petals of Blood," in *The World of Ngugi wa Thiong'o*, ed. Charles Cantalupo, Trenton, NJ: African World Press, 1975, pp. 73–92.
2 *Ibid.*, p. 73.
3 Ngugi takes up what he calls "the wider issues and problems of the
   existence, the origins, the growth and the development of the African
   novel" in *Decolonising the Mind*, London: James Currey, 1986, pp. 63–
   86.
4 The classic study of the politics of underdevelopment in Kenya is
   Colin Leys, *Underdevelopment in Kenya: The Political Economy of Neo-
   Colonialism 1964–1971*, London: Heinemann, 1974. See especially
   Chapter 7, "The Politics of Neo-Colonialism."
5 See the preface to *Secret Lives*, London: Heinemann, 1975.
6 Frantz Fanon's critique of the culture of neo-colonialism can be
   found in *The Wretched of the Earth*, trans. Constance Farrington, New
   York: Grove Press, 1968.
7 Frederic Jameson, "Third World Literature in the Era of Multinational Capitalism," *Social Text* 15 (Fall 1986), 65–88.
8 *Secret Lives*, p. 82. Further references to this edition will be made in the
   text in parenthesis.
9 *Wretched*, p. 149.
10 *Ibid.*
11 *Petals of Blood*, London, Heinemann, 1977, p. 110. Further references
   to this edition will be made in the text in parenthesis.
12 *Wretched*, p. 148.
13 *Ibid.* pp. 149–50.
14 *Writers in Politics*, London: Heinemann, 1981, p. 71.
15 *Homecoming: Essays on African and Caribbean Literature and Politics*. Westport, CT: Lawrence and Hill, 1972, p. 65.
16 *Writers in Politics*, p. 78.
17 *Homecoming*, pp. 65–66.
18 *Writers in Politics*, p. 94.
19 *Decolonising*, p. 72.
20 *Ibid.*, p. 65.
21 *Ibid.*, p. 77.
22 For Marxist perspectives on the novel and African literature in
   general, see the essays collected in *Marxism and African Literature*, ed. G.
   M. Gugelberger, Trenton, NJ: Africa World Press, 1986; see also
   Chidi Amuta, "The Revolutionary Imperative in the Contemporary
   African Novel: Ngugi's *Petals of Blood* and Armah's *The Healers*."

Commonwealth Novel in English 3.2 (1990), 130–42.

23 Ngugi was writing the final sections of *Petals of Blood* when J. M.
Kariuki, a populist Kenyan politician, was abducted from a Nairobi
hotel by – it was claimed – agents of the state, murdered in the most
brutal of circumstances and dumped in the wilderness. Readers
familiar with Kenyan politics will recognize J. M. Kariuki's life and
politics in the figure of the lawyer in Ngugi's novel. Ngugi's tribute to
Kariuki can be found in *Writers in Politics*, pp. 82–93.

24 Georg Lukács, *The Theory of the Novel*, Cambridge, MA: MIT Press,
1971, p. 56.

25 *Ibid.*, p. 6.

26 For the novel and the desire for an organic community, see *ibid.*,
p. 122.

27 *Ibid.*, p. 78.

28 *Ibid.*

29 *Ibid.*, p. 70.

30 The early European and American reviews of the novel tended to
dismiss it as a piece of polemic. See McLaren, "Ideology and Form,"
pp. 73–79.

31 Lukács, *The Theory of the Novel*, p. 75.

32 *Ibid.*

33 *Ibid.*, pp. 112–31.

34 *Ibid.*, p. 117.

35 Raymond Williams, *The Country and the City*, London: Oxford University Press, 1973, p. 196.

6. PERFORMANCE AND POWER: THE PLAYS

1 Ngugi wa Thiong'o, *Barrel of a Pen: Resistance to Repression in Neo-
Colonial Kenya*, Trenton, NJ: Africa World Press, 1983, p. 42. For one
of the most influential notions of the public sphere see Jürgen Haber-
mas, *The Structural Transformation of the Public Sphere: An Inquiry into a
Category of Bourgeois Society*, trans. Thomas Burger, Cambridge, MA:
MIT Press, 1991. The book was originally published in 1962 as
Strukturwandel der Öffentlicheit.

2 My information here comes from a private conversation I had with
Ngugi soon after his release from detention in 1979.

3 David Hecht and Maliqalim Simone, *Invisible Governance: The Art of
African Micropolitics*, New York: Autonomedia, 1994, p. 12. For a
controversial study of the state in African, see Achille Mbembe, "The
Banality of Power and the Aesthetics of Vulgarity in the Postcolony,"
Public Culture 4.2 (1992), 1–30. The paradigm of counter-discourse
used here is borrowed from Richard Terdiman, *Discourse/Counter-*

Discourse, Ithaca, NY: Cornell University Press, 1985.

4 David Cohen, *The Combing of History*, Chicago: University of Chicago Press, 1994, p. 60.

5 Michel de Certeau, *The Practice of Everyday Life*, Berkeley: University of California Press, 1984, p. 169.

6 Johannes Fabian, *Power and Performance: Ethnographic Explorations through Proverbial Wisdom and Theater in Shaba, Zaire*, Madison: University of Wisconsin Press, 1990, p. 5.

7 *Ibid.*, pp. 6–7.

8 Ngugi wa Thiong'o, *Ngaahika Ndeenda*, Nairobi: Heinemann, 1980, p. 5. Where I make references to this edition, the translations are my own. My references for most of this chapter are to *I Will Marry When I Want*, London: Heinemann, 1982, the English translation by Ngugi wa Thiong'o. All further references to this edition will be included in parenthesis in the text.

9 De Certeau, *The Practice of Everyday Life*, p. 171.

10 Johanes Fabian, "Popular Culture in Africa: Findings and Conjectures," *Africa* 48 (1978), 316.

11 *Barrel of a Pen*, p. 44.

12 Ngugi wa Thiong'o, *The Black Hermit: A Play*, London: Heinemann, 1968, p. 2. All further references to this edition will be included in parenthesis in the text.

13 Ross Chambers, *Room for Maneuver: Reading (the) Oppositional (in) Narrative*, Chicago: University of Chicago Press, 1991, pp. 104–10.

14 One of the best explorations of the location of women in the symbolic language of nationalism can be found in Jean Franco, *Plotting Women: Gender and Representation in Mexico*, London, Verso, 1989.

15 Ngugi wa Thiong'o, *Homecoming: Essays on African and Caribbean Literature and Politics*, Westport, CT:, Lawrence and Hill, 1972, p. 25.

16 Ngugi wa Thiong'o, *This Time Tomorrow: Three Plays*, Nairobi: Kenya Literature Bureau, 1970, p. 3. All further references to the three plays in this collection will be included in parenthesis in the text.

17 A complete bibliographical listing of Ngugi's early journalism can be found in Carol Sicherman, *Ngugi wa Thiong'o: A Bibliography of Primary and Secondary Sources 1957–1987*, London: Hans Zell, 1989, pp. 9–15.

18 Ngugi wa Thiong'o, *The Trial of Dedan Kimathi*, London: Heinemann, 1976, pp. 84–85. All further references to this edition will be included in parenthesis in the text.

19 Frantz Fanon, *The Wretched of the Earth*, trans. Constance Farrington, New York: Grove Press, 1968, p. 39

20 David Cook and Michael Okenimpke, *Ngugi wa Thiong'o: An Exploration of His Writings*, London, Heinemann, 1983, p. 161.

21 For Ngugi's view of the politics surrounding the production of the

play, see *Writers in Politics*, London: Heinemann, 1981, pp. 42–52.

22 My discussion here is indebted to Fabian's *Power and Performance*.

23 See Ngugi wa Thiong'o, *Decolonising the Mind*, London: James Currey, 1986, pp. 39–40.

24 For a discussion of the relationship between oppositionality and the scene of reading, see Chambers, *Room for Maneuver*, pp. 17–18.

25 Ngugi discusses the Kenyan state's imposition of a culture of a silence in his introduction to *Barrel of a Pen*, pp. 1–4. For the place of "Mau Mau" in the debate on Kenyan pasts and futures, see Cohen's *The Combing of History*, pp. 60–64.

26 Fabian, "Popular Culture," p. 8.

27 *Ibid.*, p. 9.

28 For a collection of Gikuyu proverbs see G. Barra, *1000 Kikuyu Proverbs*, Nairobi: Kenya Literature Bureau, 1939 and Ngumbu Njururi, *Gikuyu Proverbs*, revised edition, Nairobi: Oxford University Press, 1968, 1983.

29 As noted earlier, this was the gist of many of Kenyatta's first speeches as Prime Minister. See Jomo Kenyatta, *Suffering Without Bitterness: The Founding of the Kenyan Nation*, Nairobi: East African Publishing House, 1968.

7. THE PRISONHOUSE OF CULTURE: *DETAINED* AND *DEVIL ON THE CROSS*

1 This information comes from a conversation I had with Okot p'Bitek at the University of Nairobi sometime in 1977.

2 Okot p'Bitek was speaking as a guest lecturer in Owour Anyumba's undergraduate seminar on African Oral Literature at the University of Nairobi in the first term of 1977. I was a student in this seminar and the information provided here is based on my recollections.

3 Ngugi wa Thiong'o, *Decolonising the Mind*, London: James Currey, 1986, p. 44.

4 *Ibid.*, p. 45.

5 *Detained: A Writer's Prison Diary*, London: Heinemann, 1981, p. 15. All further references to this edition will be included in parenthesis in the text.

6 See Michael Taussig, *The Nervous System*, London and New York: Routledge, 1992.

7 This image of the postcolonial state is discussed in Achille Mbembe, "The Banality of Power and the Aesthetics of Vulgarity in the Postcolony," *Public Culture* 4.2 (1992), 1–30.

8 This is the basic premise Ngugi maintains in the essays on literary theory collected in *Writers in Politics*, London: Heinemann, 1981. See

especially pp. 3–33.

9 See Barbara Harlow, *Resistance Literature*, London and New York: Methuen, 1987, pp. 122–33.

10 See Orlando Patterson, *Slavery and Social Death*, Cambridge, MA: Harvard University Press, 1982.

11 In his lectures at the University of Nairobi in the 1970s, Ngugi did not conceal his preference for what he considered to be radical and committed writers. His attitude toward writers who seemed to valorize the bourgeois ideal of aesthetic detachment and reflection is discernible in the following comment on the role of the artist in Wole Soyinka's works: "The artist in Soyinka's world gets away unscathed. He is seen as the conscience of the nation . . . Soyinka's good man is the uncorrupted individual: his liberal humanism leads him to admire an individual's lone act of courage, and thus often he ignores the creative struggle of the masses." See *Homecoming: Essays on African and Caribbean Literature and Politics*, Westport, CT: Lawrence and Hill, 1972, p. 65.

12 See Nicholas Dirks, "Introduction: Colonialism and Culture," in *Colonialism and Culture*, ed. Nicholas Dirks, Ann Arbor: University of Michigan Press, 1992, pp. 1–25.

13 Alamin Mazrui and Lupenga Mphande, "Orality and the Literature of Combat: Ngugi and the Legacy of Fanon," in *The World of Ngugi wa Thiong'o*, ed. Charles Cantalupo, Trenton, NJ: Africa World Press, 1995, p. 171.

14 *Decolonising*, p. 83.

15 *Ibid.*, p. 81.

16 Cook and Okenimpke read this novel as as "both thematically and stylistically a logical development from Ngugi's earlier fiction" and "a startling new departure." See David Cook and Michael Okenimpke, *Ngugi wa Thiong'o: An Exploration of His Writings*, London: Heinemann, 1983, p. 121.

17 My reference here is to *Caitaani Mutharaba-ini*, Nairobi: Heinemann, 1980, preface (my translation). All further references to this edition will be included in parenthesis in the text.

18 T. G. Benson, *Kikuyu–English Dictionary*, Oxford: Oxford University Press, 1964.

19 Eileen Julieen, *African Novels and the Question of Orality*, Bloomington: Indiana University Press, 1992, pp. 141–53.

20 Ngugi wa Thiong'o, *Devil on the Cross*, London: Heinemann, 1982, p. 7. All further references to this edition will be included in parenthesis in the text.

21 Gitahi Gititi, "Recuperating a 'Disappearing' Art Form: Resonances of 'Gicaandi' in Ngugi wa Thiong'o's *Devil on the Cross*," in *The World*

of *Ngugi wa Thiong'o*, ed. Charles Cantalupo, Trenton, NJ: Africa World Press, 1995, p. 117.

22 My thinking on rumors and vampires has been influenced by conversations with Louise White. See her *Blood and Fire: Rumor and History in East and Central Africa* (Berkeley: University of California Press, forthcoming).

23 Gititi, "Recuperating a 'Disappearing' Art Form," p. 117.

24 M. M. Bakhtin, *The Dialogical Imagination*, Austin: University of Texas Press, 1981, p. 318.

25 Given the significance of multivalency in *Devil on the Cross*, Bahktin's famous formulation on double-voicedness in the novel is worth quoting at some length: "Heteroglossia, once incorporated into the novel (whatever the forms for its incorporation), is *another's speech in another's language*, serving to express authorial intentions but in a refracted way. Such speech constitutes a special type of *double-voiced discourse*. It serves two speakers at the same time and expresses simultaneously two different intentions: the direct intention of the character who is speaking, and the refracted intention of the author. In such discourse there are two voices, two meanings and two expressions." See *The Dialogical Imagination*, p. 324.

26 Jean Franco, *Plotting Women: Gender and Representation in Mexico*, London, Verso: 1989, p. 131.

27 This is an English translation of the chorus to the song, "Twathiaga Tūkeneete" ("We Travelled in Happiness"): "We traveled in happiness / We returned in happiness / Our journey was without problems / Both on our departure and return." The original can be found in Gakaara wa Wanjau, *Nyimbo Cia Mau Mau*, Karatina, Kenya: Gakaara Press, no date, p. 29.

8. THE WORK OF ART IN EXILE: *MATIGARI*

1 For some critical perspectives on *Matigari* see F. O. Balogun, "Ngugi's *Matigari* and the Refiguration of the Novel as Genre," in *The World of Ngugi wa Thiong'o*, ed. Charles Cantalupo, Trenton, NJ: Africa World Press, 1995, pp. 185–96; and *"Matigari* and the Reconceptualization of Realism in the Novel," in *Ngugi wa Thiong'o: Texts and Contexts*, ed. Charles Cantalupo, Trenton, NJ: Africa World Press, 1995, p. 356; see also the essays by Anne Biersteker, Lewis Nkosi, Alamin Mazrui, and Lupenga Mphande in *The World of Ngugi wa Thiong'o*. On the problem of translation in the novel, see Simon Gikandi, "The Epistemology of Translation: Ngugi, *Matigari*, and the Politics of Language," *Research in African Literatures* 22.4 (1991), 161–67.

2 My discussion here is indebted to Walter Benjamin. See "The

Storyteller: Reflections on the Works of Nikolai Leskov," in *Illuminations: Essays and Reflections*, trans. Harry Zohn, New York: Schocke, 1968. Ngugi's reflections on time and space can be found in the overture to the novel itself. See *Matigari*, Oxford: Heinemann, 1987, p. vii. Further references to this edition will be made in parenthesis in the text. Where I refer to the original Gikuyu edition (*Matigari ma Njiruungi*, Nairobi: Heinemann, 1986), the translations are my own unless otherwise stated.

3 Balogun makes perhaps the strongest case for a reading of "formal realism" in the novel. See "Ngugi's *Matigari* and the Refiguration of the Novel as Genre." My argument in this chapter is that while the novel contains a lot of details drawn from everyday life, it is unique in its attempt to collapse the distinction between "life" and "fiction." Ngugi writes of a world in which the real has acquired the character of the fictional and fiction the authority of reality.

4 Ngugi wa Thiong'o, *Homecoming: Essays on African and Caribbean Literature and Politics*, Westport, CT: Lawrence and Hill, 1972, p. 44.

5 *Ibid.*, see Frantz Fanon, *The Wretched of the Earth*, trans. Constance Farrington, New York: Grove Press, 1968, p. 225.

6 *Wretched*, p. 225.

7 *Ibid.*

8 *Ibid.*

9 *Ibid.* As we shall see in the next chapter, the critical works Ngugi produced in the 1970s privilege an aesthetic that is committed to revolution and socialism. See especially *Writers in Politics*, London: Heinemann, 1981, p. 31.

10 Miriam Hansen, "Foreword" to Oskar Negt and Alexander Kluge, *Public Sphere and Experience: Toward an Analysis of the Bourgeois and Proletarian Public Sphere*, Minneapolis: University of Minnesota Press, 1993.

11 For a study of the ways in which popular culture in Africa "*asks* questions and *creates* conditions," see Johannes Fabian, "Popular Culture in Africa: Findings and Conjectures," *Africa* 48 (1978), 315–34, p. 316.

12 For a detailed account on the status of *Matigari* as a novel produced in exile see Ngugi wa Thiong'o, *Moving the Centre: The Struggle for Cultural Freedoms*, London: James Currey, 1993, pp. 154–76.

13 This is the argument Ngugi makes in *Decolonising the Mind*, London, James Currey, 1986, p. 77.

14 See the report by Ali Mazrui in Carol Sicherman, *Ngugi wa Thiong'o: The Making of a Rebel, A Source Book in Kenyan Literature and Resistance*, London: Hans Zell, 1990, p. 34.

15 There is perhaps no better evidence of Ngugi's desire to hold on to

the culture of the nation and the hearth than his establishment of a Gikuyu language journal called *Mũtiiri* at New York University.

16 In the Gikuyu edition, Matigari is looking for "Nyũmba" which is more than a house; it is a homestead, a family, and a community.

17 On the relation between writing and genealogy, see Michel de Certeau, *The Writing of History*, trans. Tom Conley, New York: Columbia University Press, 1988, p. 320.

18 It is important that while Ngugi had used his author's notes or prefaces to call attention to the historical references of his fictional works or their "reality effect" in the 1970s, his preface to both the Gikuyu and English editions of *Matigari* underscored the fictionality of his narrative and its dispensation with two key integers of realism – time and space.

19 Benedict Anderson has provided us with a memorable formulation of the relationship between forgetfulness and narrative: "All profound changes in consciousness, by their very nature, bring with them characteristic amnesias. Out of such oblivions, in specific historical circumstances, spring narratives." See *Imagined Communities: Reflections on the Origin and Spread of Nationalism*, London: Verso, 1991, p. 204.

20 See Balogun, "*Matigari* and the Reconceptualization of Realism in the Novel," p. 356.

21 My argument here is indebted to Jean Franco, *Plotting Women: Gender and Representation in Mexico*. London: Verso, 1989; and Doris Sommer, *Foundational Fictions: The National Romances of Latin America*, Berkeley: University of California Press, 1991.

22 Franco, *Plotting Women*, p. 129.

23 For a discussion of the opposition between allegory and symbolism see Paul de Man, *The Rhetoric of Temporality*, Minneapolis: University of Minnesota Press, 1983, pp. 187–88; and Hans-Georg Gadamer, *Truth and Method*, trans. Ganett Barden and John Cumming, New York: Seabury Press, 1975, p. 67.

24 Franco, *Plotting Women*, p. 81; p. 129.

25 There are many versions of this folktale, but most Gikuyu readers are familiar with Benson Gakahu's version which was widely used in adult literacy classes in the 1950s. See Benson Gakahu "*Mũthuri Wetagwo Thĩrũ Waarĩ Mũndũ Mũgo na Kanyoni*" ("An Old Medicineman Called Thiiru and a Little Bird"), in *Ng'ano Cia Ũ Gĩkũyũ* ("Gikuyu Stories"), ed. W. Sandler, Nairobi: Kenya Literature Bureau, 1957, pp. 34–39. For comparative purposes, see the version collected by Rose Mwangi in *Kikuyu Folktales: Their Nature and Value*, Nairobi: Kenya Literature Bureau, 1970, pp. 14–119.

26 Hansen, "Foreword," p. xvii.

27 The Gospel According to St. Matthew, 19:14.

28 Hansen, "Foreword," pp. xvi–xvii.

9. WRITING FREEDOM: ESSAYS AND CRITICISM

1 Ngugi wa Thiong'o, *Homecoming: Essays on African and Caribbean Literature and Politics*, Westport, CT: Lawrence and Hill, 1972, p. xv. Further references to this edition will be made in parenthesis in the text.

2 For a general discussion of the concept of overdetermination, see Ben Brewster's glossary to Louis Althusser and Etienne Balibar, *Reading Capital*, trans. Ben Brewster, London: Verso, 1977, p. 315.

3 The real greatness of England, argued Matthew Arnold, did not lie in its coal production or industrial progress but in its culture; against the coarse opacity of things such as coal or iron, culture was a salutary friend "bent on seeing things as they are" and "dissipating delusions" engendered by materialism. See "Sweetness and Light," in *Prose of the Victorian Period*, ed. William E. Buckler, Boston: Houghton, 1958, p. 463. While Leavis valued the literary text for its "vital capacity for experience," he considered the best works of art to be the ones that were marked by a moral intensity that transcended "raw" experience. See F. R. Leavis, *The Great Tradition*, New York: New York University Press, 1973, p. 9.

4 See *African Writers Talking*, eds. Dennis Duerden and Cosmo Pierterse, London: Heinemann, 1972, p. 121.

5 *Ibid.*, p. 122.

6 See Carol Sicherman, *Ngugi wa Thiong'o: The Making of a Rebel, A Source Book in Kenyan Literature and Resistance*, London: Hans Zell, 1990.

7 Quoted in *ibid.*, p. 392.

8 Ngugi wa Thiong'o, *Decolonising the Mind*, London: James Currey, 1986. Further references to this edition will be made in parenthesis in the text.

9 Carol Sicherman, "Ngugi's Colonial Education: 'The Subversion . . . of the African Mind,'" *African Studies Review* 38.3, (December 1995), 19.

10 For Ngugi, as for Arnold, culture was the agent of a universal moral character. See Arnold, "Sweetness and Light," p. 460.

11 For a detailed and incisive portrait of Carey Francis and his uneasy relation to Africans, and especially African nationalists, see B. E. Kipkorir, "Carey Francis at the A. H. S., Kikuyu – 1940–62," in *Biographical Essays on Imperialism and Collaboration in Colonial Kenya*, ed. B. E. Kipkorir, Nairobi: Kenya Literature Bureau, 1980, pp. 112–59.

12 For Ngugi at Leeds, see Sicherman's "Ngugi's Colonial Education," pp. 32–33.

13 Ngugi wa Thiong'o, *Moving the Centre: The Struggle for Cultural Freedoms*,

London: James Currey, 1993, p. 3. Further references to this edition will be made in parenthesis in the text.

14 Frantz Fanon, *The Wretched of the Earth*, trans. Constance Farrington, New York: Grove Press, 1968, p. 217.

15 A vivid portrait of the drama at the Kenyatta "court" at his ancestral home can be found in Colin Leys, *Underdevelopment in Kenya: The Political Economy of Neo-Colonialism 1964–1971*, London: Heinemann, 1974, pp. 246–49.

16 Fanon, *Wretched*, p. 209.

17 *Ibid.*, p. 210.

18 *Ibid.*, p. 211.

19 Jaques Derrida, *Specters of Marx: The State of Debt, the Work of Mourning, and the New International*, New York: Routledge, 1994, p. 10.

20 Ngugi wa Thiong'o, *Writers in Politics*, London: Heinemann, 1981, p. 34. Further references to this edition will be made in parenthesis in the text.

21 For other perspectives on Ngugi's "epistemological break" see Anthony Appiah, *In My Father's House: Africa in the Philosophy of Culture*, New York and Oxford: Oxford University Press, 1992, p. 61; and Terence Ranger, "The Invention of Tradition in Colonial Africa," in *The Invention of Tradition*, eds. Eric Hobsbawn and Terence Ranger, Cambridge: Cambridge University Press, 1983, pp. 261–62. My discussion on the question of language in Ngugi's criticism is adopted from "Ngugi's Conversion: Writing and the Politics of Language," *Research in African Literatures*, Special Issue: "The Question of Language," 23.1 (1992), 131–44. This issue contains some excellent discussions of the question of language in African literature. See, especially, Alamin Mazrui, "Relativism, Universalism, and the Language of African Literature" (65–72).

22 Duerden and Pierterse, eds., *African Writers Talking*, pp. 121, 122.

23 *Ibid.*, p. 128.

24 See "Kĩ̃ngeretha: Rũthiomi rwa Thĩ Yoothe? Kaba Gĩtwaĩri [*sic*]" ("English as A Global Language? Perhaps Swahili"), *Yale Journal of Criticism* 5.1 (Fall 1991), 269–94.

25 My assessment of *Mũtiiri* is based on three issues of the first volume published in 1994.

26 Ngugi spent some time training to be a film-maker in Europe in the 1980s and has since collaborated with Manthia Diawara in the making of a documentary on Sembene Ousmane, the Senegalese novelist and film-maker.

27 For an examination of state and society in Marxist thought, see Etienne Balibar, *Masses, Classes, Ideas: Studies on Politics and Philosophy Before and After Marx*, trans. James Swenson, New York and London:

Routledge, 1994.

28 Ngugi wa Thiong'o, *Penpoints, Gunpoints, and Dreams: Toward a Critical Theory of the Arts and the State in Africa*, Clarendon Lectures in English Literature 1996, Oxford: Clarendon Press, 1998, p. 2. Further references to this edition will be made in parenthesis in the text.

29 For this argument see Martin Jay, "'The Aesthetic Ideology' as Ideology; or, What Does It Mean to Aestheticize Politics?" *Cultural Critique* (Spring 1992), 41–61.

CONCLUSION

1 In his discussion of the problem of language in African literature, Ngugi notes how he accepted the "fatalistic logic" that African writers had no choice but to use the European language: "We were guided by it [this logic] and the only question which preoccupied us was how best to make the borrowed tongues carry the weight of our African experience." See *Decolonising the Mind*, London: James Currey, 1986, p. 7.

2 Frantz Fanon, *The Wretched of the Earth*, trans. Constance Farrington, New York: Grove Press, 1968, p. 39. The works of Peter Abrahams and Ferdinard Oyono are similarly preoccupied with the violent regulation of everyday life in a colonial situation, but the crucial difference in the cultural politics of colonial Francophone Africa and what Mahmood Mamdani has aptly called the "exceptionalism" of South Africa in colonial culture do not allow for the comparison I want to make here, hence my use of Achebe as a better counterpoint. See Mamdani's *Citizen and Subject: Contemporary Africa and the Legacy of Late Colonialism*, Princeton, NJ: Princeton University Press, 1996, pp. 27–32.

3 C. L. Innes, *Chinua Achebe*, Cambridge: Cambridge University Press, 1990, p. 169.

4 Ngugi wa Thiong'o, *Moving the Centre: The Struggle for Cultural Freedom*, London: James Currey, 1993, p. 163.

5 For a very subtle discussion of history and the dialectic of order and disorder, coherence and discontinuity, see Jean and John Comaroff, *Of Revelation and Revolution: Christianity, Colonialism, and Consciousness in South Africa*, vol. 1, Chicago: University of Chicago Press, 1991, pp. 14–17.

6 For a discussion of the problems and possibilities provided by the author in interpretation, see Michel Foucault's "What is an Author?" in *Language, Counter-Memory, Practice: Selected Essays and Interviews*, ed. Donald F. Bouchard, trans, Donald F. Bouchard and Sherry Simon, Ithaca, NY: Cornell University Press, 1977, pp. 113–38.

7 John Frow, *Marxism and Literary History*, Cambridge, MA: Harvard University Press, 1986, p. 186.

8 *Moving the Centre*, p. 175.

9 From *Marxism and Literary History*, p. 186. For a more elaborate discussion of reading and (as) oppositionality, see *Room for Maneuver: Reading (the) Oppositional (in) Narrative*, Chicago: University of Chicago Press, 1991.

10 See Barbara Hernstein Smith, *Contingencies of Value: Alternative Perspectives for Critical Theory*, Cambridge, MA: Harvard University Press, 1988, and Terry Eagleton, *The Ideology of the Aesthetic*, Oxford: Basil Blackwell, 1990.

11 *Moving the Centre*, p. 108.

Bibliography

NGUGI'S MAJOR WORKS

Weep Not, Child, London: Heinemann, 1964.
The River Between, London: Heinemann, 1965.
A Grain of Wheat, London: Heinemann, 1967.
The Black Hermit: A Play, London: Heinemann, 1968.
This Time Tomorrow: Three Plays, Nairobi: Kenya Literature Bureau, 1970.
Homecoming: Essays on African and Caribbean Literature and Politics, London: Heinemann, 1972; Westport, CT: Lawrence and Hill, 1972.
Secret Lives, London: Heinemann, 1975.
The Trial of Dedan Kimathi (with Micere Mugo), London: Heinemann, 1976.
Petals of Blood, London: Heinemann: 1977; New York: Penguin, 1977.
Caitaani Mutharaba-ini, Nairobi: Heinemann, 1980.
Detained: A Writer's Prison Diary, London: Heinemann, 1981.
Writers in Politics, London: Heinemann, 1981.
Devil on the Cross, London: Heinemann, 1982.
Ngaahika Ndeenda: Ithaako ria Ngerekano (with Ngugi wa Mirii), Nairobi: Heinemann, 1980.
I Will Marry When I Want (with Ngugi wa Mirii), London: Heinemann, 1982.
Barrel of a Pen: Resistance to Repression in Neo-Colonial Kenya, Trenton, NJ: African World Press, 1983.
Decolonising the Mind, London: James Currey, 1986.
Matigari ma Njiruungi, Nairobi: Heinemann, 1986.
Matigari, trans. Wangui wa Goro, Oxford: Heinemann, 1987.
Moving the Centre: The Struggle for Cultural Freedoms, London: James Currey, 1993.
Writers in Politics: A Re-engagement with Issues of Literature and Society, revised and enlarged edition, London: James Currey, 1997.
"Kīīngeretha: Rūthiomi rwa Thī Yoothe? Kaba Gītwaīri [*sic*]," ("English as A Global Language? Perhaps Swahili"), *Yale Journal of Criticism* 5.1 (Fall 1991), 269–94.

Penpoints, Gunpoints, and Dreams: Toward a Critical Theory of the Arts and the State in Africa, Oxford: Clarendon Press, 1998.

SECONDARY WORKS AND SOURCES

Althusser, Louis, *For Marx*, trans. Ben Brewster, London: New Left Books, 1977.

Althusser, Louis and Etienne Balibar, *Reading Capital*, trans. Ben Brewster, London: Verso, 1977.

Ambler, Charles, "'What is the World Coming To?' Prophecy and Colonialism in Central Kenya," in *Revealing Prophets: Prophecy in Eastern African History*, eds. David M. Anderson and Douglas H. Johnson, Oxford: James Currey, 1995, pp. 221–39.

Amuta, Chidi, "The Revolutionary Imperative in the Contemporary African Novel: Ngugi's *Petals of Blood* and Armah's *The Healers*," *Commonwealth Novel in English* 3.2 (1990), 130–42.

Anderson, Benedict, *Imagined Communities: Reflections on the Origin and Spread of Nationalism*. London, Verso, 1991.

Appadurai, Arjun, "The Past as a Scarce Resource," *Man* 16 (1981), 201–19.

Appiah, Anthony, *In My Father's House: Africa in the Philosophy of Culture*, New York and Oxford: Oxford University Press, 1992.

Bakhtin, M. M., *The Dialogical Imagination*, Austin: University of Texas Press, 1981.

Balandier, Georges, *The Sociology of Black Africa: Social Dynamics in Central Africa*, trans. Douglas Garman, New York: Praeger (1955), 1970.

Balibar, Etienne, *Masses, Classes, Ideas: Studies on Politics and Philosophy Before and After Marx*, trans. James Swenson, New York and London: Routledge, 1994.

Balogun, F. O., "Ngugi's *Matigari* and the Refiguration of the Novel as Genre," in *The World of Ngugi wa Thiong'o*, ed. Charles Cantalupo, Trenton, NJ: Africa World Press, 1995, pp. 185–96.

"*Matigari* and the Reconceptualization of Realism in the Novel," in *Ngugi wa Thiong'o: Texts and Contexts*, ed. Charles Cantalupo, Trenton, NJ: Africa World Press, 1995.

Barnett, Donald I., and Karari Njama, *Mau Mau from Within*, New York: Monthly Review Press, 1966.

Barra, G., *1000 Kikuyu Proverbs*, Nairobi: Kenya Literature Bureau, 1939.

Benjamin, Walter, "The Storyteller: Reflections on the works of Nikolai Leskov," in *Illuminations: Essays and Reflections*, trans. Harry Zohn, New York: Schocken, 1968.

Benson, T. G., *Kikuyu–English Dictionary*, Oxford: Oxford University Press, 1964.

Berman, Bruce and John Londsdale, *Unhappy Valley: Conflict in Kenya and Africa*, London: James Currey, 1992.

Bhabha, Homi, *The Location of Culture*, London and New York: Routledge, 1994.

Biersteker, Anne, "*Matigari ma Njiruungi*: What Grows from Leftover Seeds of 'Chat' Trees," in *Ngugi wa Thiong'o: Texts and Contexts*, ed. Charles Cantalupo, Trenton, NJ: Africa World Press, 1995, pp. 141–58.

Buckler, William E., *Prose of the Victorian Period*, Boston: Houghton, 1958.

Buijtenhuijs, Robert, *Essays on Mau Mau: Contributions to Mau Mau Historiography*, Leiden: African Studies Center, 1982.

Cantalupo, Charles, ed., *The World of Ngugi wa Thiong'o*, Trenton, NJ: Africa World Press, 1995.

Ngugi wa Thiong'o: Texts and Contexts, Trenton, NJ: Africa World Press, 1995.

Chambers, Ross, *Room for Maneuver: Reading (the) Oppositional (in) Narrative*, Chicago: University of Chicago Press, 1991.

Clough, Marshall S, *Fighting Two Sides: Kenyan Chiefs and Politicians, 1918–1940*, Boulder: University Press of Colorado, 1990.

Cohen, David W., *The Combing of History*, Chicago: University of Chicago Press, 1994.

Comaroff, Jean and John, *Of Revelation and Revolution: Christianity, Colonialism, and Consciousness in South Africa*, vol. 1, Chicago: University of Chicago Press, 1991.

Cook, David, *Origin East Africa: A Makerere Anthology*, London: Heinemann, 1965.

Cook, David and Michael Okenimpke, *Ngugi wa Thiong'o: An Exploration of His Writings*, London: Heinemann, 1983.

Cooper, Frederick, "Mau Mau and the Discourses of Decolonization," *Journal of African History* 29 (1988), 313–20.

Corfield, F. D., *Historical Survey of the Origins of Mau Mau*, London: HMSO, 1960.

Culler, Jonathan, *Flaubert: The Uses of Uncertainty*, Ithaca, NY: Cornell University Press, 1974.

De Certeau, Michel, *The Practice of Everyday Life*, Berkeley: University of California Press, 1984.

The Writing of History, trans. Tom Conley, New York: Columbia University Press, 1988.

De Man, Paul, *The Rhetoric of Temporality*, Minneapolis: University of Minnesota Press, 1983.

Deleuze, Giles and Felix Guattari, *Kafka: Toward a Minor Literature*, Minneapolis: University of Minnesota Press, 1972.

Derrida, Jacques, *Specters of Marx: The State of Debt. the Work of Mourning. and the New International,* New York: Routledge, 1994.

Dirks, Nicholas, "Introduction: Colonialism and Culture, " in *Colonialism and Culture,* ed. Nicholas Dirks, Ann Arbor: University of Michigan Press, 1992, pp. 1–25.

Douglas, Mary, *Purity and Danger: An Analysis of the Concepts of Pollution and Taboo,* London: Routledge, 1988.

Duerden, Dennis, and Cosmo Pierterse, *African Writers Talking,* London: Heinemann, 1972.

Eagleton, Terry, *The Ideology of the Aesthetic,* Oxford: Basil Blackwell, 1990.

Fabian, Johannes, "Popular Culture in Africa: Findings and Conjectures," *Africa* 48 (1978), 315–34.

Power and Performance: Ethnographic Explorations through Proverbial Wisdom and Theater in Shaba, Zaire, Madison: University of Wisconsin Press, 1990.

Fanon, Frantz. *The Wretched of the Earth,* trans. Constance Farrington, New York: Grove Press, 1968.

Foucault, Michel, "What is an Author?" in *Language, Counter-Memory, Practice: Selected Essays and Interviews,* ed. Donald F. Bouchard, trans, Donald F. Bouchard and Sherry Simon, Ithaca, NY: Cornell University Press, 1977, pp. 113–38.

"Of Other Spaces," *Diacritics* 16 (1986): 22–27.

Franco, Jean, *Plotting Women: Gender and Representation in Mexico,* London: Verso, 1989.

Frow, John, *Marxism and Literary History,* Cambridge: MA: Harvard University Press, 1986.

Furedi, Frank, *The Mau Mau War in Perspective,* London: James Currey, 1989.

Gadamer, Hans-Georg, *Truth and Method,* trans. Ganett Barden and John Cumming, New York: Seabury Press, 1975.

Gakahu, Benson, "Mũthuri Wetagwo Thĩĩrũ Waarĩ Mũndũ Mũgo na Kanyoni," in *Ng'ano Cia ũ Gĩkũyũ,* ed. W. Sandler, Nairobi: Kenya Literature Bureau, 1959, pp. 34–39.

Gikandi, Simon, "Moments of Melancholy: Ngugi and the Discourse of Emotions," in *The World of Ngugi wa Thiong'o,* ed. Charles Cantalupo: Trenton, NJ, Africa World Press, 1995, pp. 59–72.

Maps of Englishness: Writing Identity in the Culture of Colonialism, New York: Columbia University Press, 1996.

"The Epistemology of Translation: Ngugi, *Matigari,* and the Politics of Language," *Research in African Literatures* 22.4 (1991), 161–67.

"Ngugi's Conversion: Writing and the Politics of Language," *Research in African Literatures,* Special Issue: "The Question of Language," 23.1 (1992), 131–44.

Gititi, Gitahi, "Recuperating a 'Disappearing' Art Form: Resonances of

'Gicaandi' in Ngugi wa Thiong'o's *Devil on the Cross*," in *The World of Ngugi wa Thiong'o*, ed. Charles Cantalupo: Trenton, NJ, Africa World Press, 1995, pp. 109–28.

Gugelberger, G. M., ed. *Marxism and African Literature*, Trenton, NJ, Africa World Press, 1986.

Habermas, Jürgen, *The Structural Transformation of the Public Sphere: An Inquiry into a Category of Bourgeois Society*, trans. Thomas Burger, Cambridge, MA: MIT Press, 1991.

Hecht, David and Maliqalim Simone, *Invisible Governance: The Art of African Micropolitics*, New York: Autonomedia, 1994.

Innes, C. L. *Chinua Achebe*, Cambridge: Cambridge University Press, 1990,

Irele, Abiola, "African Letters: The Making of a Tradition," *Yale Journal of Criticism* 5.1 (1991), 69–100.

Jameson, Frederic, "Third World Literature in the Era of Multinational Capitalism, " *Social Text* 15 (Fall 1986): 65–88.

The Political Unconscious: Narrative as a Socially Symbolic Act, Ithaca: Cornell University Press, 1981.

JanMohammed, Abdul, *Manichean Aesthetics: The Politics of Literature in Colonial Africa*, Amherst, MA: University of Massachusetts Press, 1983.

Jay, Martin, "'The Aesthetic Ideology' as Ideology; or, What Does It Mean to Aestheticize Politics?" *Cultural Critique* (Spring 1992), 41–61.

Jeyifo, Biodun, "The Nature of Things: Arrested Decolonization and Critical Theory," *Research in African Literature* 21.1 (1990), 33–46.

Julieen, Eileen, *African Novels and the Question of Orality*, Bloomington: Indiana University Press, 1992.

Kaggia, Bildad, *Roots of Freedom, 1921–1963: The Autobiography of Bildad Kaggia*, Nairobi: East African Publishing House, 1975.

Kanogo, Tabitha, *Squatters and the Roots of Mau Mau*, London, James Currey, 1987.

Kariuki, Josiah Mwangi, *Mau Mau Detainee*, London: Oxford University Press, 1963.

Kenyatta, Jomo, *Facing Mount Kenya*, New York: Vintage (1938), 1965.

Suffering Without Bitterness: The Founding of the Kenyan Nation, Nairobi: East African Publishing House, 1968.

Kermode, Frank, *The Sense of an Ending*, Oxford: Oxford University Press, 1966.

Kershaw, Gert, *Mau Mau from Below*, Oxford: James Currey, 1997.

Kibicho, Samuel G., "The Continuity of the African Conception of God Into and Through Christianity: A Kikuyu Case-Study," in *Christianity in Independent Africa*, ed. Edward Fashikole-Luke, et al., Bloomington: Indiana University Press, 1978, pp. 370–88.

Killam, G. D., *An Introduction to the Writings of Ngugi wa Thiong'o*, London: Heinemann, 1980.

Kinyatti, Maina, *Thunder from the Mountains: Mau Mau Patriotic Songs*, London: Zed, 1980.

Kipkorir, B. E. "Carey Francis at the A. H. S., Kikuyu – 1940–62," in *Biographical Essays on Imperialism and Collaboration in Colonial Kenya*, ed. B. E. Kipkorir, Nairobi: Kenya Literature Bureau, 1980, pp. 112–59.

Leakey, L. S. B., *Mau Mau and the Kikuyu*, London, Methuen, 1952.

The Southern Kikuyu Before 1903, London: Academic Press, 1977.

Leavis, F. R., *The Great Tradition*, New York: New York University Press, 1973.

Leys, Colin, *Underdevelopment in Kenya: The Political Economy of Neo-Colonialism 1964–1971*, London: Heinemann, 1974.

Lonsdale, John, "The Moral Economy of Mau Mau: Wealth, Poverty and Civic Virtue in Kikuyu Political Thought," in *Unhappy Valley: Conflict in Kenya and Africa*, ed. Bruce Berman and John Londsdale, London: James Currey, 1992, vol. II, pp. 315–467.

"The Prayers of Waiyaki: Political Uses of the Kikuyu Past," in *Revealing Prophets: Prophecy in Eastern African History*, eds. David M. Anderson and Douglas H. Johnson, Oxford: James Currey, 1995, pp. 240–91.

Lukács, Georg, *The Theory of the Novel*, Cambridge, MA: MIT Press, 1971.

Mamdani, Mahmood, *Citizen and Subject: Contemporary Africa and the Legacy of Late Colonialism*, Princeton, NJ: Princeton University Press, 1996.

Maughan-Brown, David, *Land, Freedom, and Fiction: History and Ideology in Kenya*, London: Zed, 1985.

Mazrui, Alamin, "Relativism, Universalism, and the Language of African Literature," *Research in African Literatures*, Special Issue: "The Question of Language," 23.1 (1992), 65–72.

Mazrui, Alamin and Lupenda Mphande, "Orality and the Literature of Combat: Ngugi and the Legacy of Fanon," in *The World of Ngugi wa Thiong'o*, ed. Charles Cantalupo, Trenton, NJ: Africa World Press, 1995, pp. 159–84.

Mbembe, Achille, "The Banality of Power and the Aesthetics of Vulgarity in the Postcolony," *Public Culture* 4.2 (1992), 1–30.

McLaren, Joseph, "Ideology and Form: The Critical Reception of *Petals of Blood*," in *The World of Ngugi wa Thiong'o*, ed. Charles Cantalupo: Trenton, NJ: Africa World Press, 1975, pp. 73–92.

Muriuki, Godfrey, *A History of the Kikuyu, 1500–1900*, Nairobi: Oxford University Press, 1974.

Mwangi, Rose, *Kikuyu Folktales: Their Nature and Value*, Nairobi: Kenya Literature Bureau, 1970.

Nazareth, Peter, *Literature and Society in Modern Africa: Essays on Literature*,

Nairobi: East African Literature Bureau, 1972.
"Out of Darkness: Conrad and Other Third-World Writers," *Conradiana* 14.3 (1982), 173–87.
Negt, Oskar and Alexander Kluge, *Public Sphere and Experience: Toward an Analysis of the Bourgeois and Proletarian Public Sphere*, Minneapolis: University of Minnesota Press, 1993.
Njururi, Ngumbu, *Gikuyu Proverbs*, revised edition, Nairobi: Oxford University Press (1968), 1983.
Nkosi, Lewis, "Ngugi's *Matigari*: The New Novel of Post-Independence," in *The World of Ngugi wa Thiong'o*, ed. Charles Cantalupo: Trenton, NJ: Africa World Press, 1995, pp. 197–206.
Obumselu, Ben, "'A Grain of Wheat': James Ngugi's Debt to Conrad," *The Benin Review* 1 (1974), 80–91.
Patterson, Orlando, *Slavery and Social Death*, Cambridge, MA: Harvard University Press, 1982.
Ranger, Terence, "The Invention of Tradition in Colonial Africa," in *The Invention of Tradition*, eds. Eric Hobsbawn and Terence Ranger, Cambridge: Cambridge University Press, 1983, pp. 211–62.
Robson, C. B., *Ngugi wa Thiong'o*, London and New York, St. Martins Press, 1979.
Rosberg, Carl and John Nottingham, *The Myth of "Mau Mau": Nationalism in Kenya*, New York: Meridian, 1966.
Routledge, W. Scoresby, *With a Prehistoric People: The Akikuyu of East Africa*, London: Frank Cass, (1910), 1968.
Said, Edward, *Beginnings: Intention and Method*, New York: Basic Books, 1975.
Seed, Patricia, *Ceremonies of Possession in Europe's Conquest of the New World, 1492–1640*, Cambridge: Cambridge University Press, 1995.
Sicherman, Carol, *Ngugi wa Thiong'o: A Bibliography of Primary and Secondary Sources 1957–1987*, London: Hans Zell, 1989.
Ngugi wa Thiong'o: The Making of a Rebel, A Source Book in Kenyan Literature and Resistance, London, Hans Zell, 1990.
"Ngugi's British Education," in *Ngugi wa Thiong'o: Texts and Contexts*, ed. Charles Cantalupo, Trenton, NJ: Africa World Press, 1995, pp. 35–46.
"Ngugi's Colonial Education: 'The Subversion ... of the African Mind'" *African Studies Review* 38.3 (December 1995), 11–41.
Smith, Barbara Hernstein, *Contingencies of Value: Alternative Perspectives for Critical Theory*, Cambridge, MA: Harvard University Press, 1988.
Sommer, Doris, *Foundational Fictions: The National Romances of Latin America*, Berkeley: University of California Press, 1991.
Taussig, Michael, *The Nervous System*, London and New York: Routledge, 1992.

Terdiman, Richard, *Discourse / Counter-Discourse*, Ithaca, NY: Cornell University Press, 1985.

Throup, David W., *Economic and Social Origins of Mau Mau 1945–53*, London: James Currey, 1987.

Tignor, Robert L., *The Colonial Transformation of Kenya: The Kamba, Kikuyu and Maasai from 1900 to 1939*, Princeton: Princeton University Press, 1976.

Wa Wanjau, Gakaara, *Nyimbo Cia Mau Mau*, Karatina, Kenya: Gakaara Press, n. d.

Mau Mau Author in Detention, trans. Ngugi wa Njoroge, Nairobi: Heinemann, Kenya, 1988.

Wastberg, P., *The Writer in Modern Africa*, Uppsala: Scandinavian Institute of African Studies, 1968.

Welbourn, F. B., *East African Rebels: A Study of Some Independent Churches*, London: SCM Press, 1961.

Williams, Raymond, *The Country and the City*, London: Oxford University Press, 1973.

Index

325